SINGAPORE
THROUGH THE LOOKING GLASS

A PHOTOGRAPHIC EXPLORATION

HAE WON SHIN

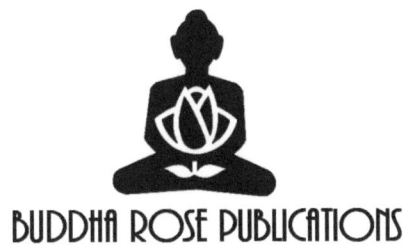

BUDDHA ROSE PUBLICATIONS

Singapore Through the Looking Glass
Copyright © 2019 by Hae Won Shin
All Rights Reserved

First Edition 2019

No part of this book may be reproduced
in any manner without the expressed
permission of the author or the publishing company.

ISBN: 978-1-949251-18-0

Printed in the United States of America

10 9 8 7 6 5 4 3 2 1

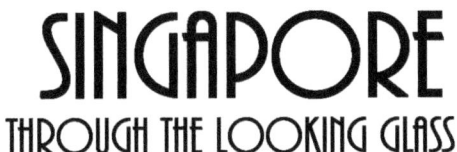

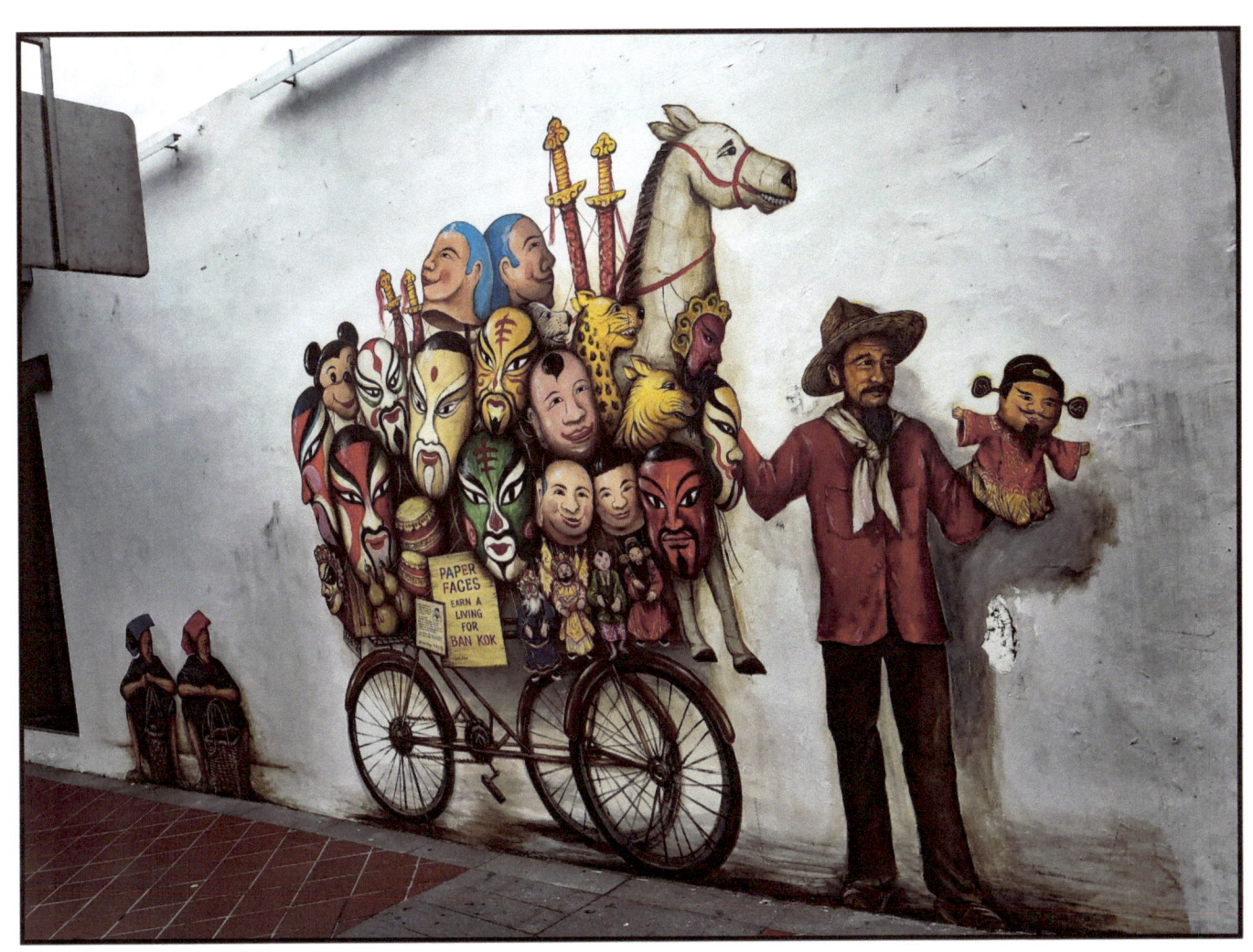

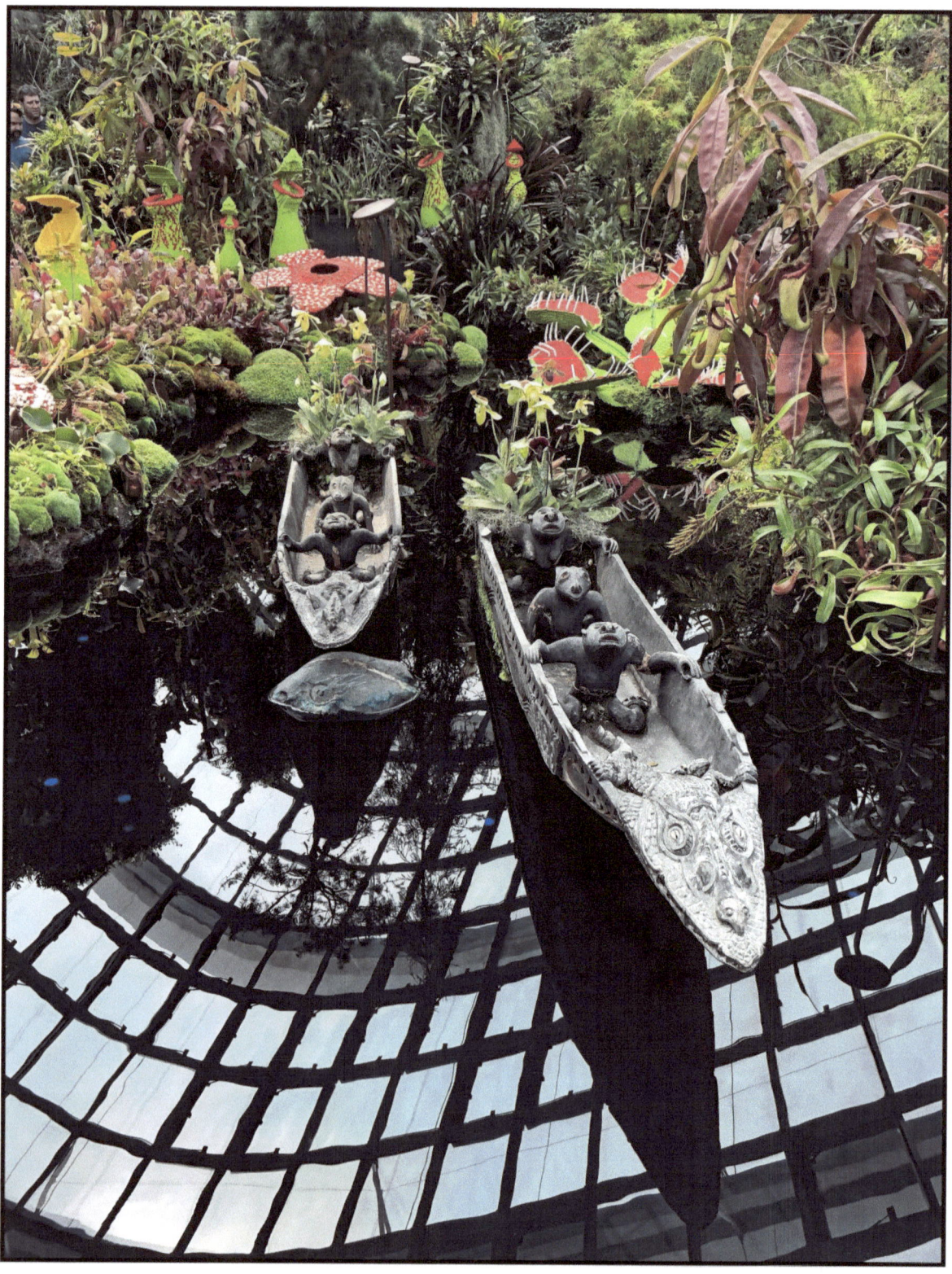

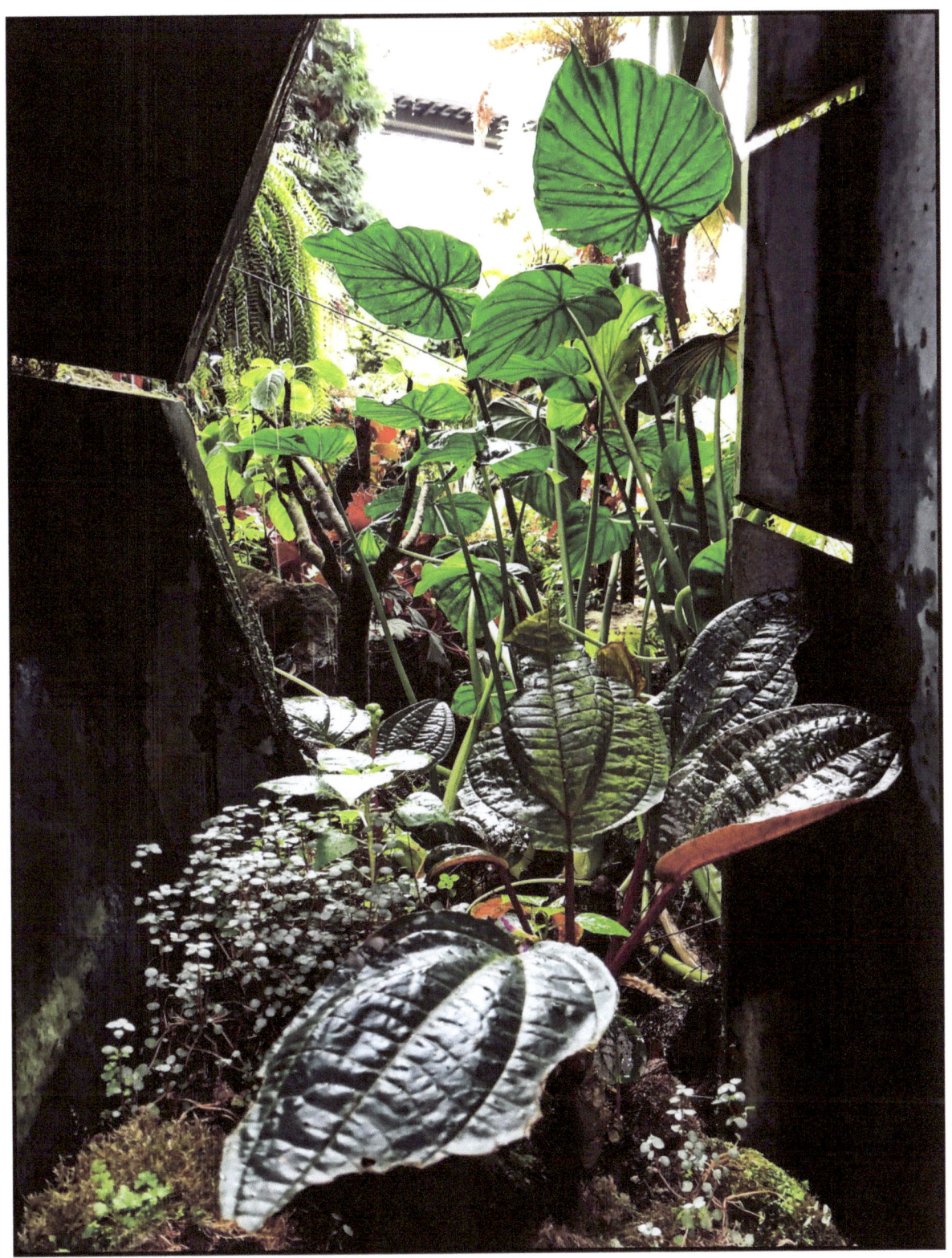

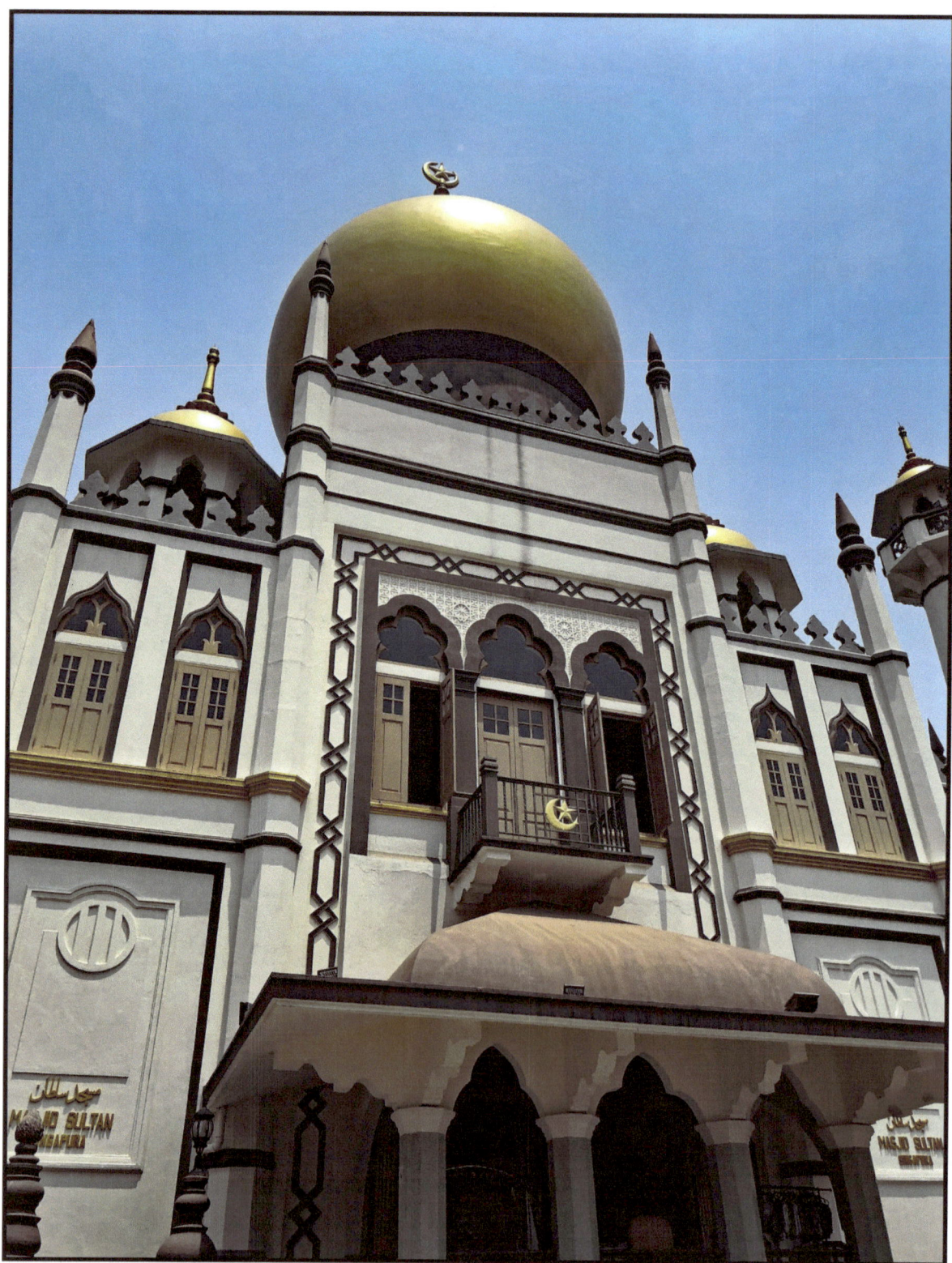

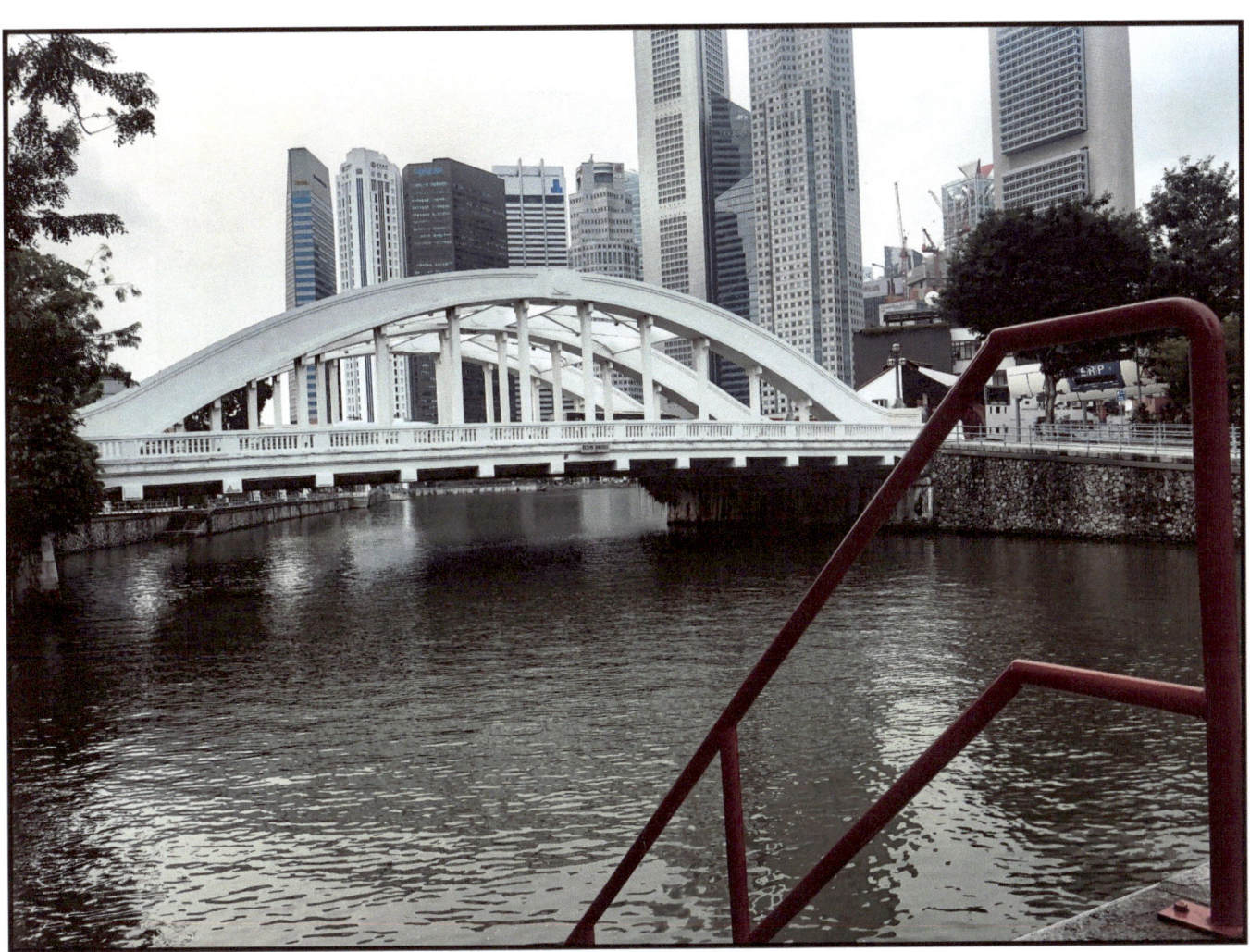

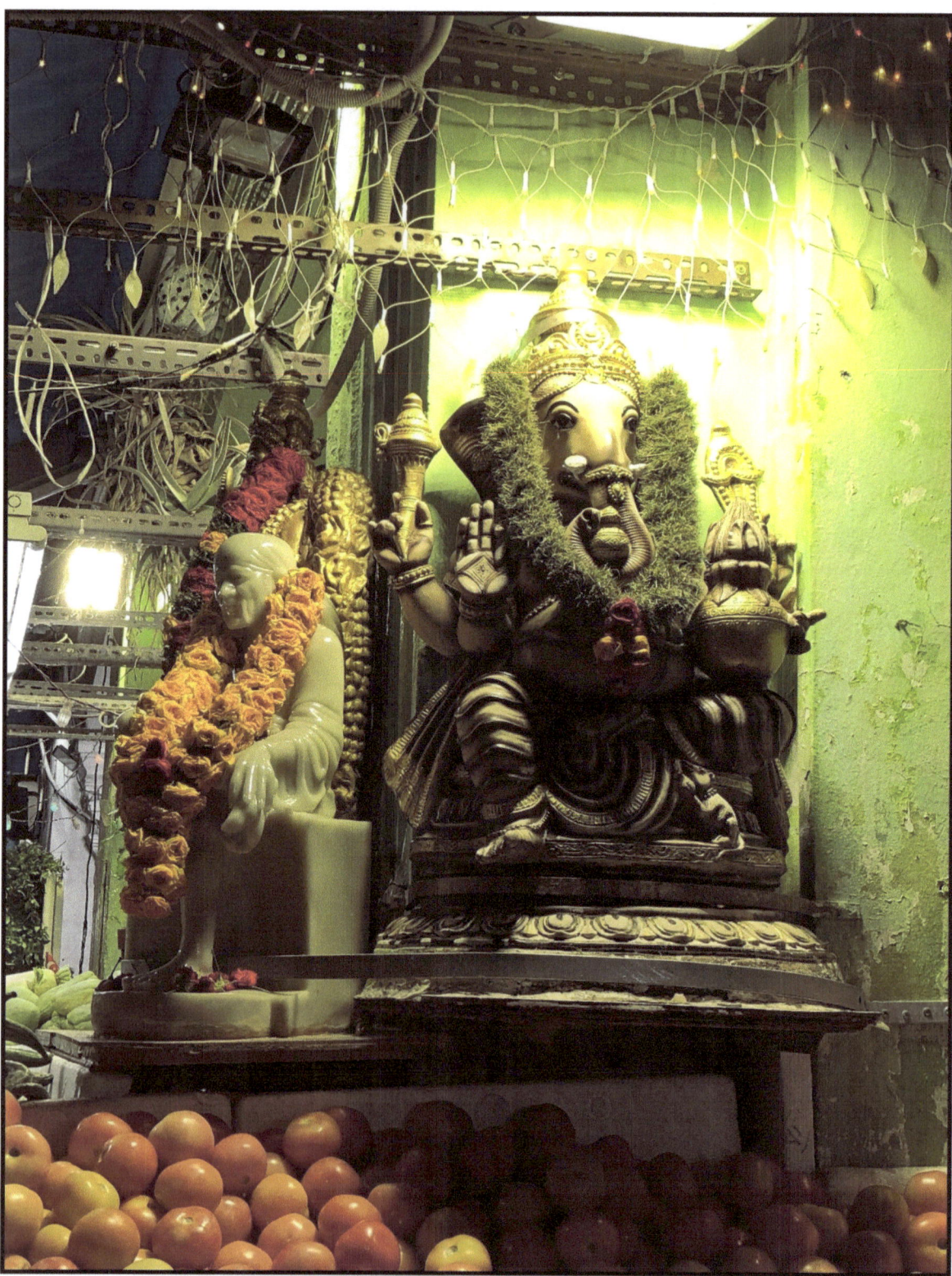

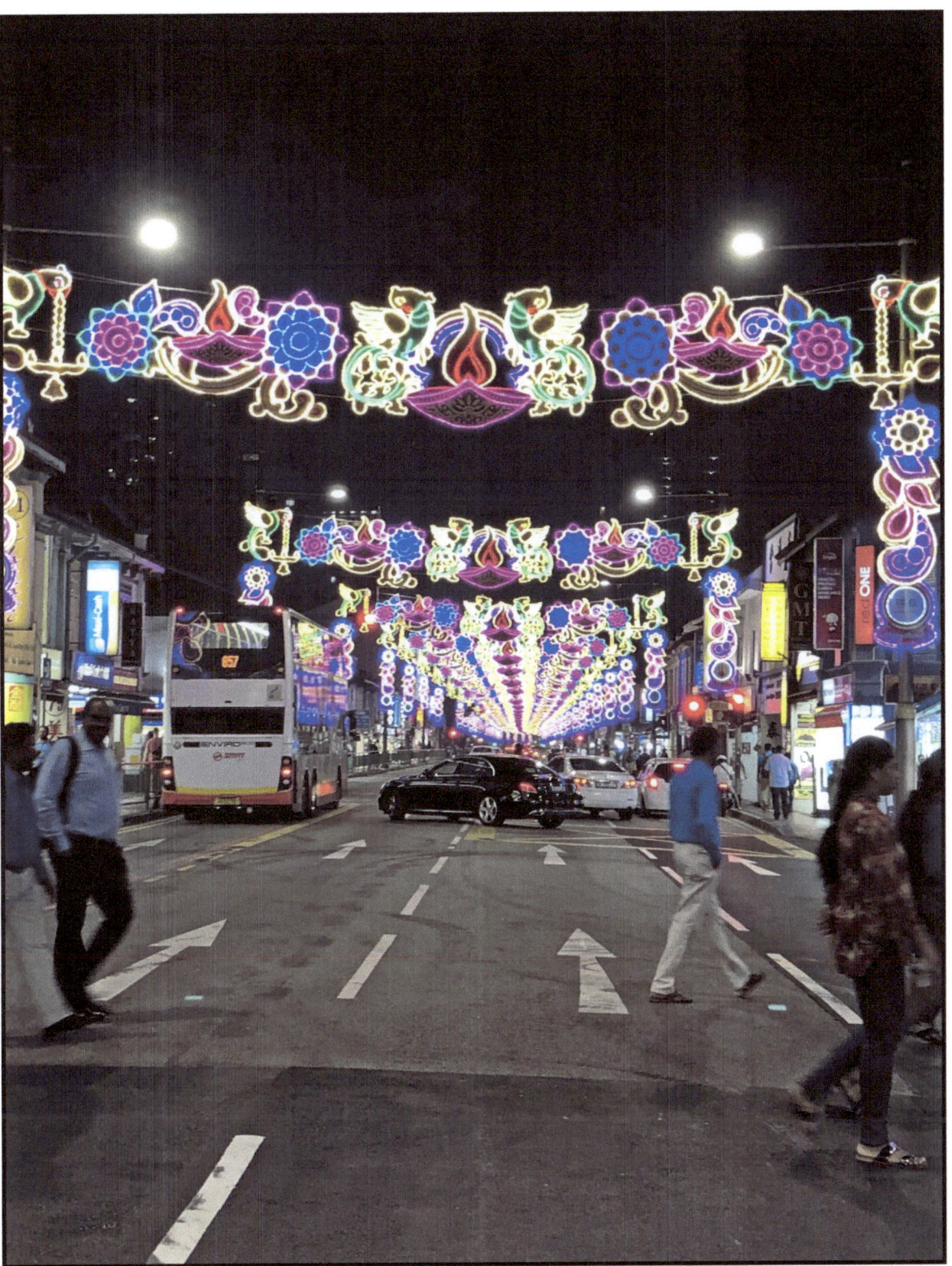

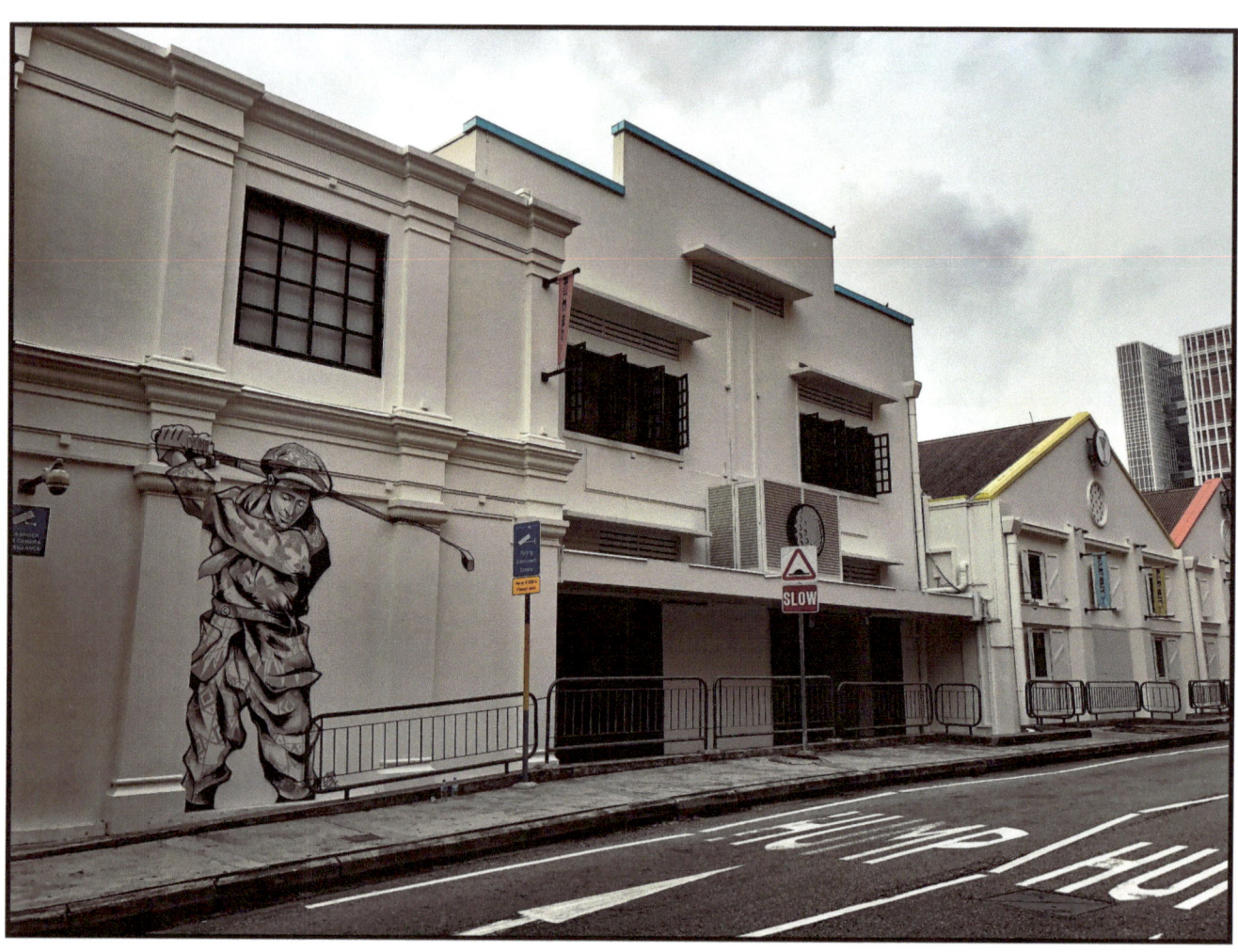

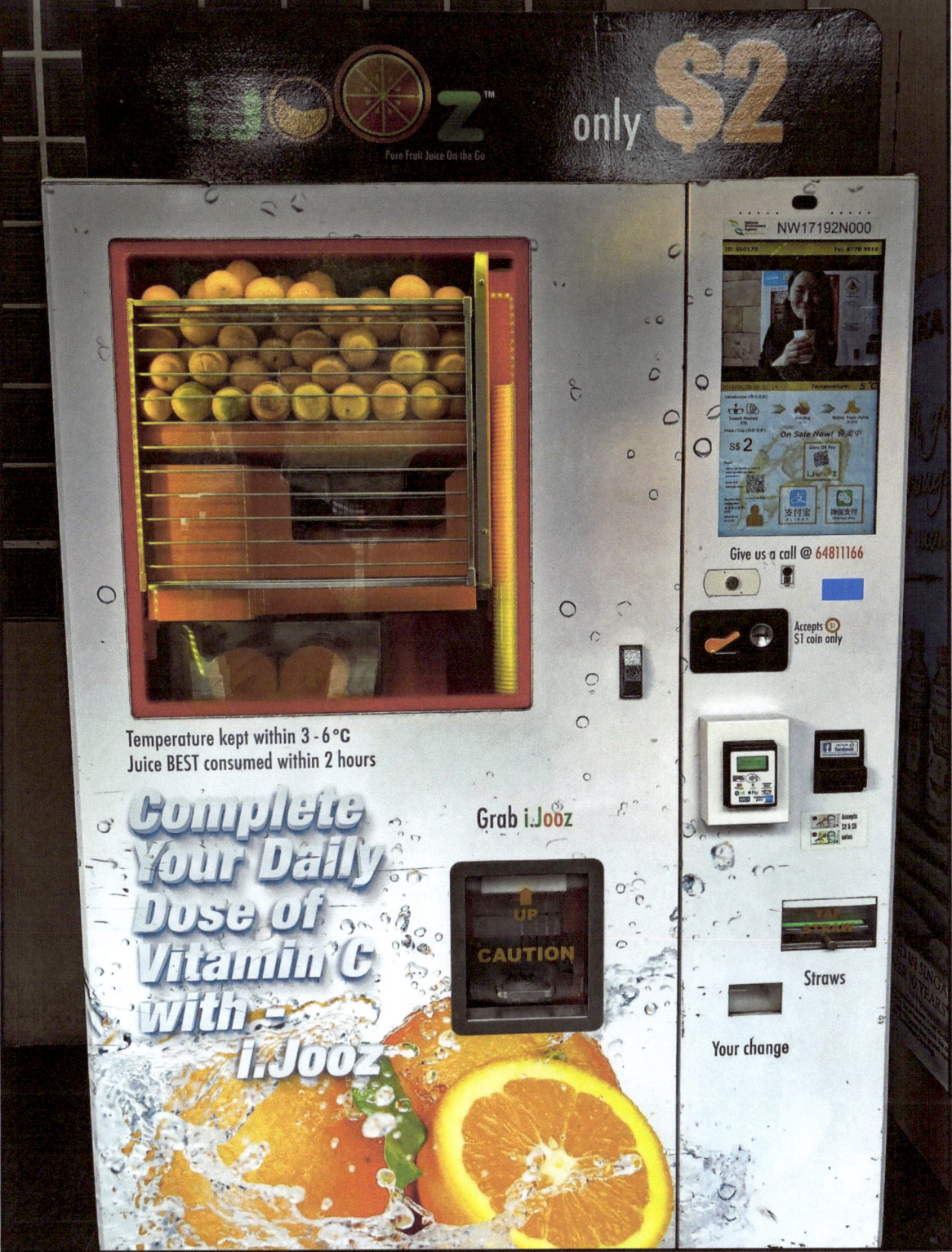

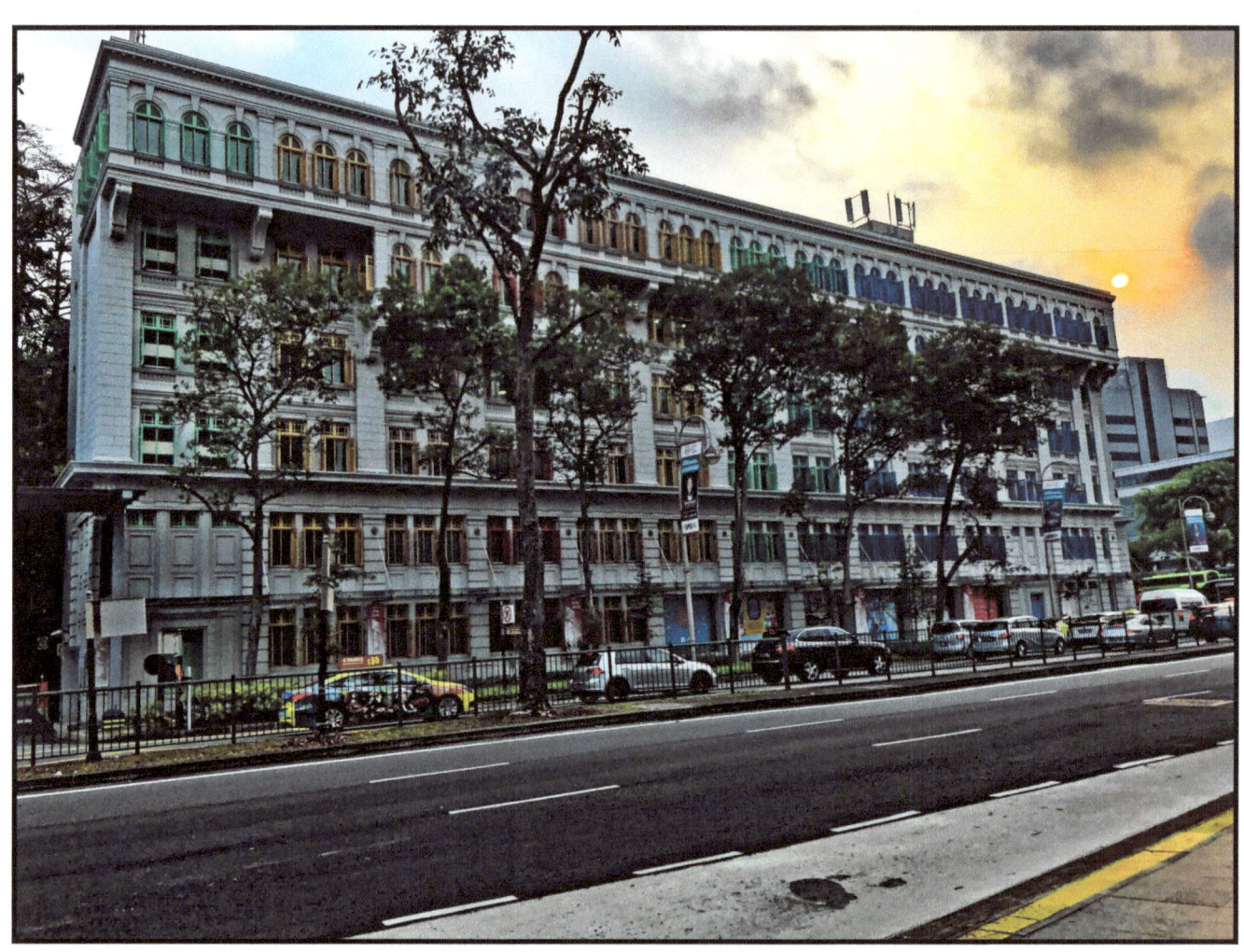

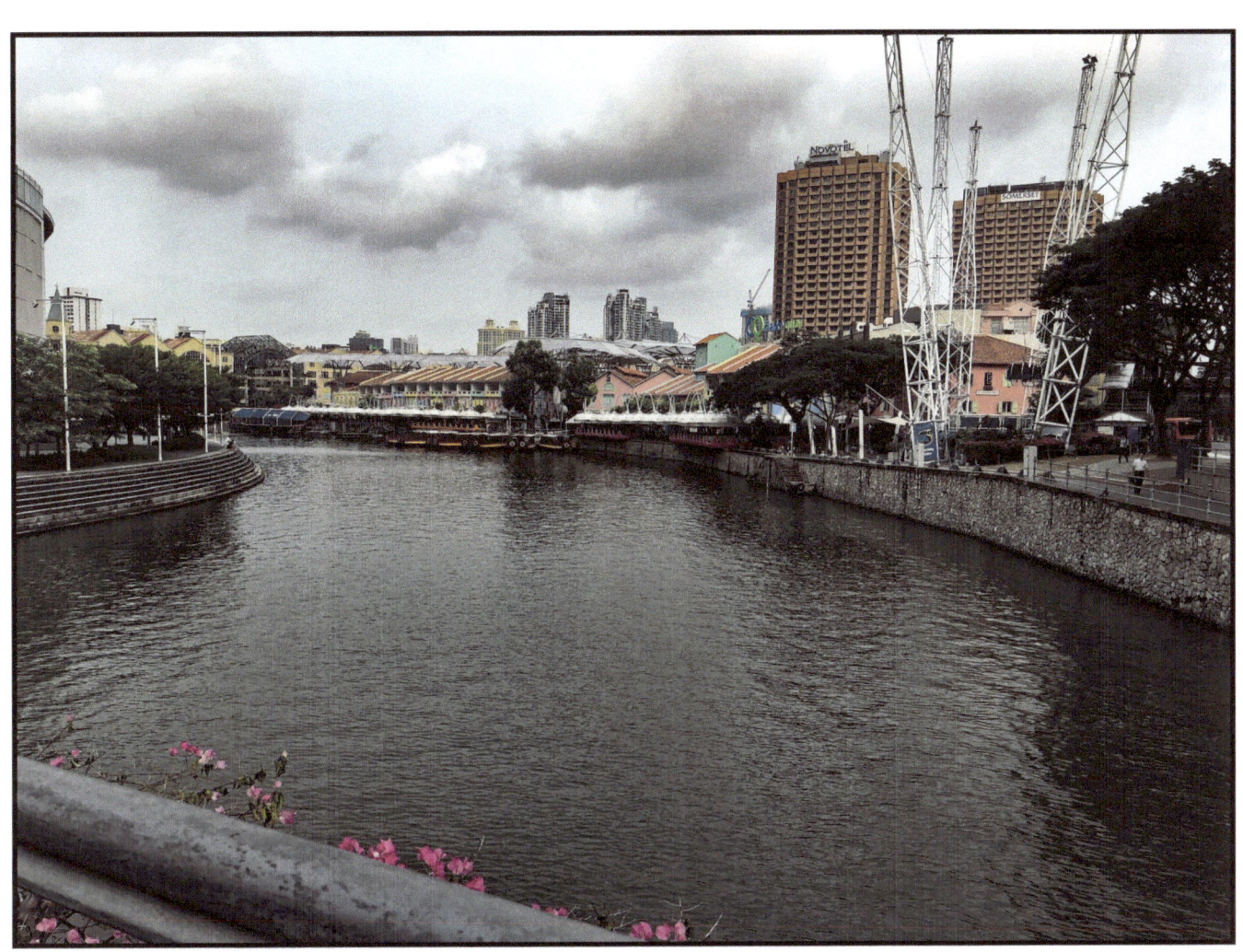

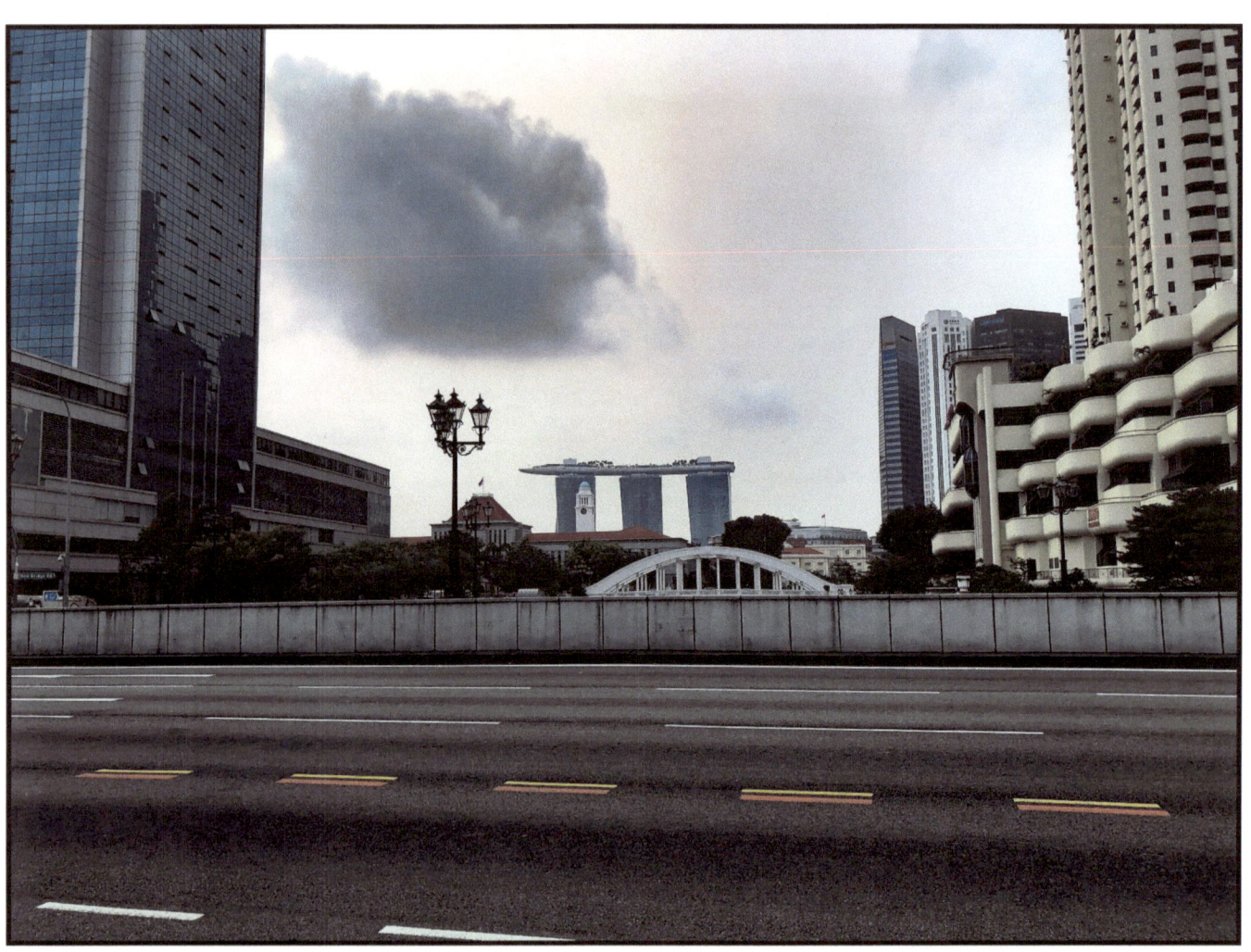

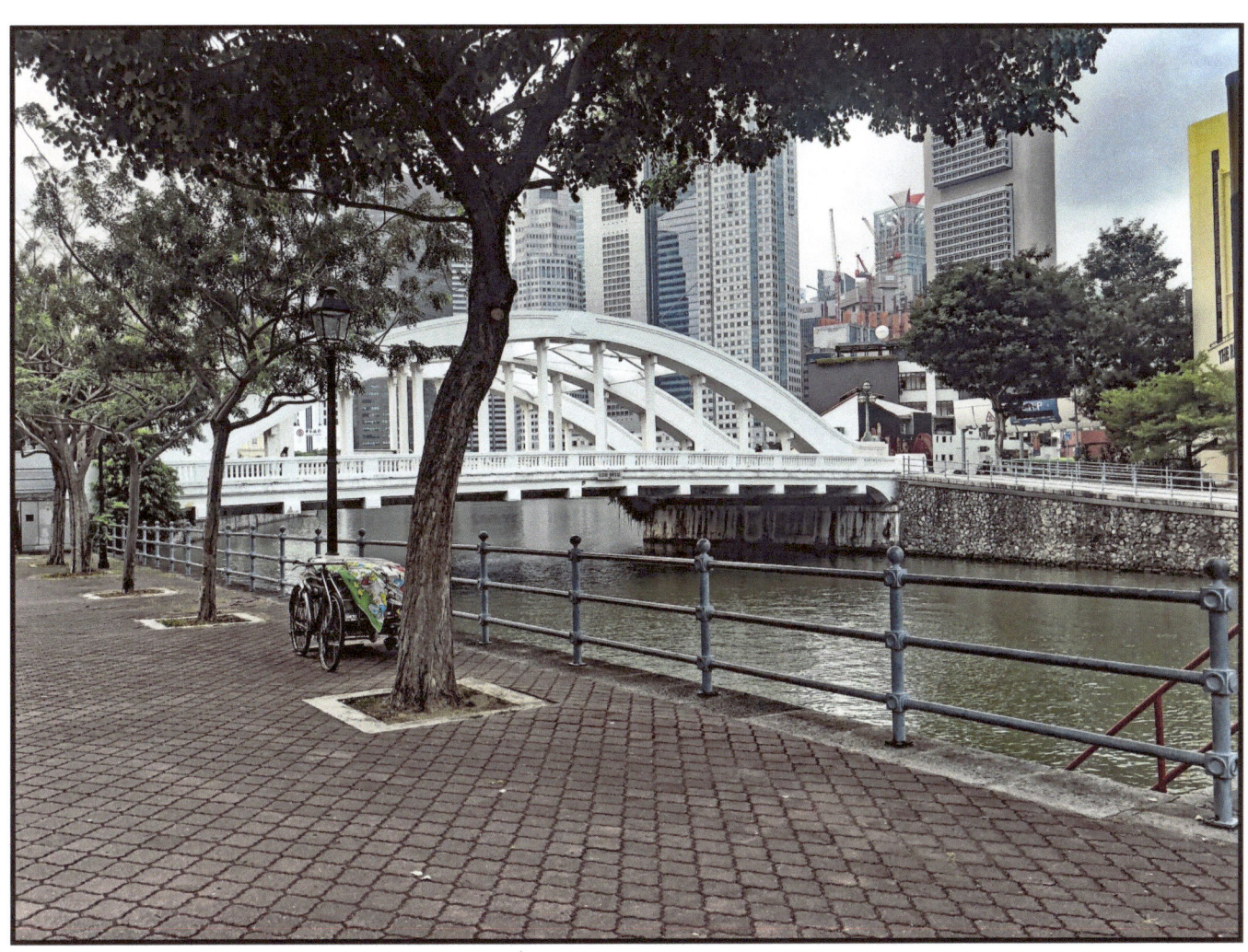

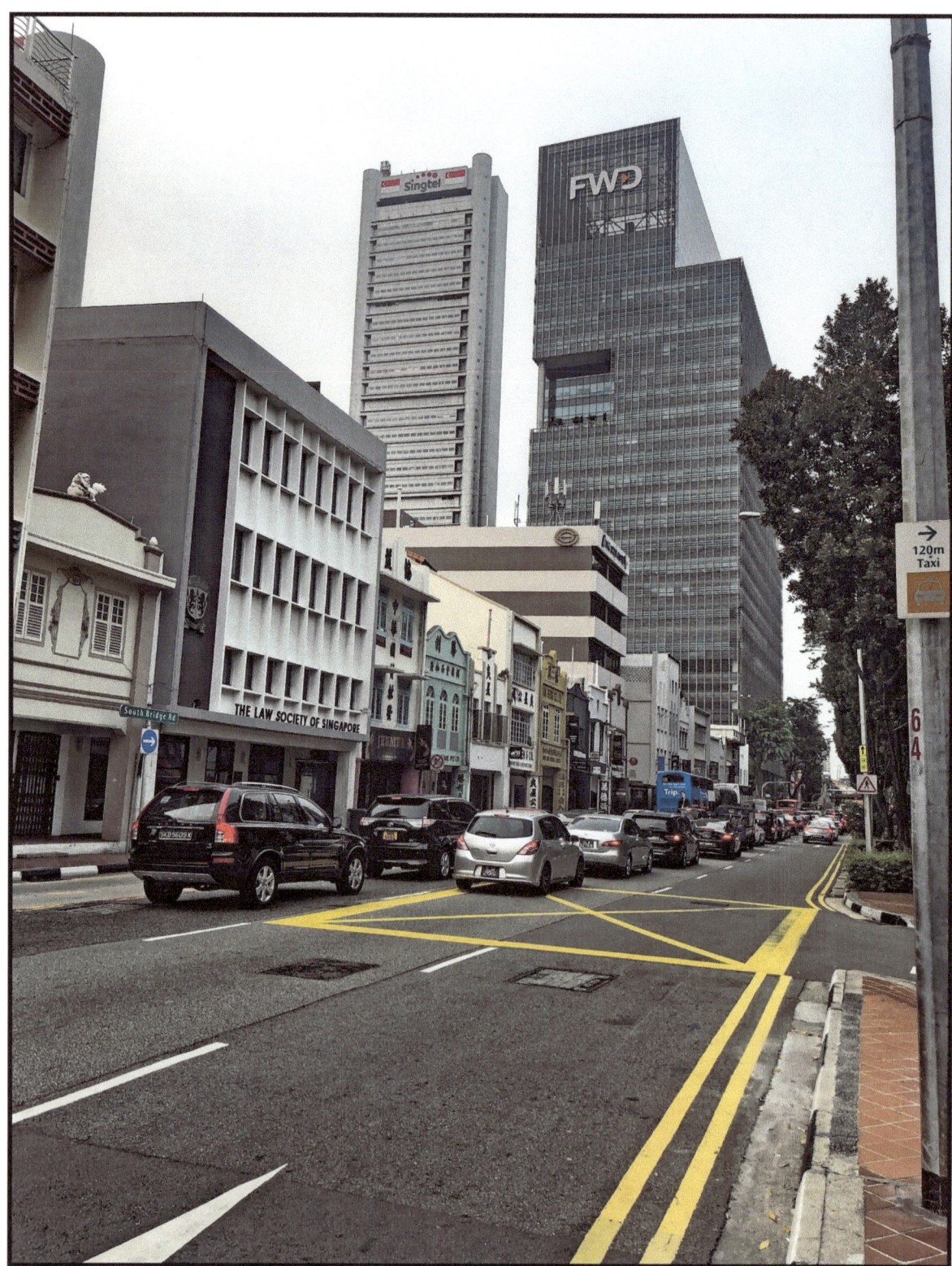

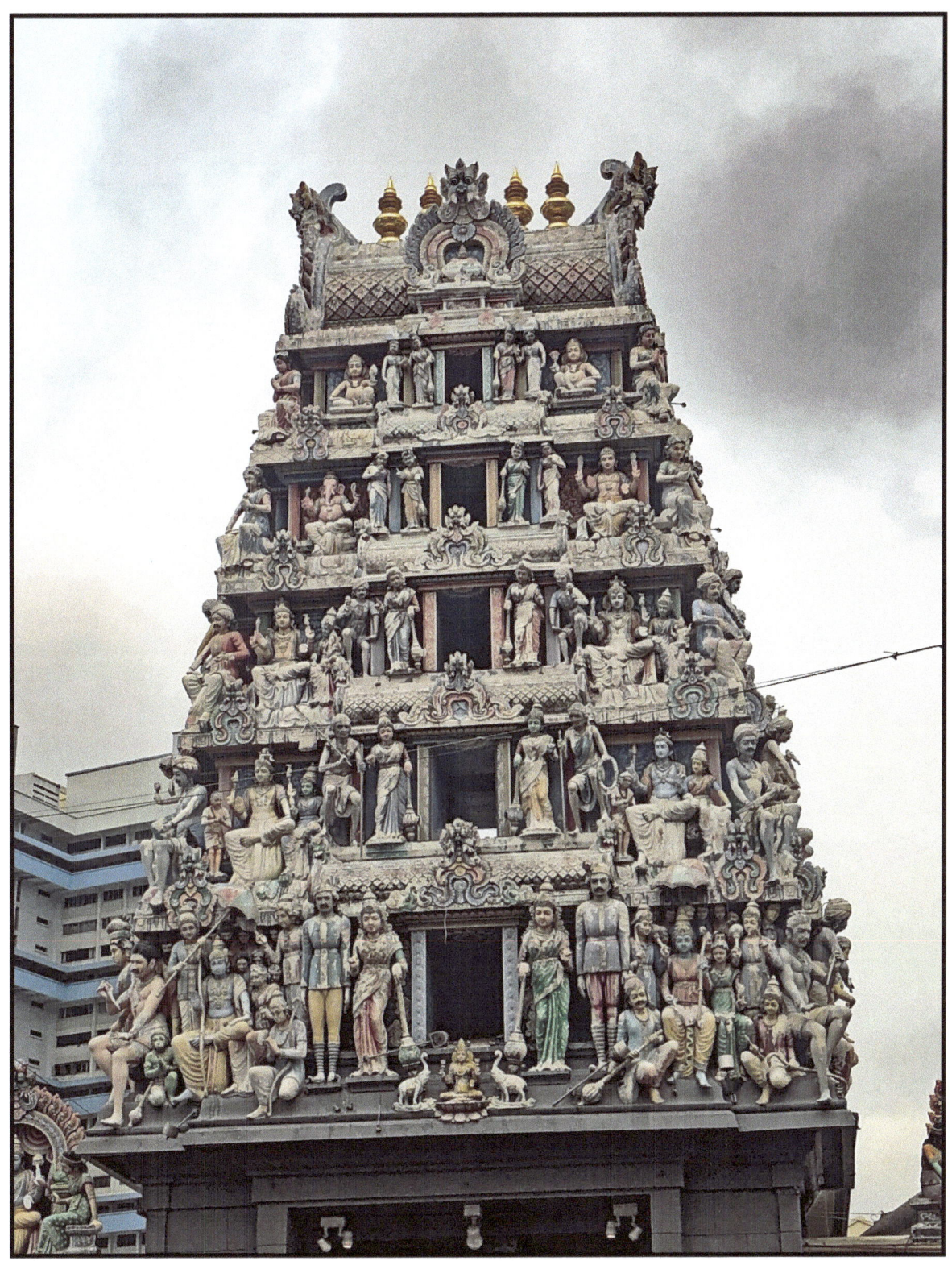

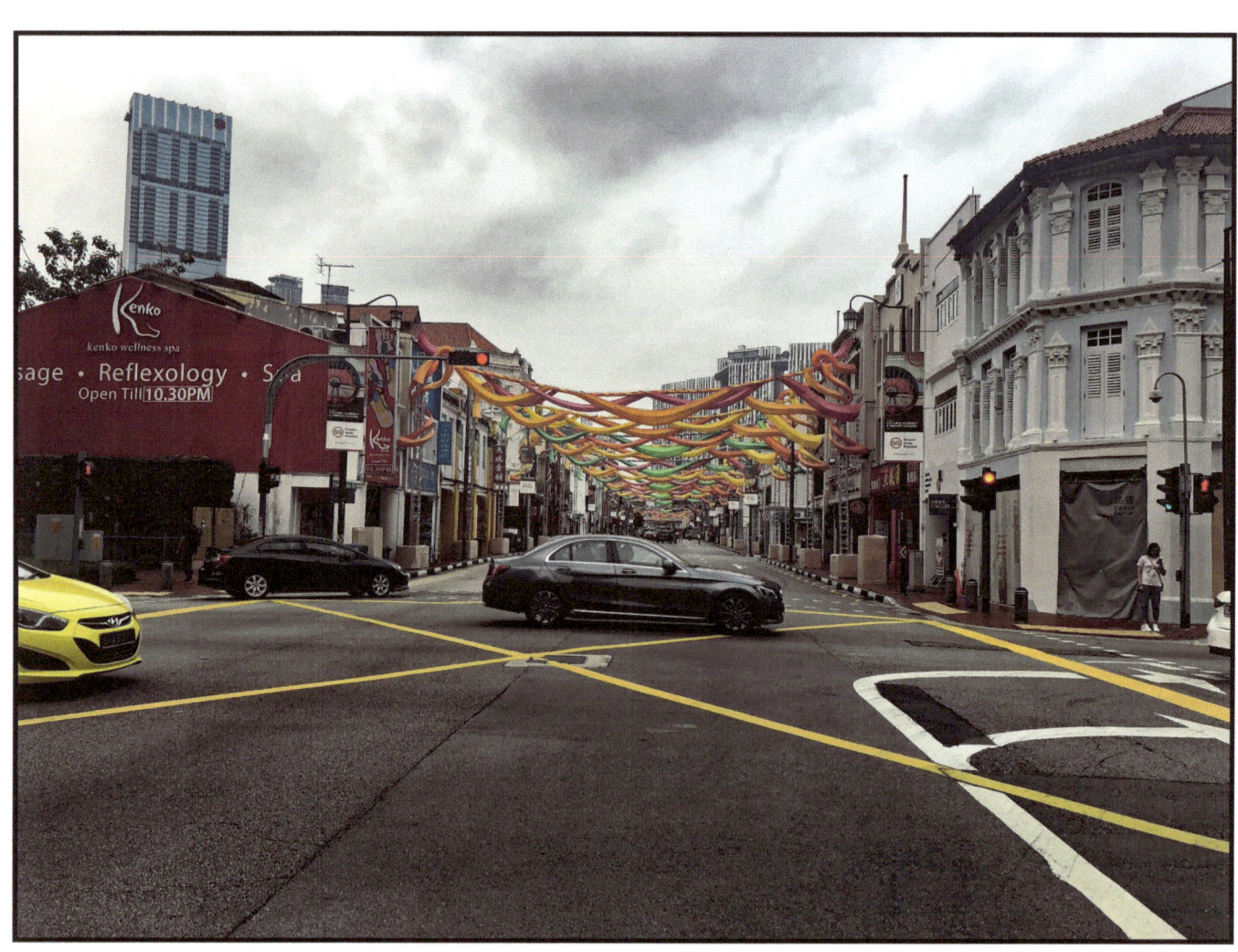

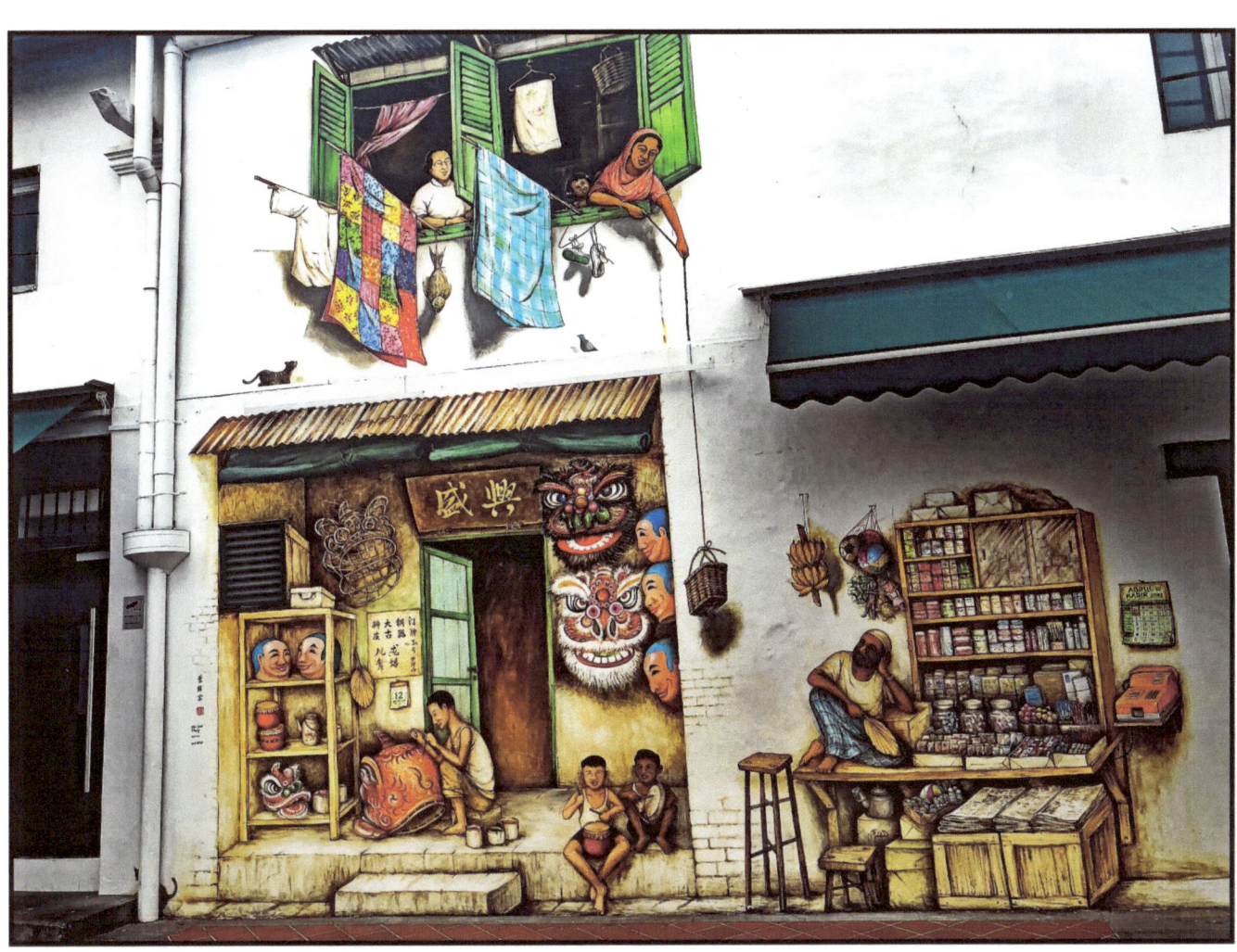

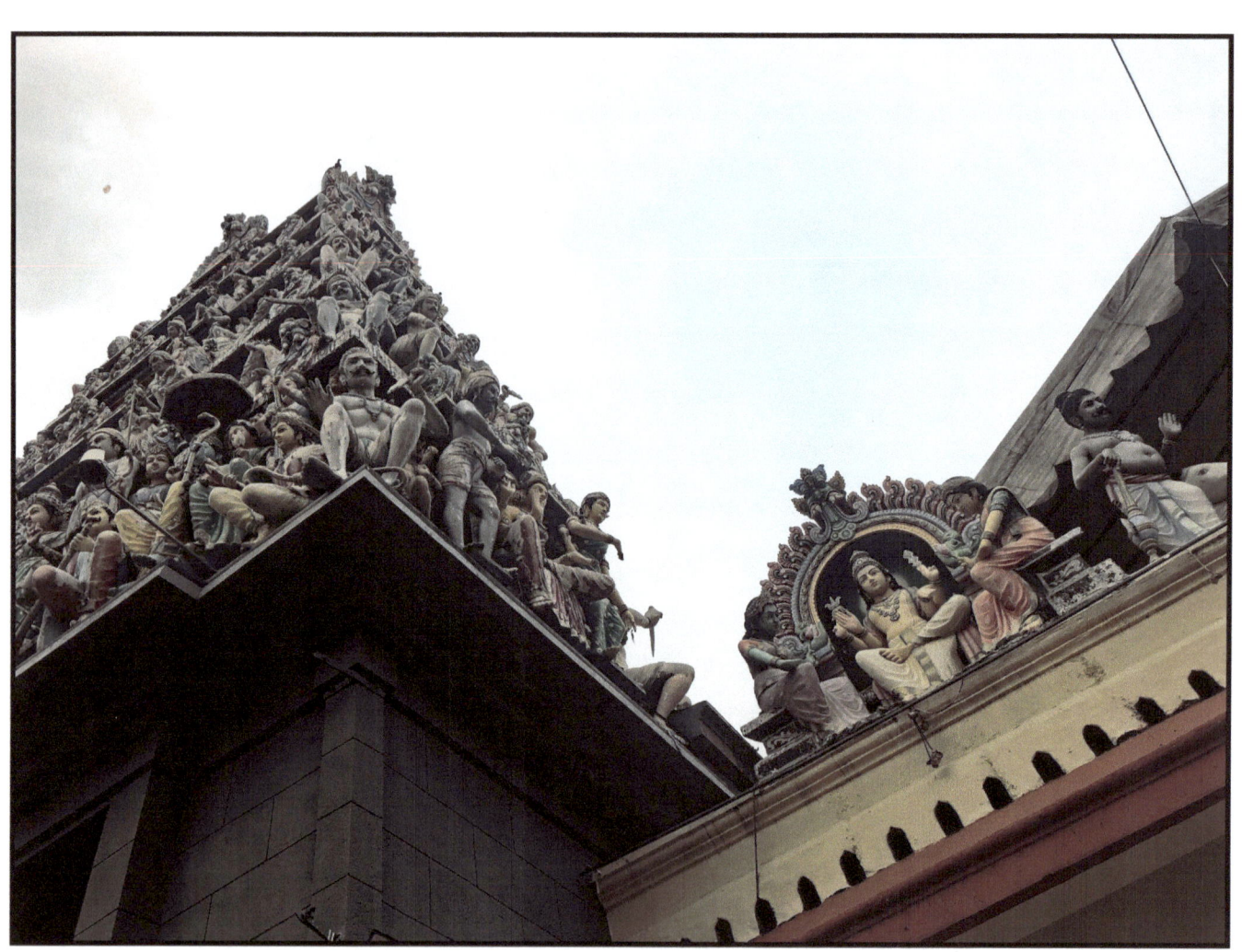

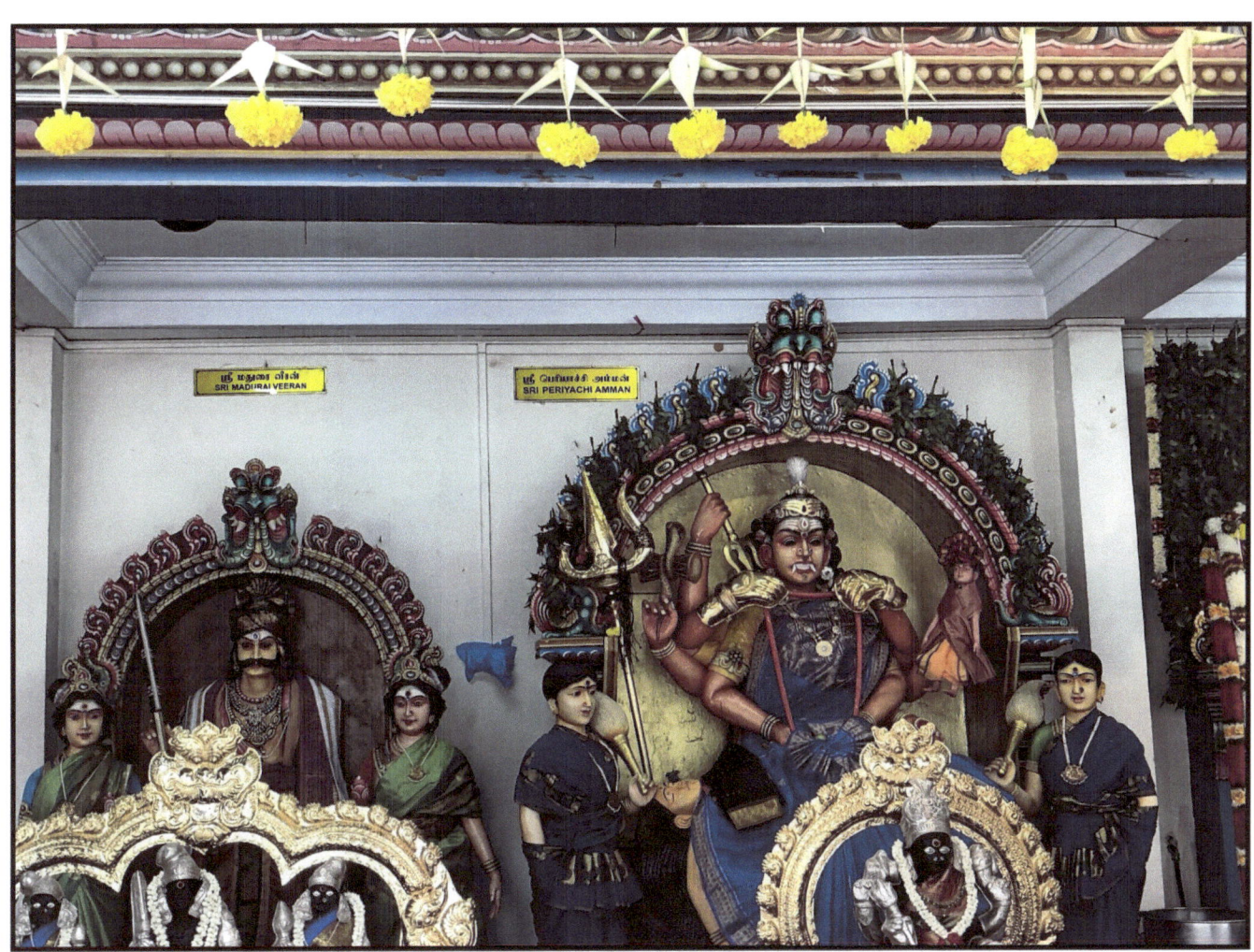

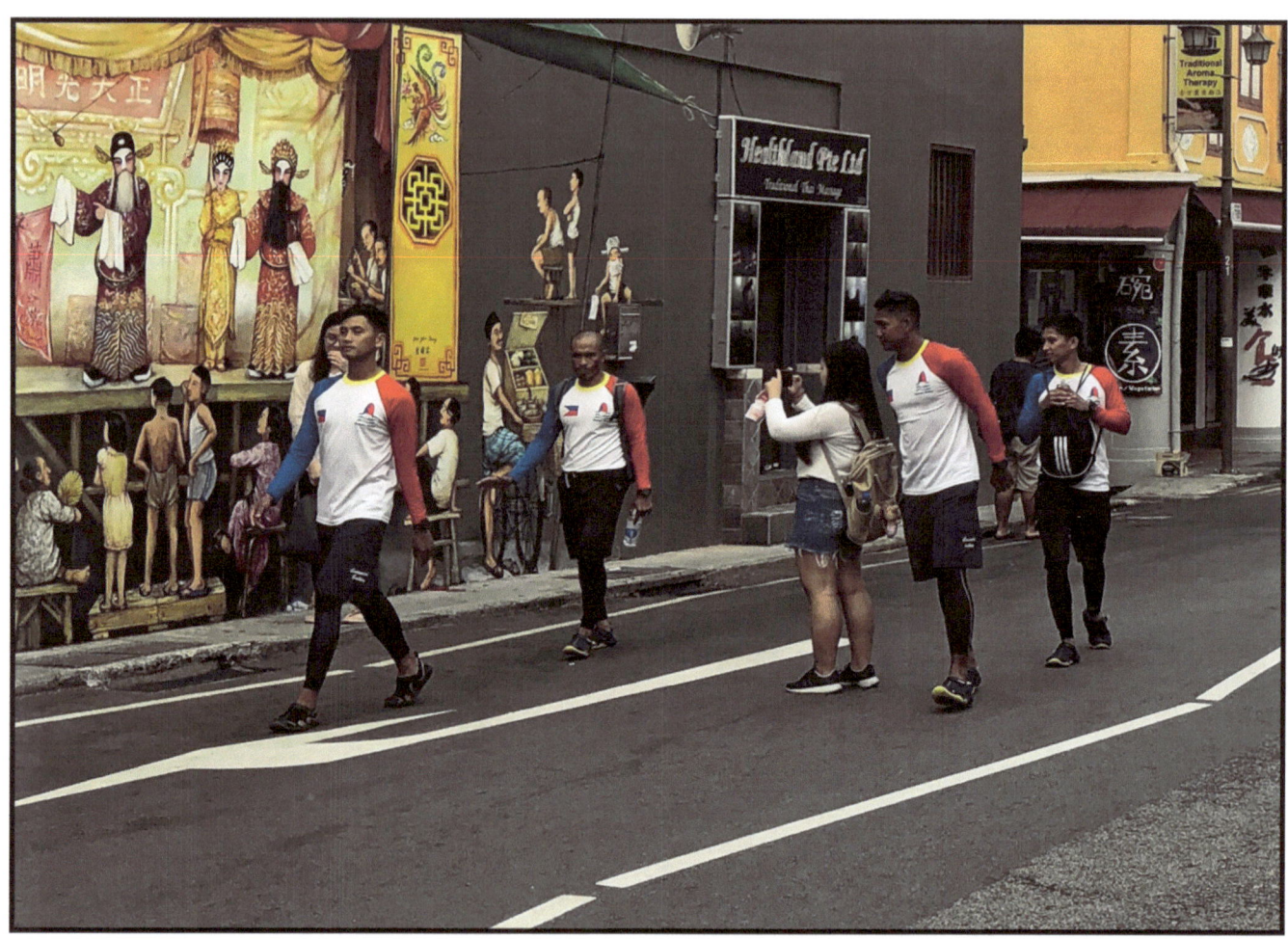

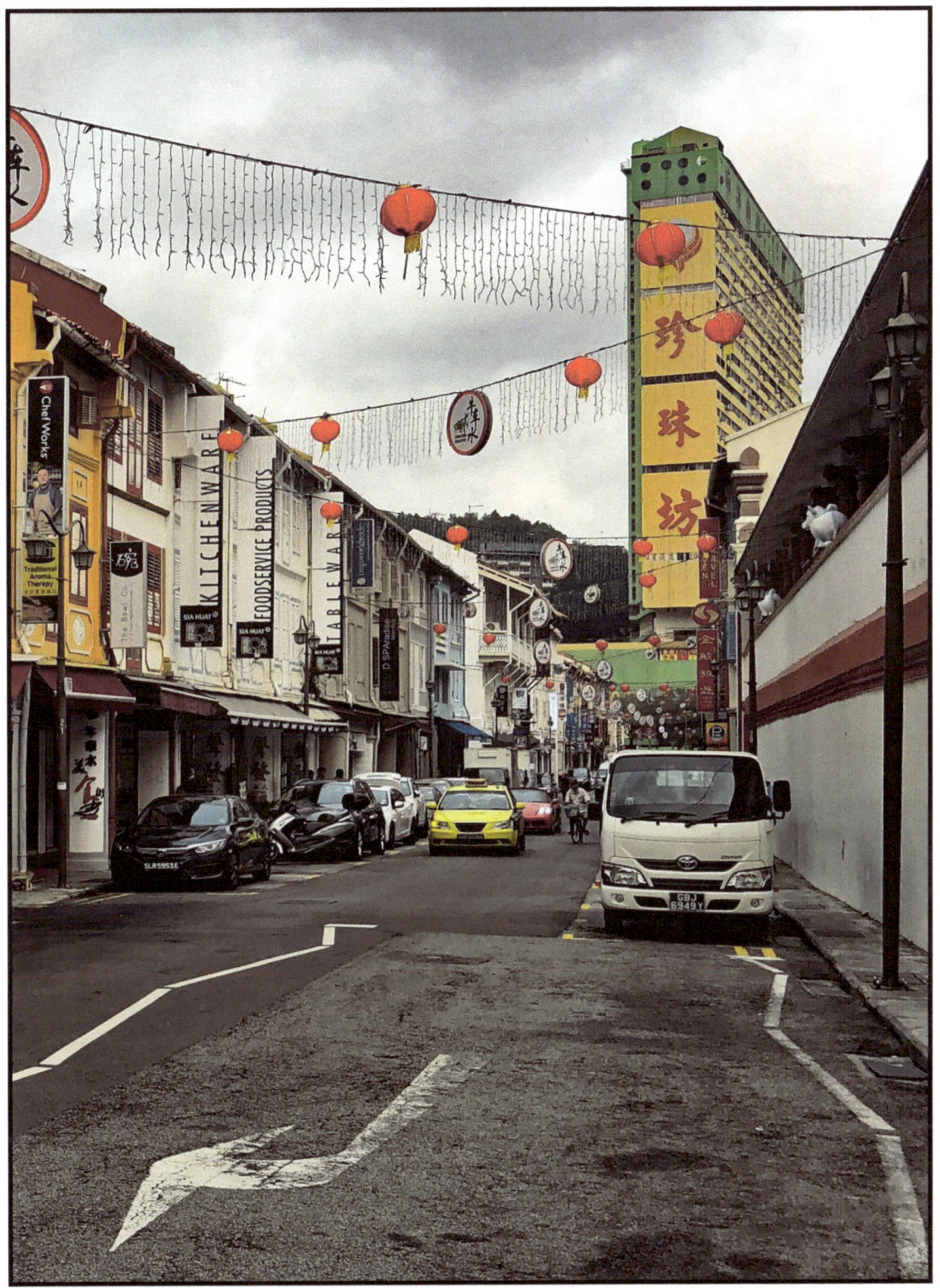

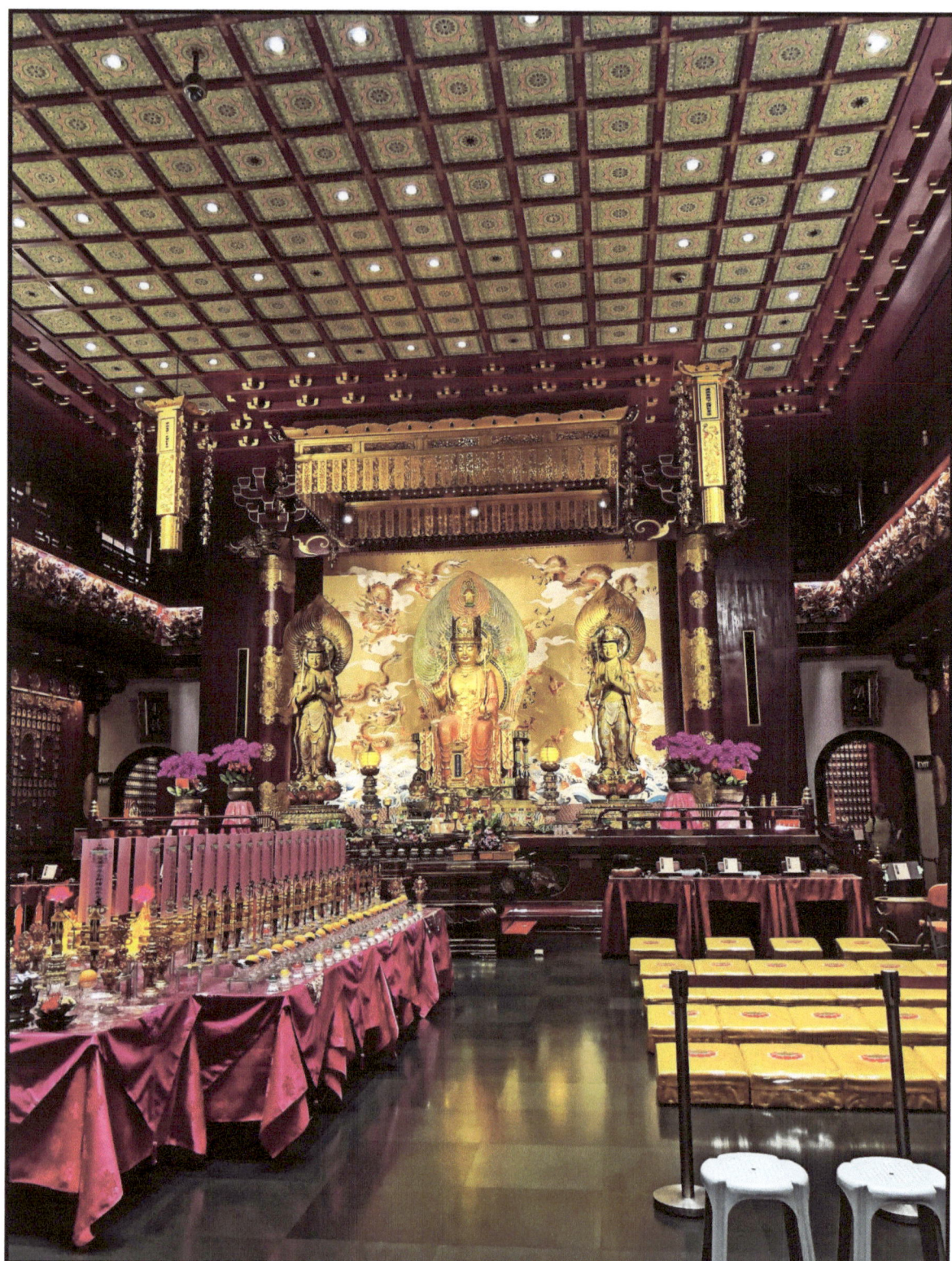

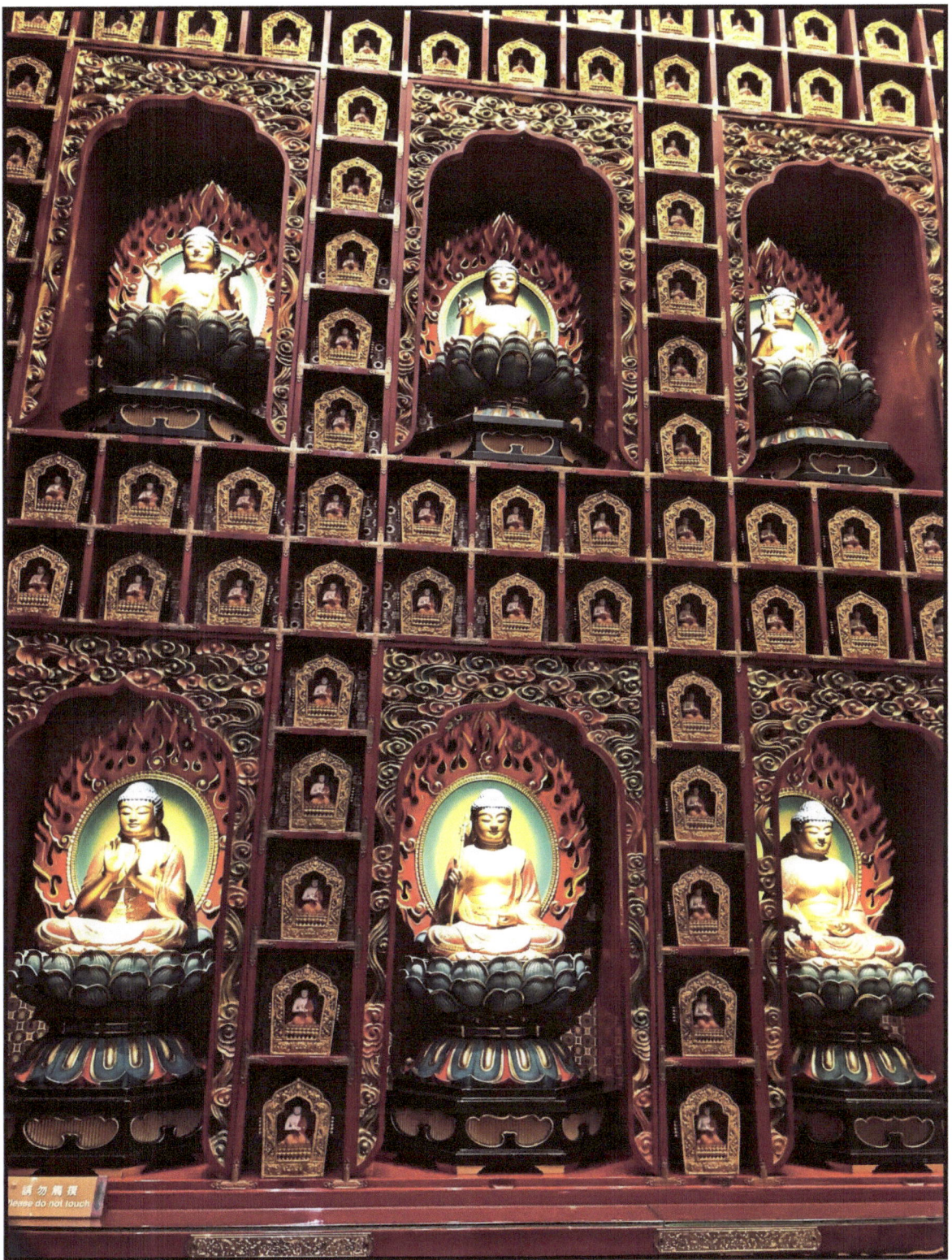

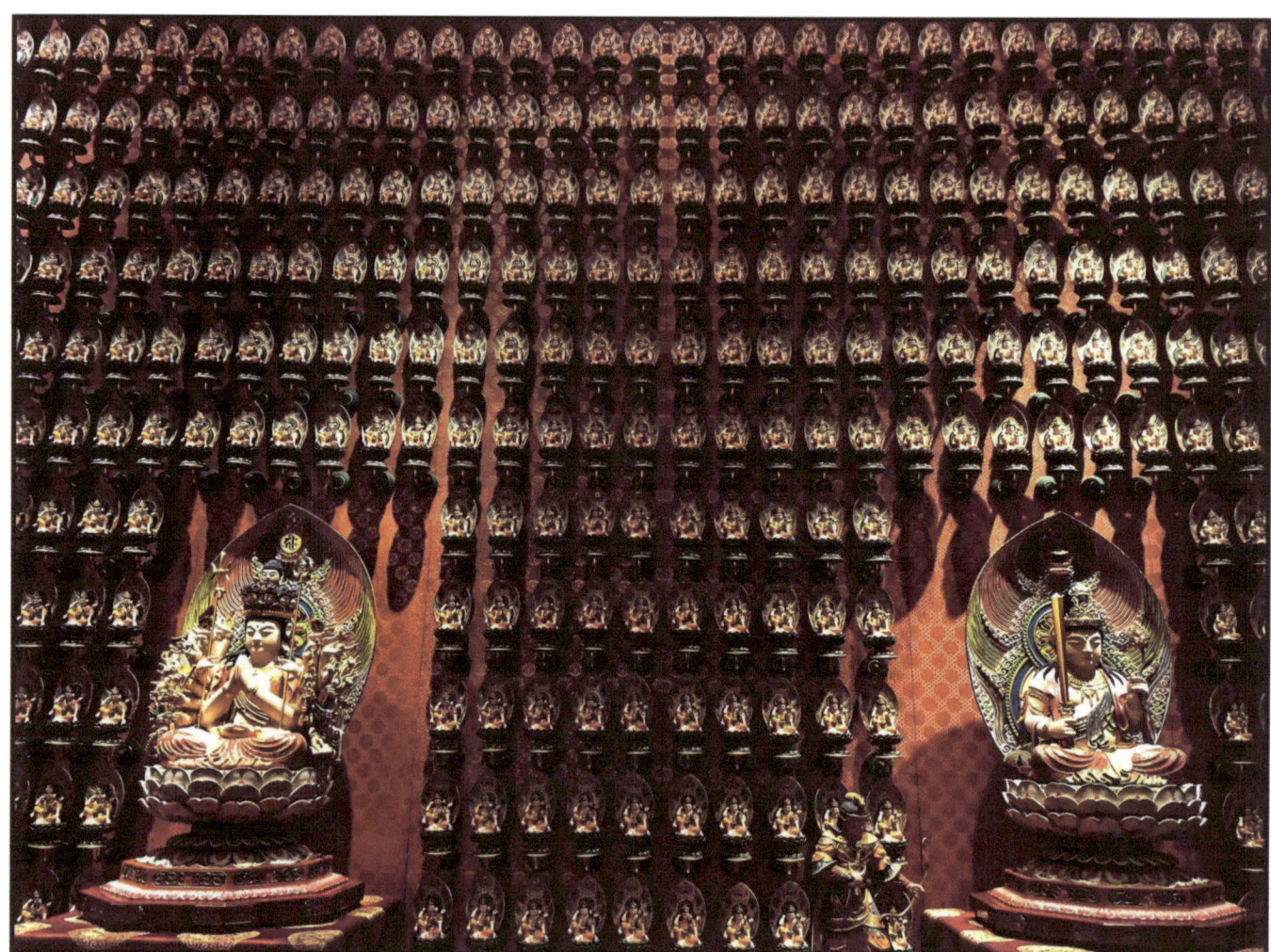

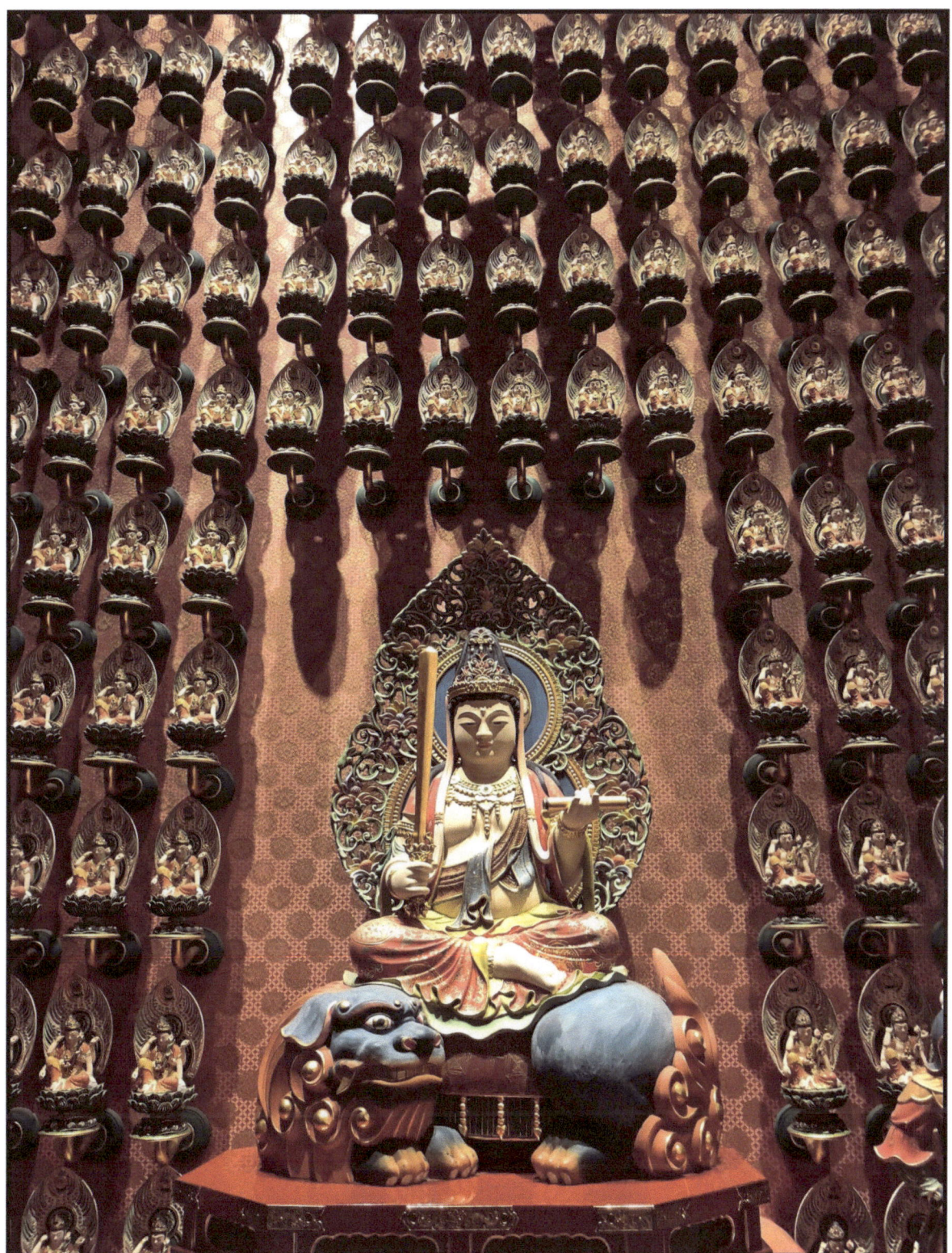

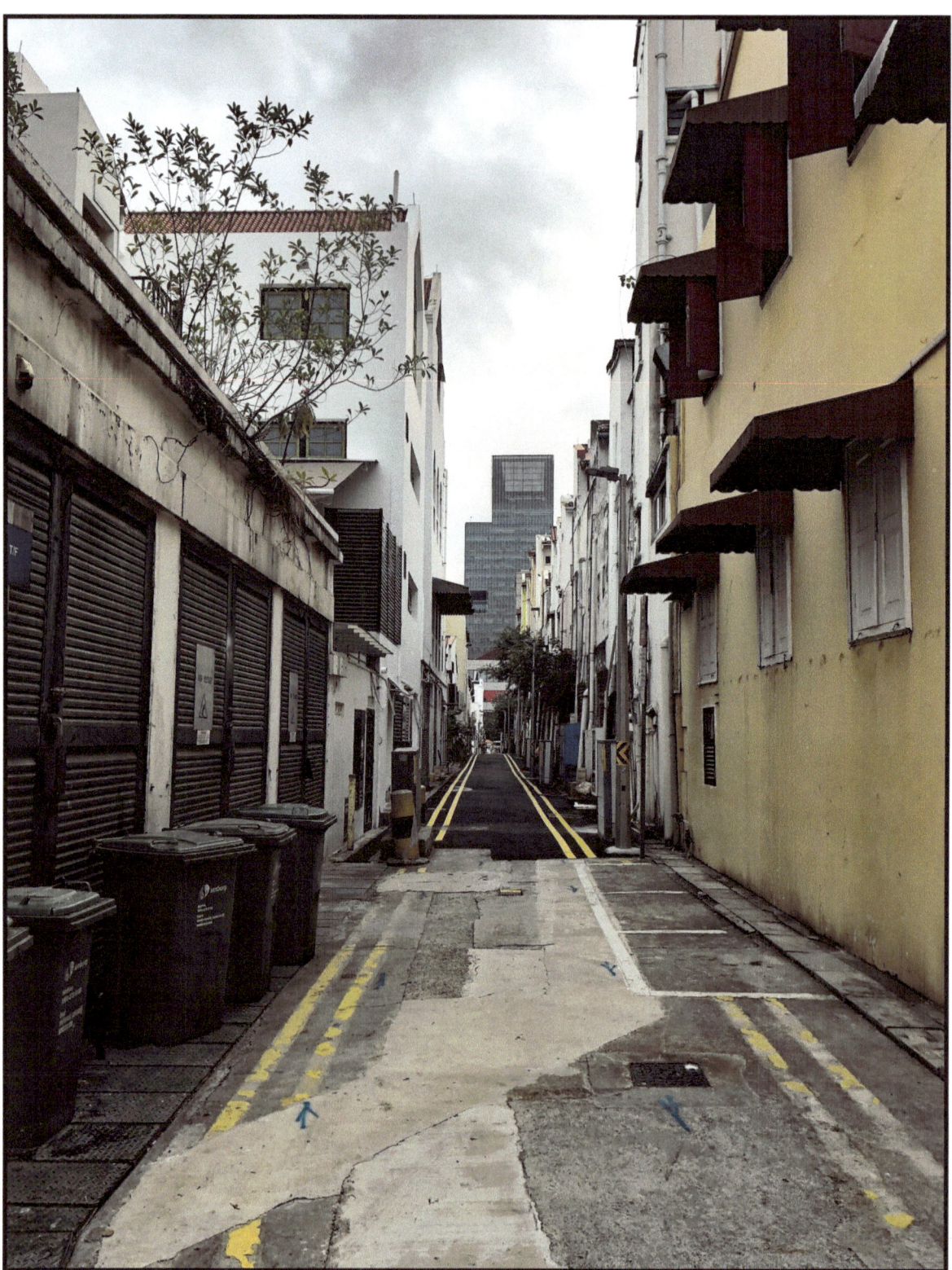

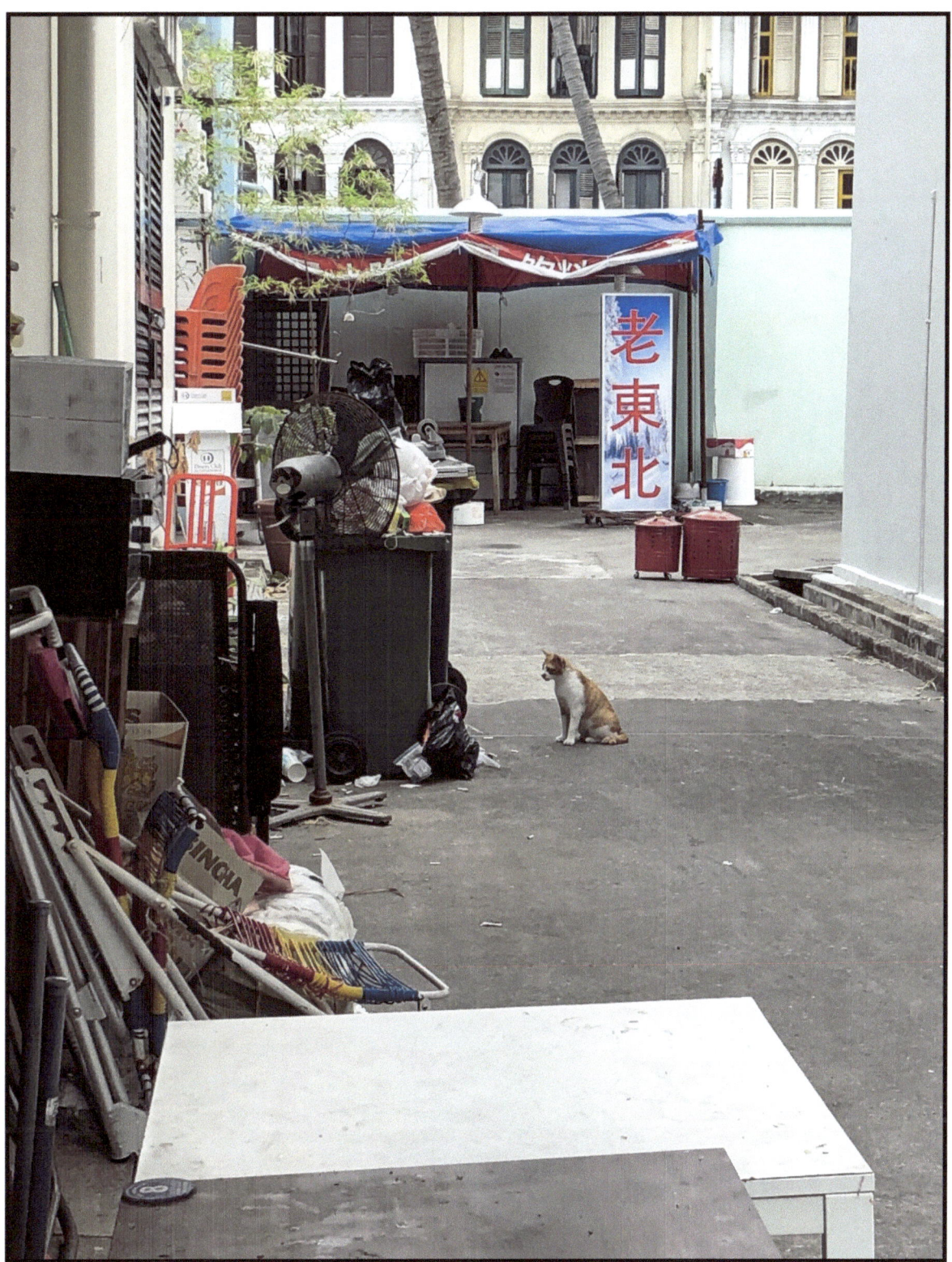

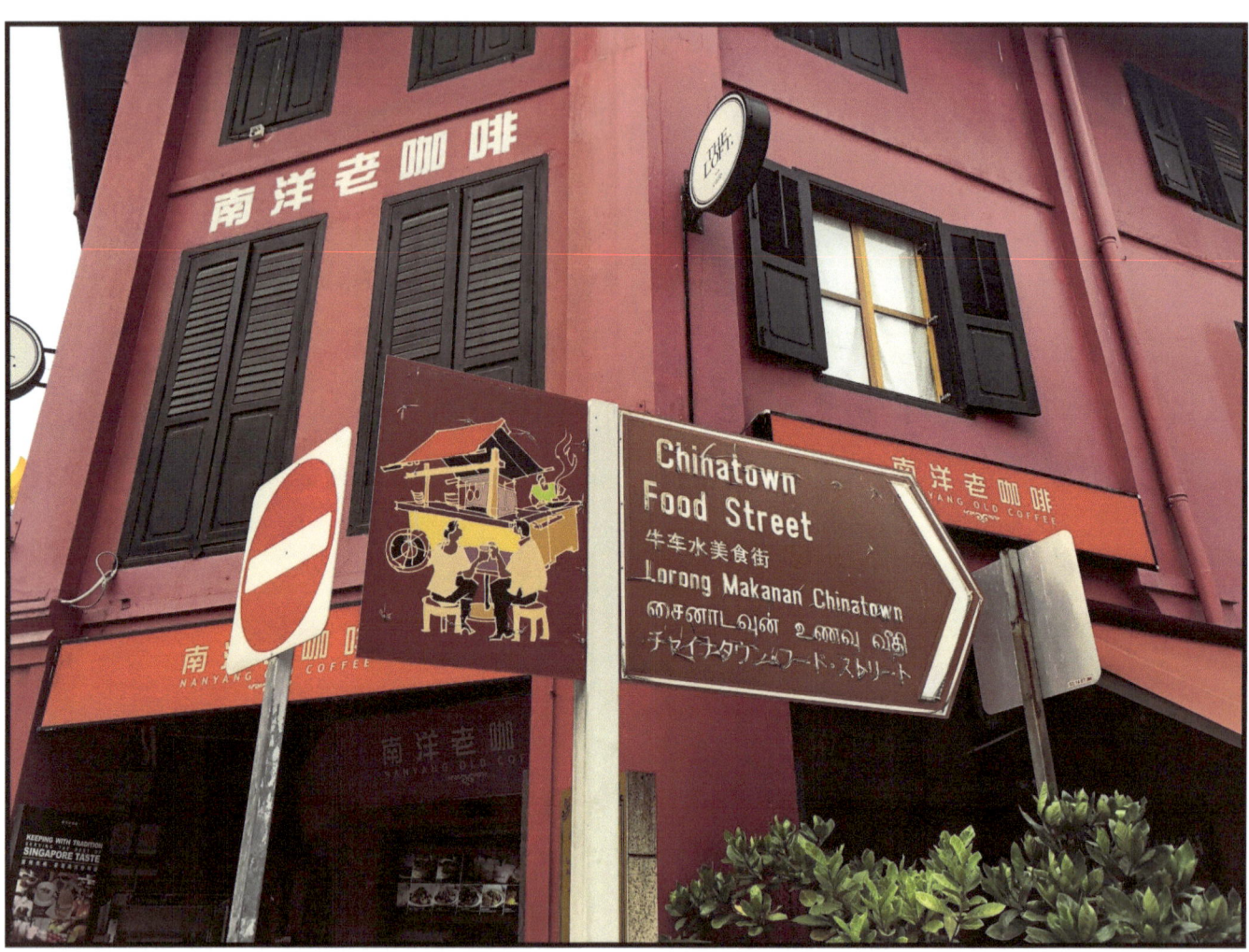

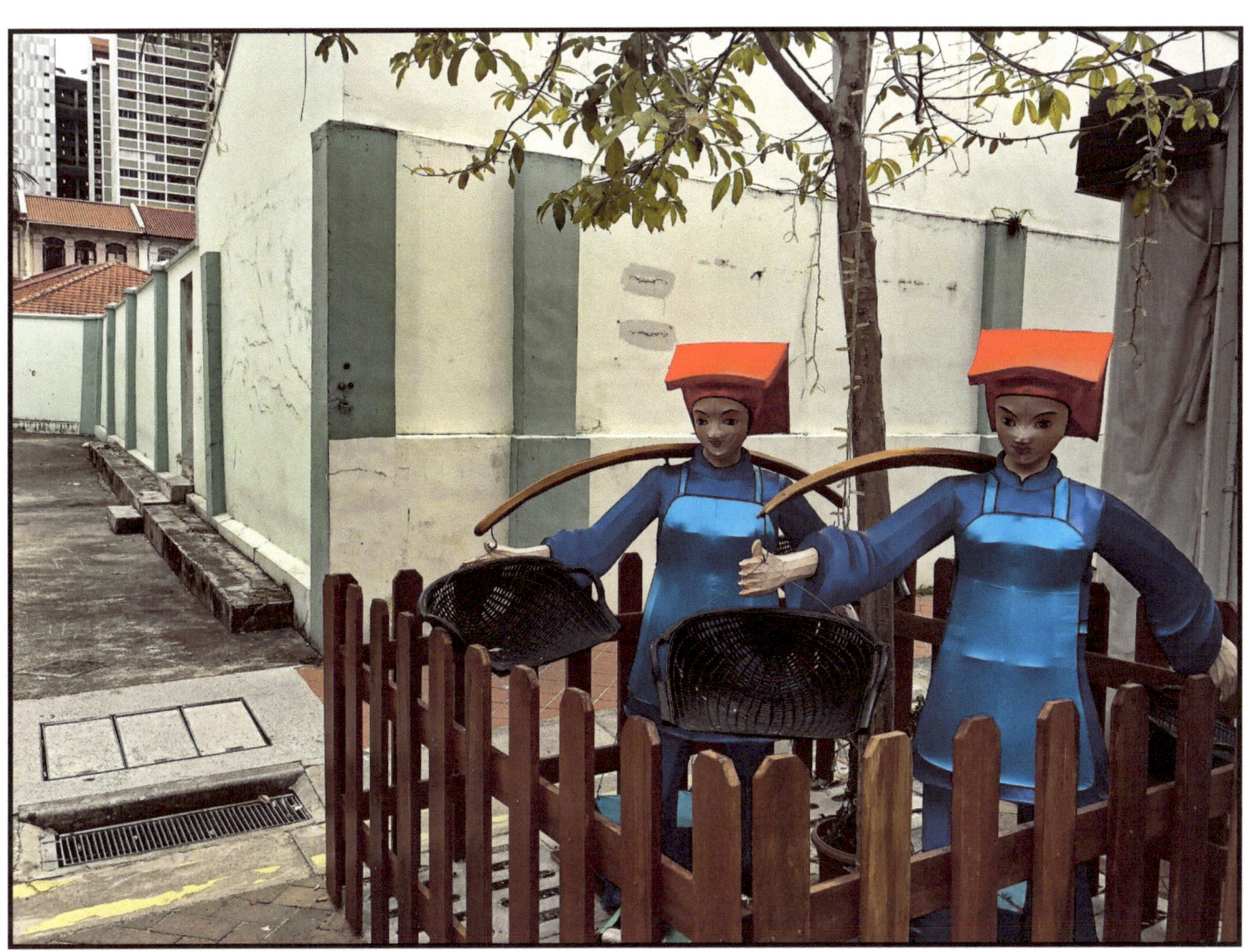

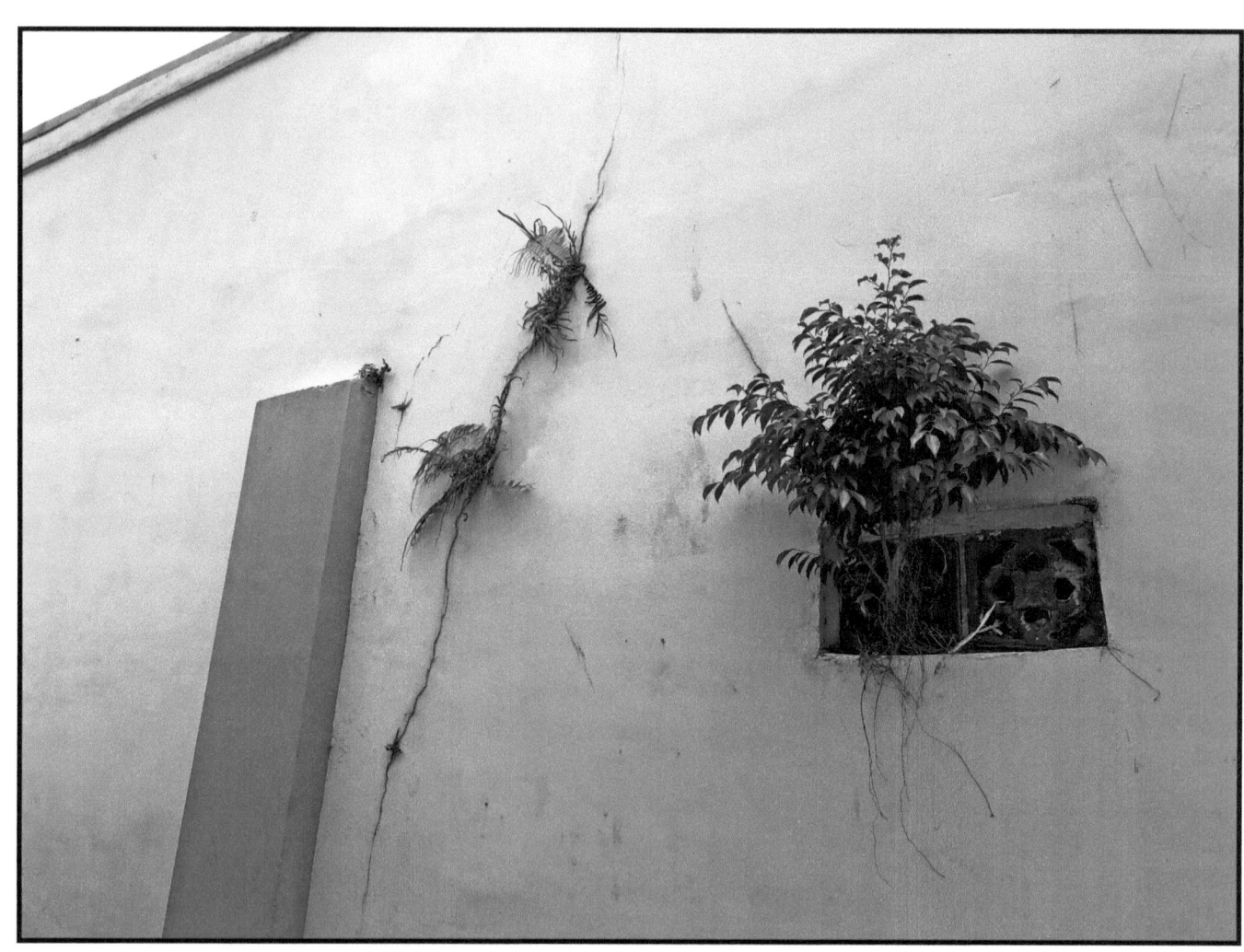

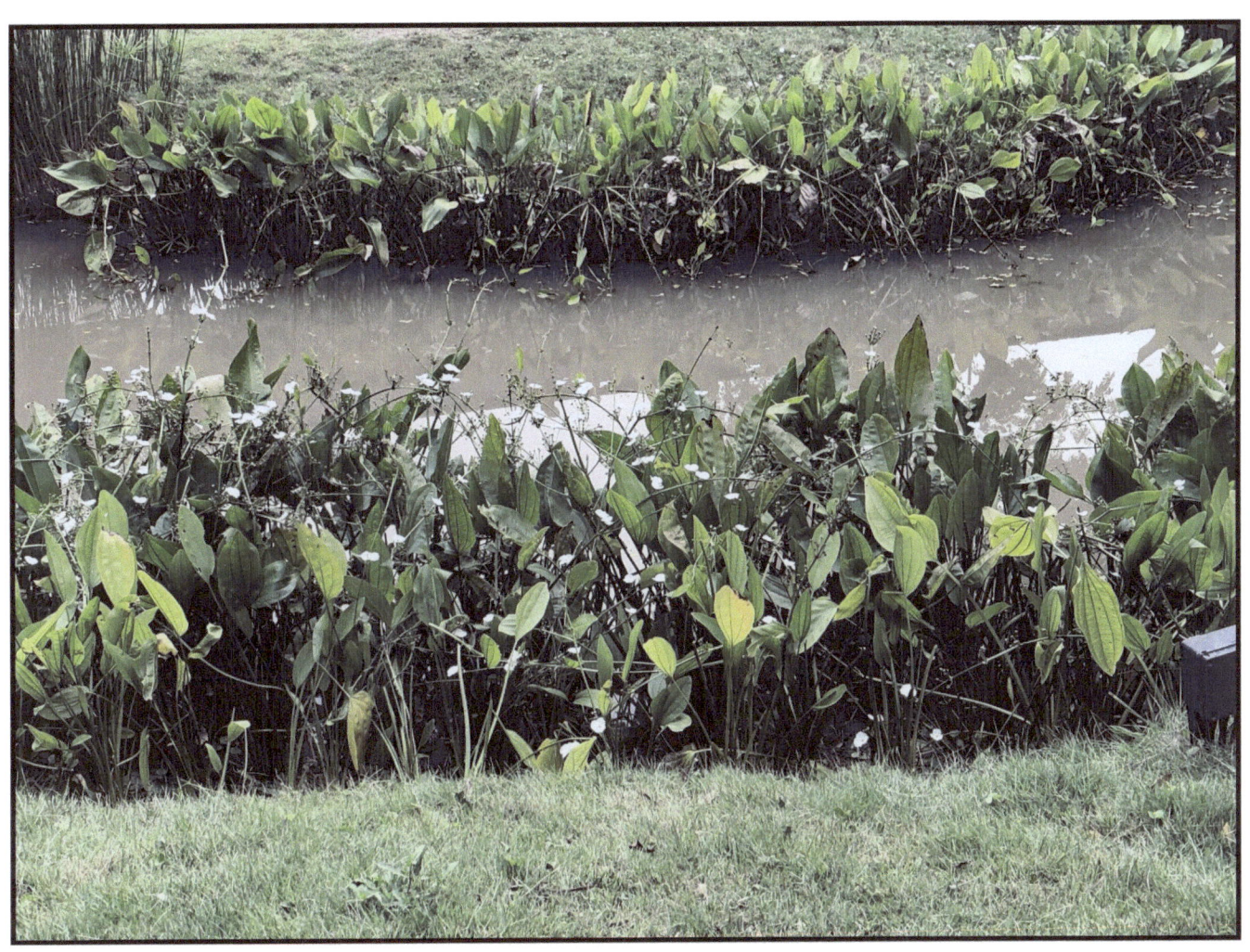

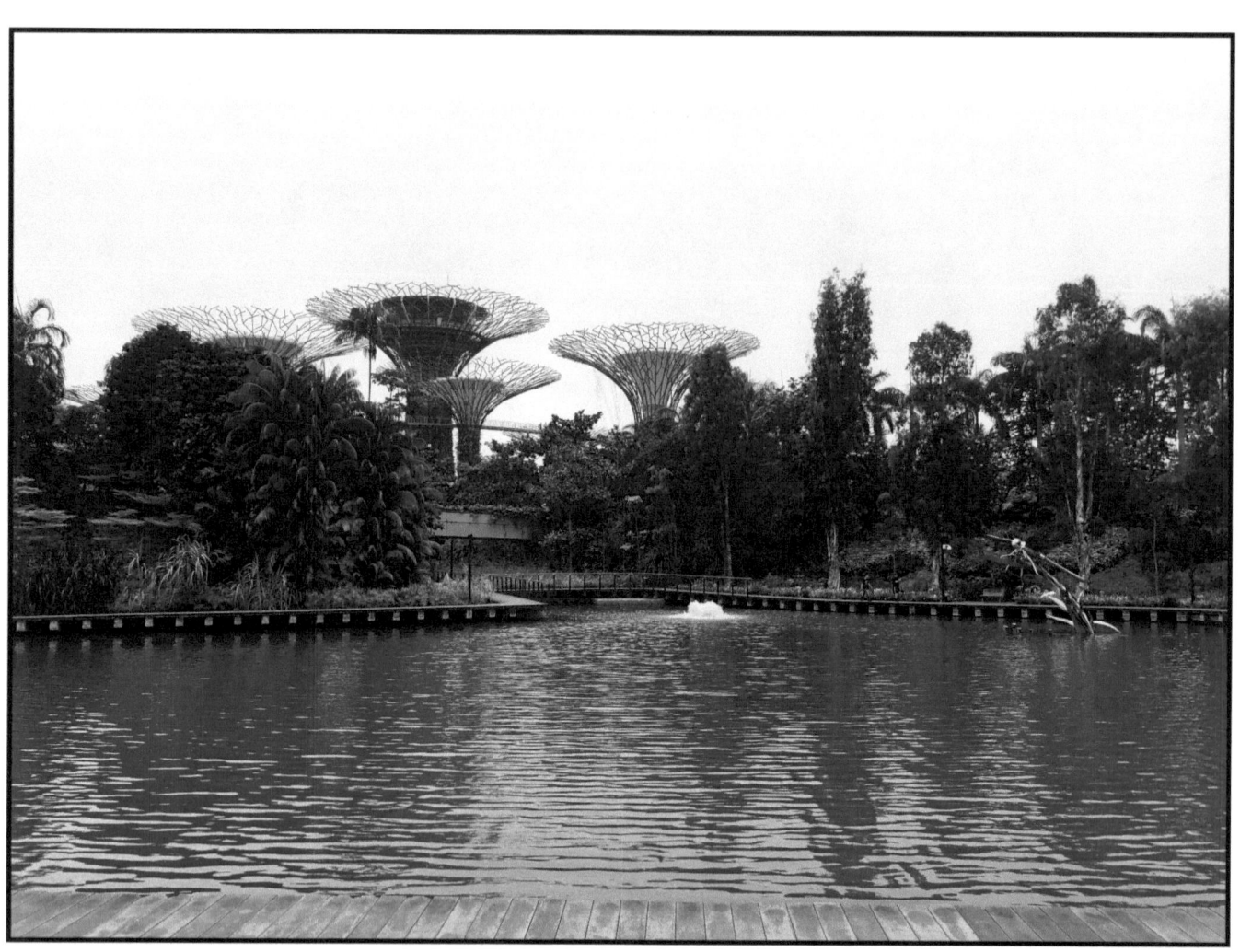

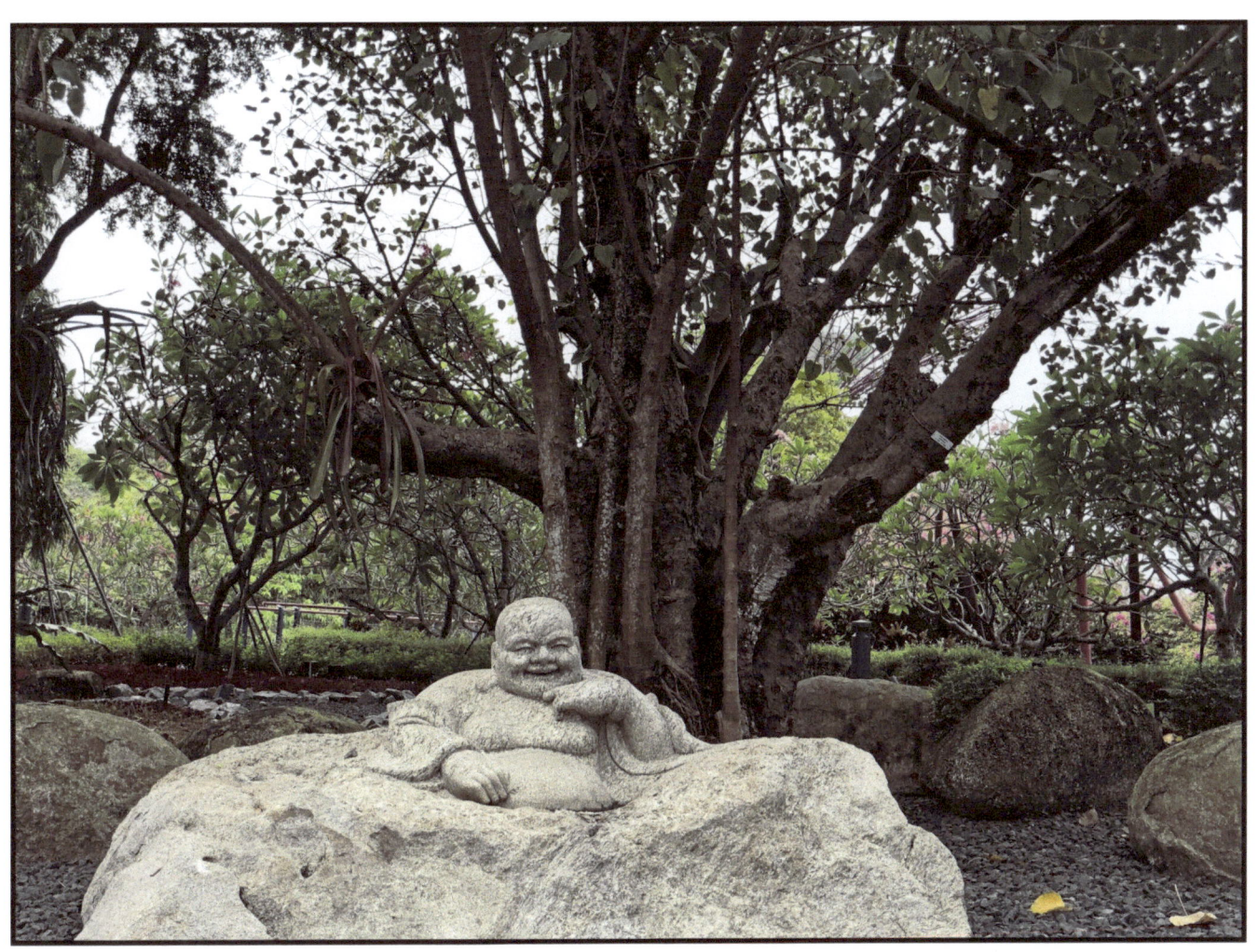

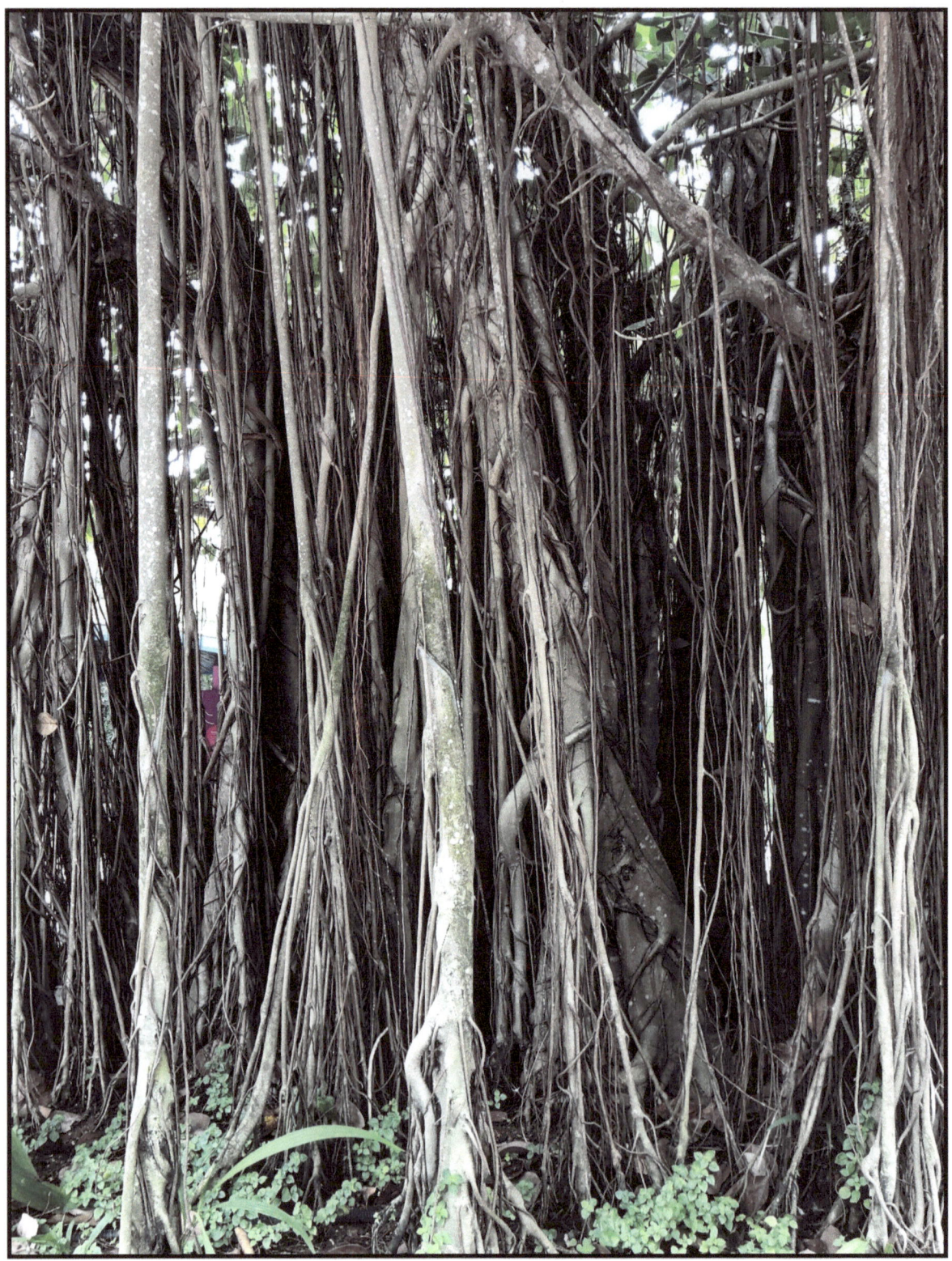

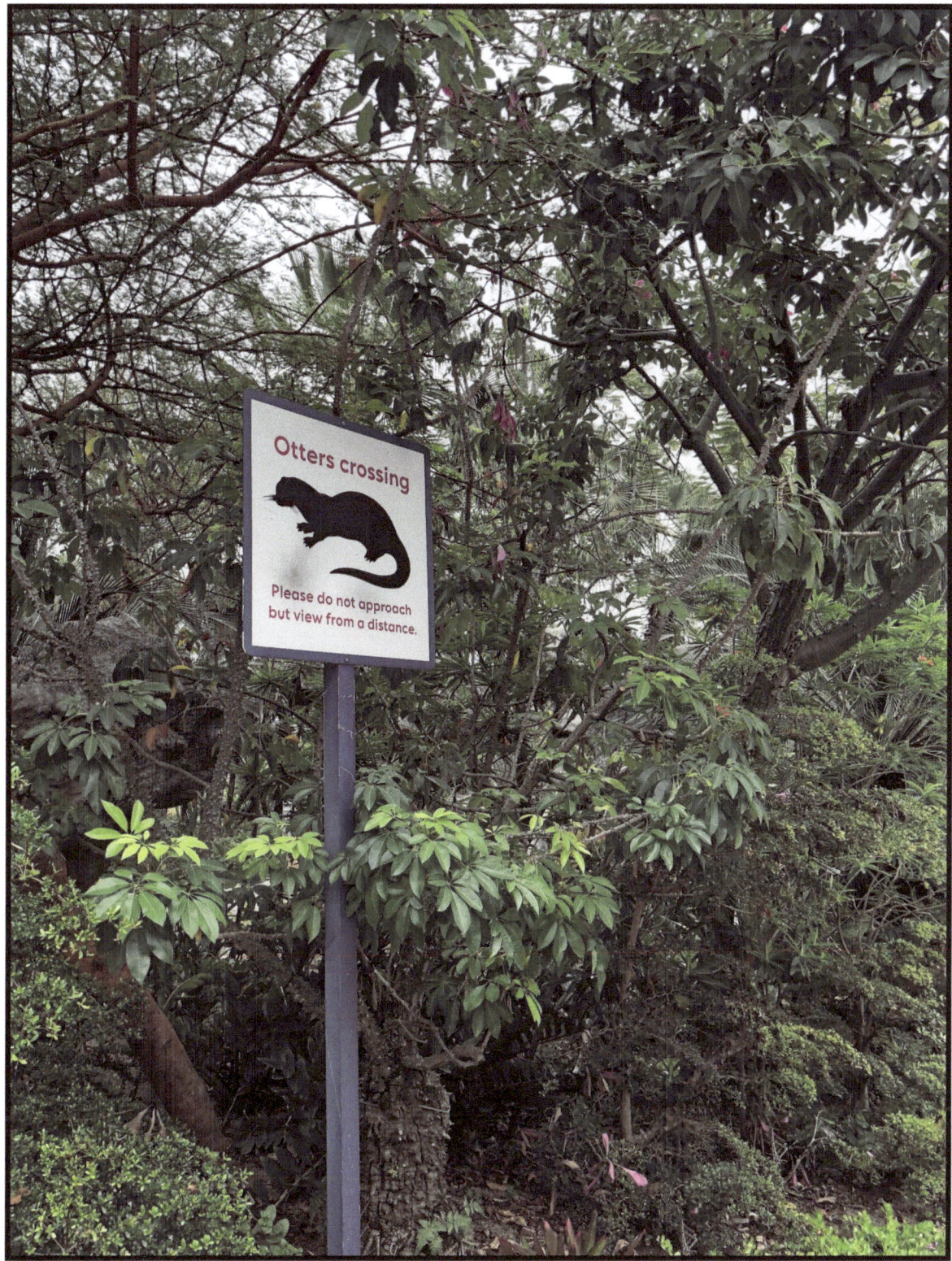

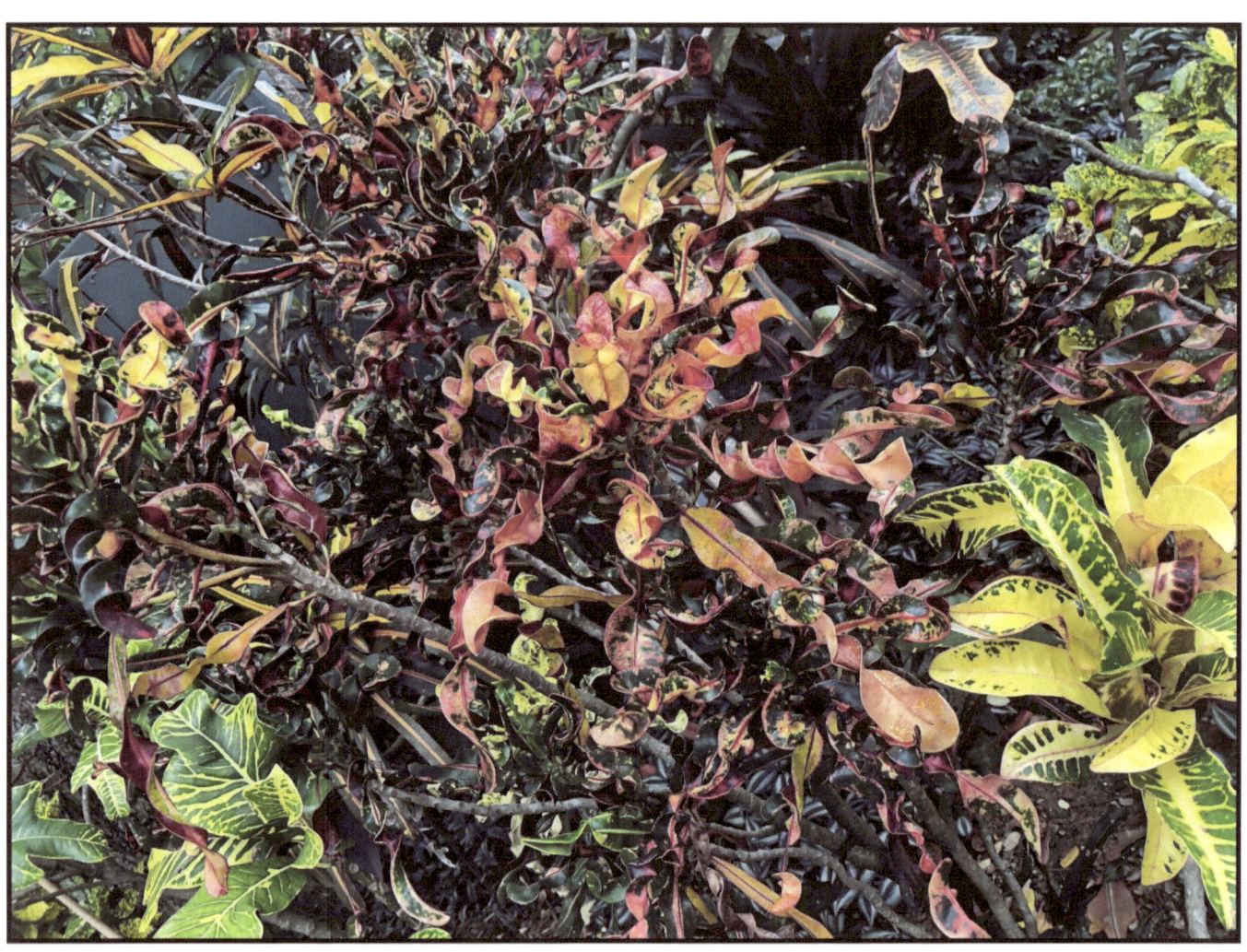

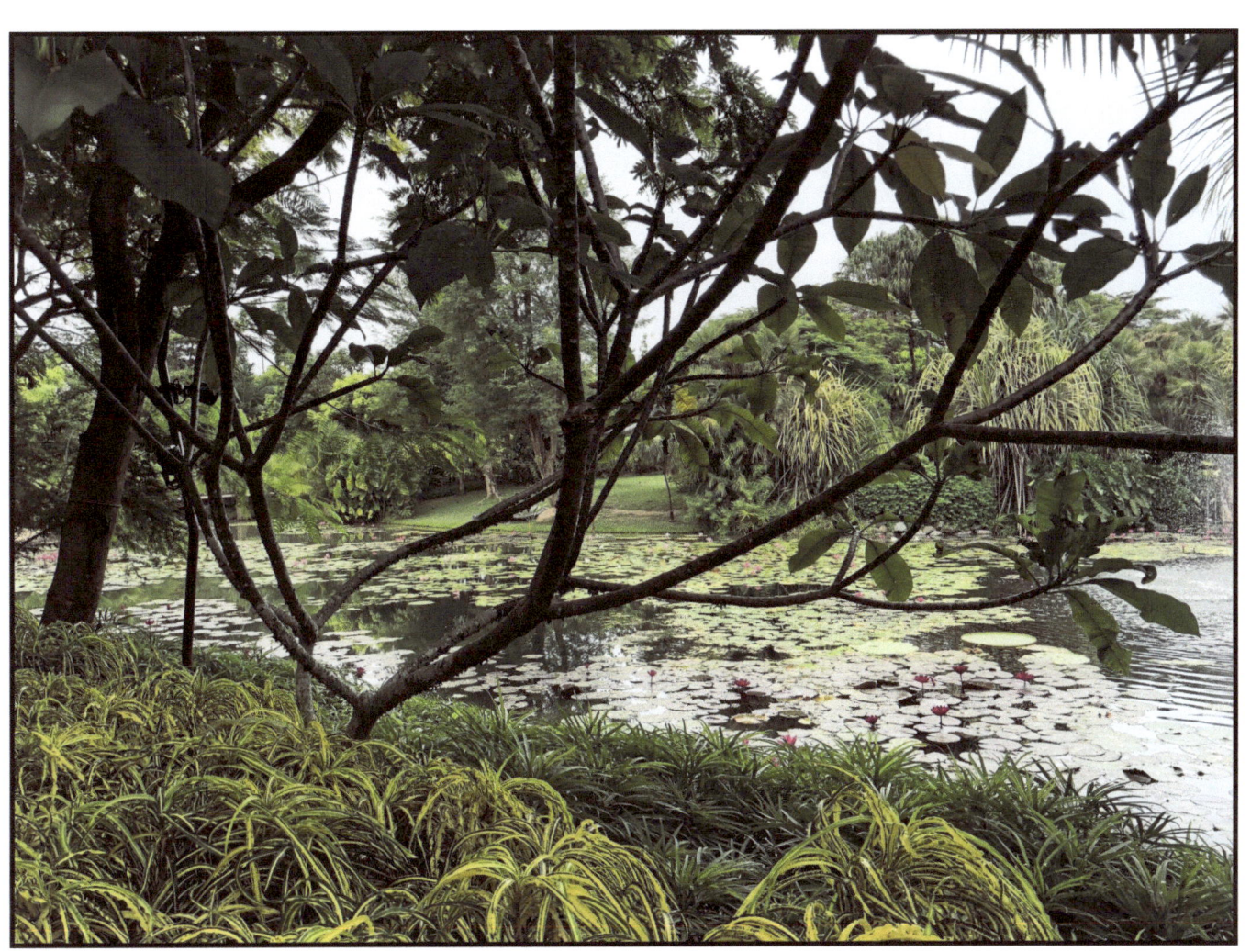

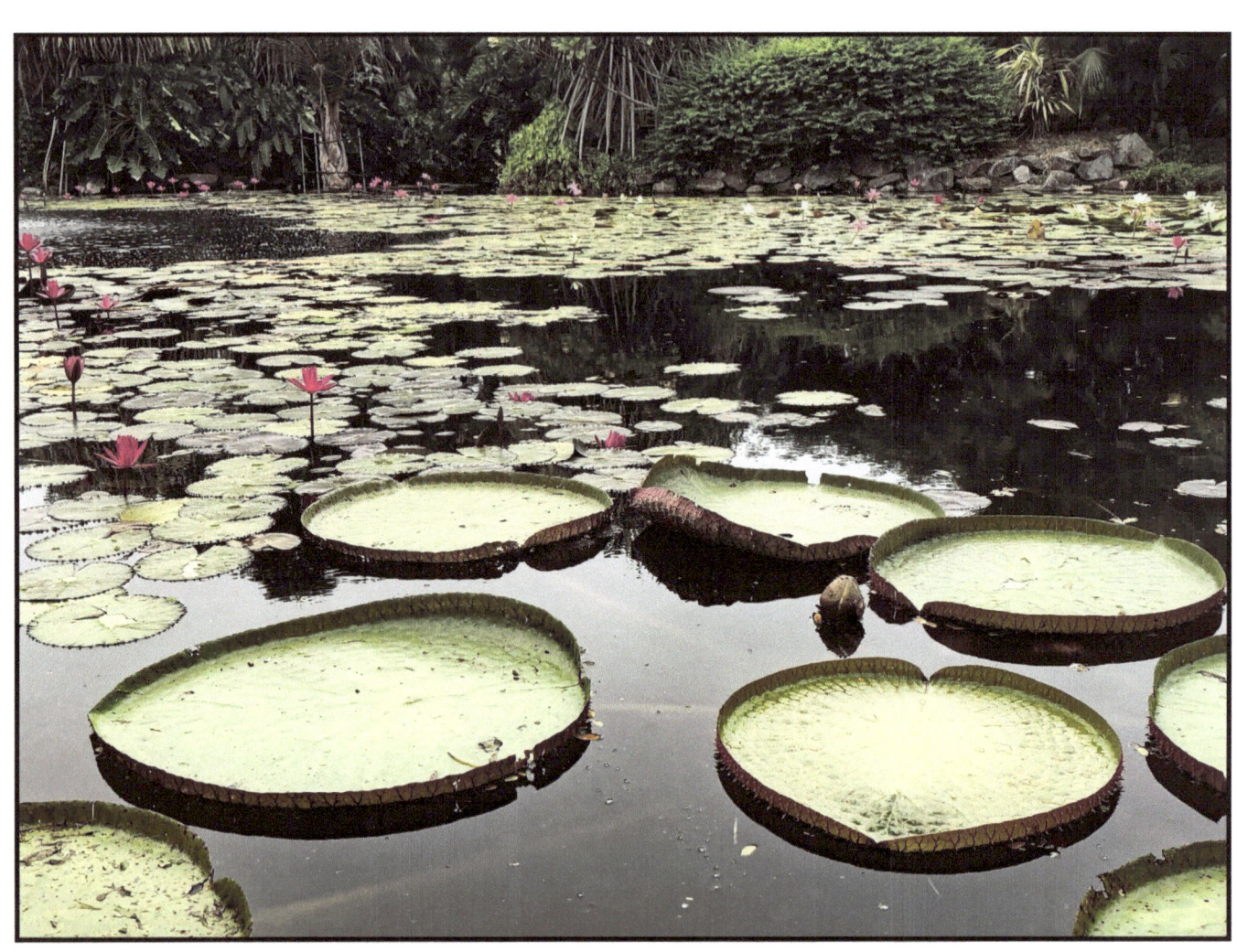

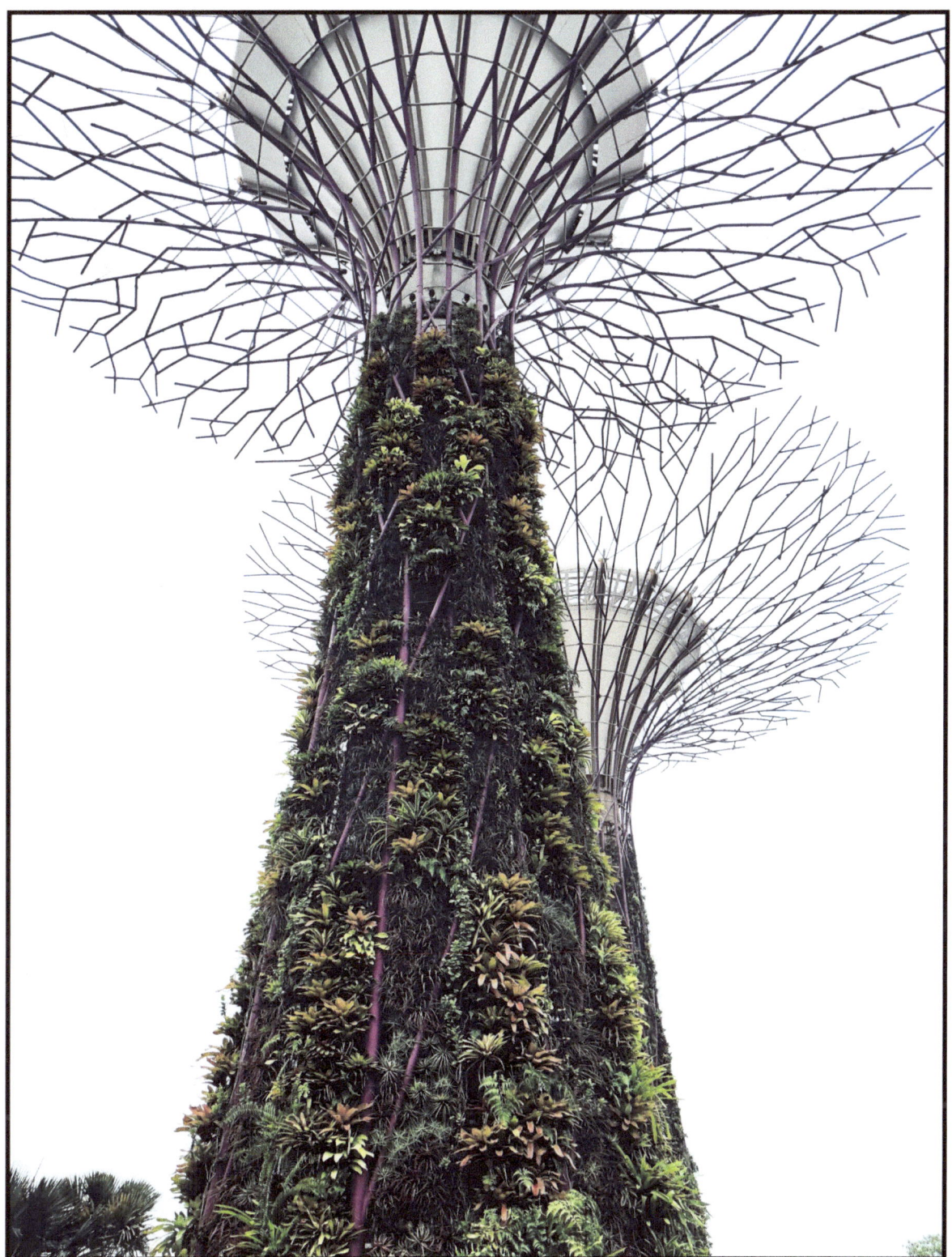

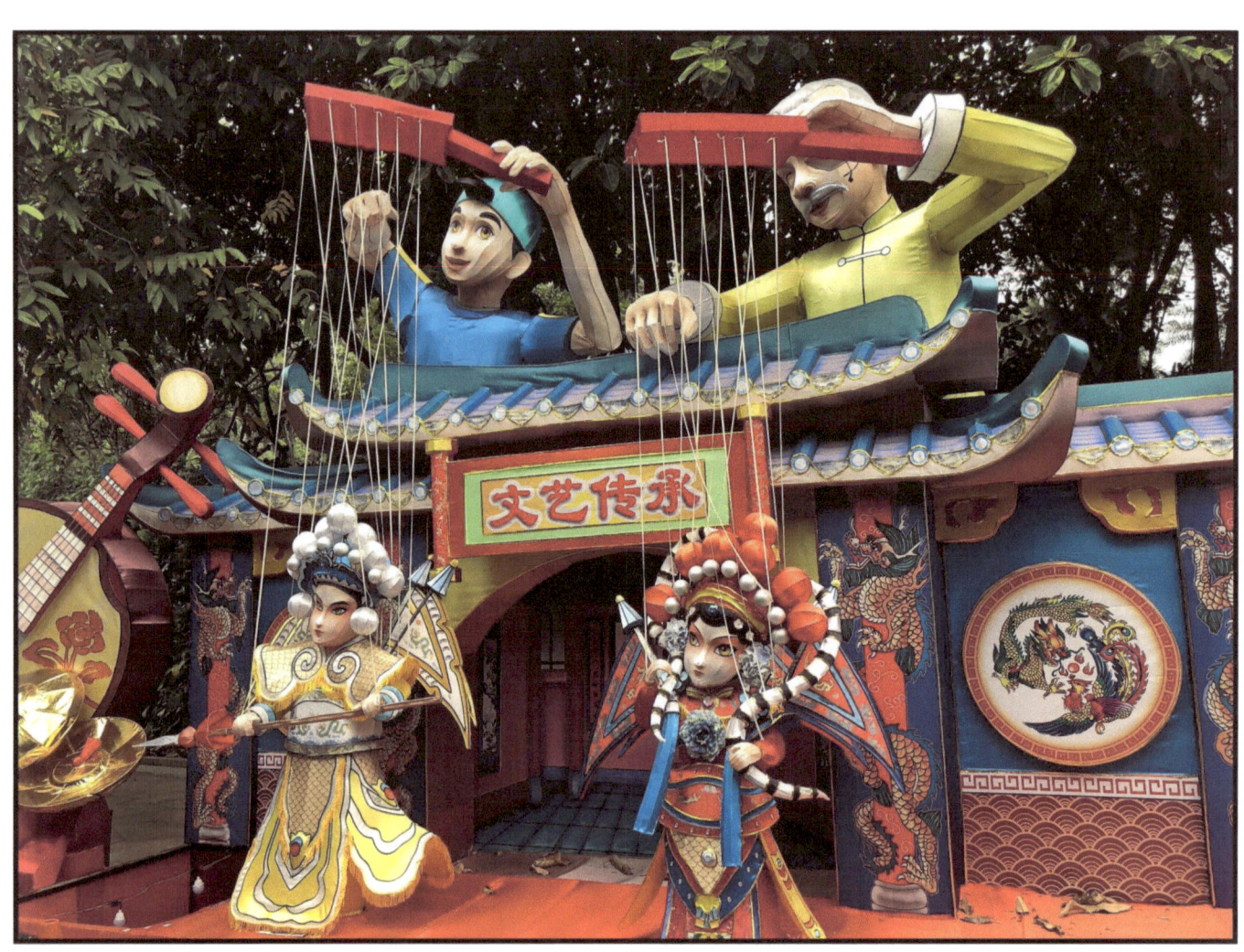

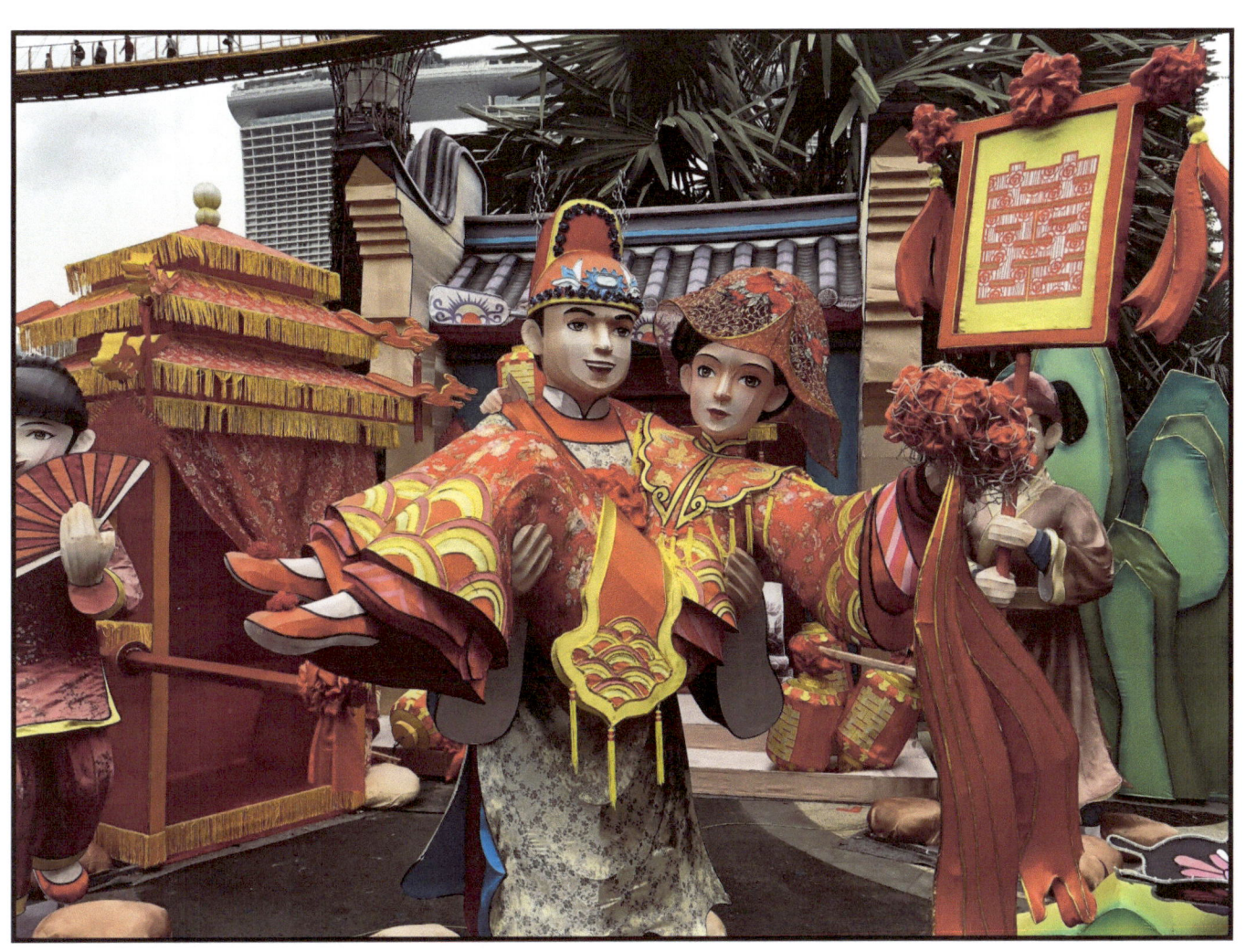

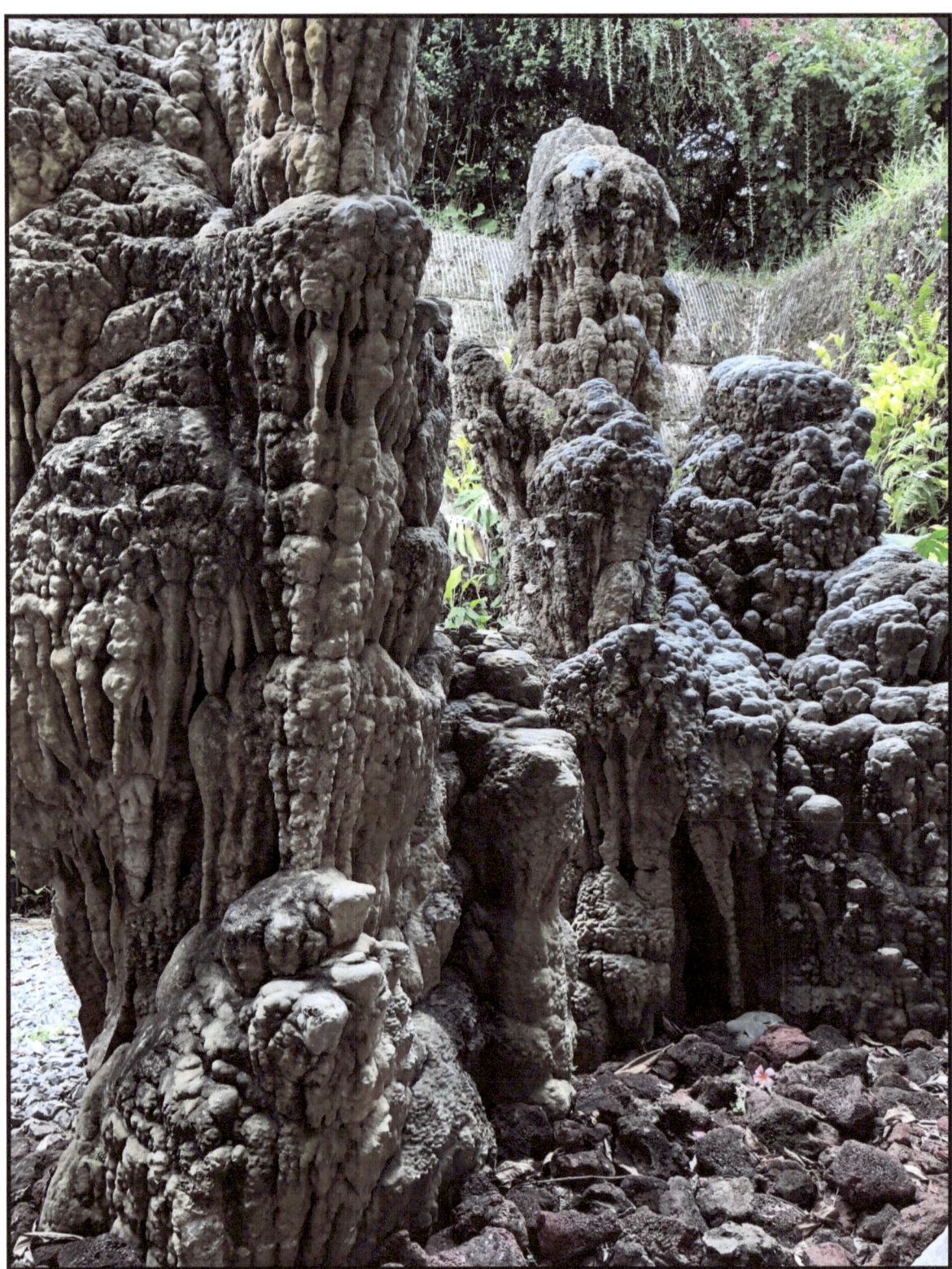

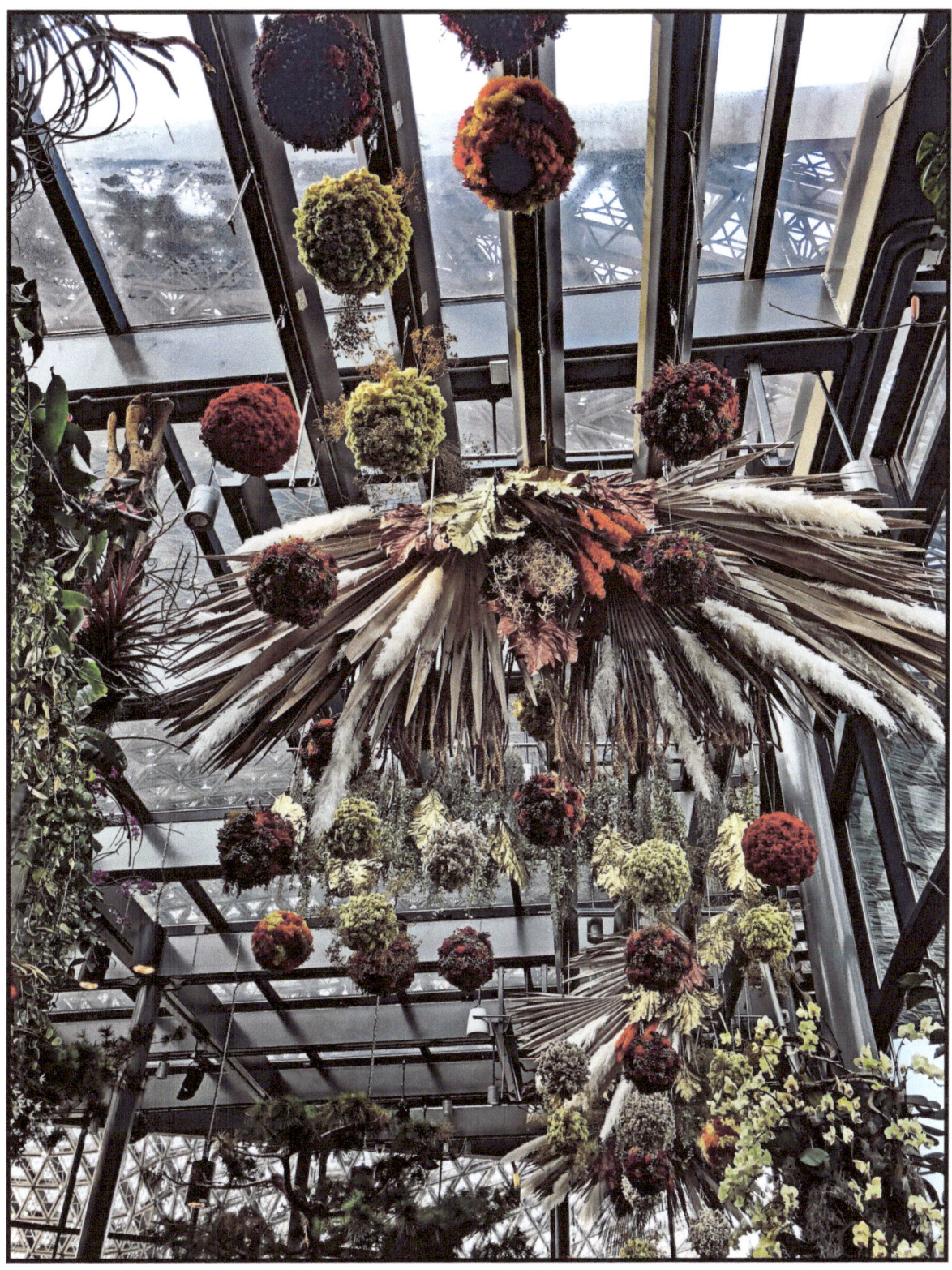

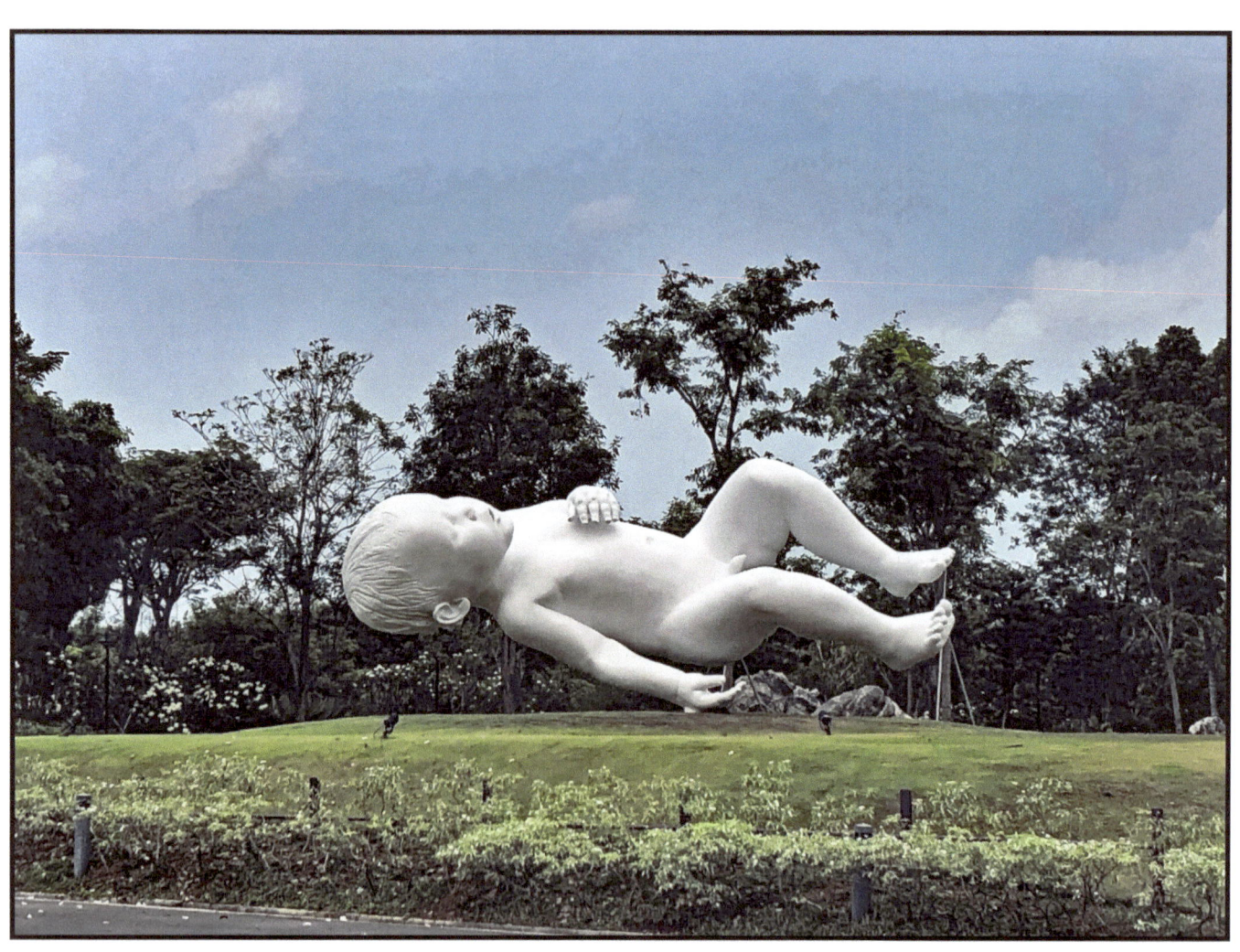

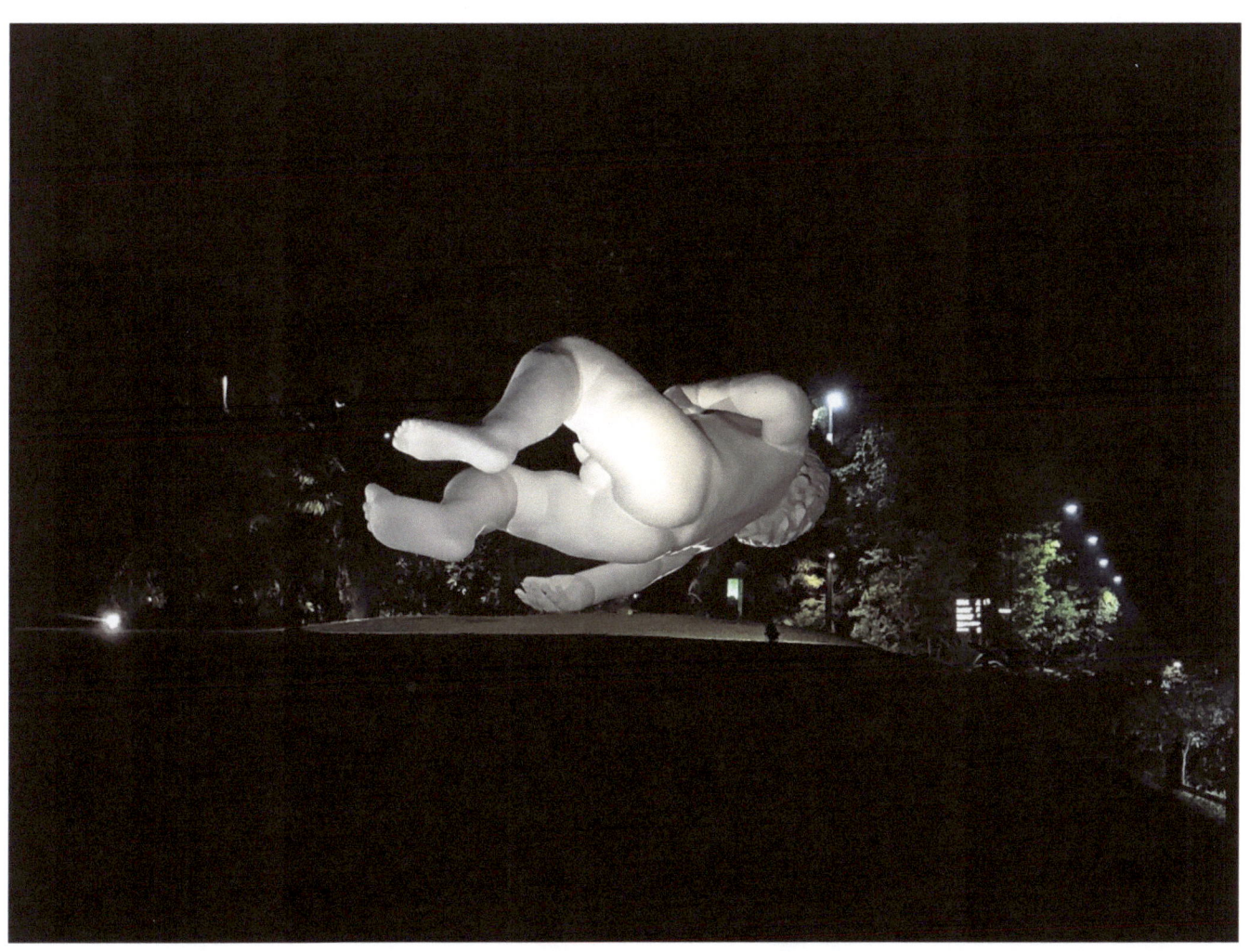

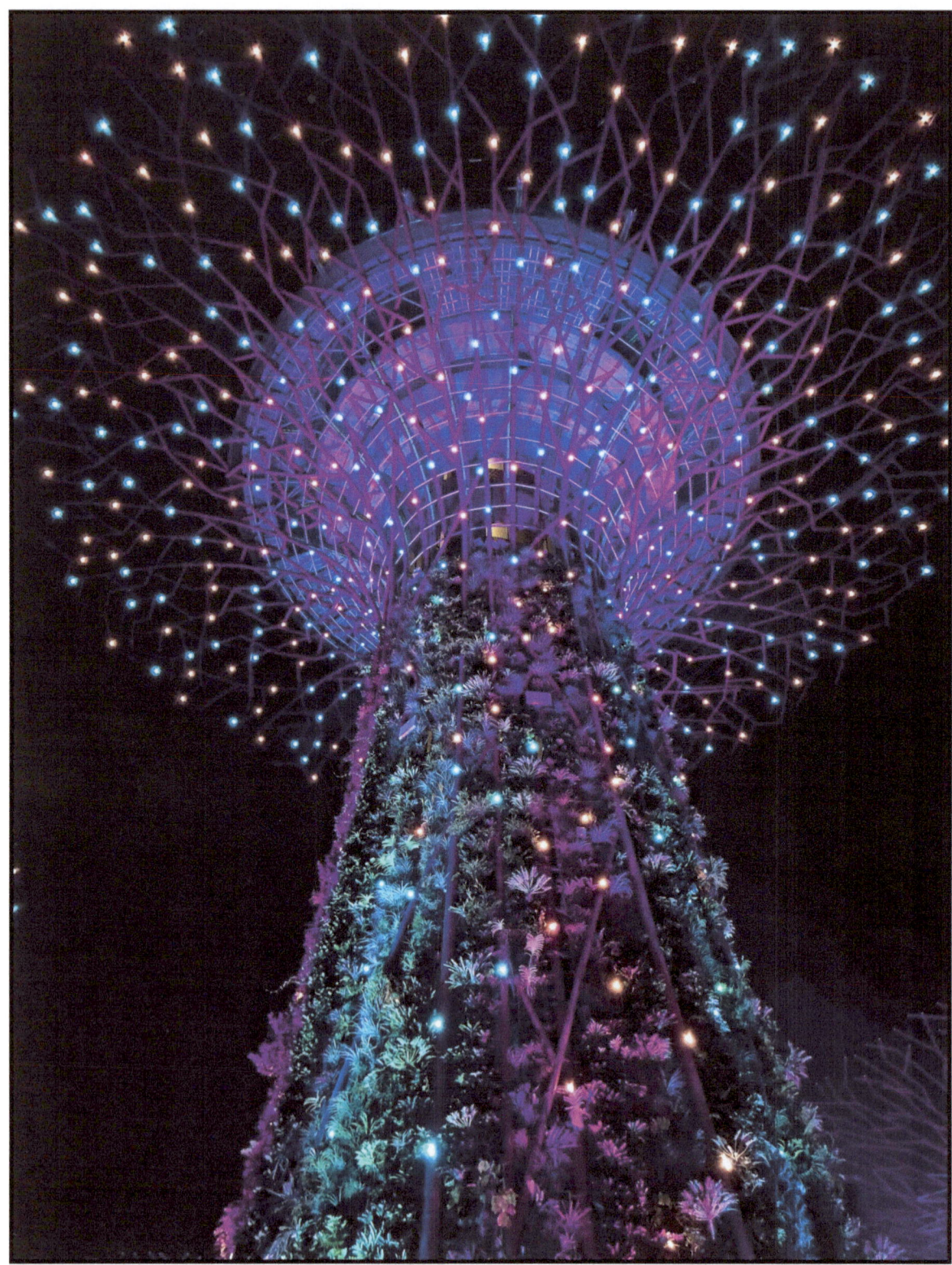

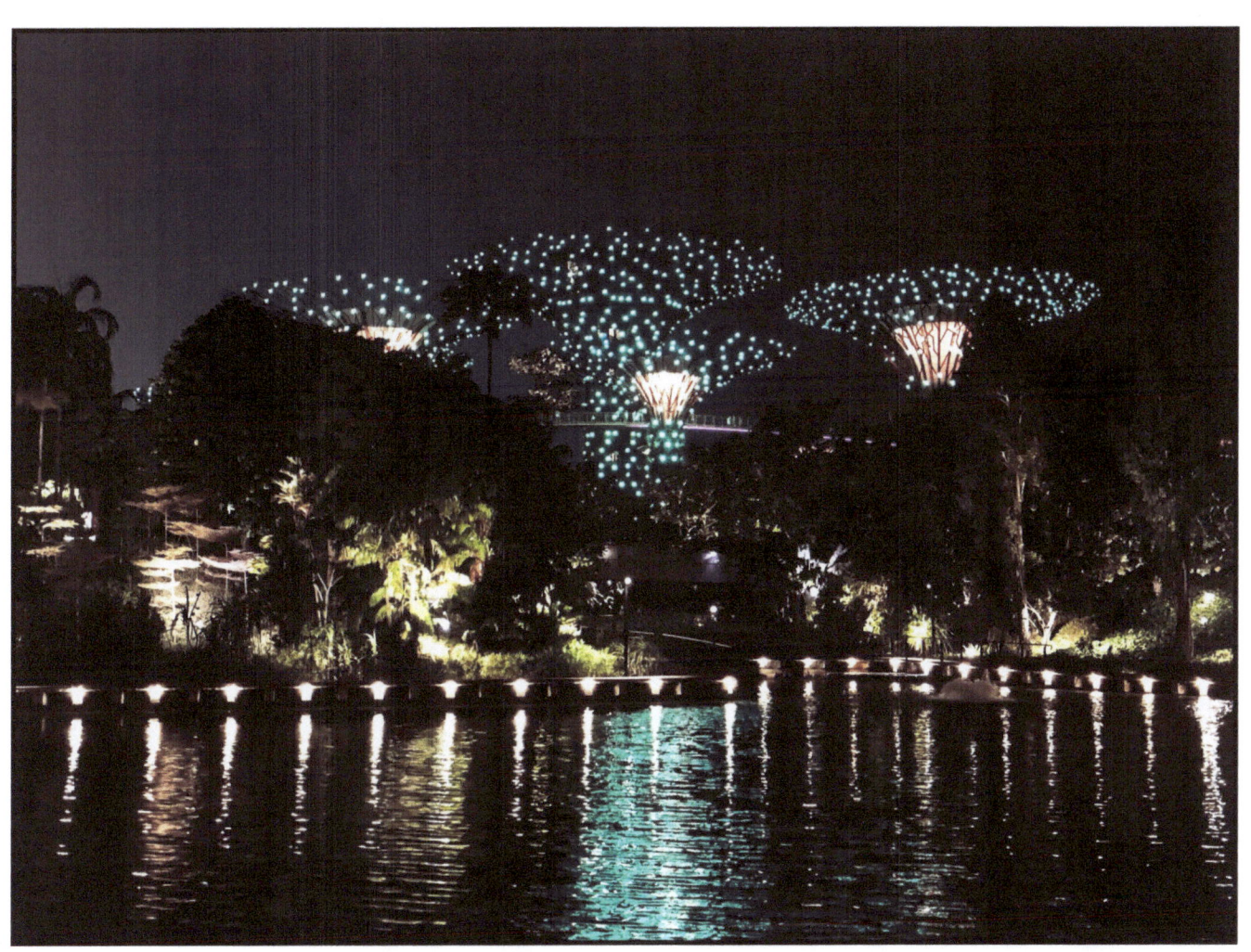

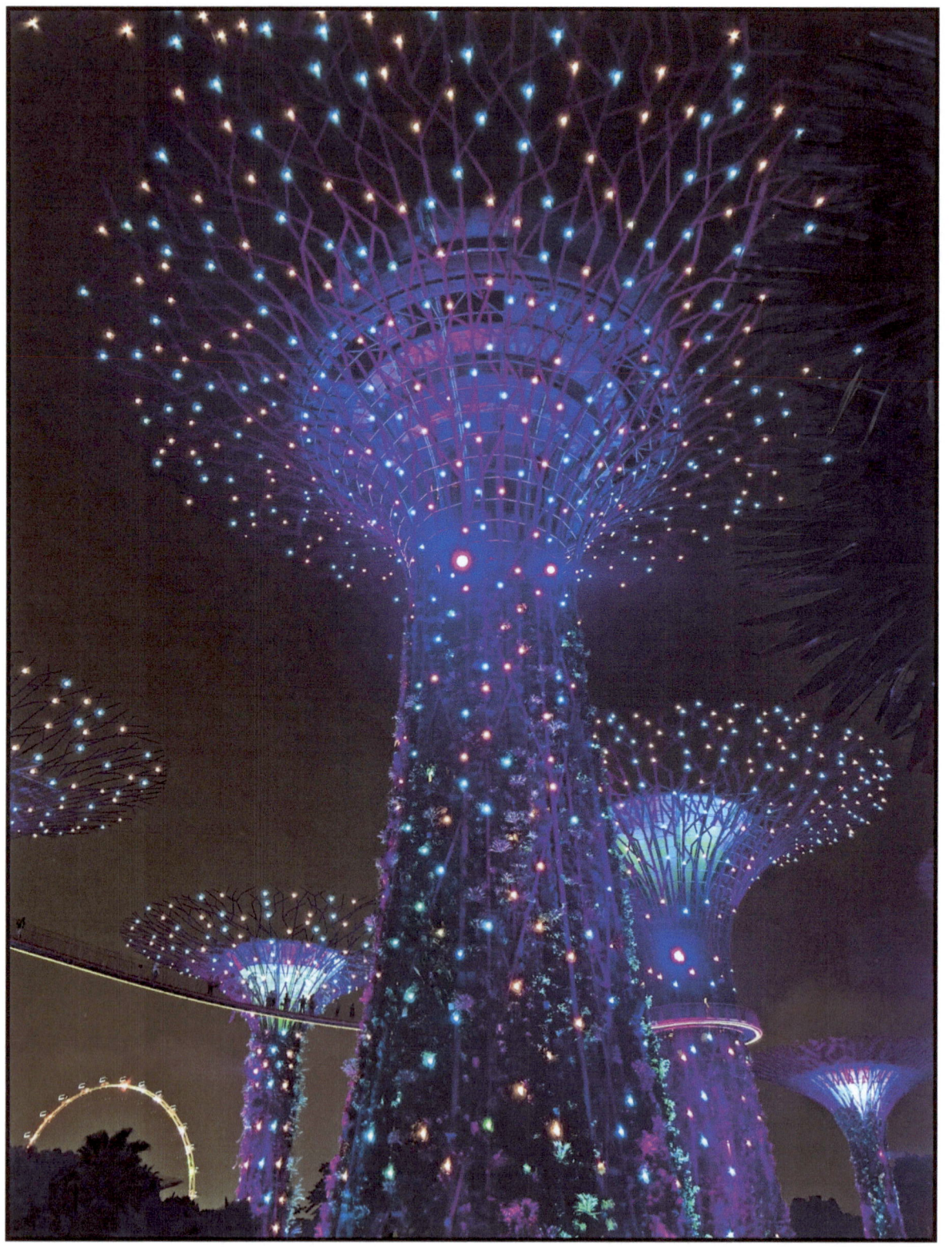

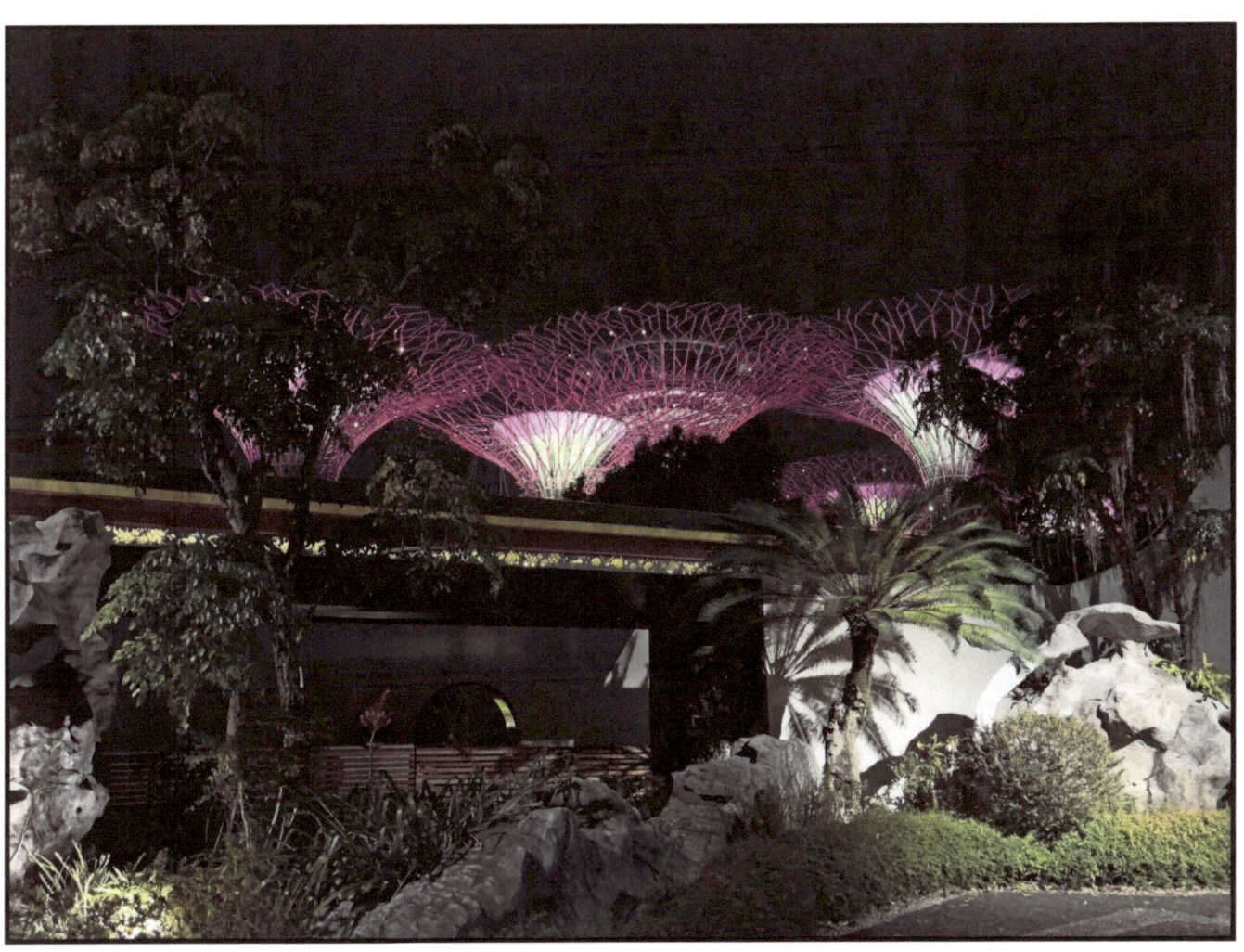

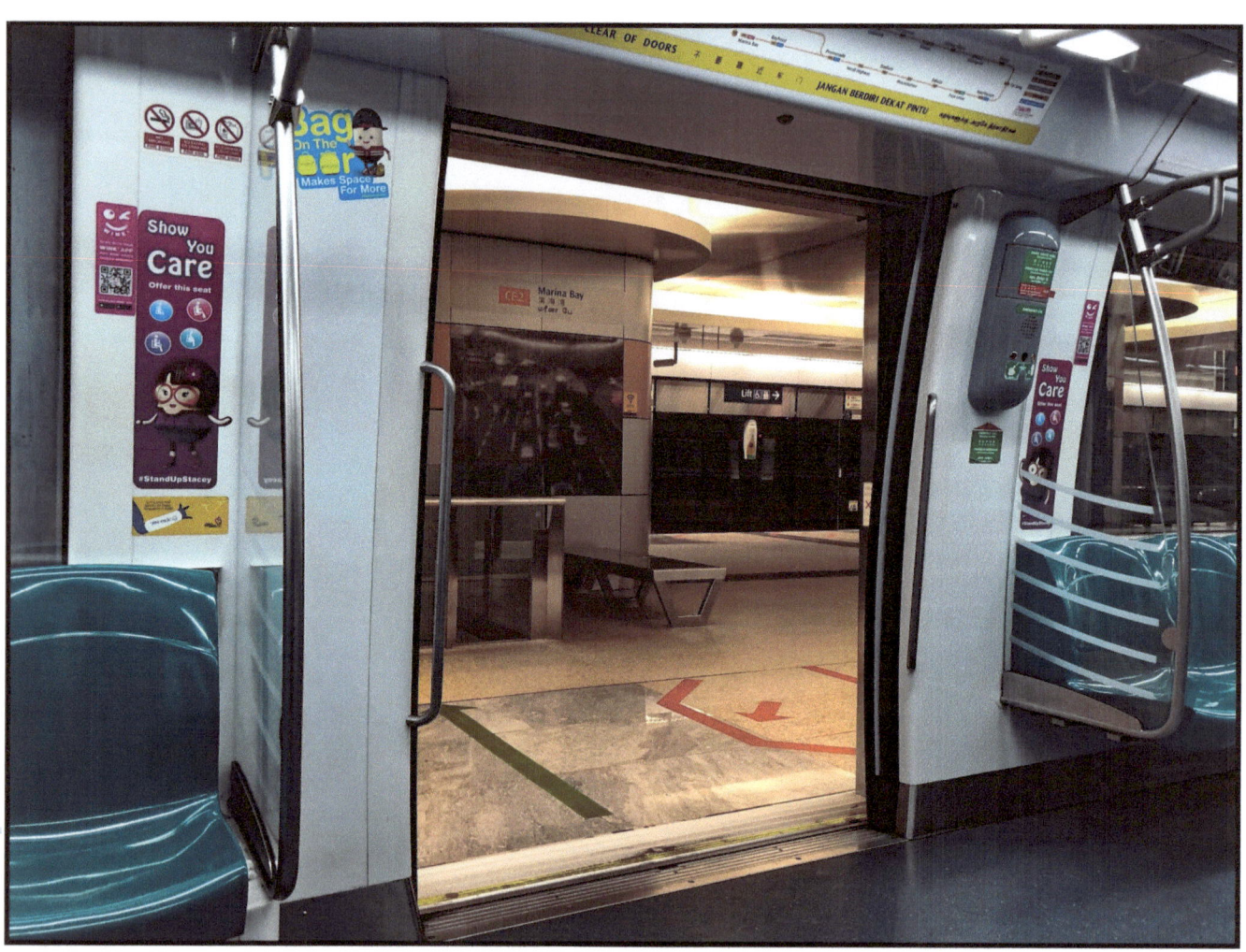

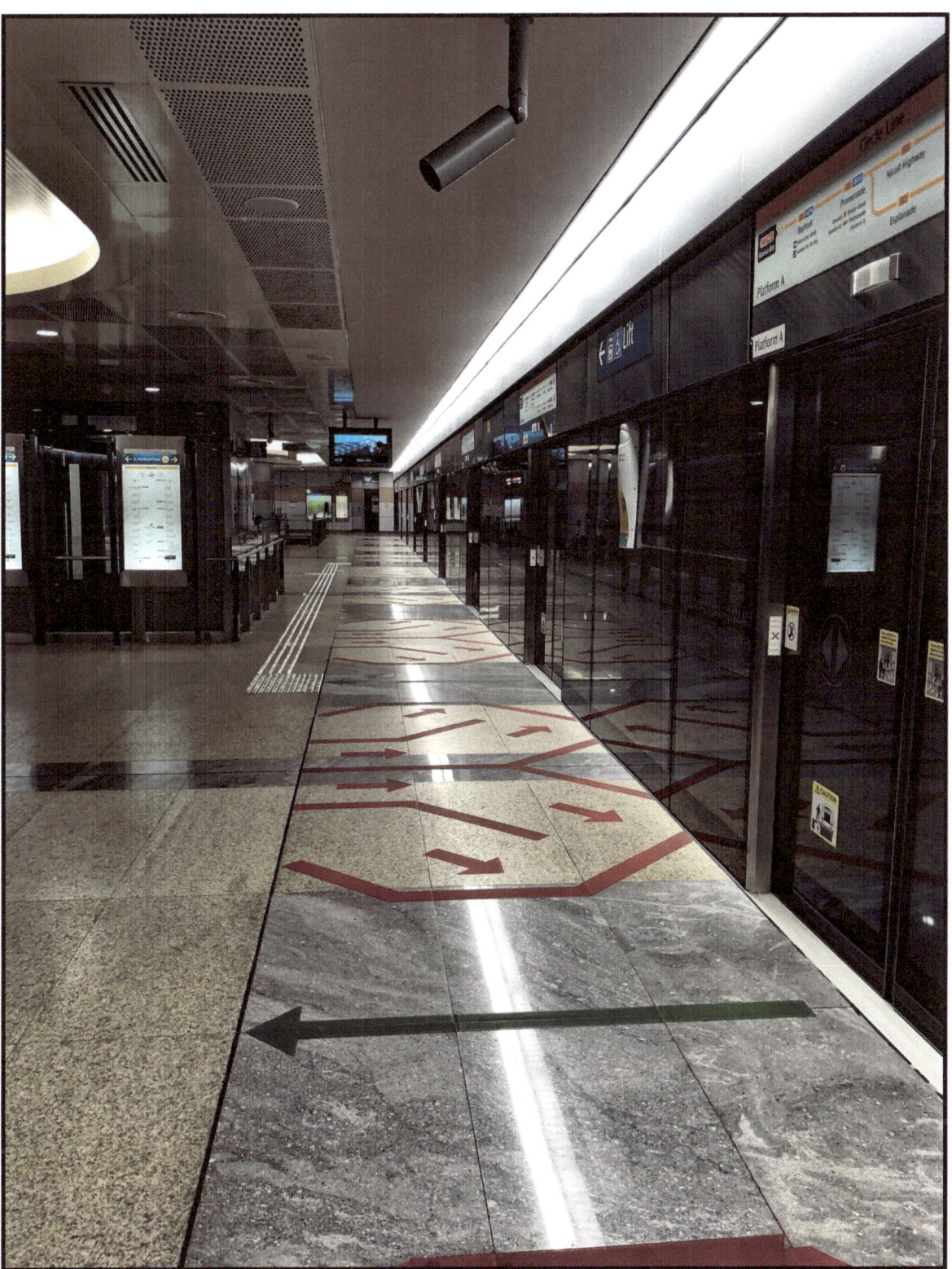

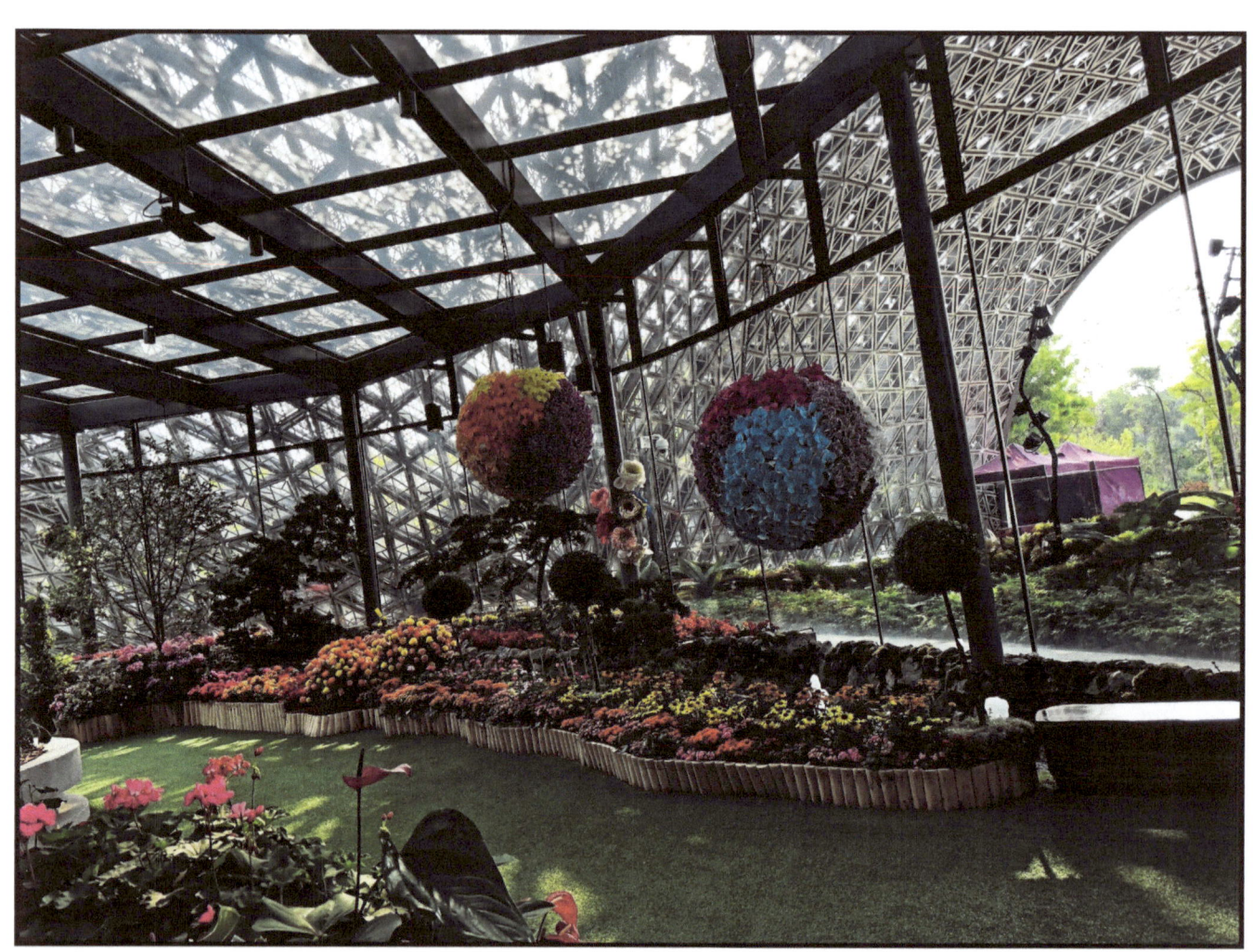

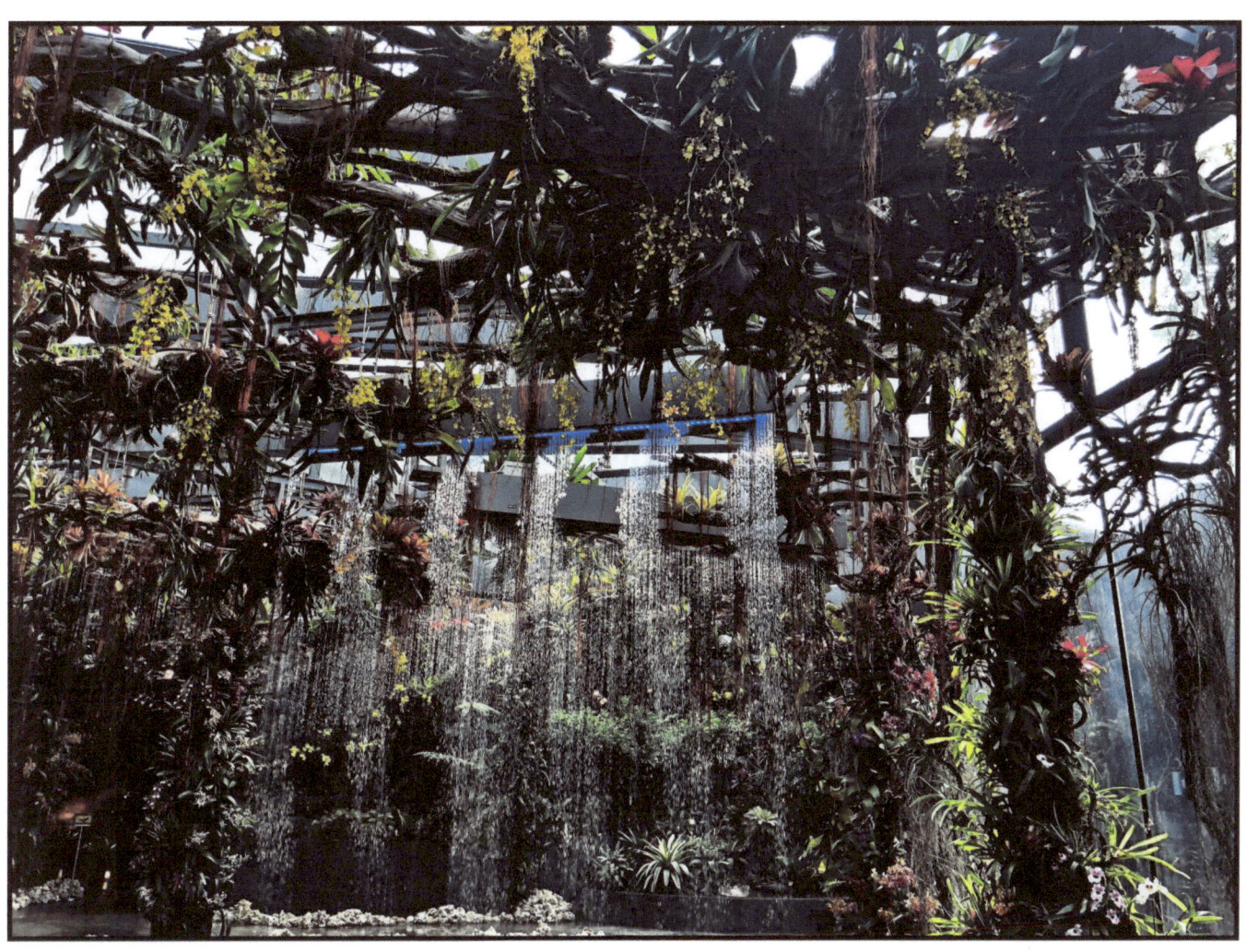

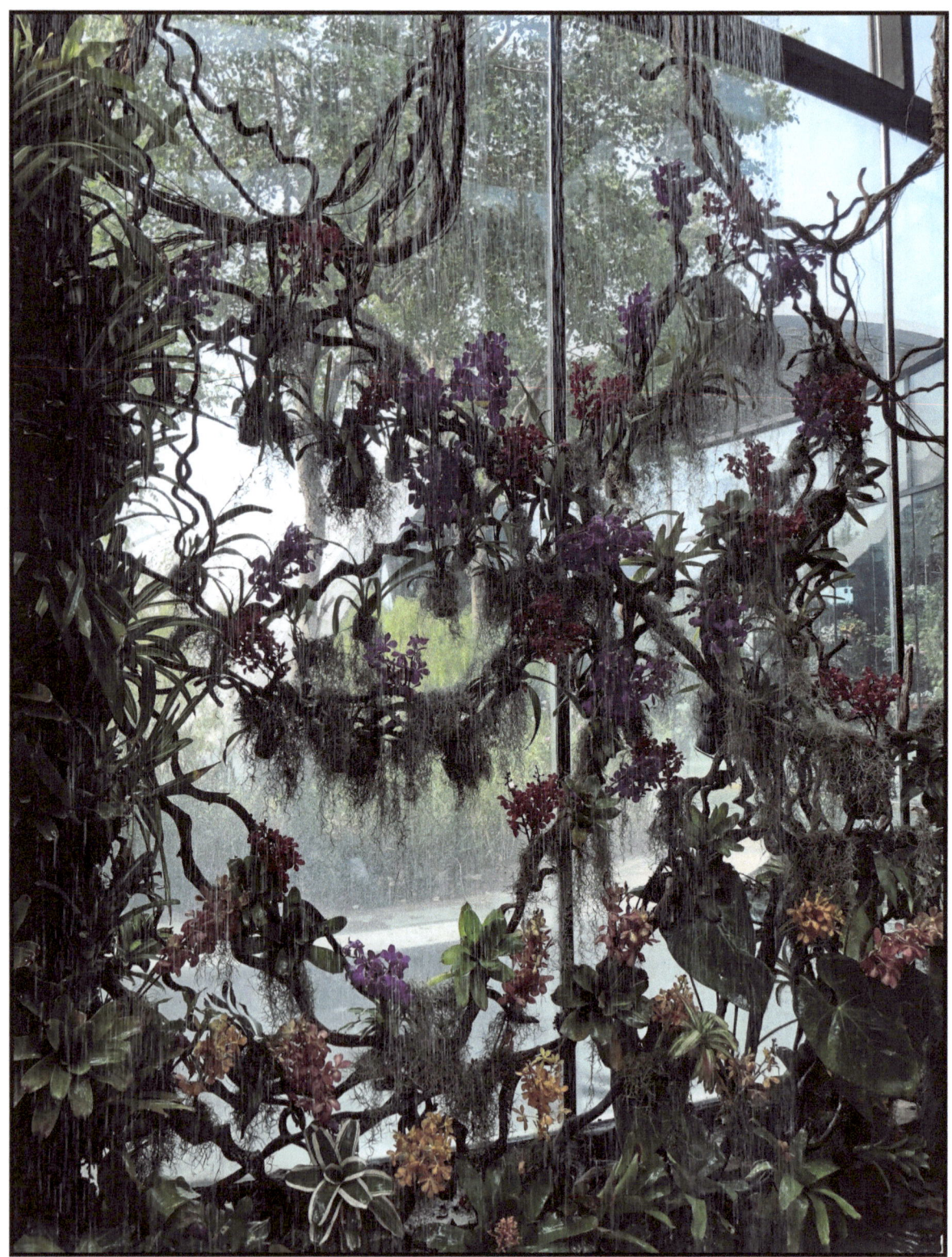

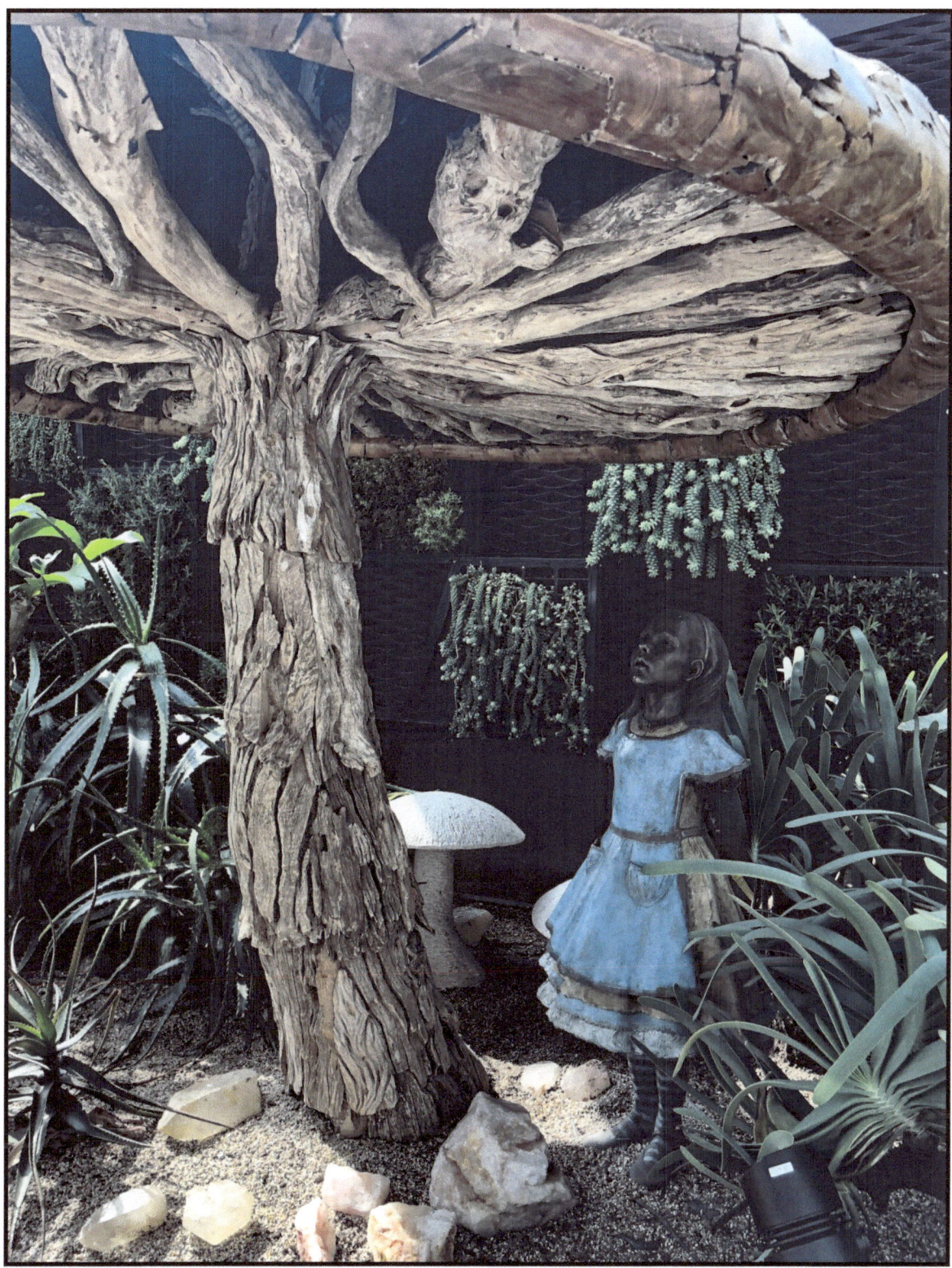

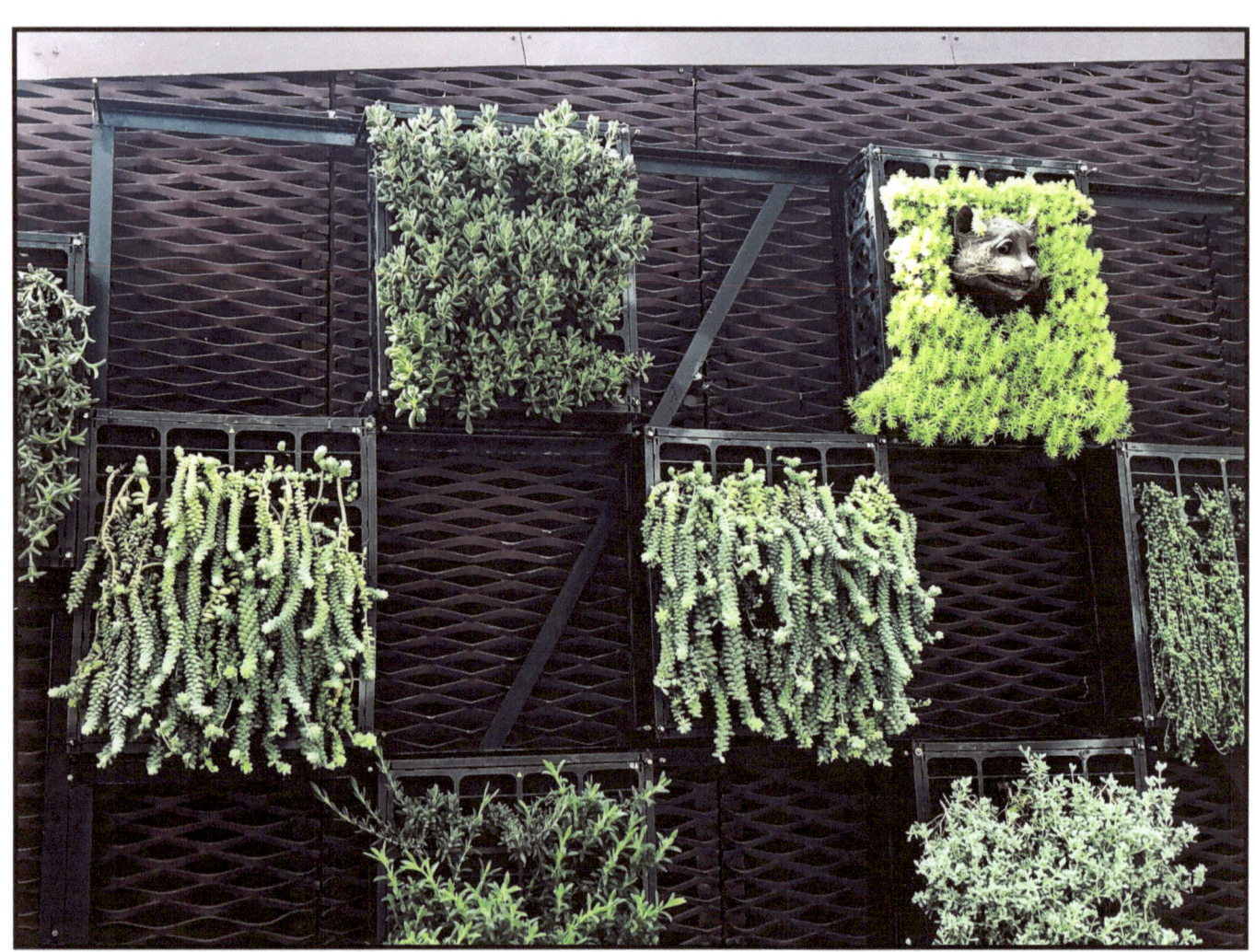

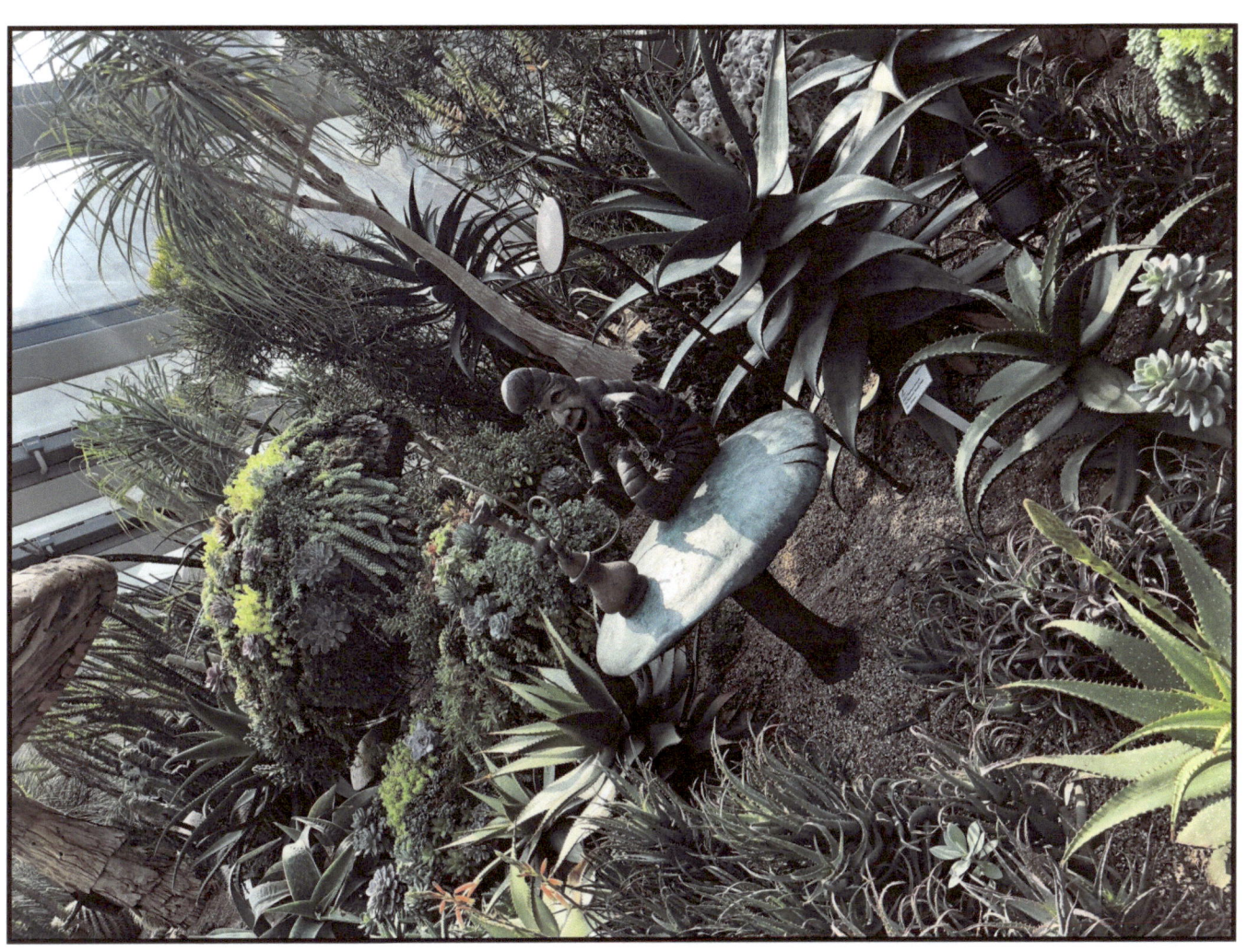

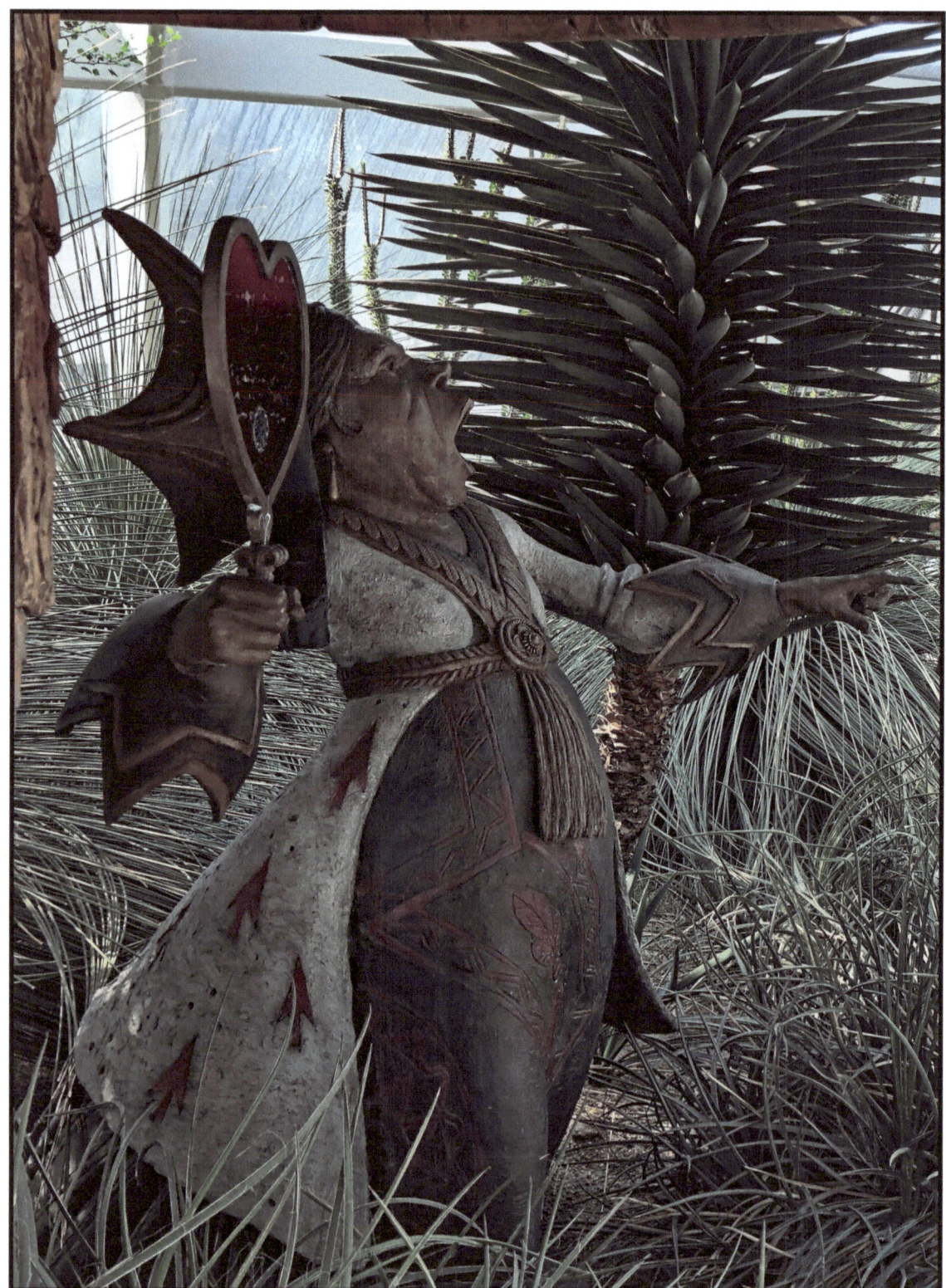

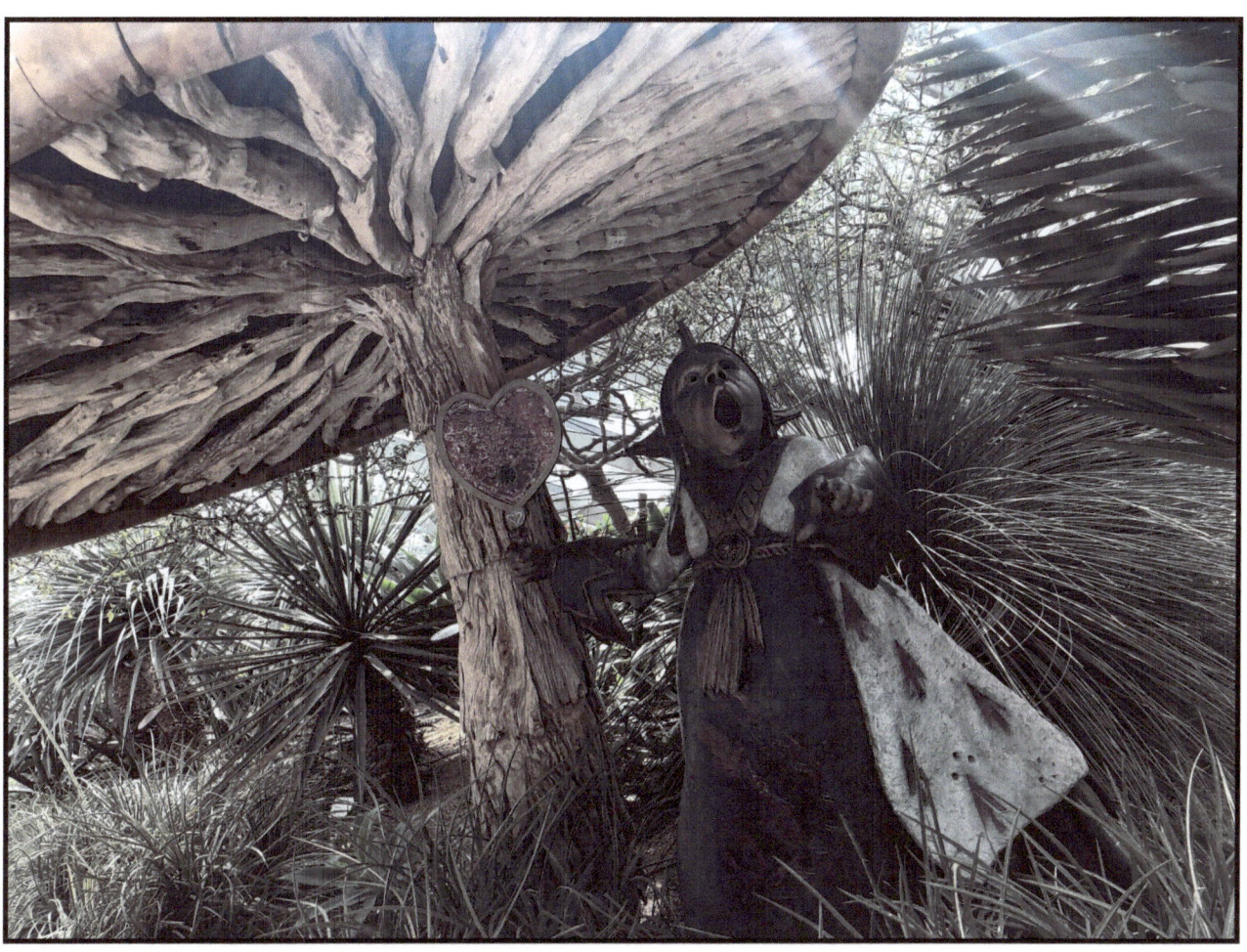

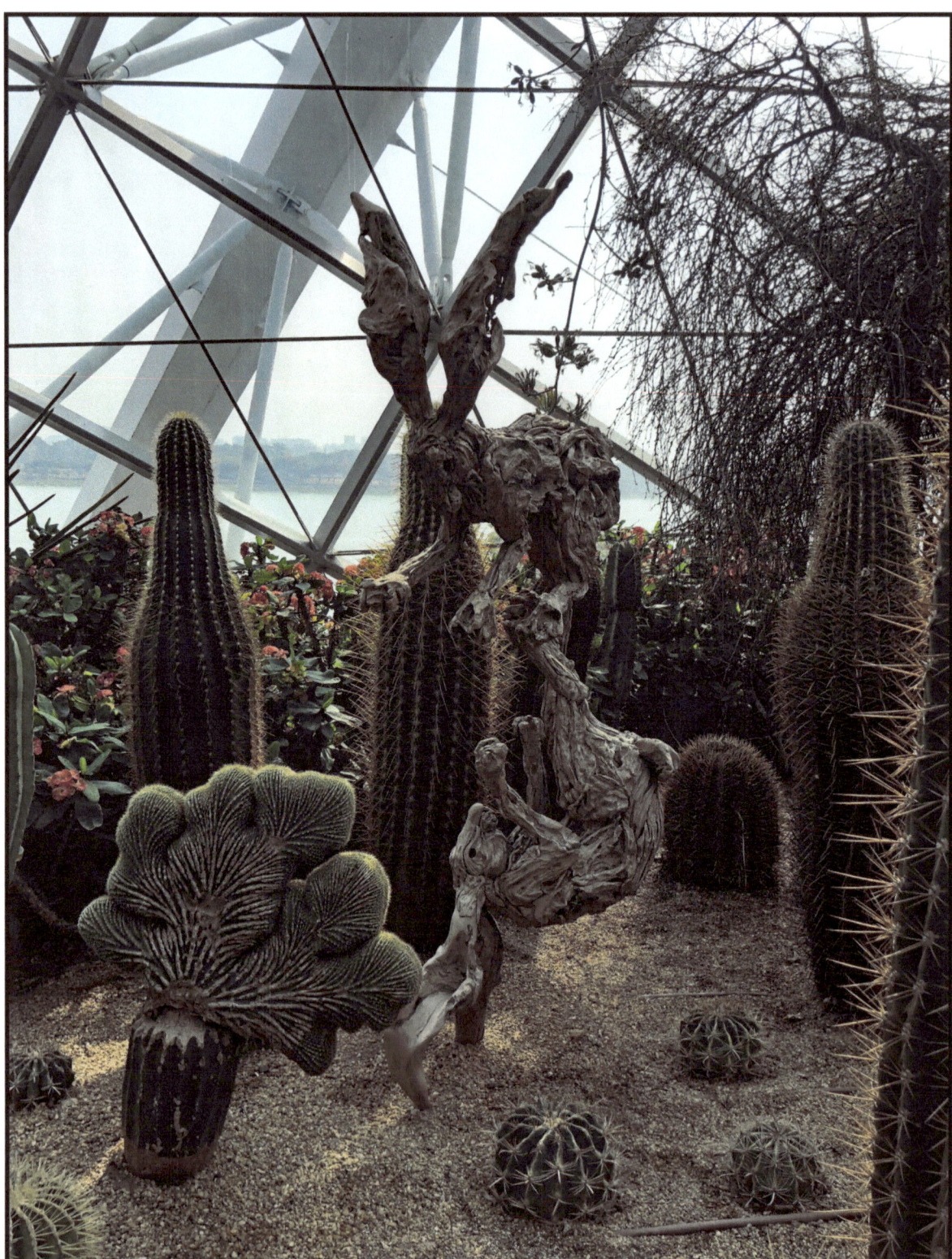

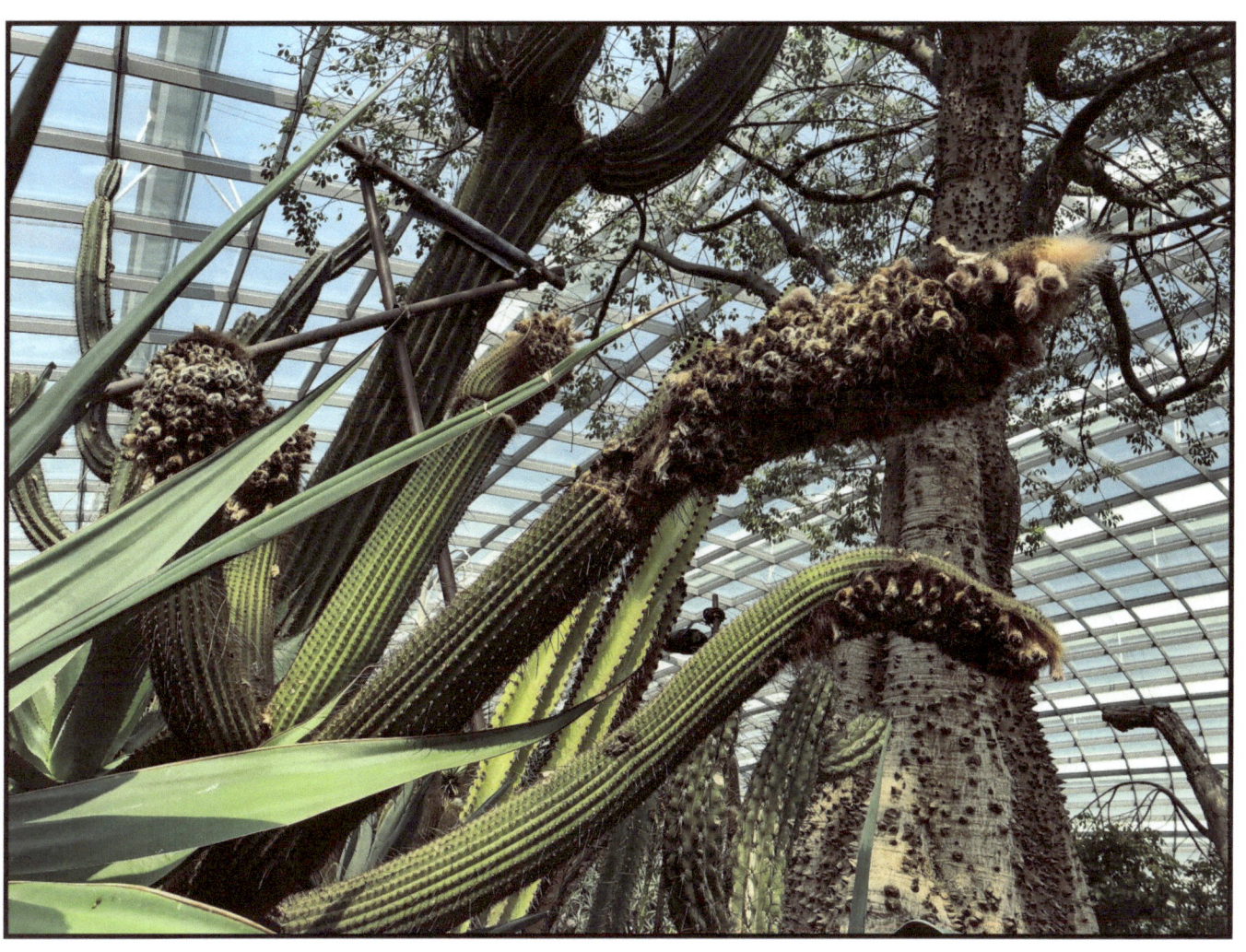

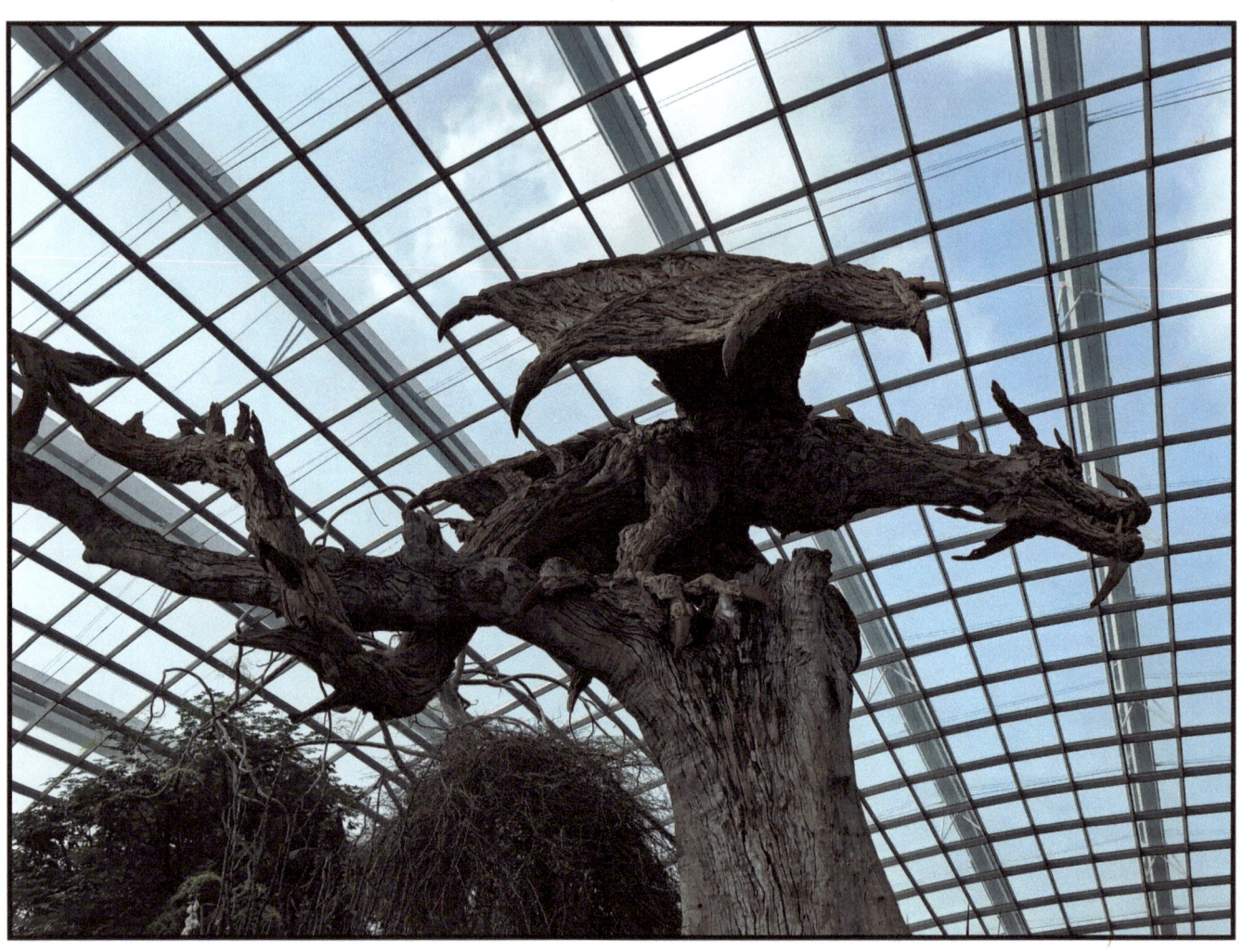

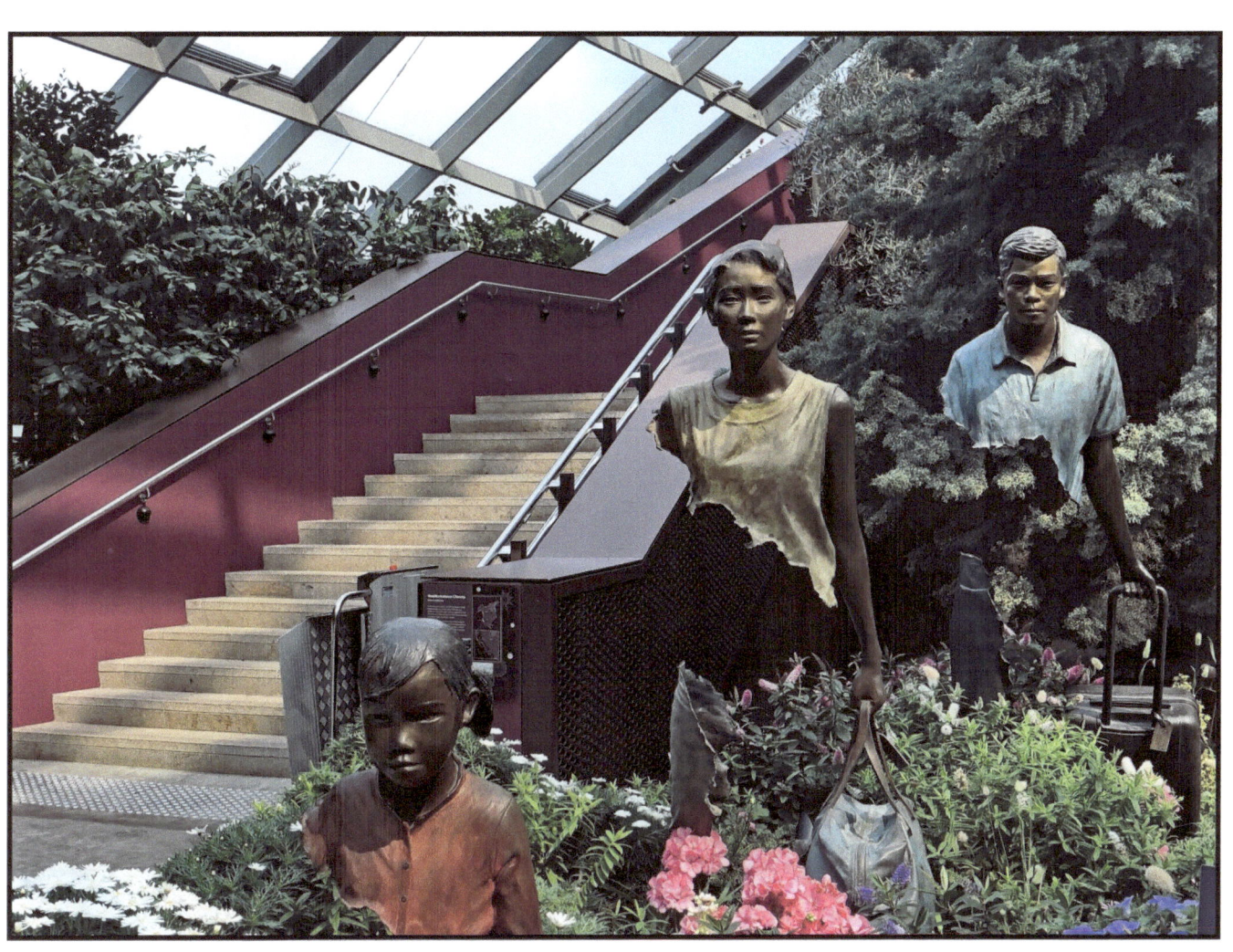

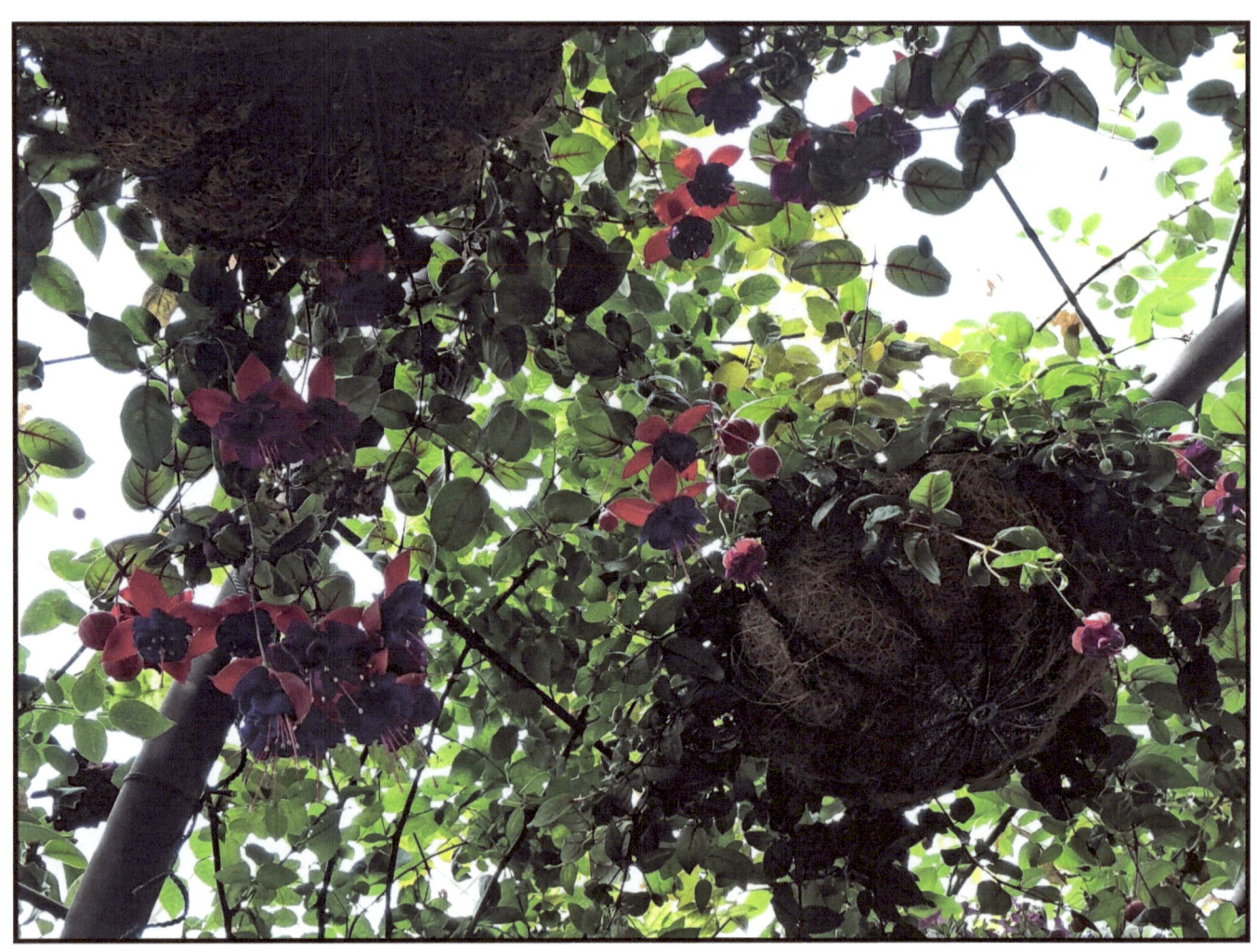

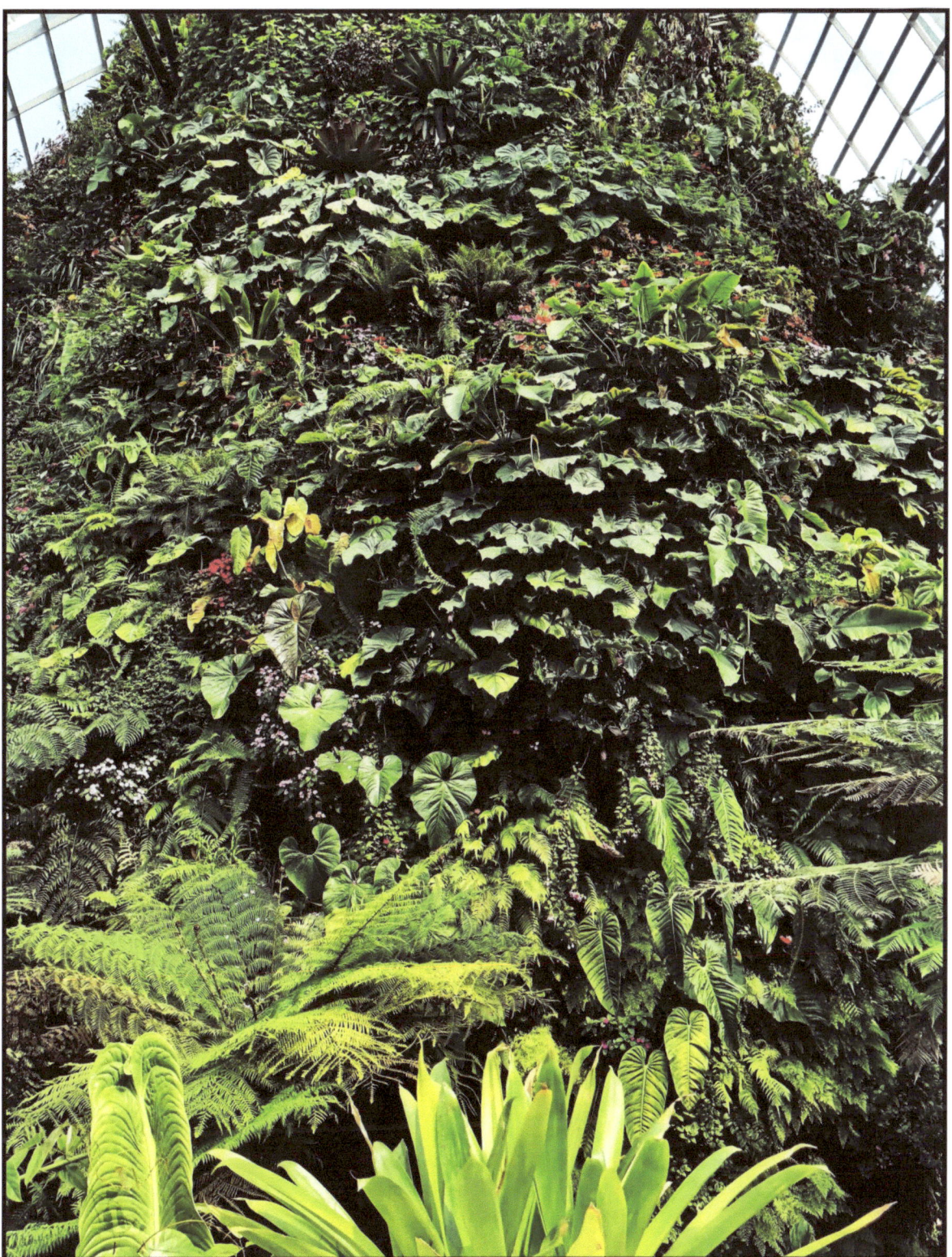

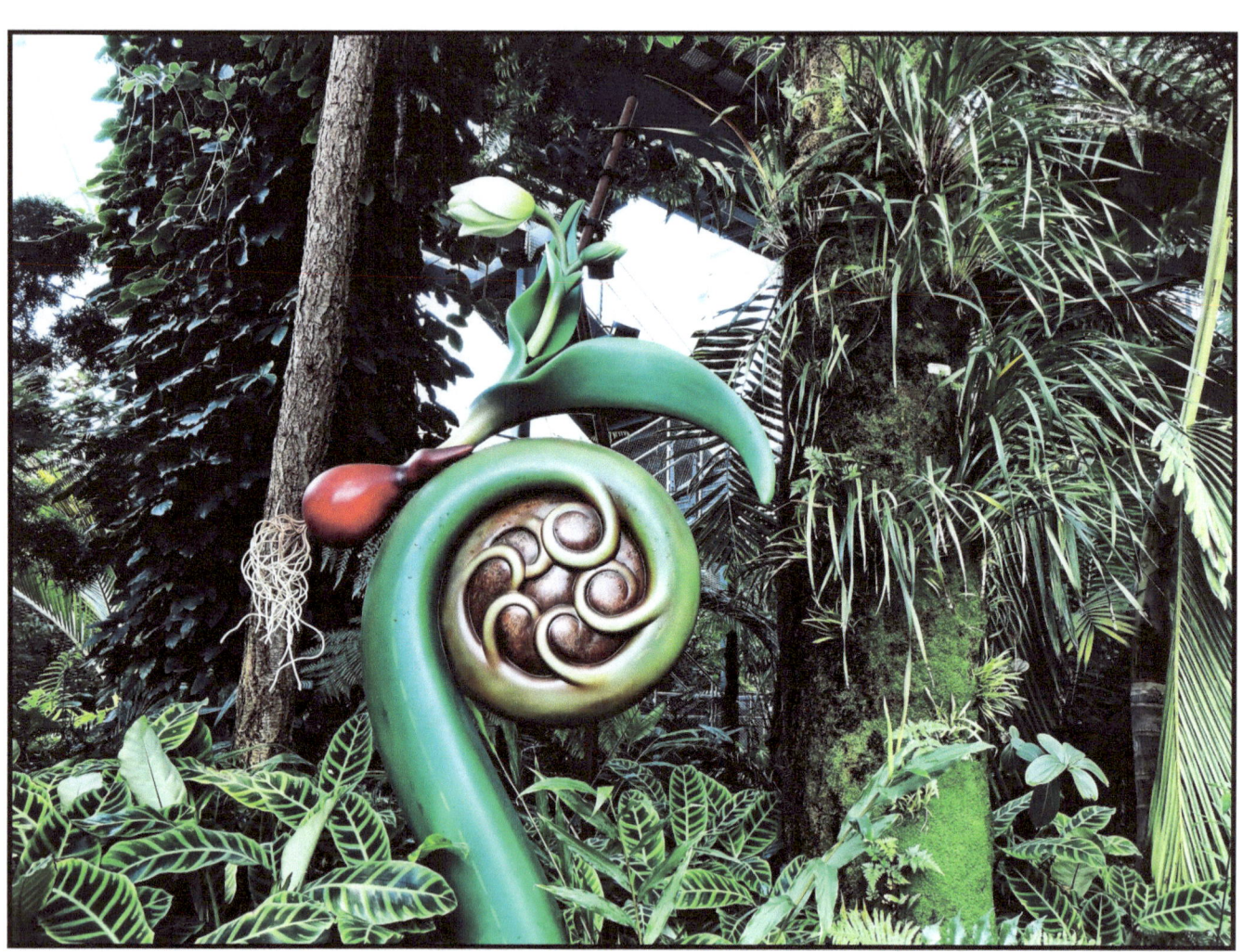

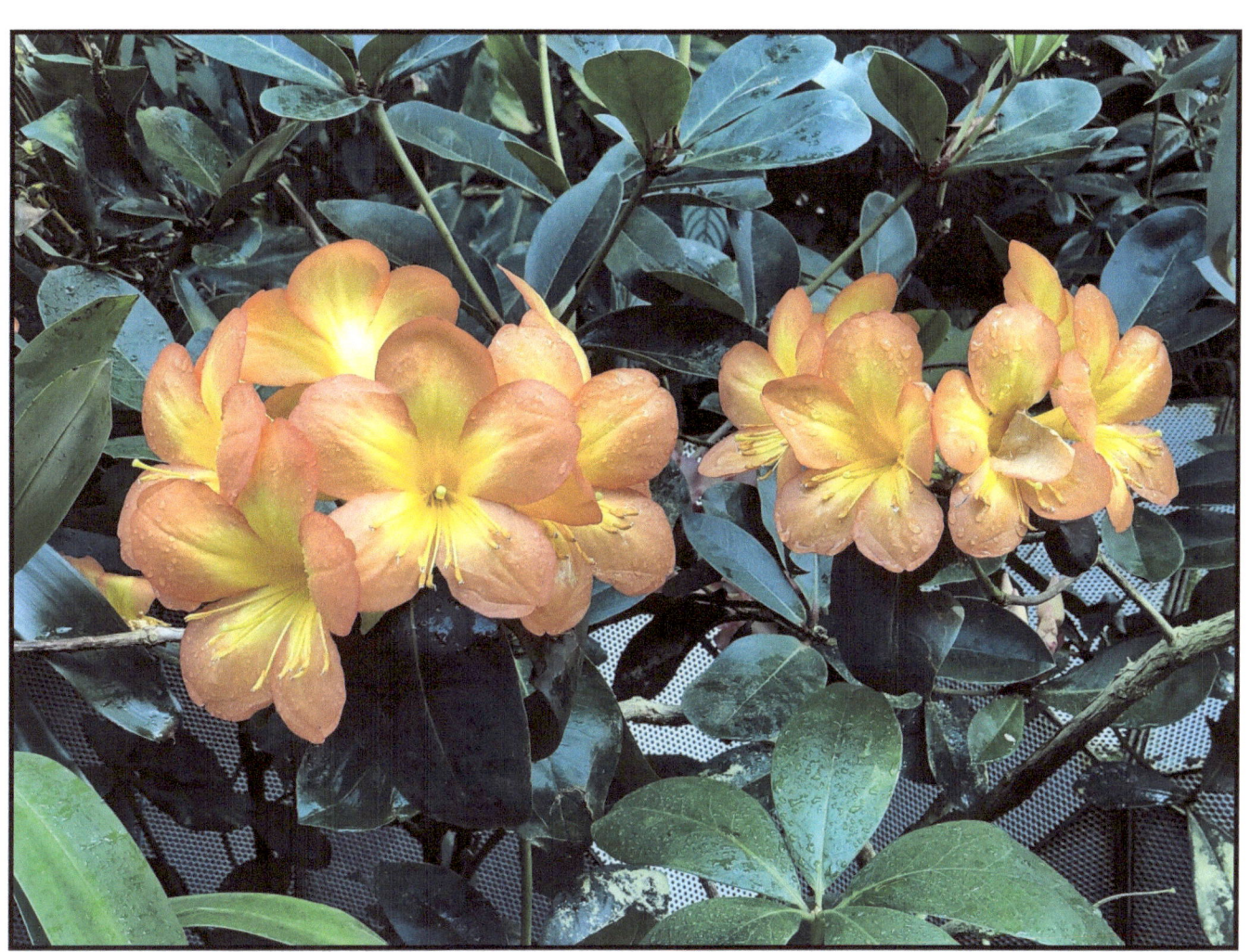

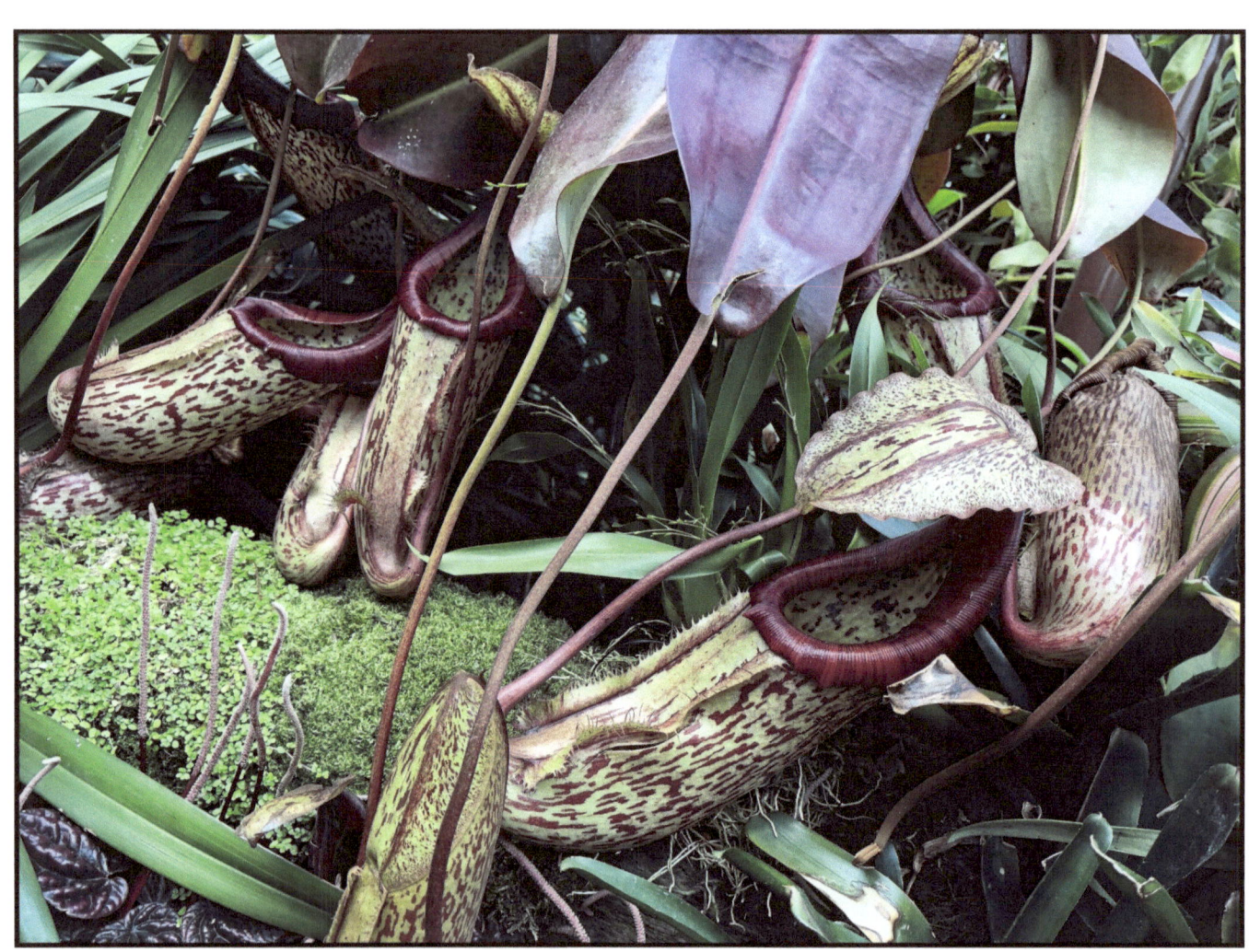

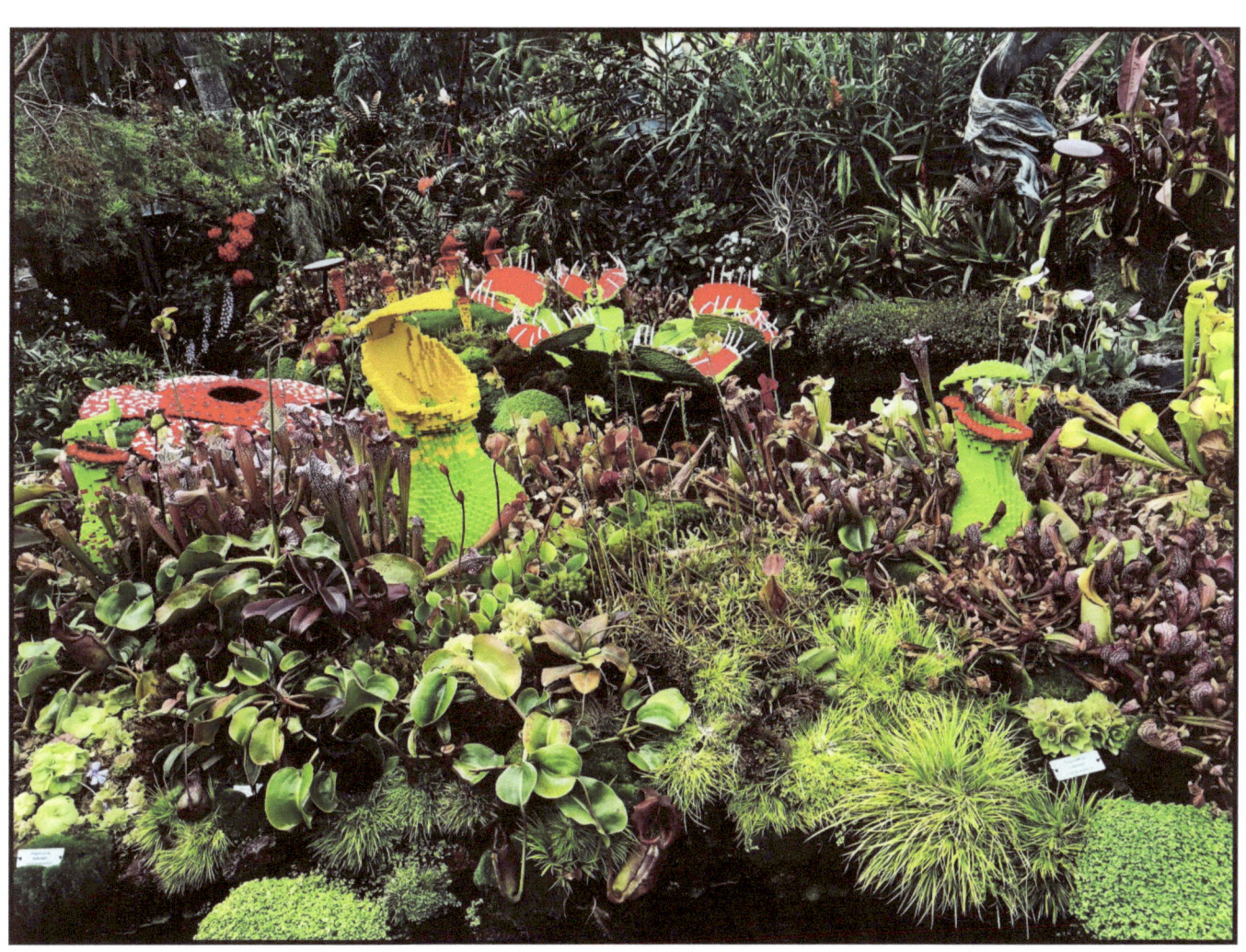

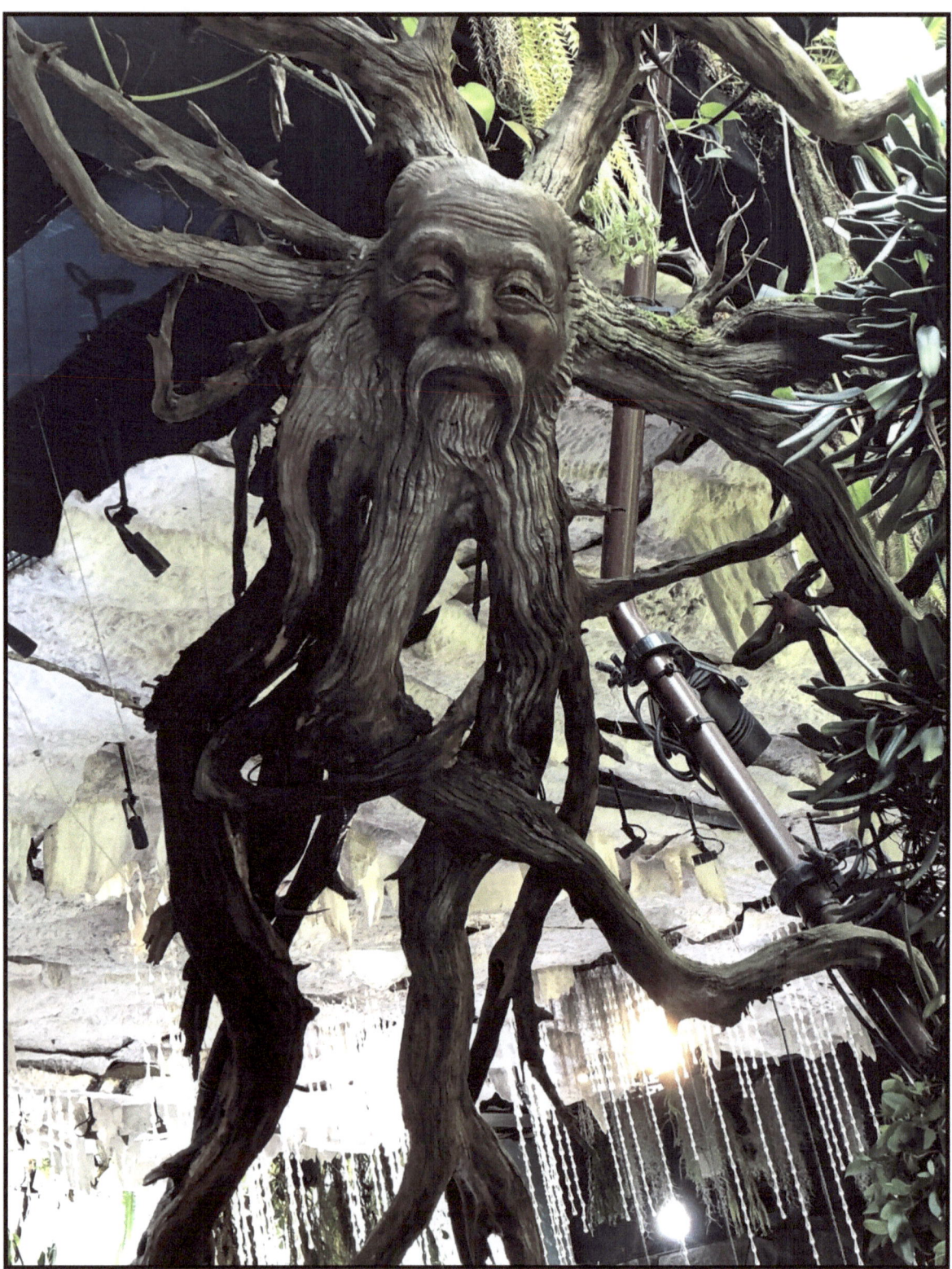

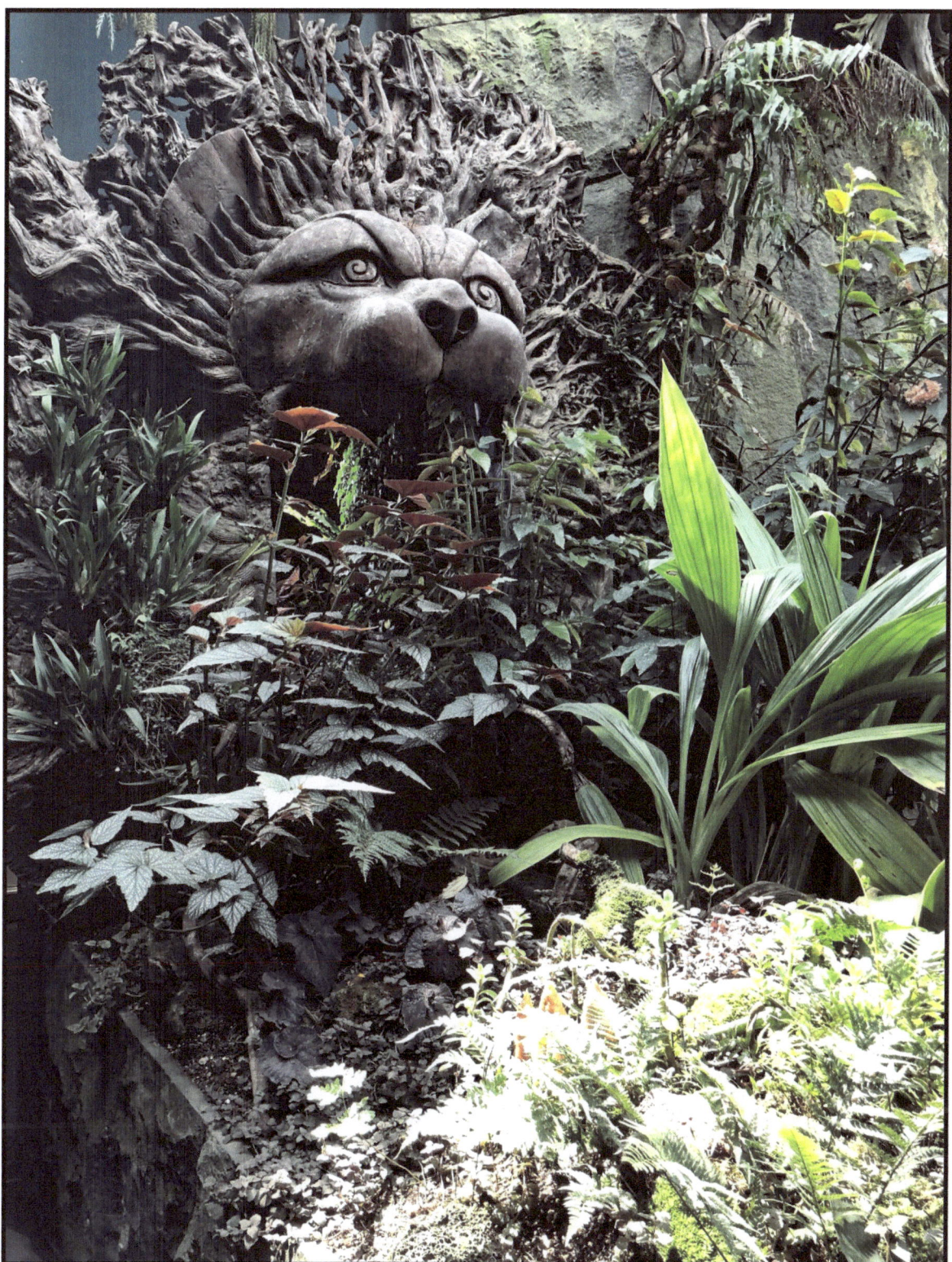

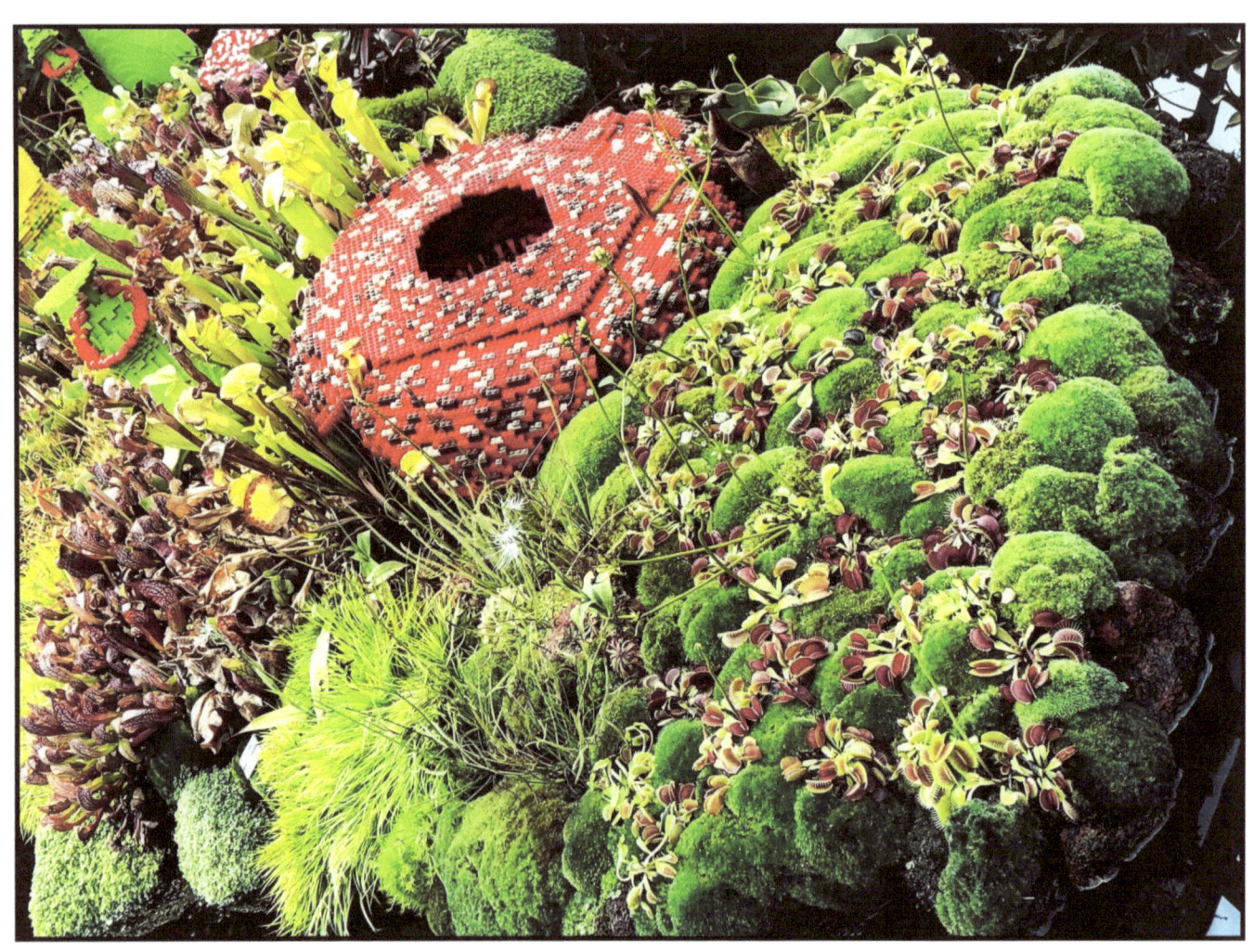

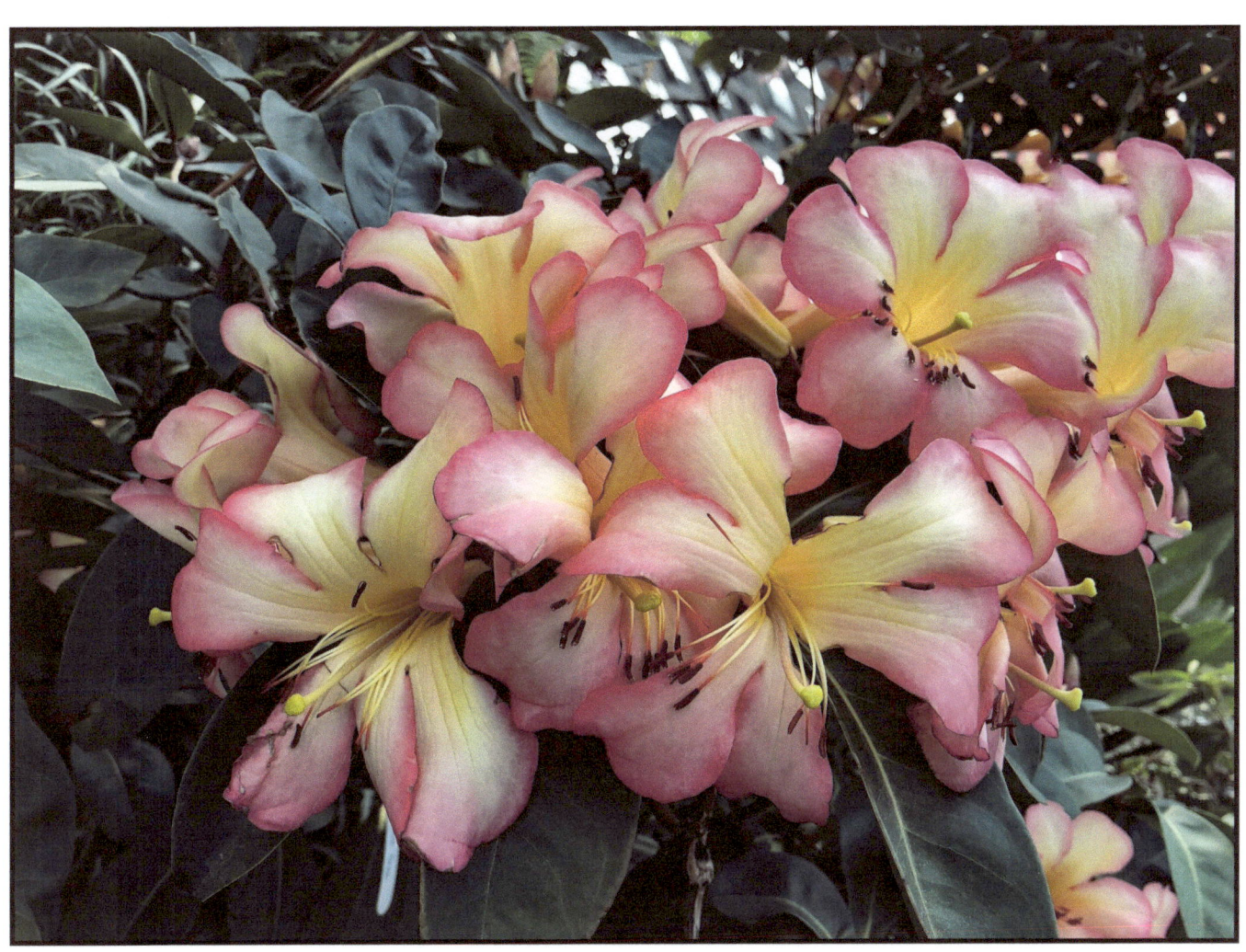

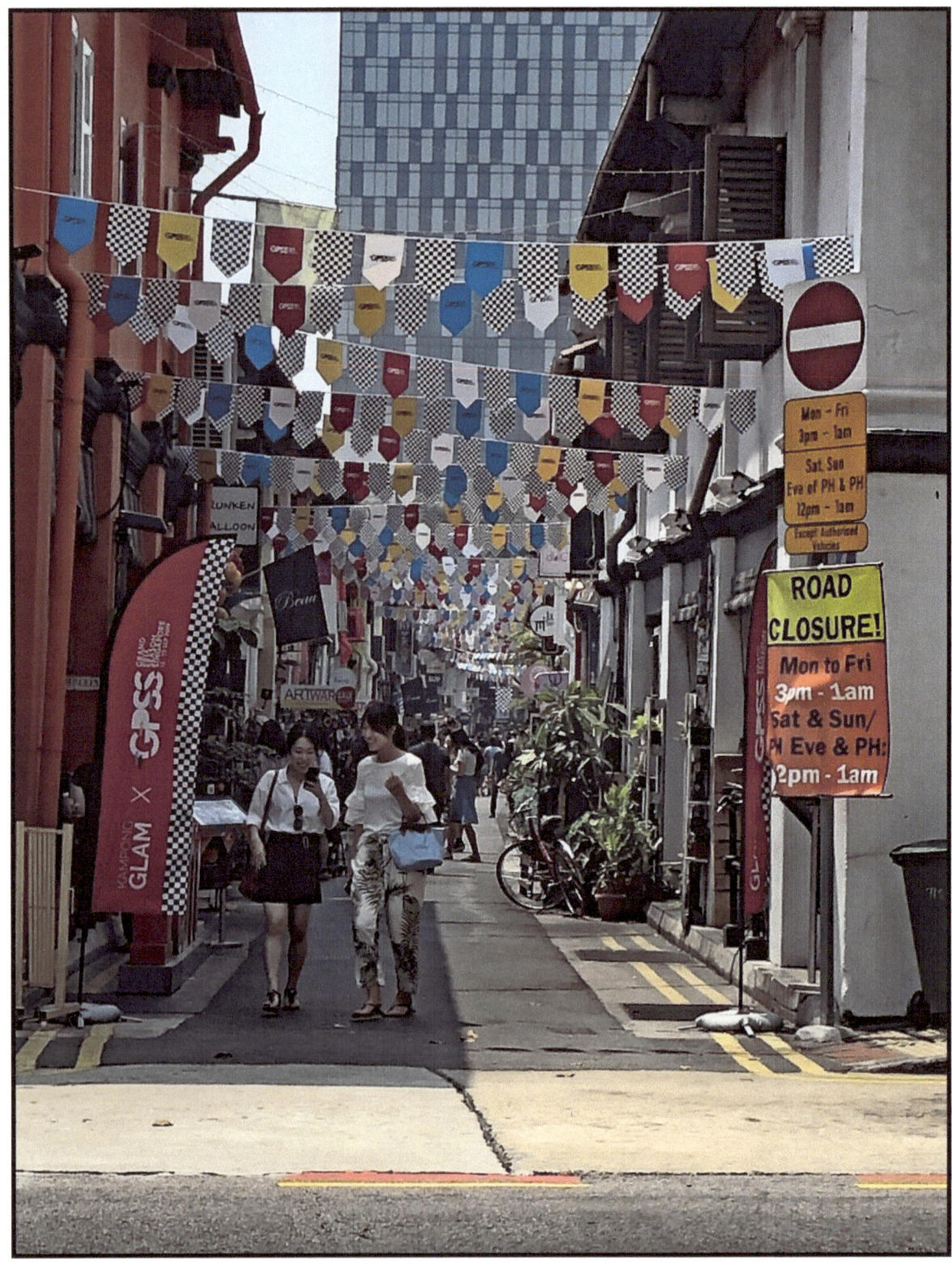

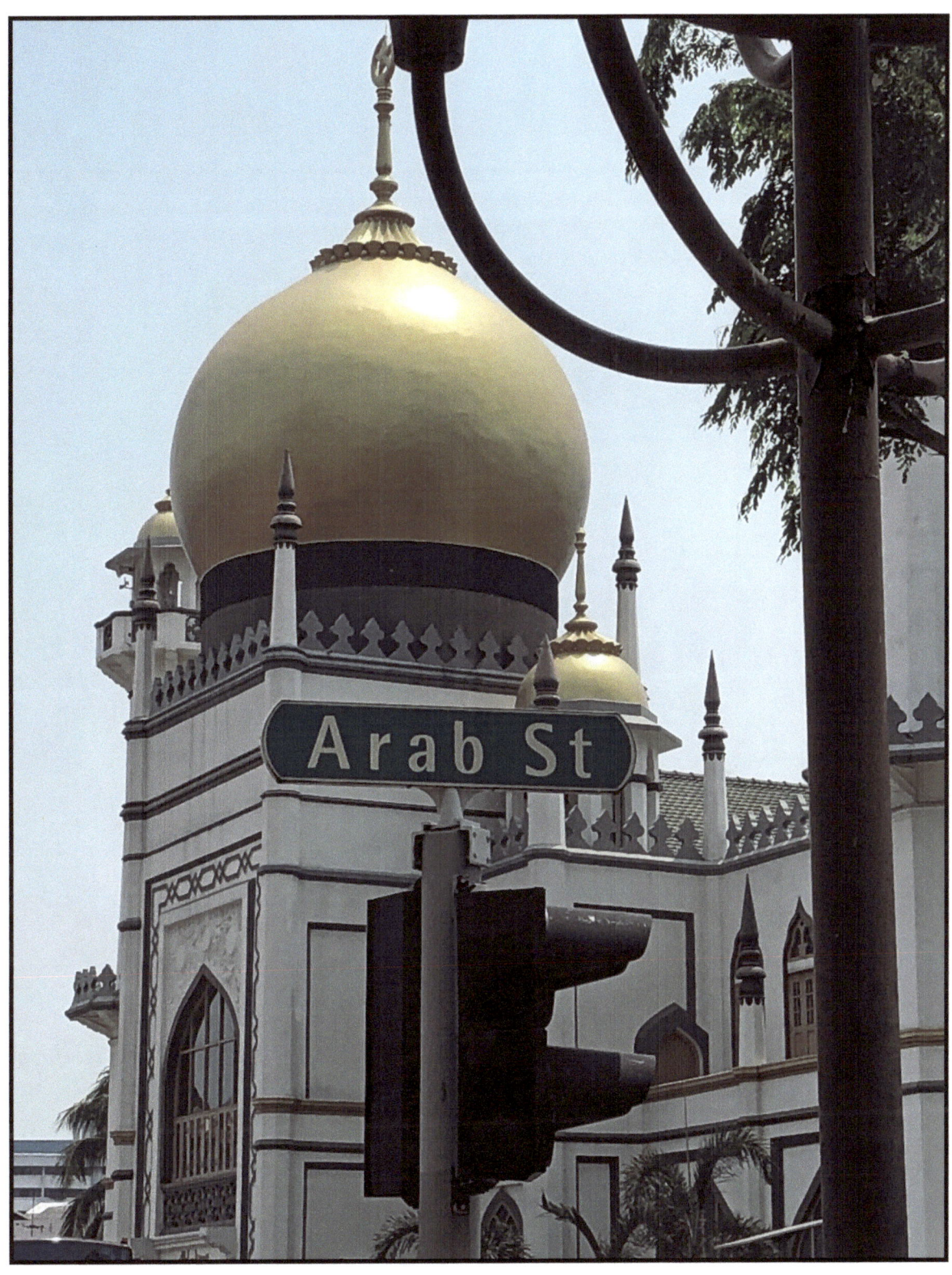

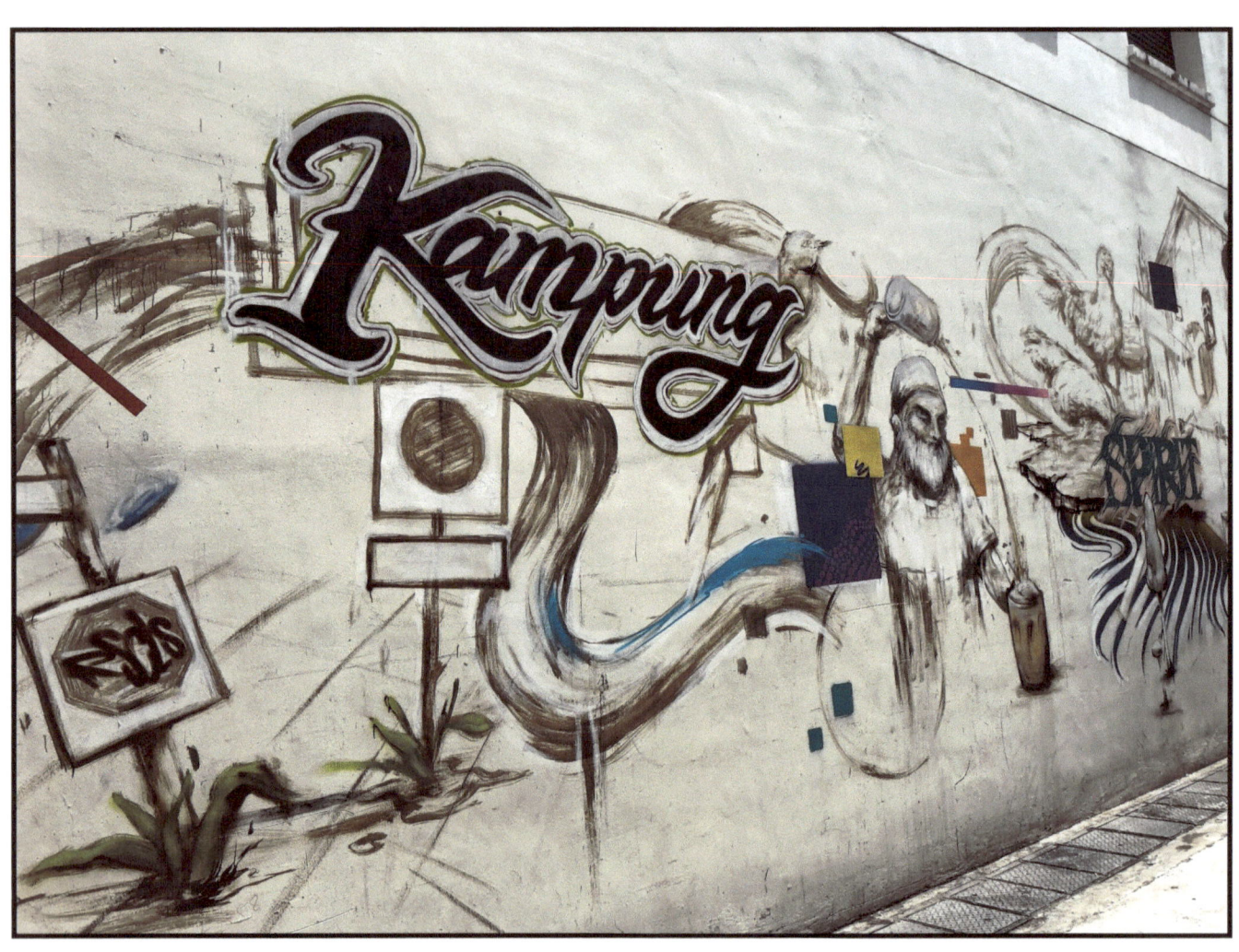

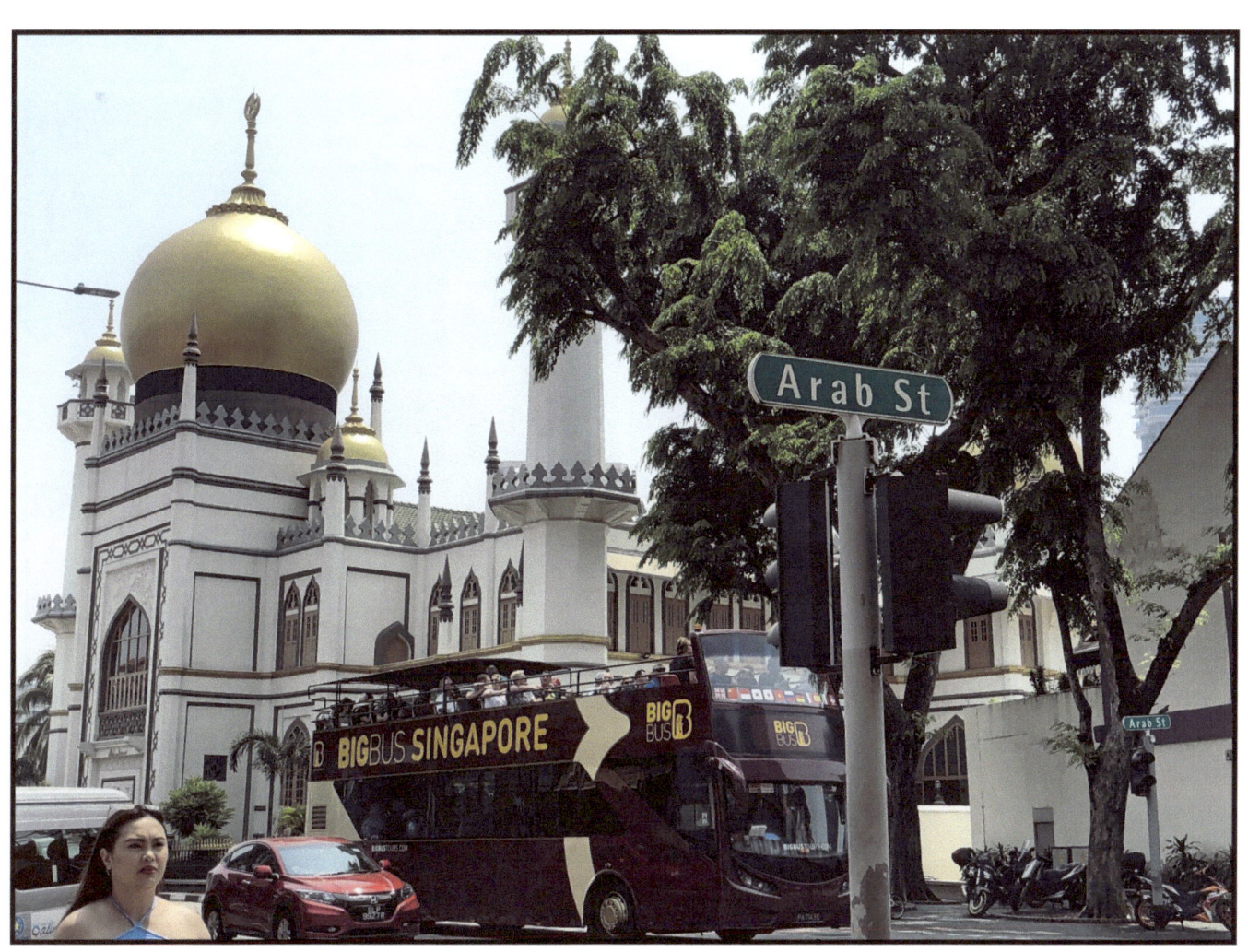

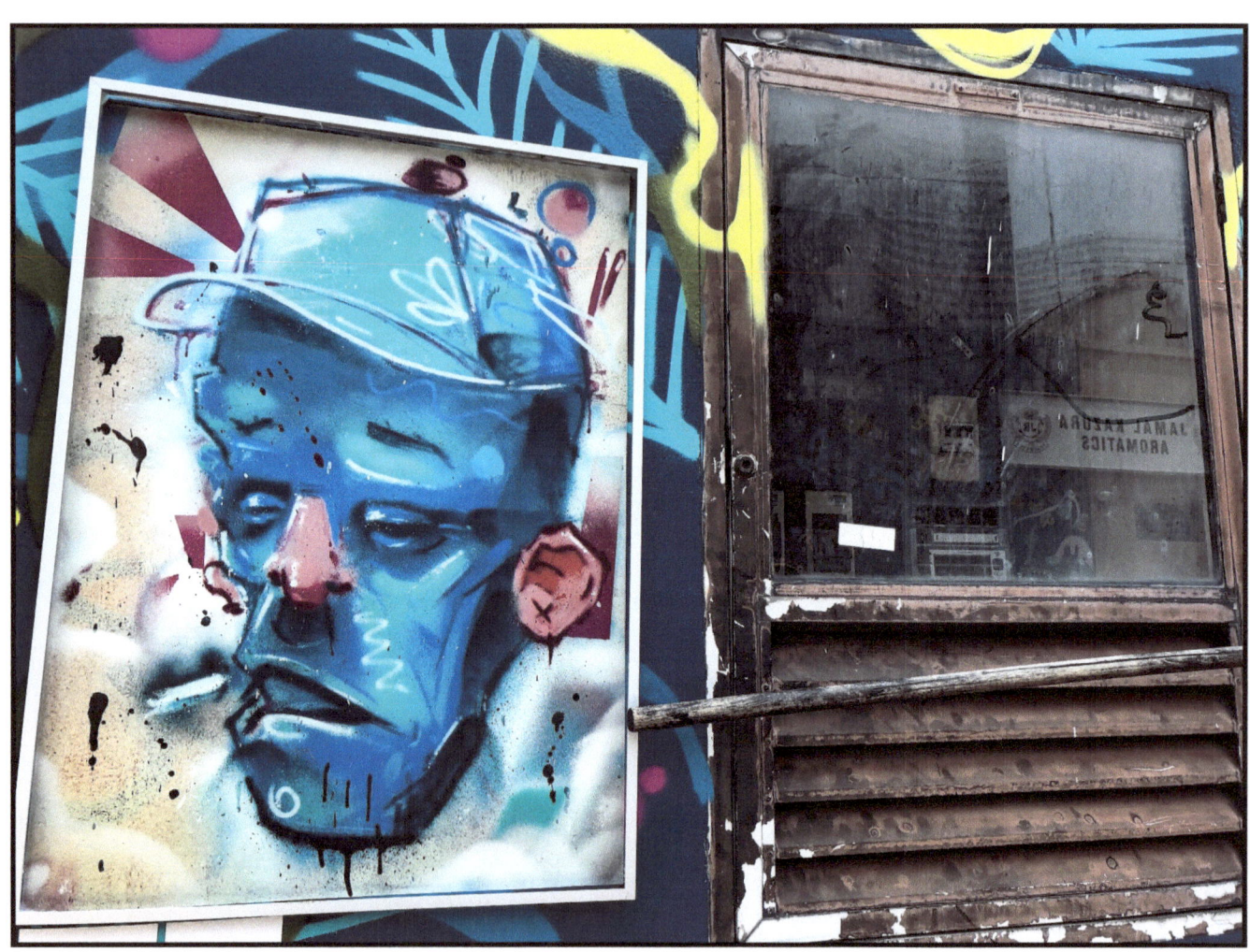

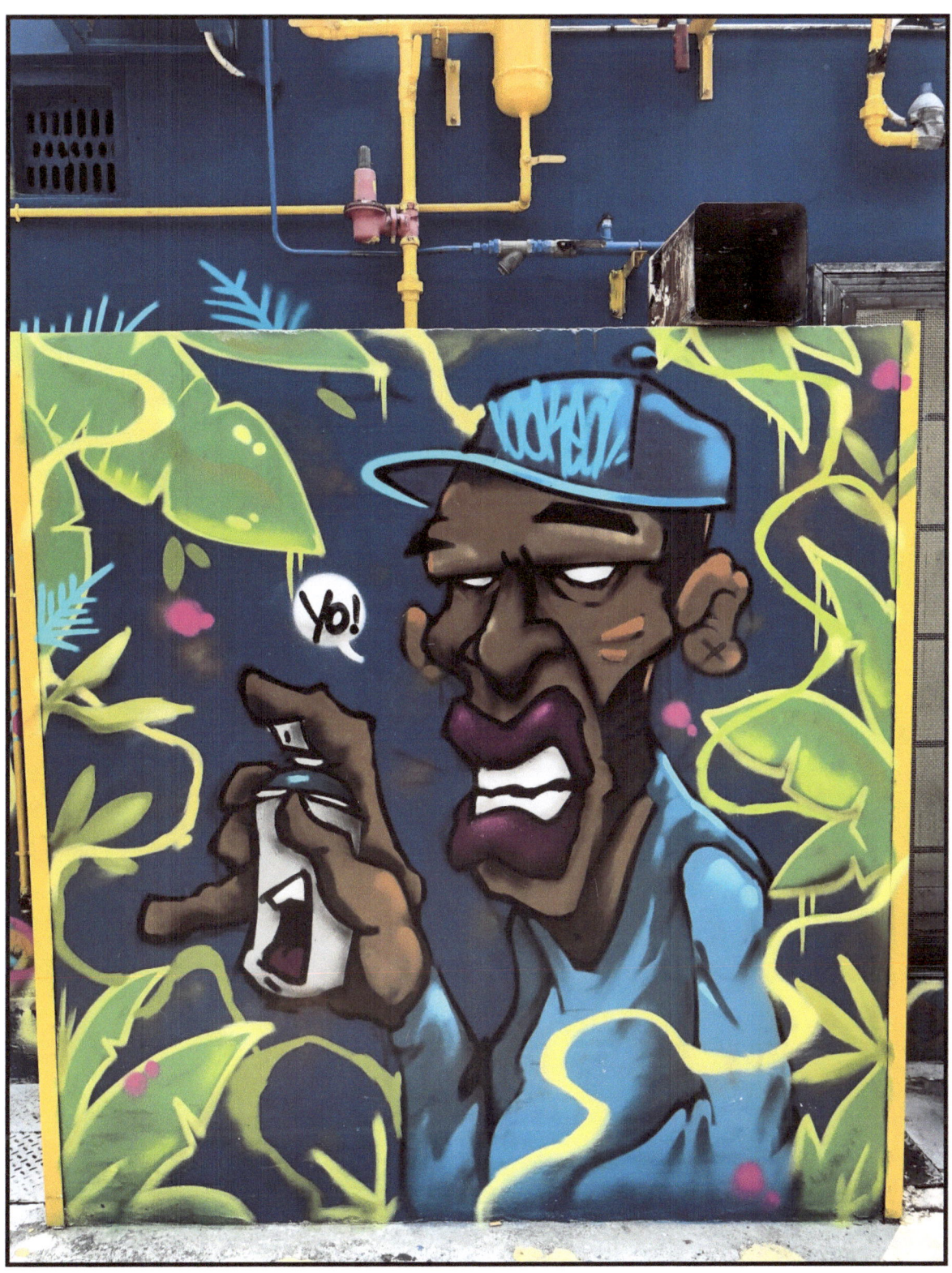

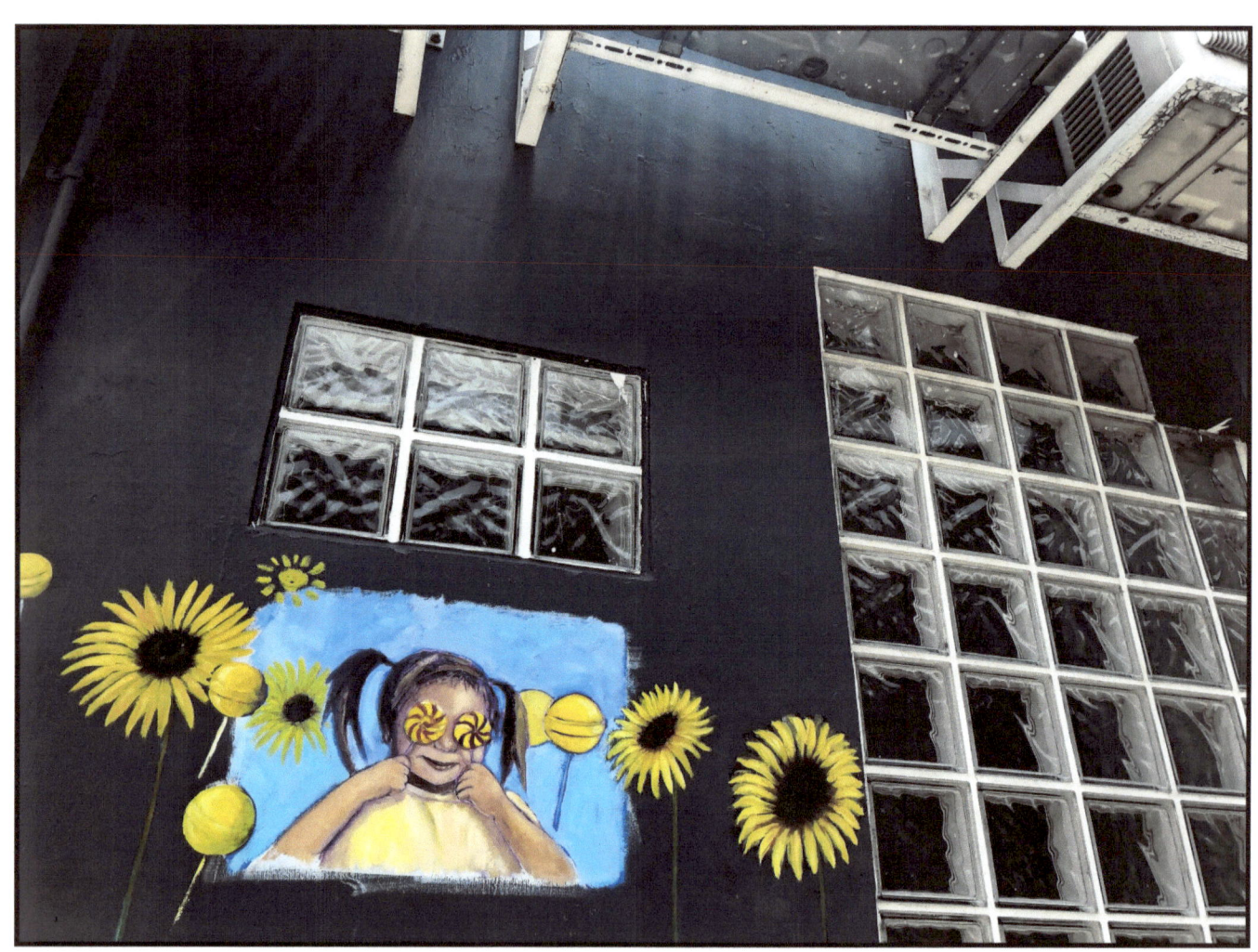

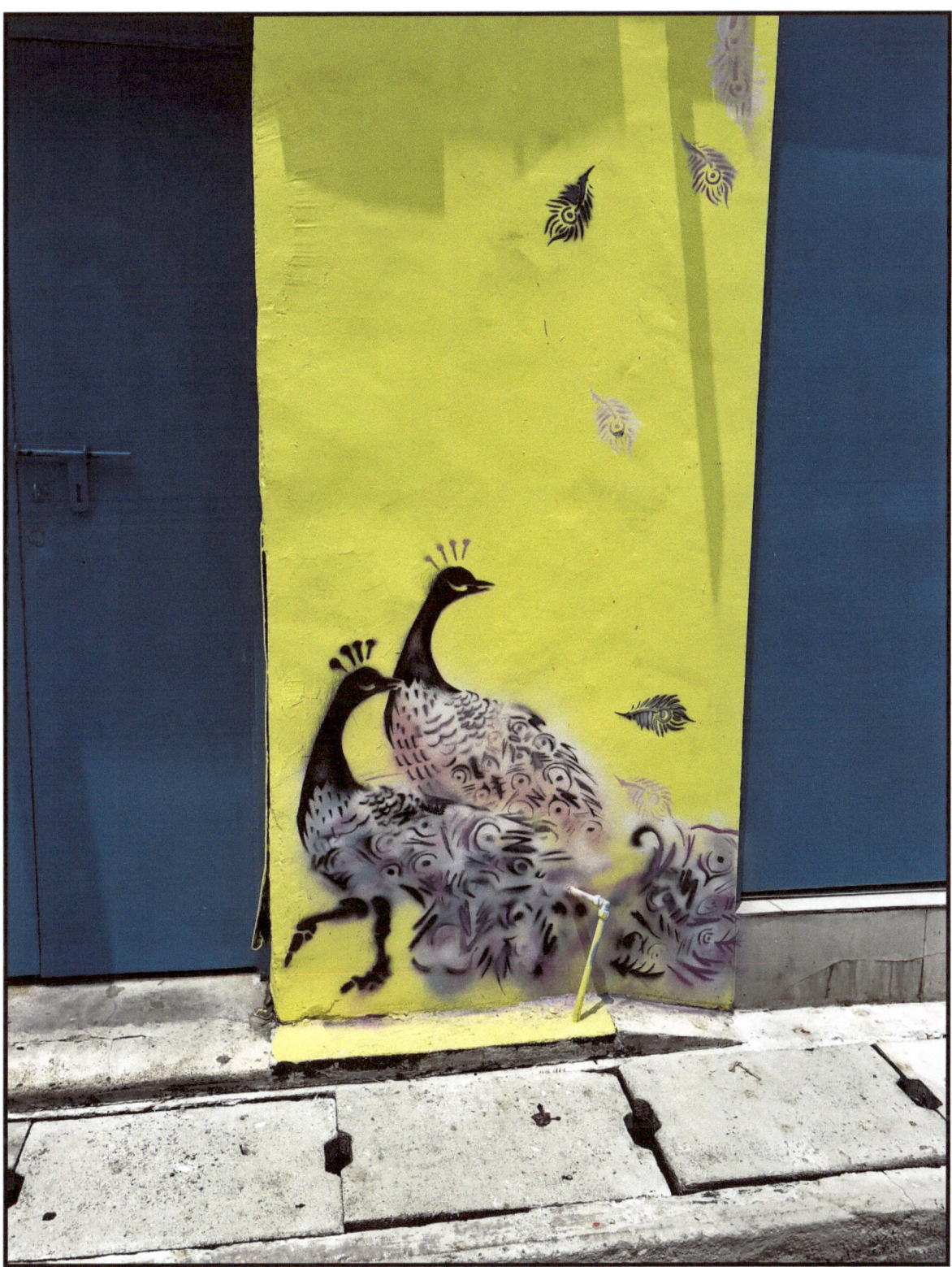

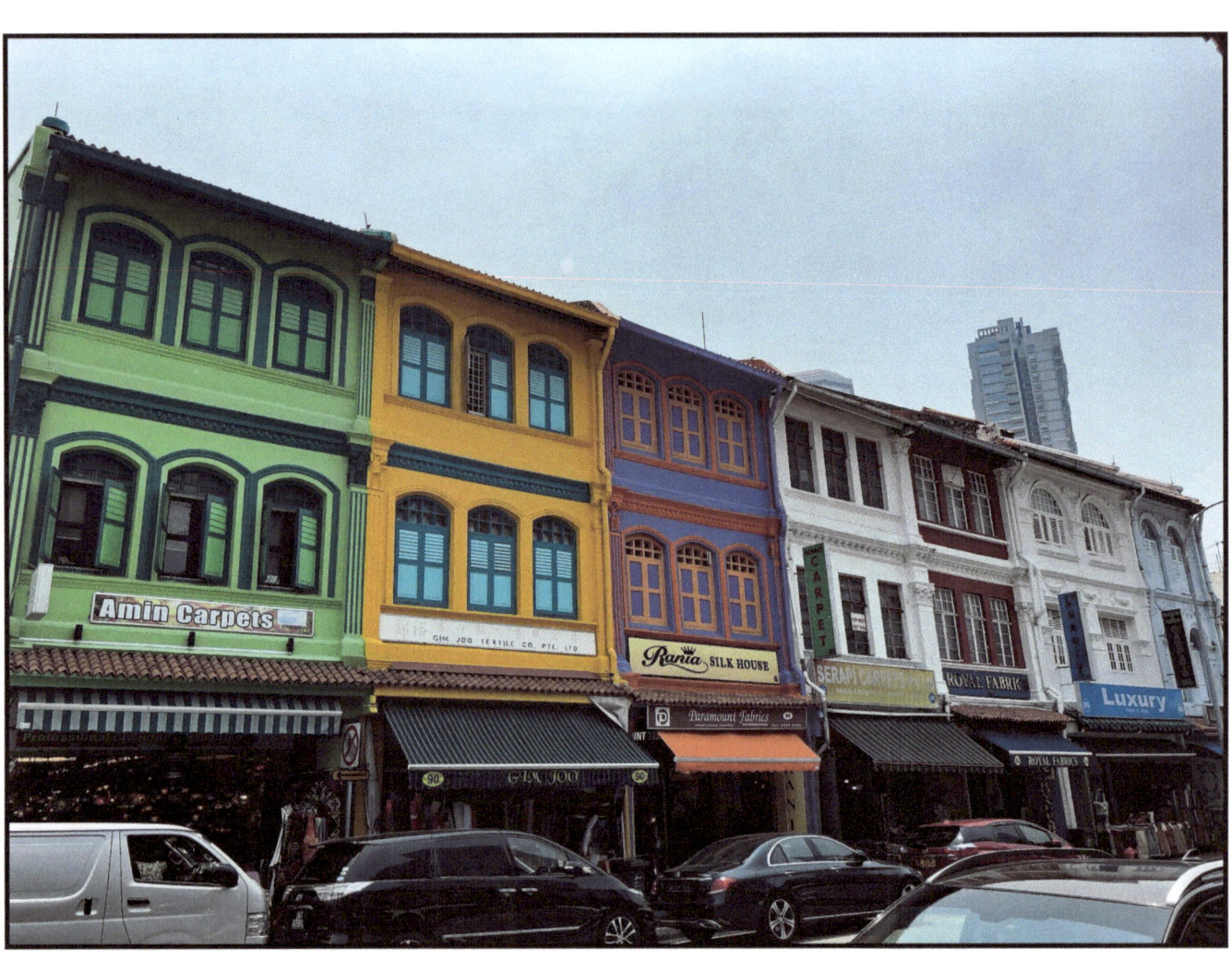

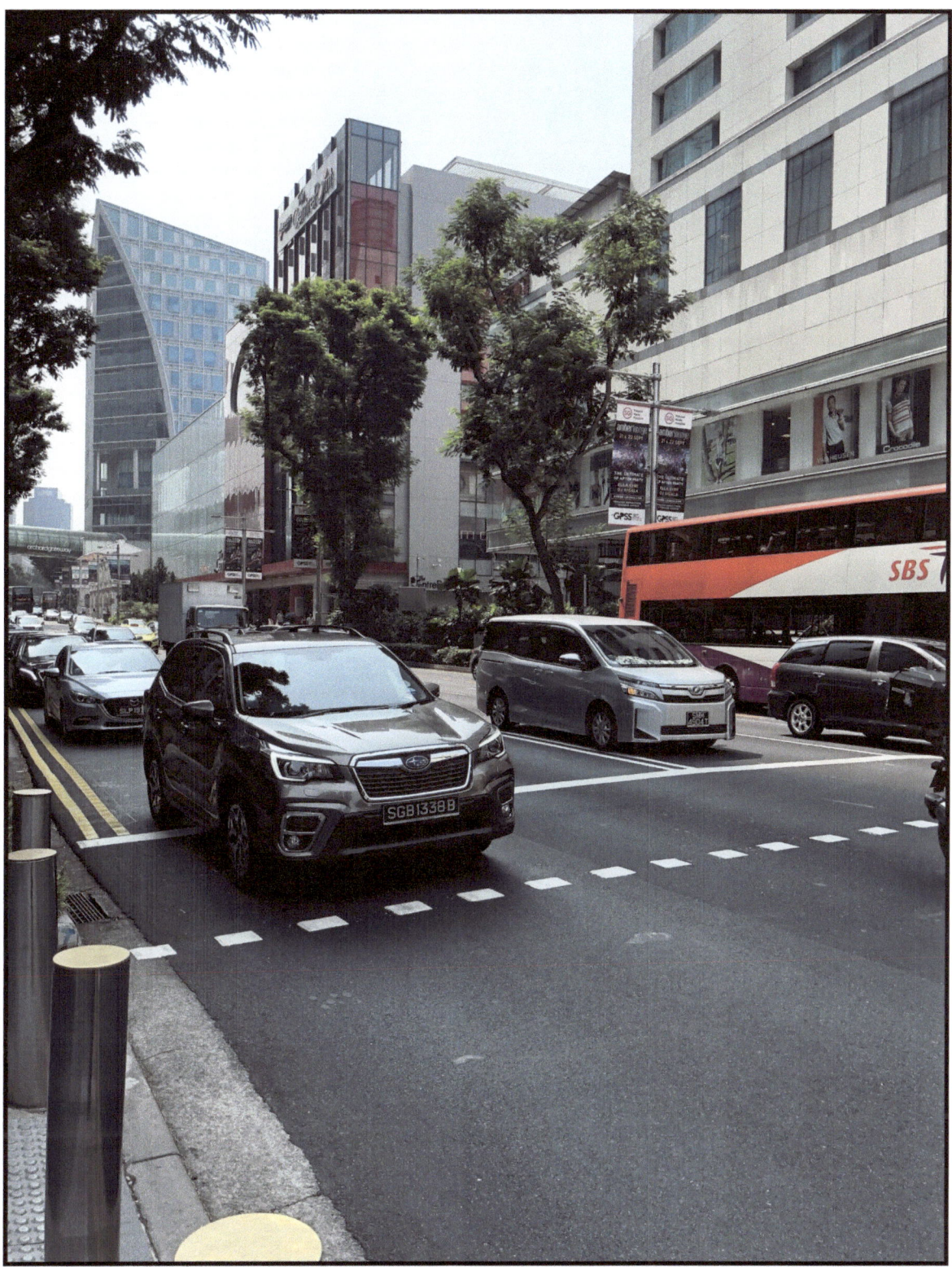

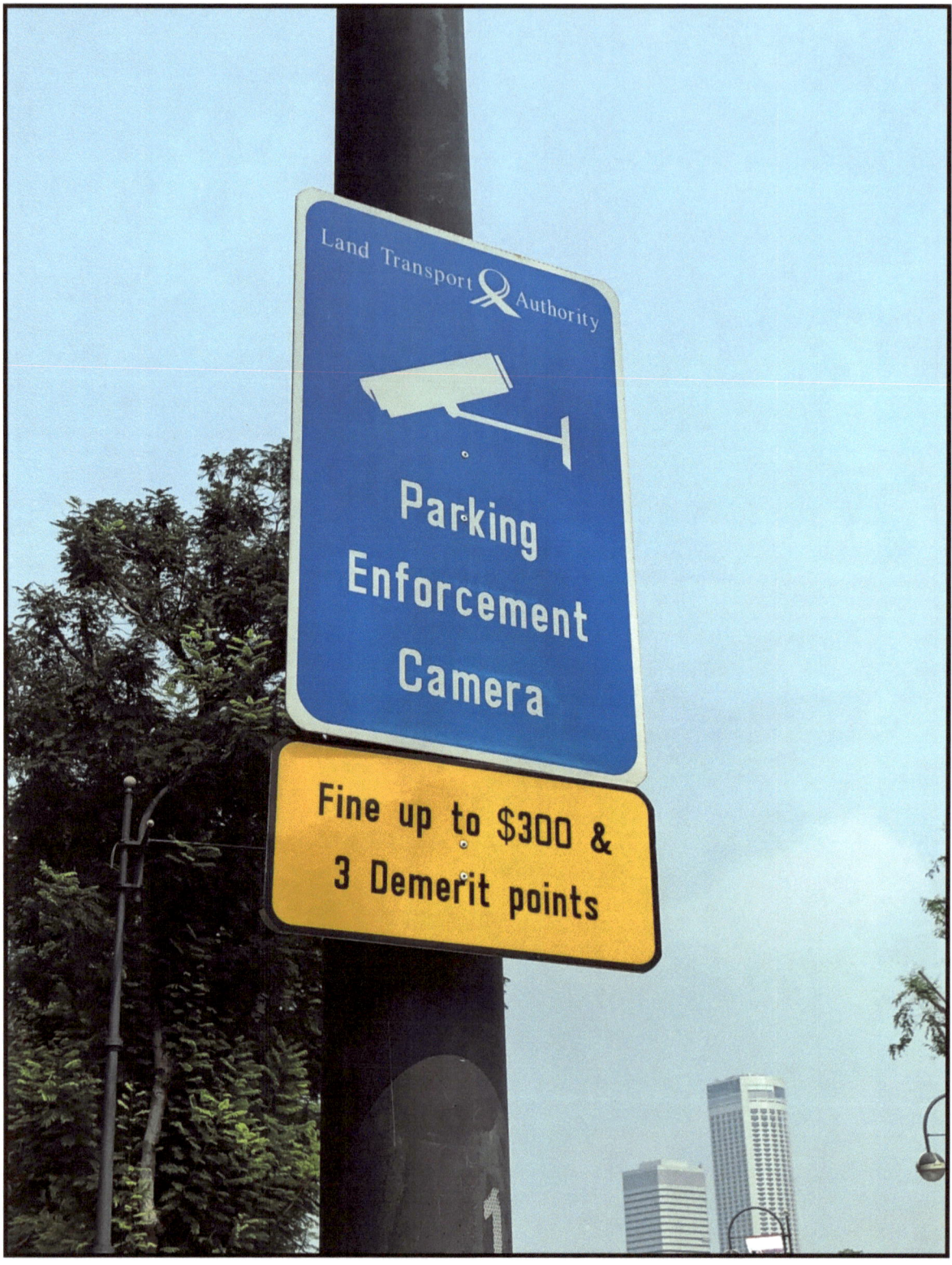

Street Of The Dead
死人街
Jalan Orang Mati
மரண வீதி

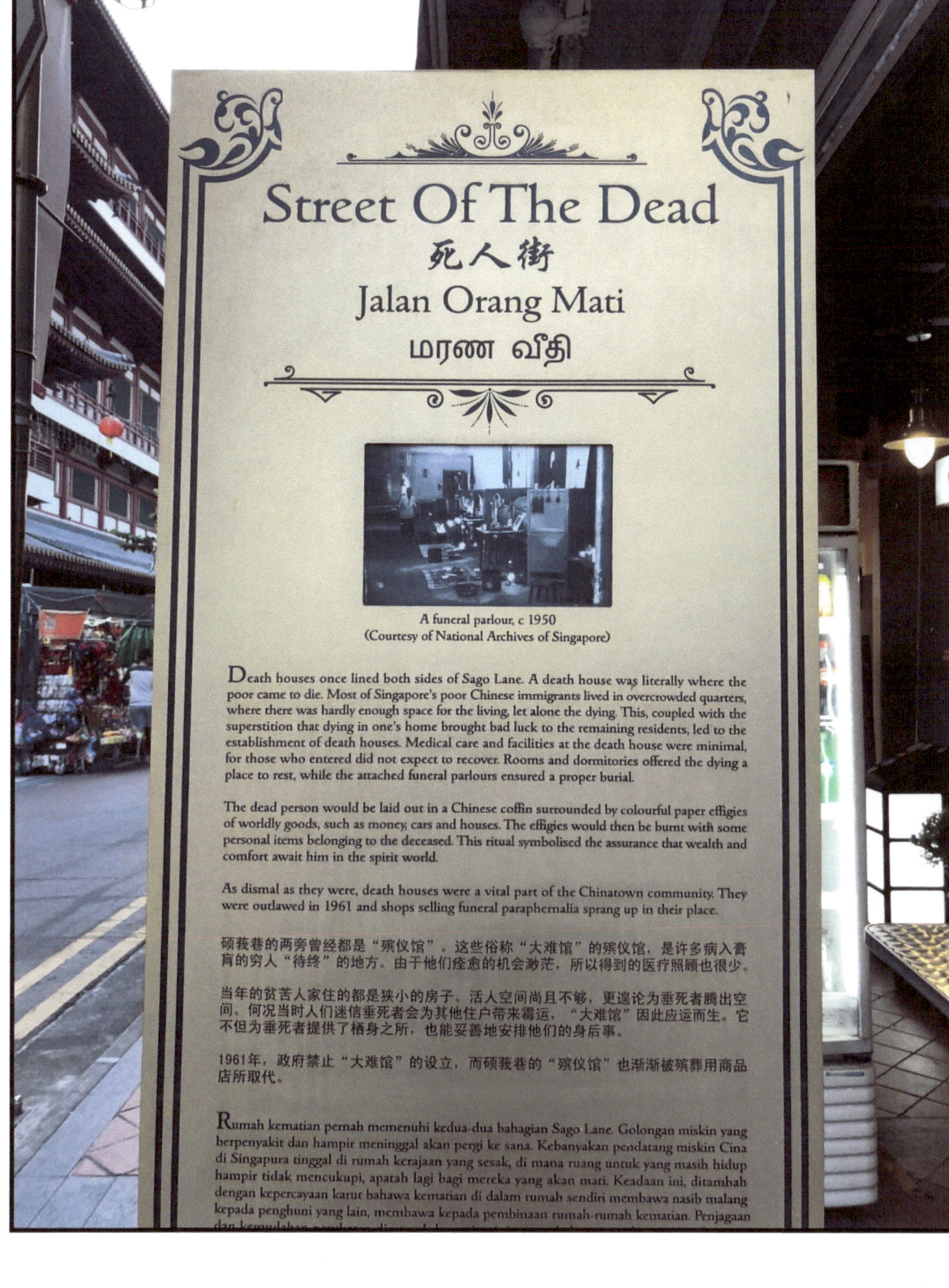

A funeral parlour, c 1950
(Courtesy of National Archives of Singapore)

Death houses once lined both sides of Sago Lane. A death house was literally where the poor came to die. Most of Singapore's poor Chinese immigrants lived in overcrowded quarters, where there was hardly enough space for the living, let alone the dying. This, coupled with the superstition that dying in one's home brought bad luck to the remaining residents, led to the establishment of death houses. Medical care and facilities at the death house were minimal, for those who entered did not expect to recover. Rooms and dormitories offered the dying a place to rest, while the attached funeral parlours ensured a proper burial.

The dead person would be laid out in a Chinese coffin surrounded by colourful paper effigies of worldly goods, such as money, cars and houses. The effigies would then be burnt with some personal items belonging to the deceased. This ritual symbolised the assurance that wealth and comfort await him in the spirit world.

As dismal as they were, death houses were a vital part of the Chinatown community. They were outlawed in 1961 and shops selling funeral paraphernalia sprang up in their place.

硕莪巷的两旁曾经都是"殡仪馆"。这些俗称"大难馆"的殡仪馆,是许多病入膏肓的穷人"待终"的地方。由于他们痊愈的机会渺茫,所以得到的医疗照顾也很少。

当年的贫苦人家住的都是狭小的房子。活人空间尚且不够,更遑论为垂死者腾出空间。何况当时人们迷信垂死者会为其他住户带来霉运,"大难馆"因此应运而生。它不但为垂死者提供了栖身之所,也能妥善地安排他们的身后事。

1961年,政府禁止"大难馆"的设立,而硕莪巷的"殡仪馆"也渐渐被殡葬用商品店所取代。

Rumah kematian pernah memenuhi kedua-dua bahagian Sago Lane. Golongan miskin yang berpenyakit dan hampir meninggal akan pergi ke sana. Kebanyakan pendatang miskin Cina di Singapura tinggal di rumah kerajaan yang sesak, di mana ruang untuk yang masih hidup hampir tidak mencukupi, apatah lagi bagi mereka yang akan mati. Keadaan ini, ditambah dengan kepercayaan karut bahawa kematian di dalam rumah sendiri membawa nasib malang kepada penghuni yang lain, membawa kepada pembinaan rumah-rumah kematian. Penjagaan

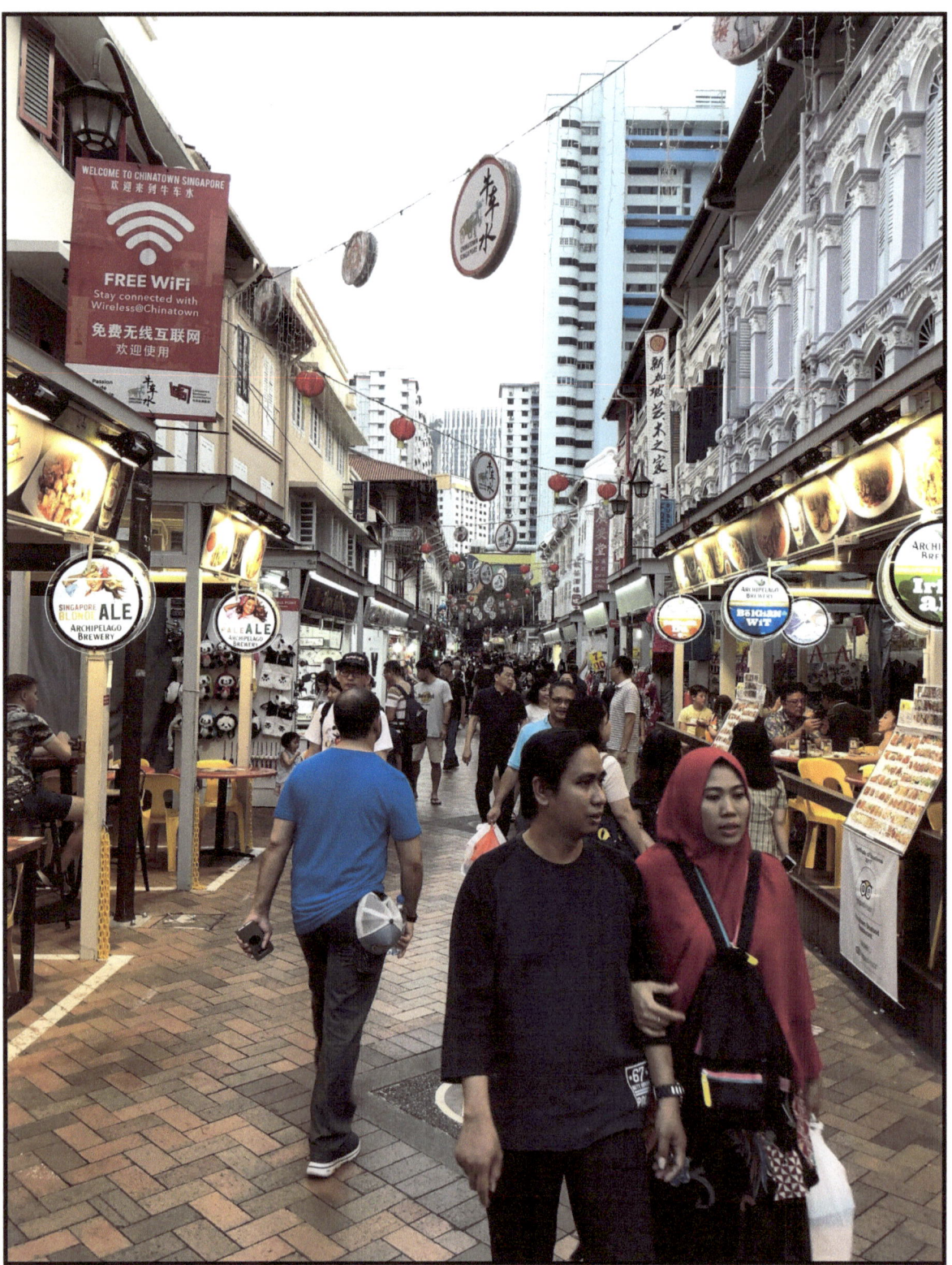

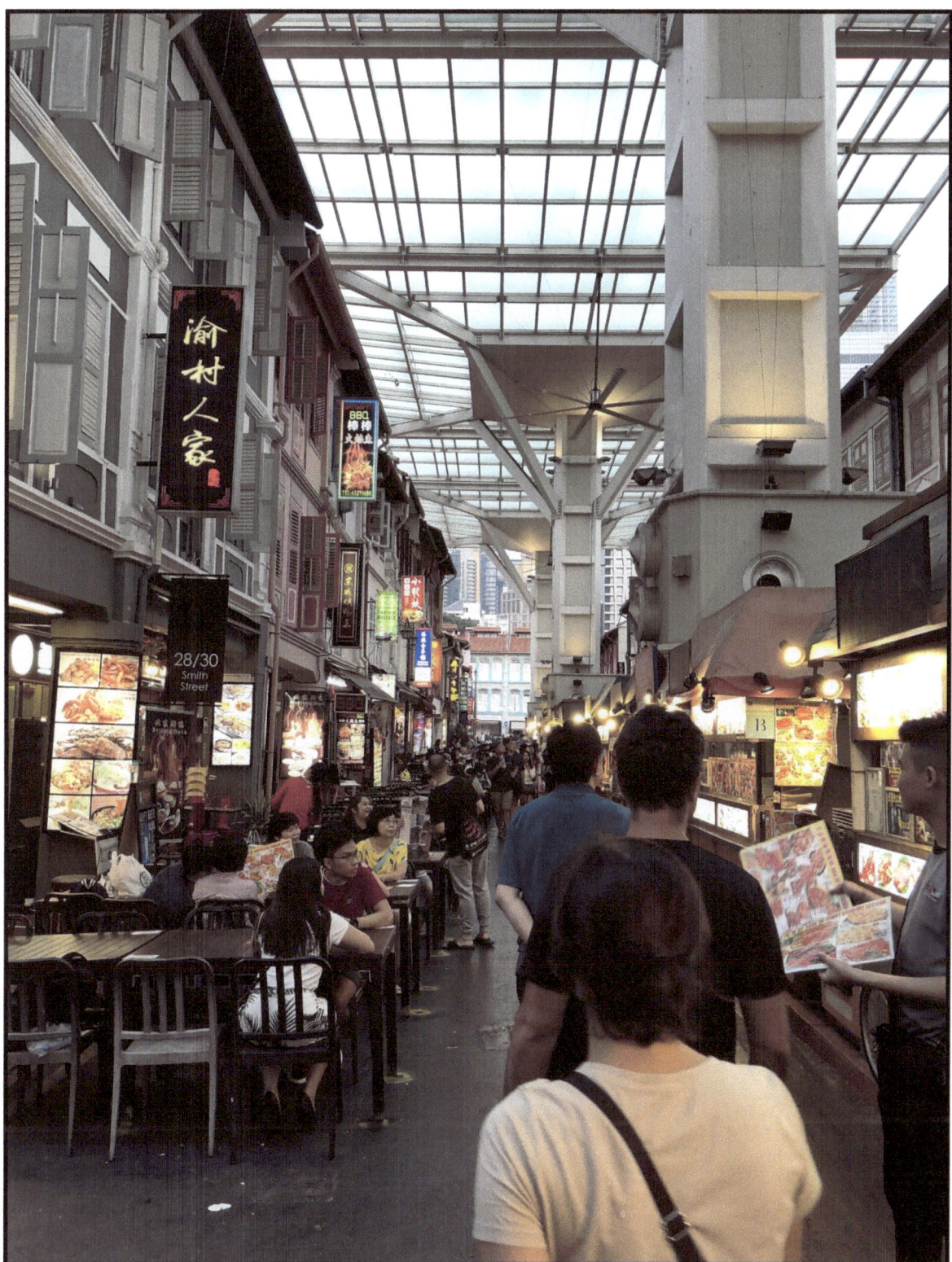

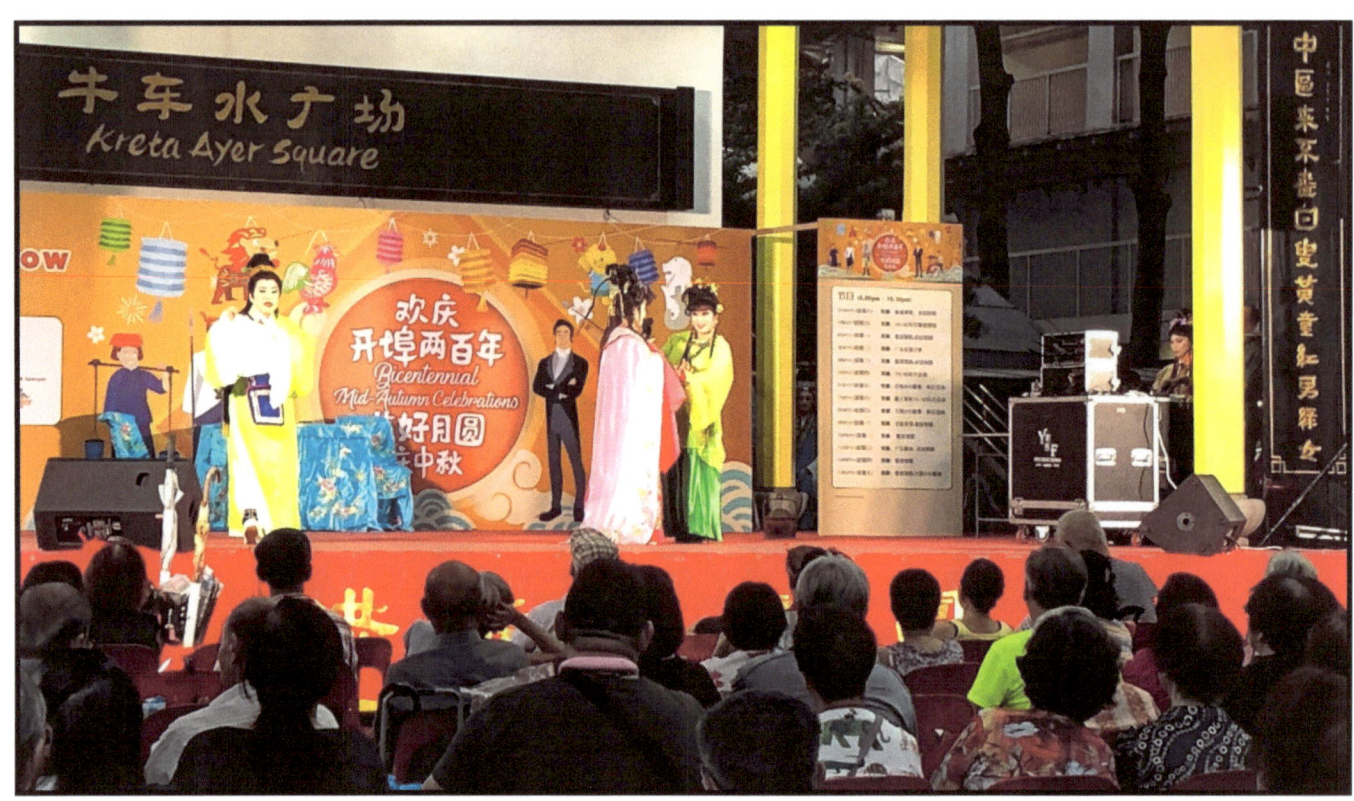

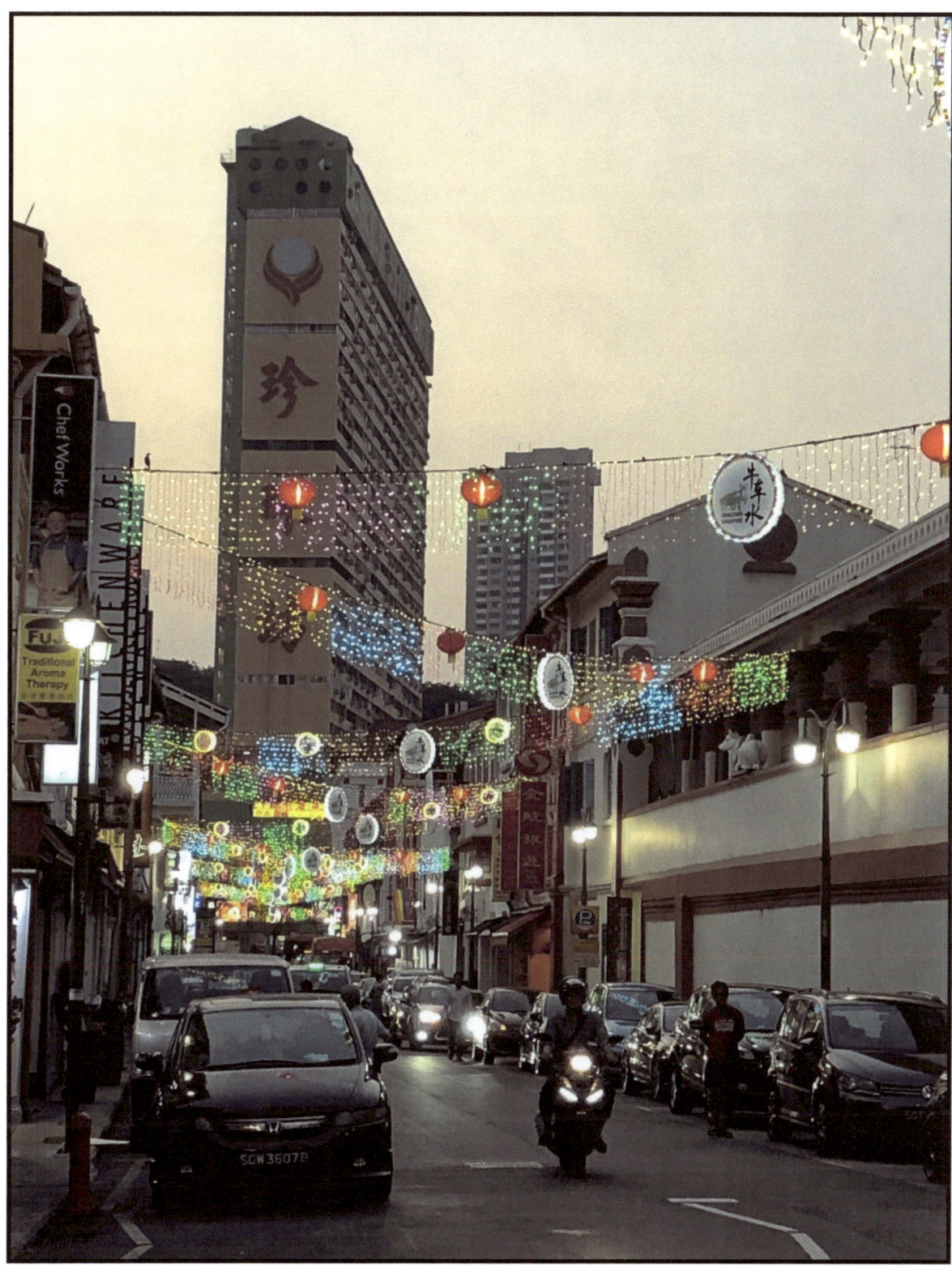

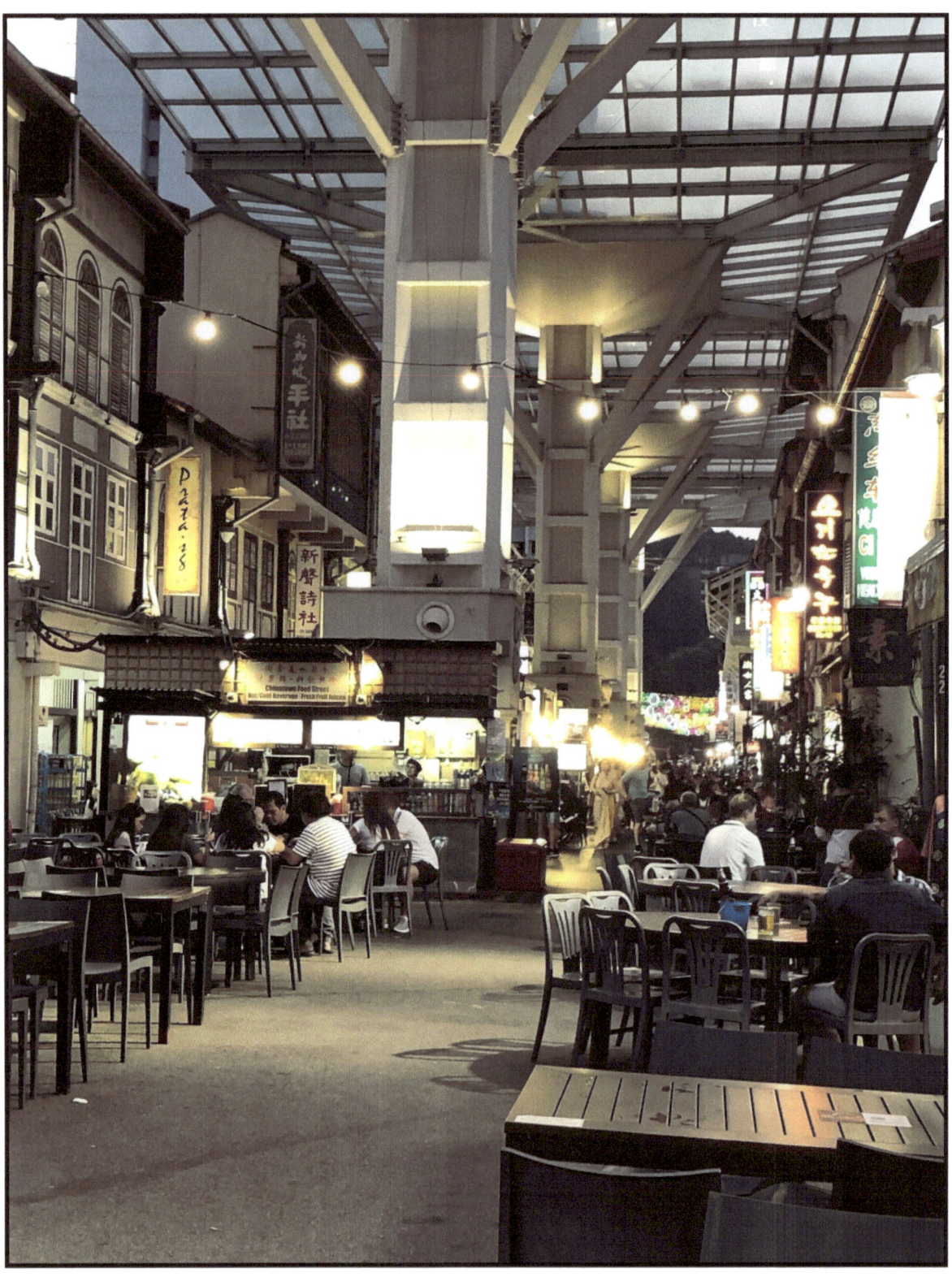

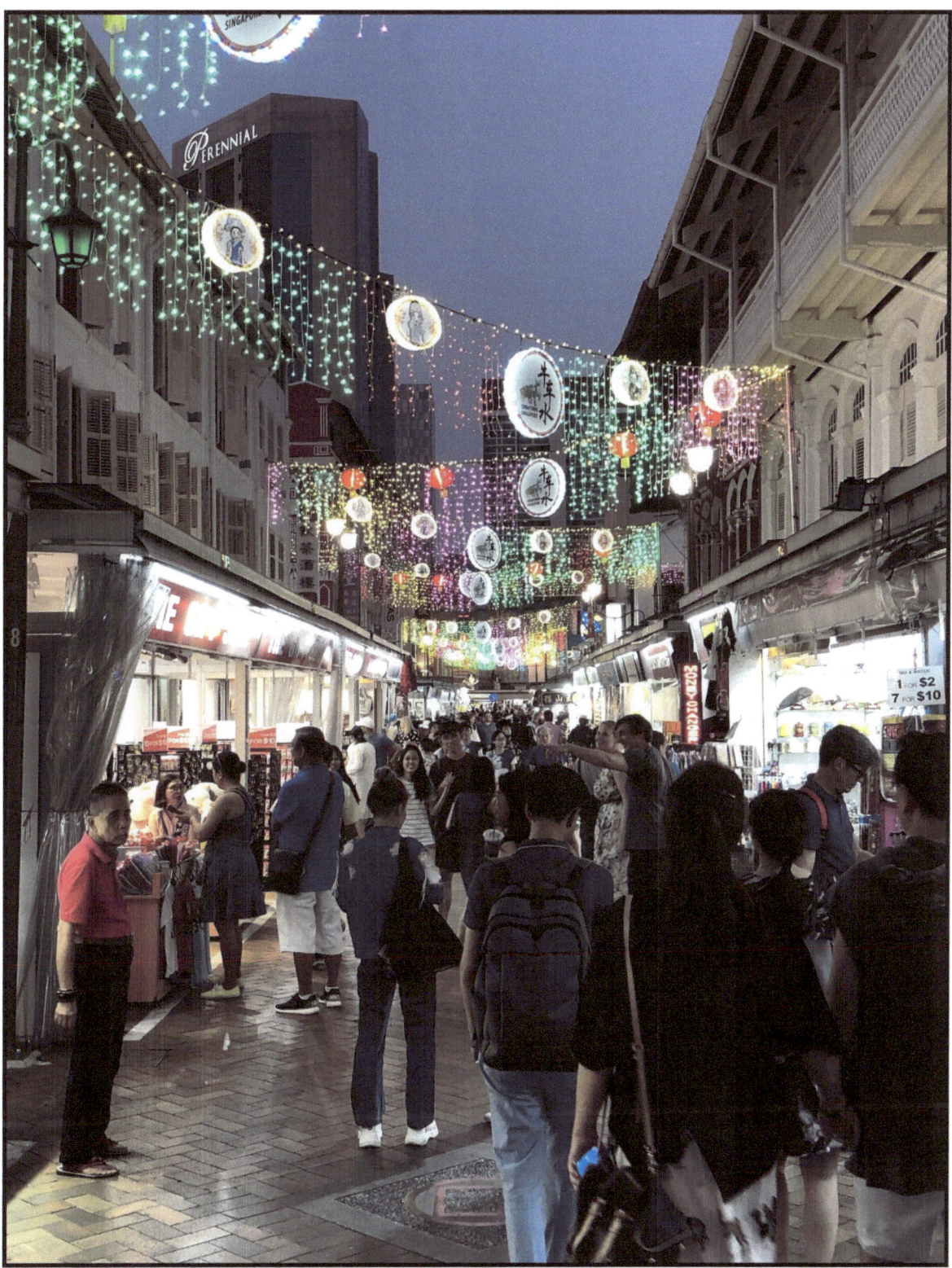

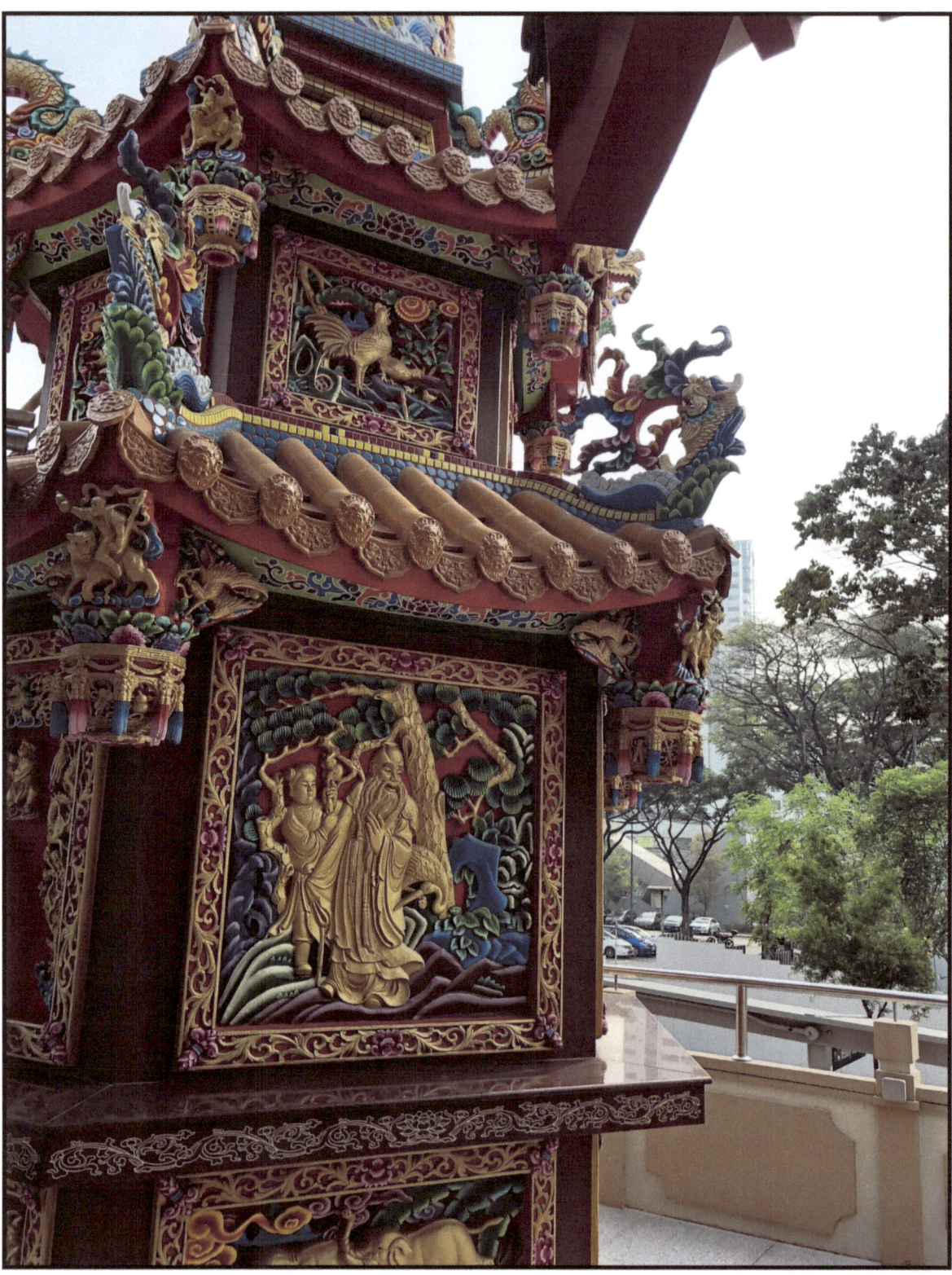

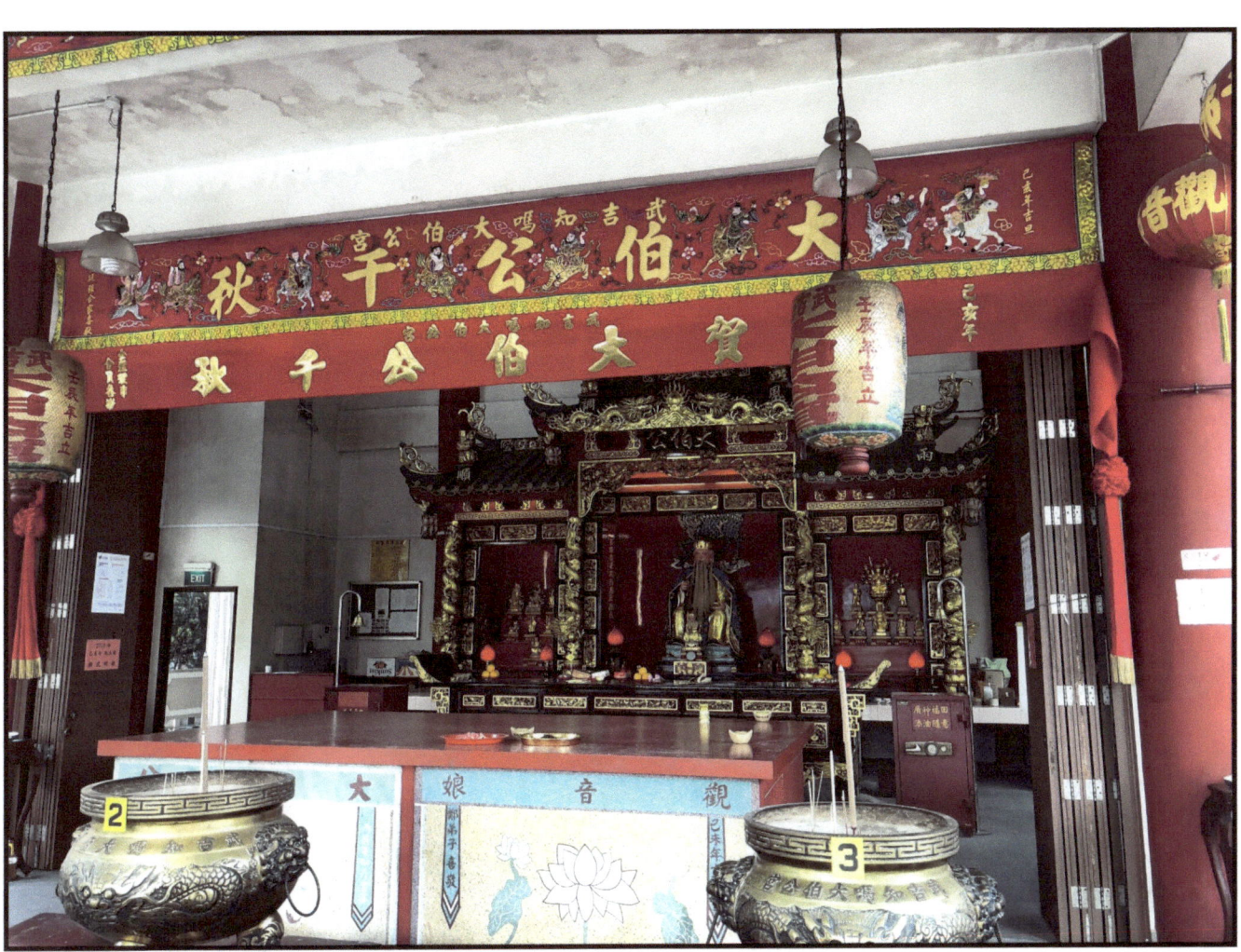

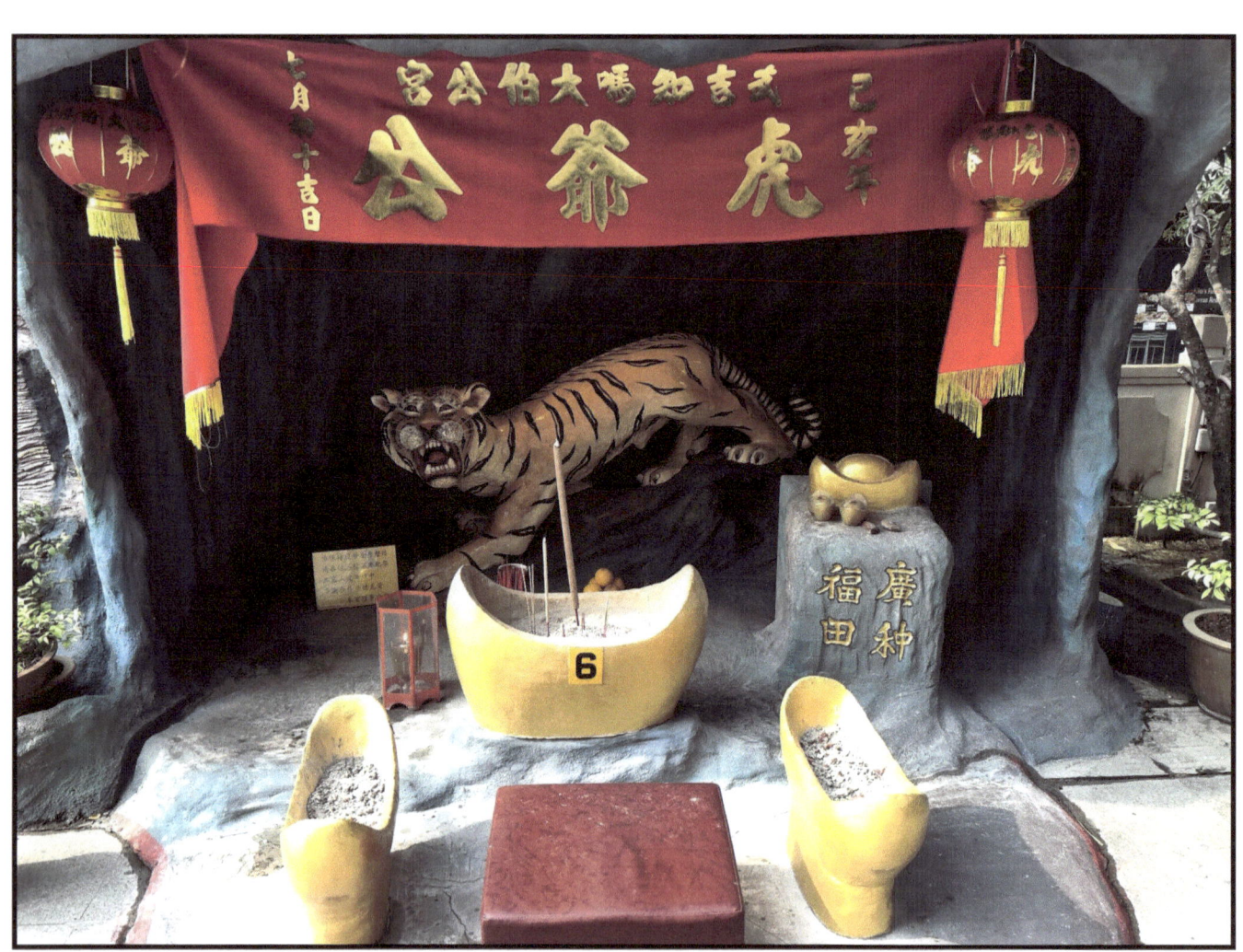

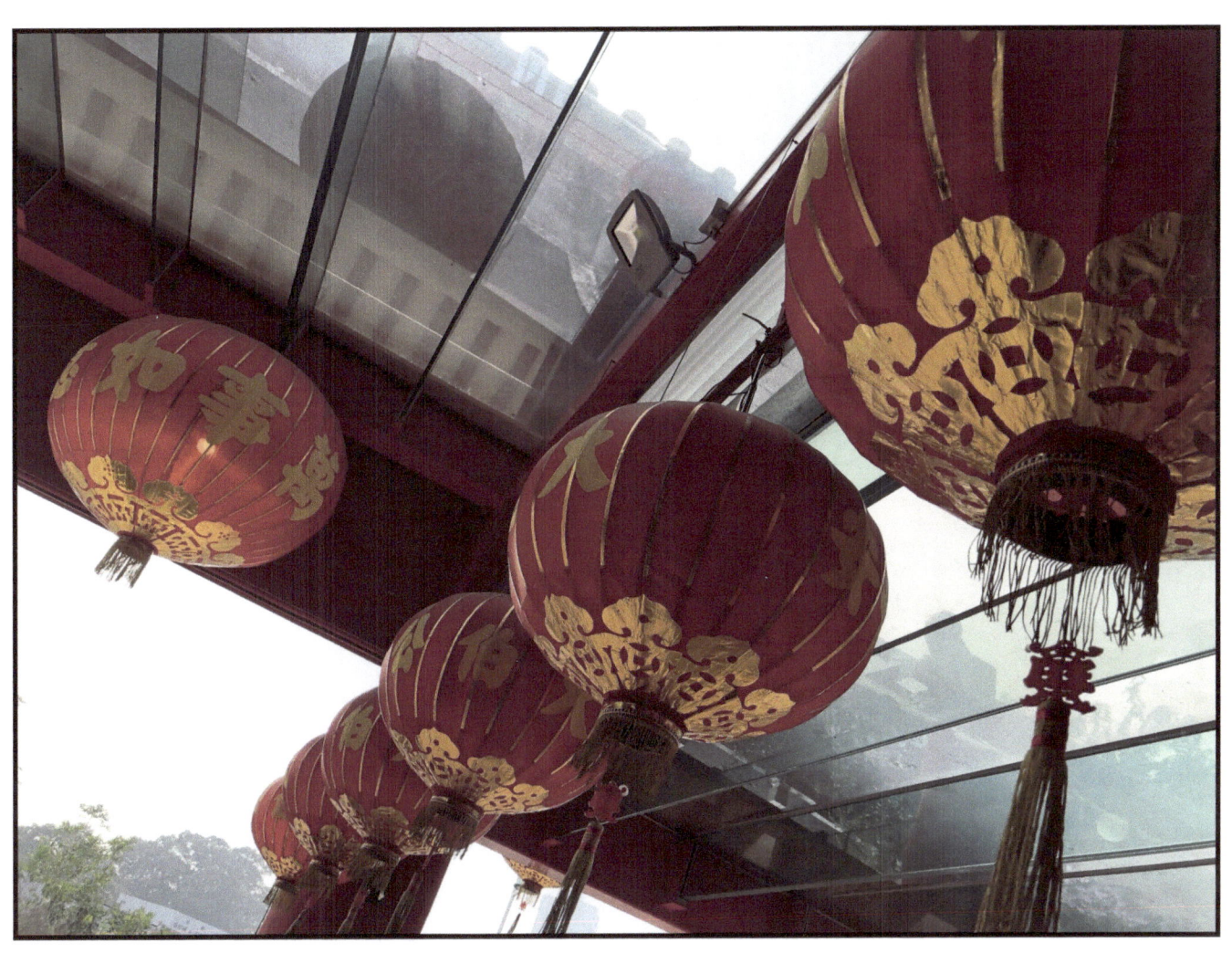

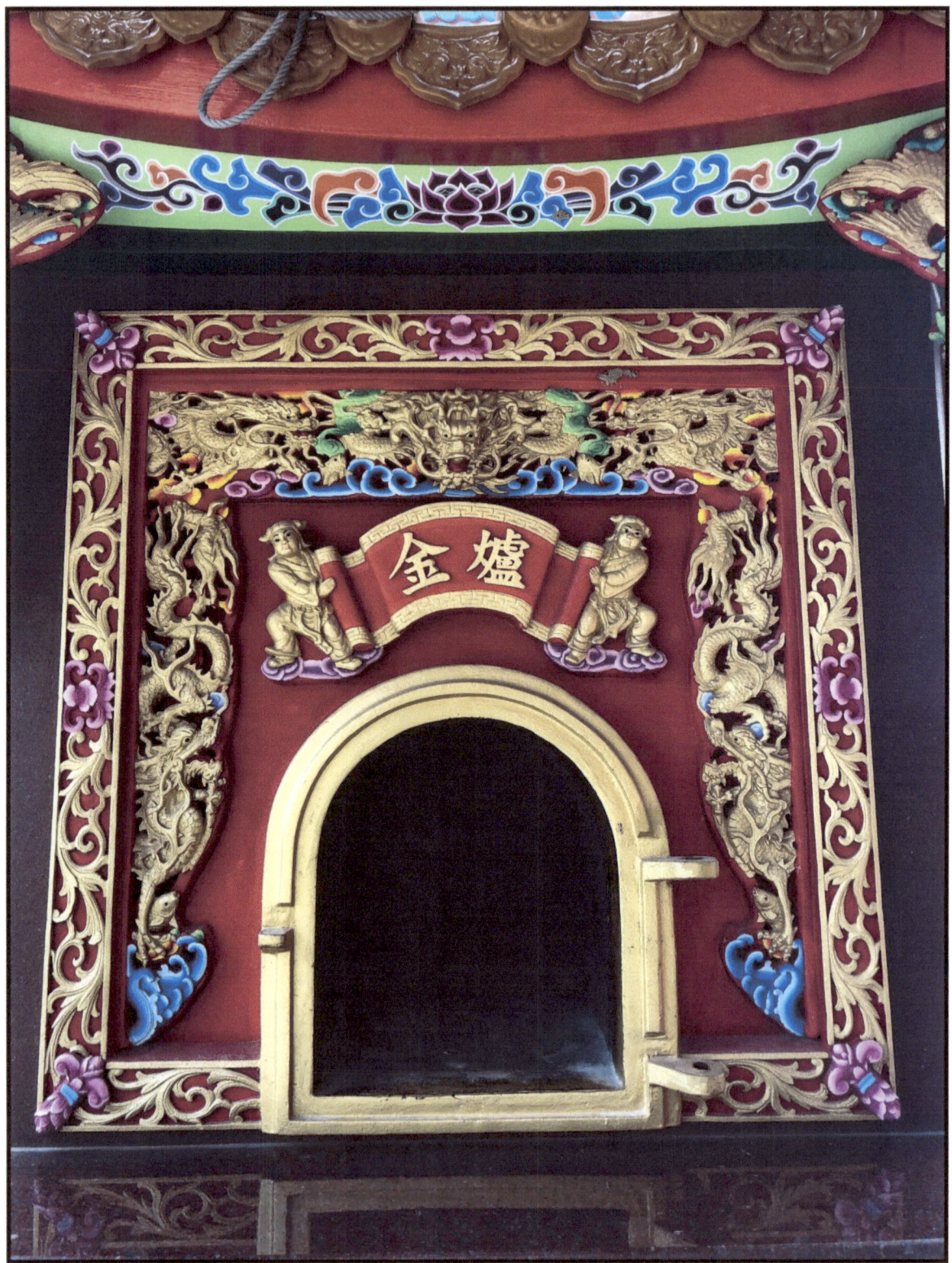

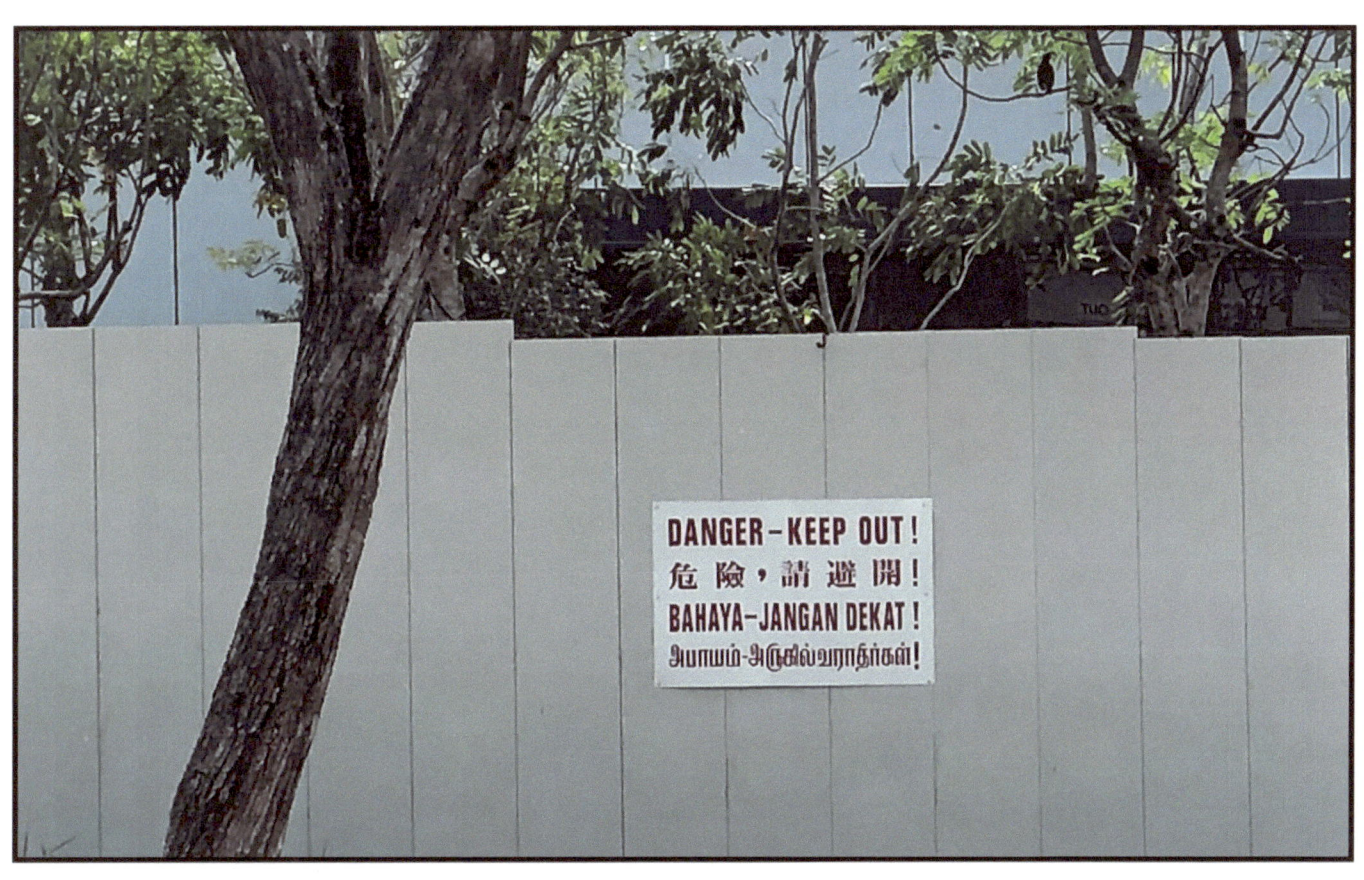

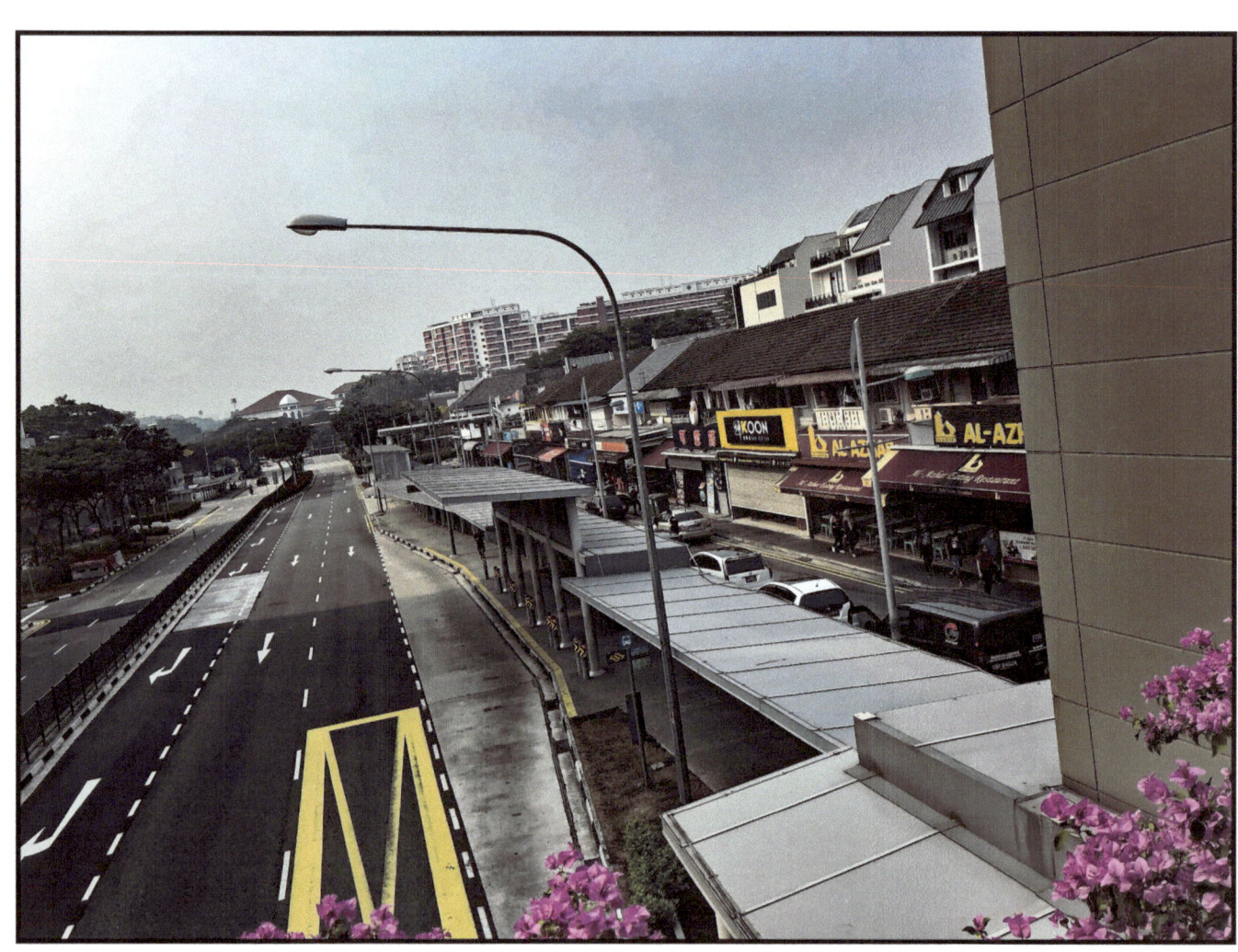

NO OPEN FIRES AND NO BARBECUING

NO SMOKING

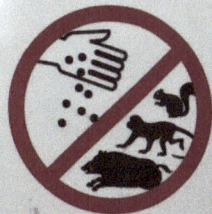
NO FEEDING OF WILD ANIMALS

NO LITTERING

NO PETS

NO FISHING OR POACHING

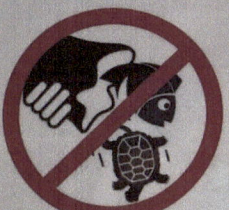
NO RELEASING OF ANIMALS

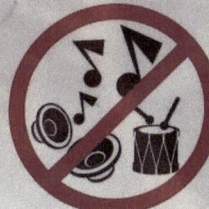
NO PLAYING OF MUSIC

NO PLUCKING OF PLANTS

NO FEEDING OF MONKEYS
FINE UP TO $50,000 AND/OR JAIL

NO BICYCLE

NO FLYING OF MODEL AIRCRAFT

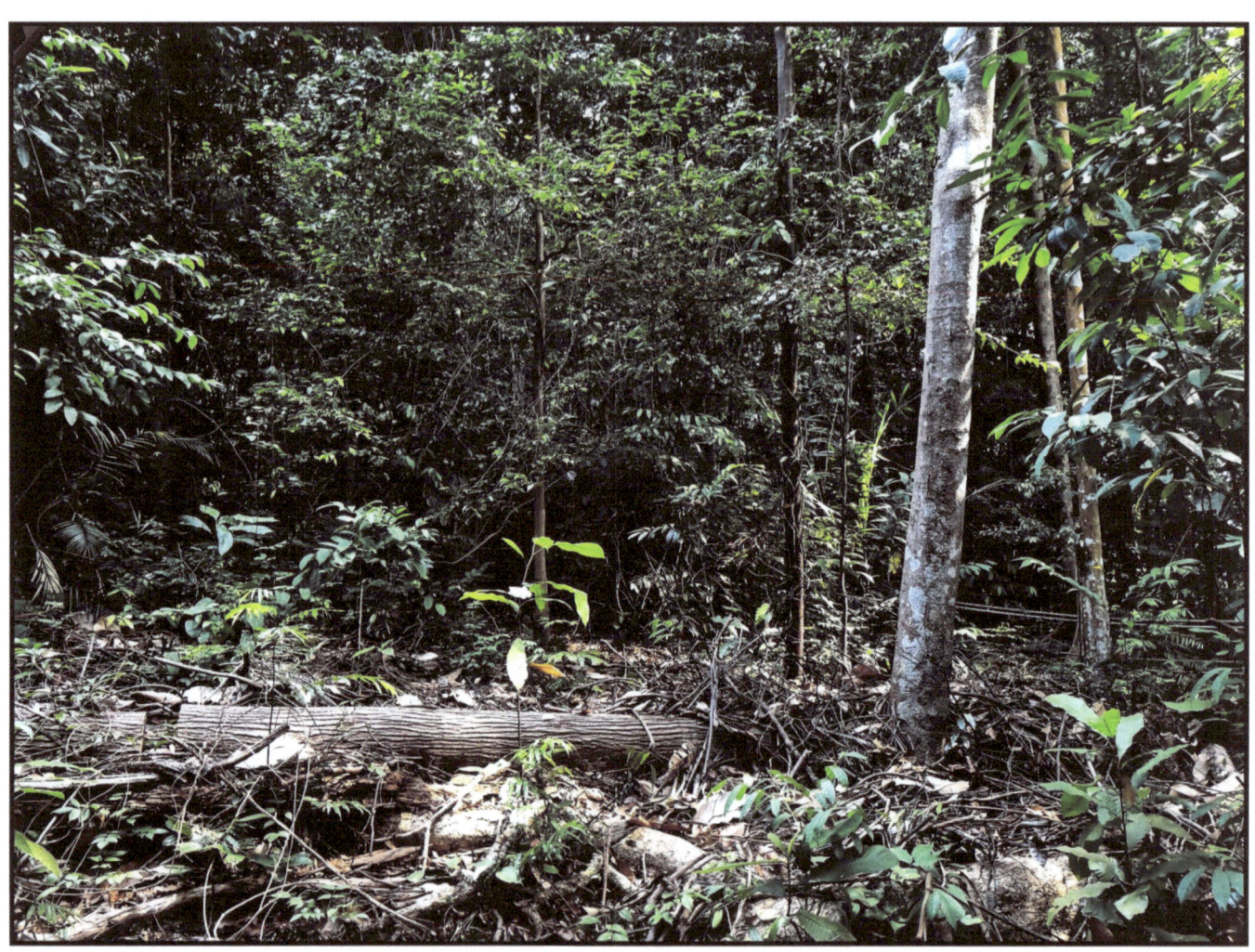

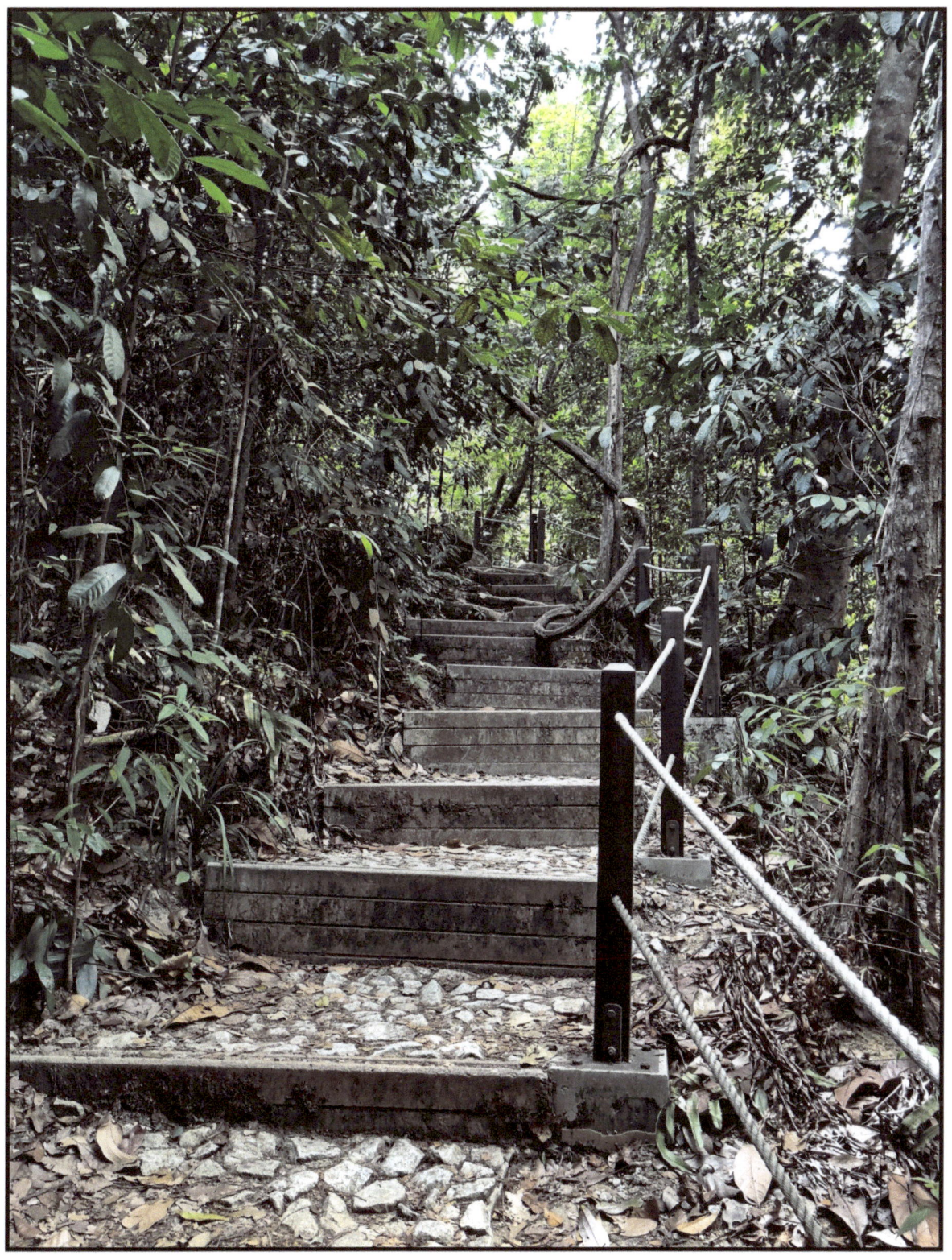

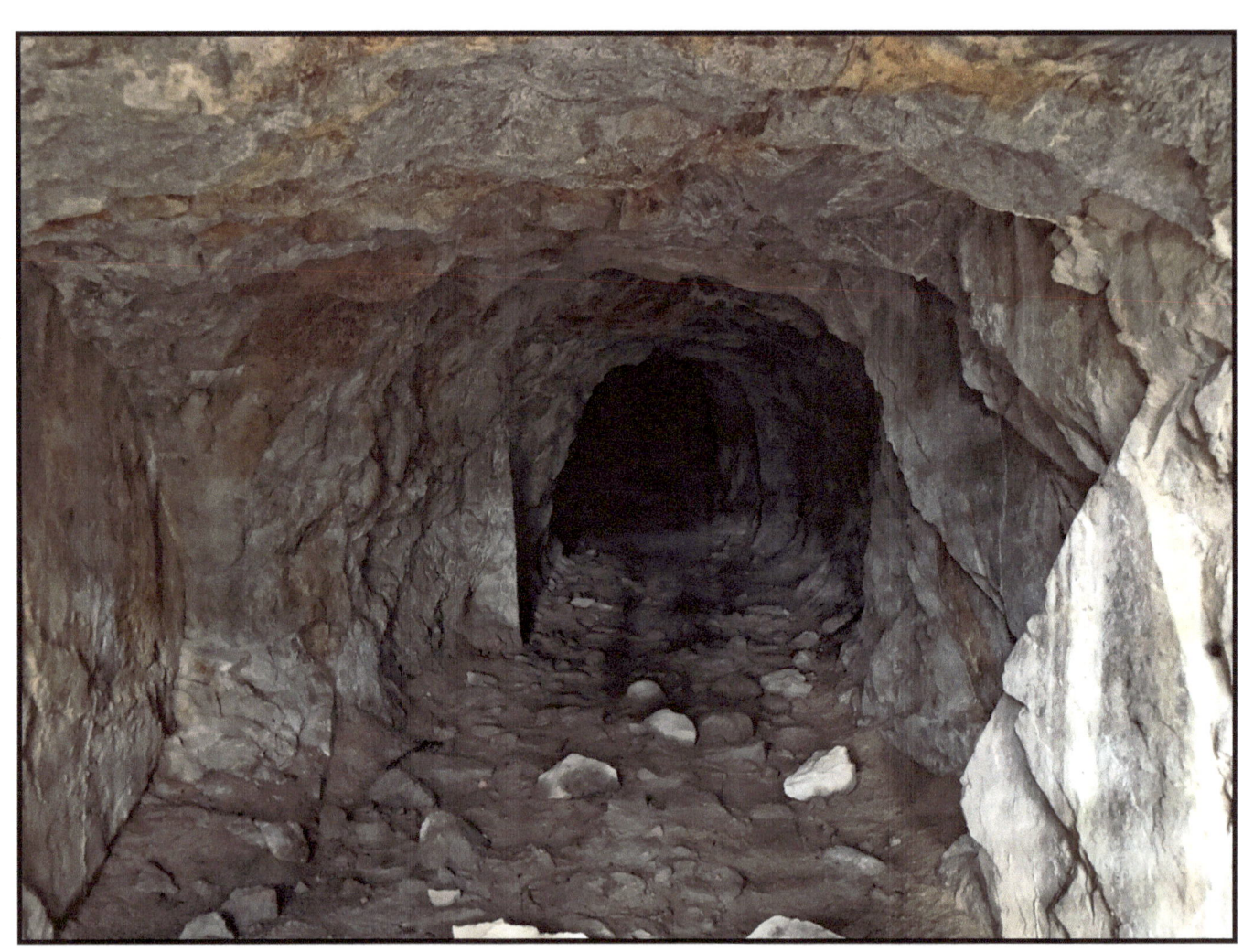

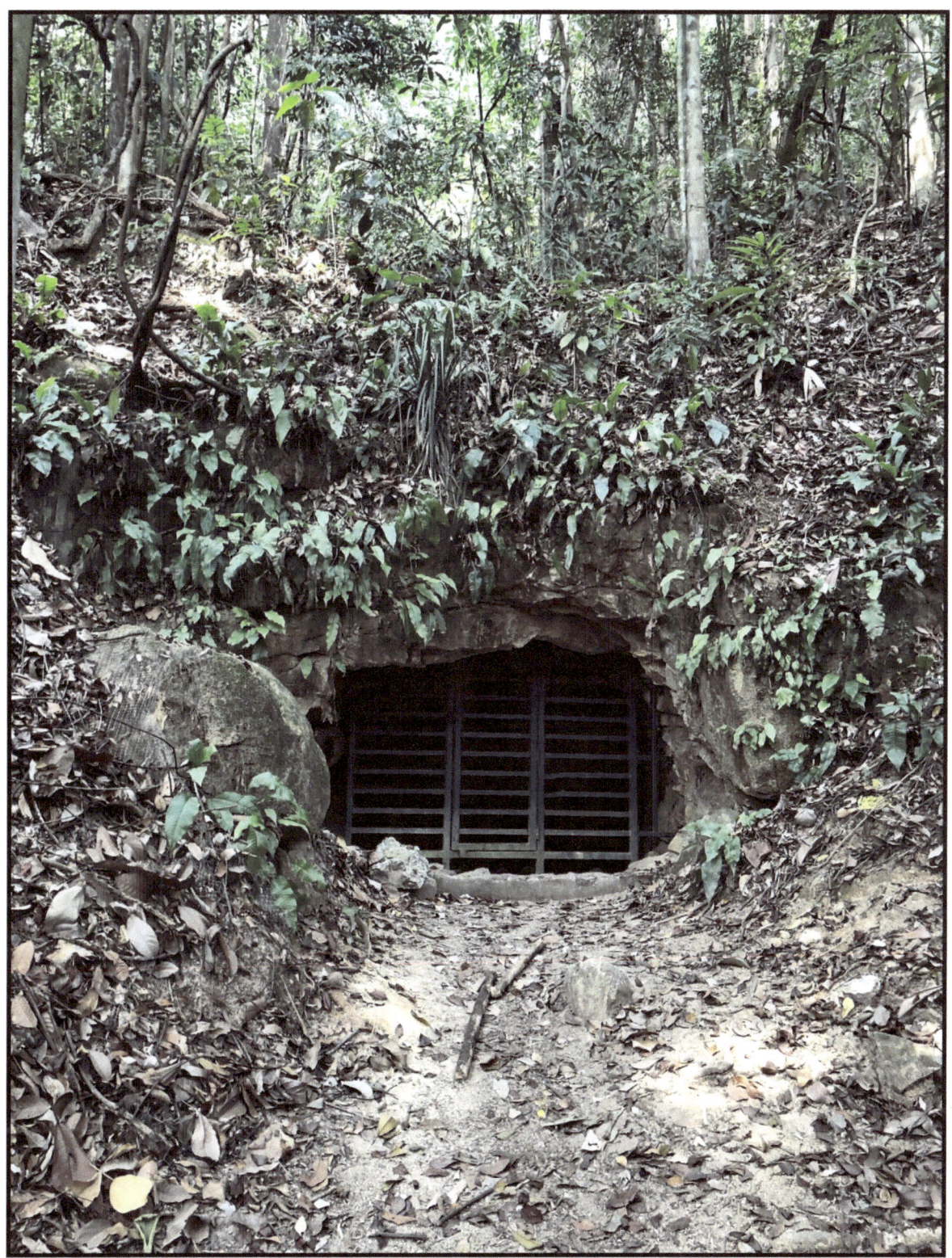

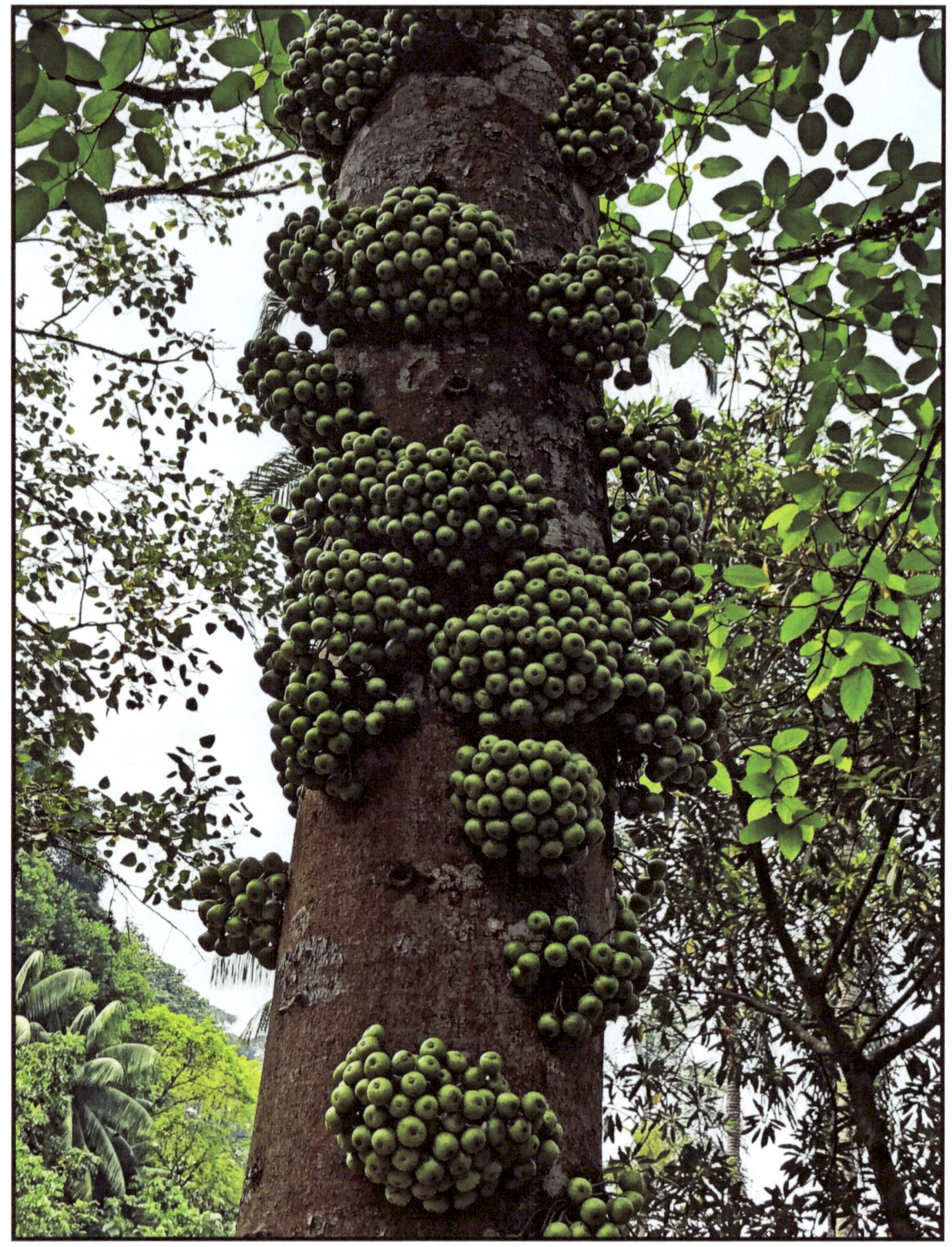

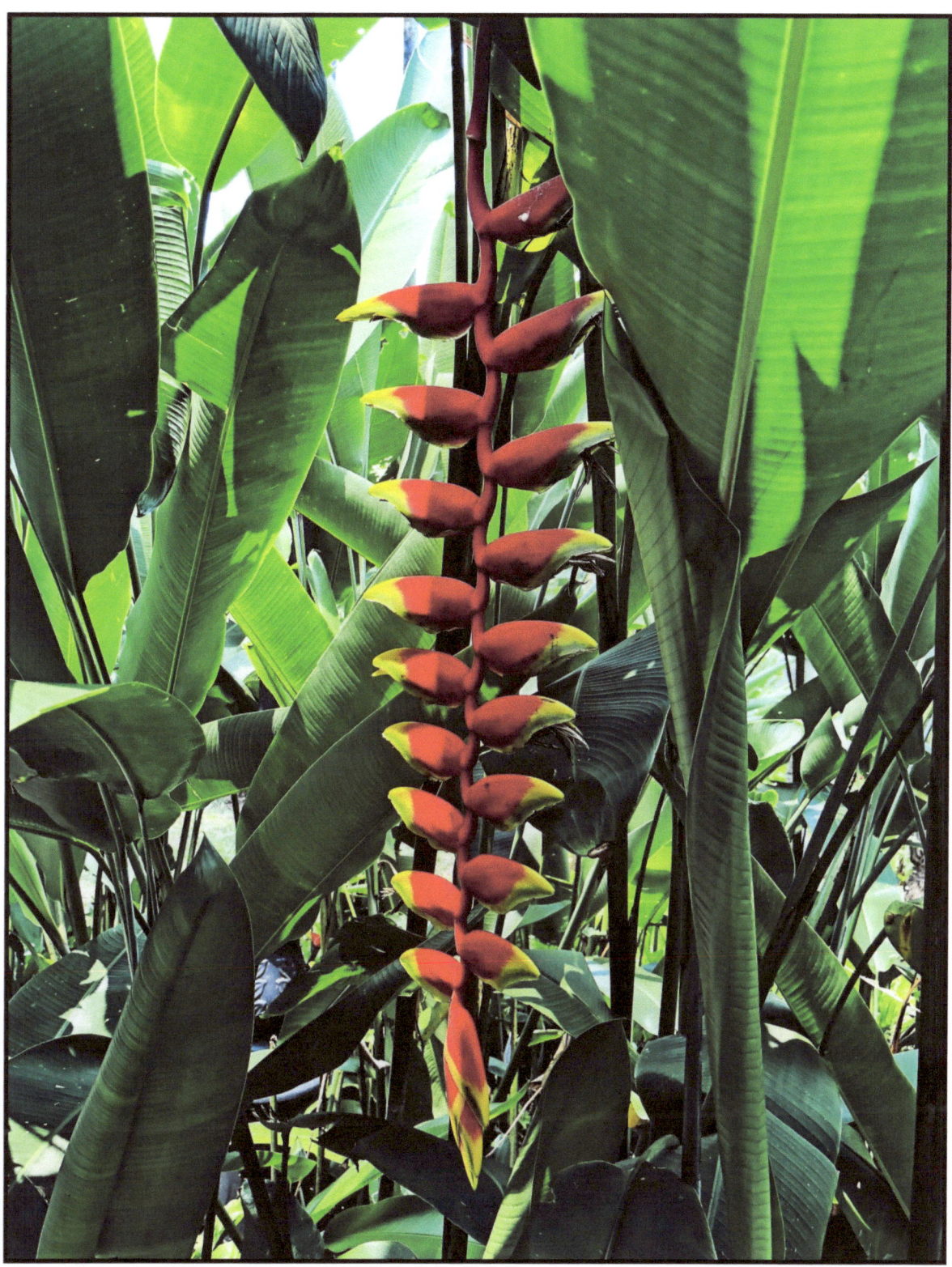

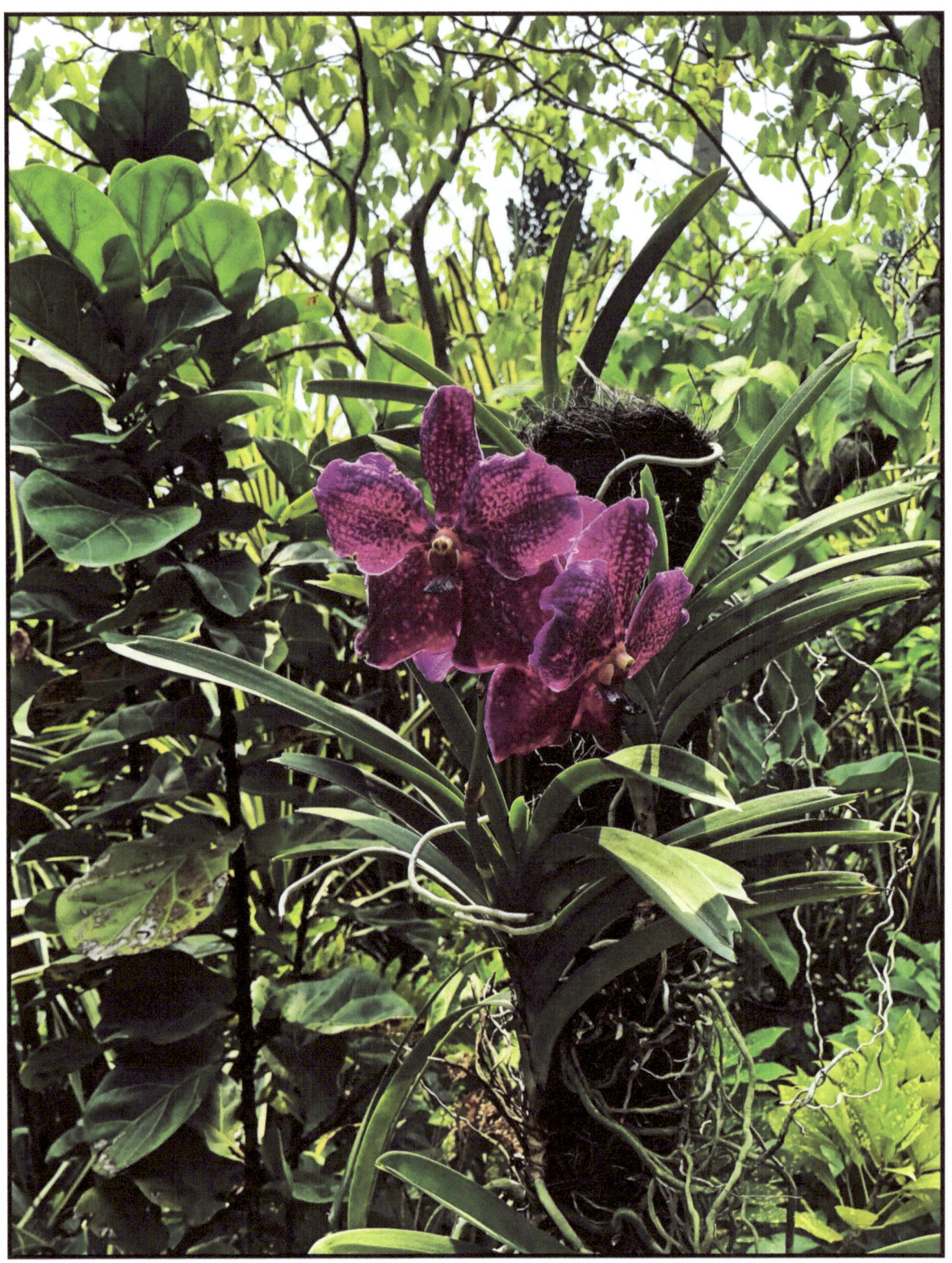

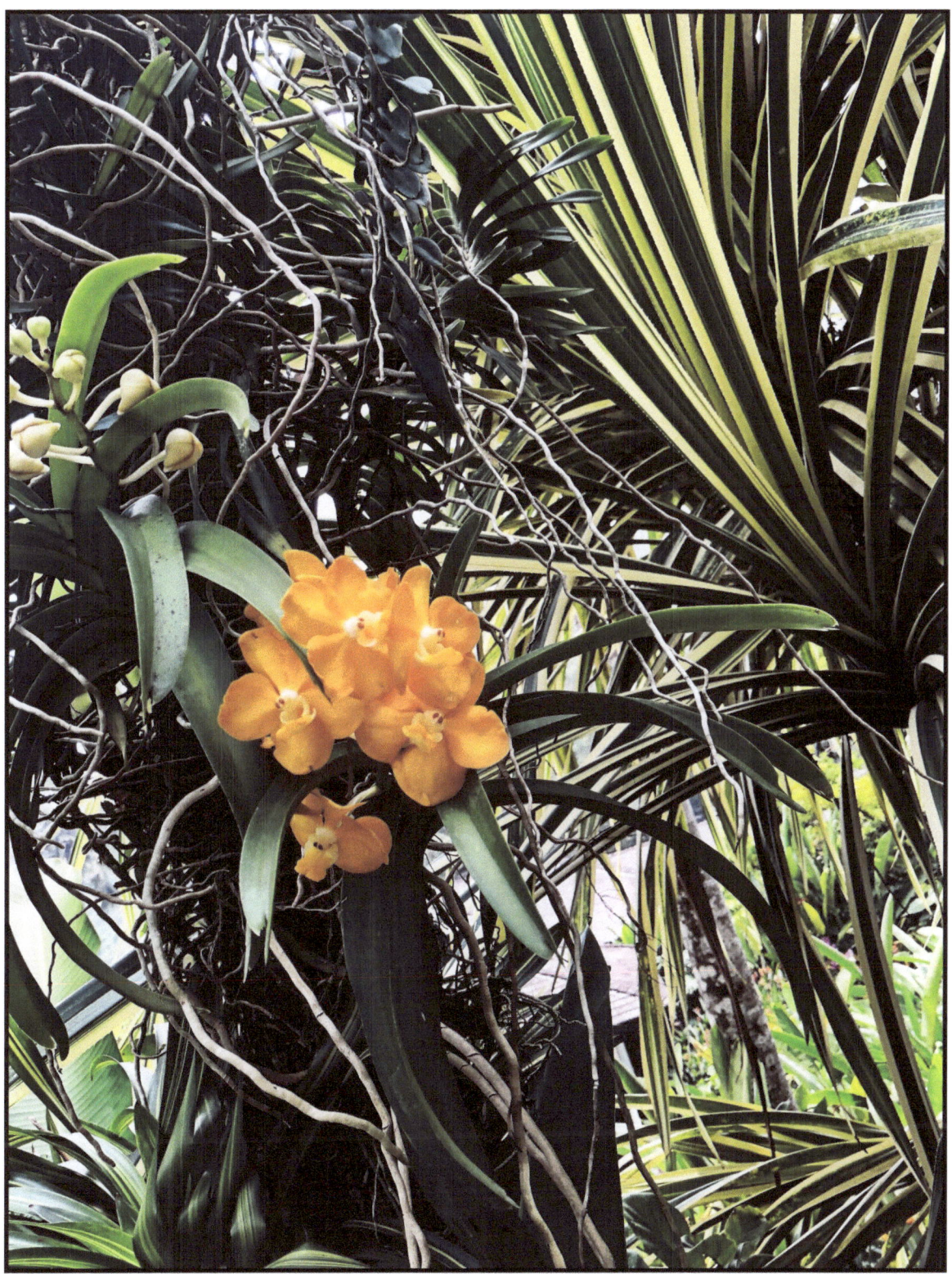

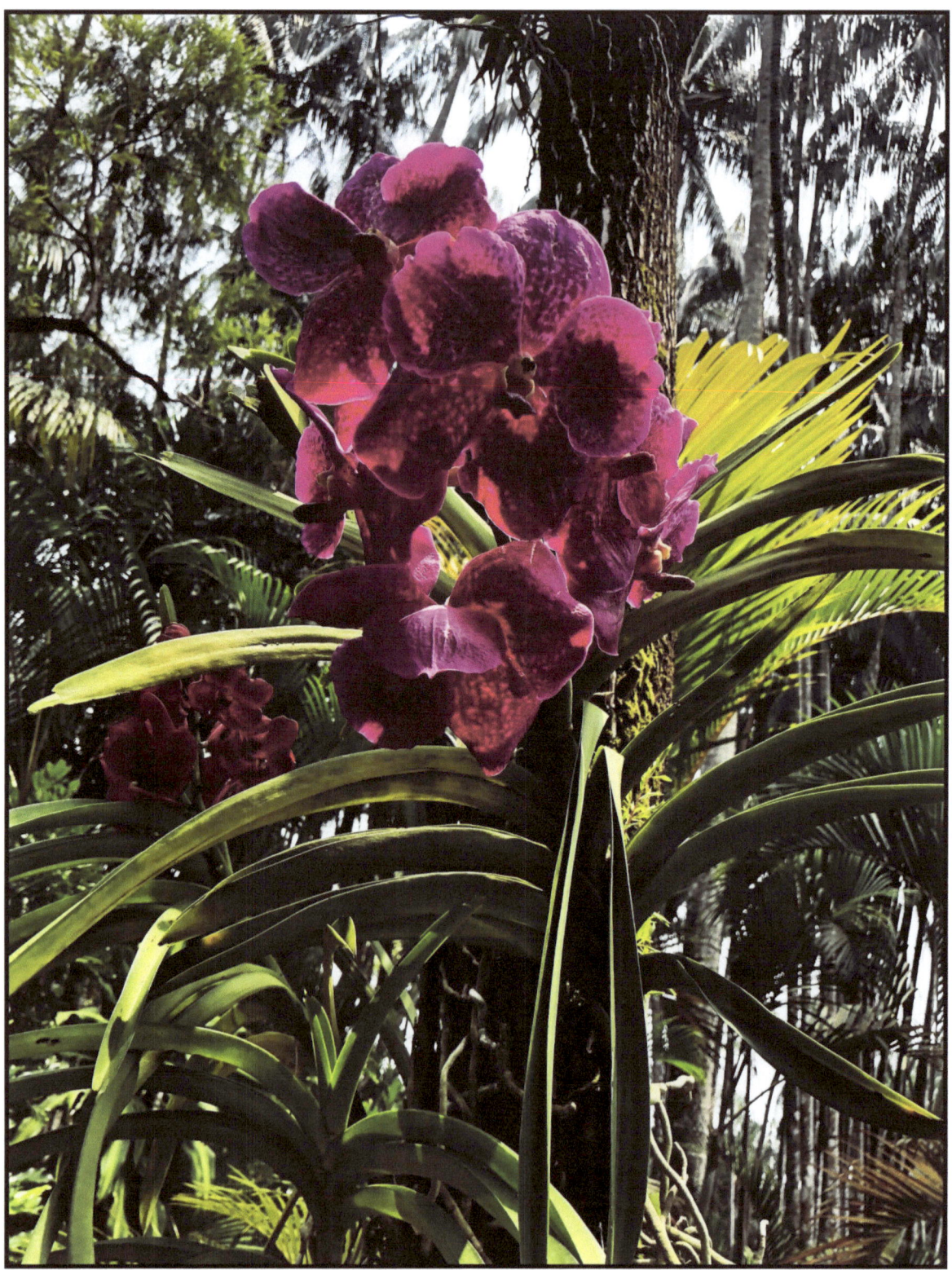

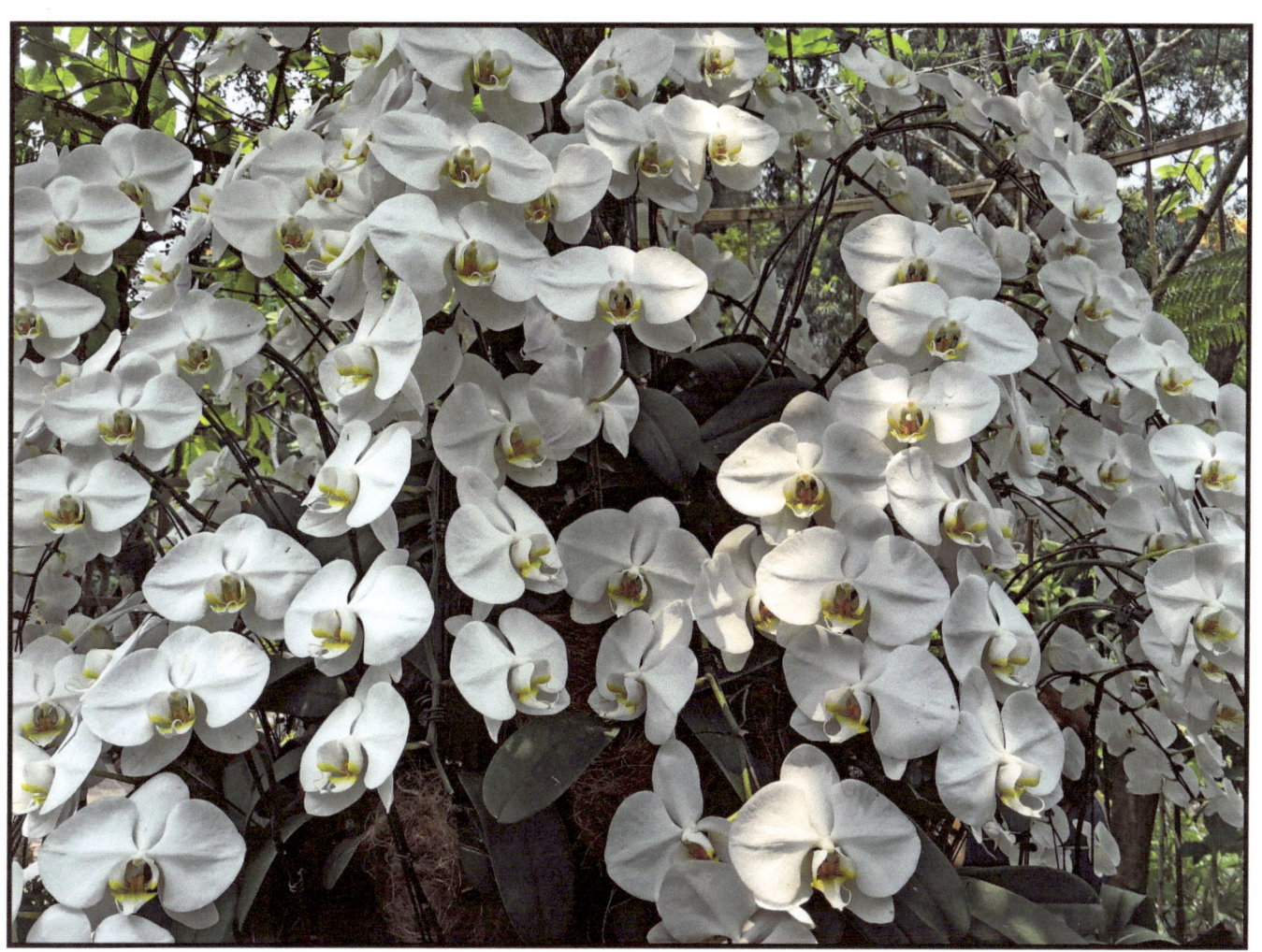

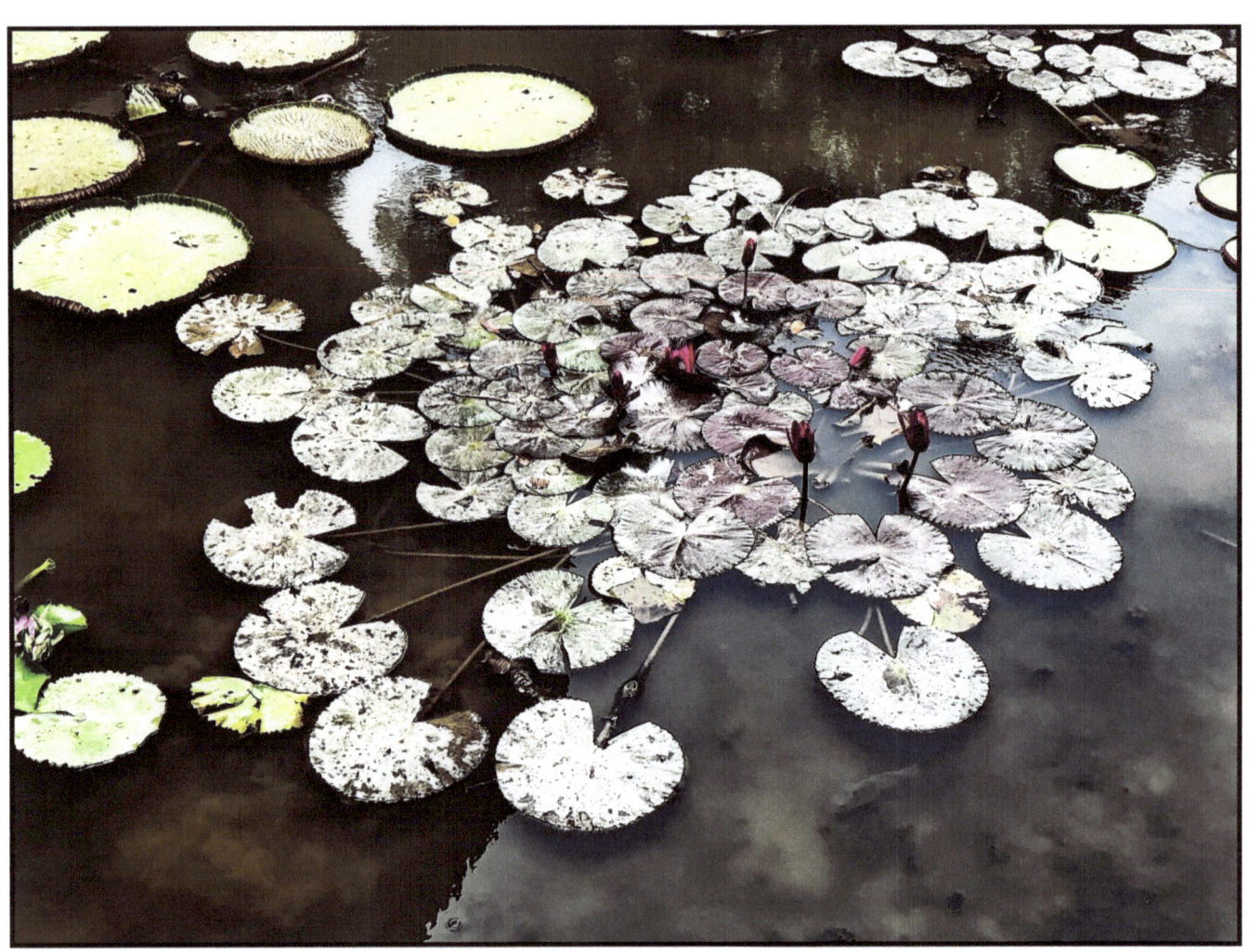

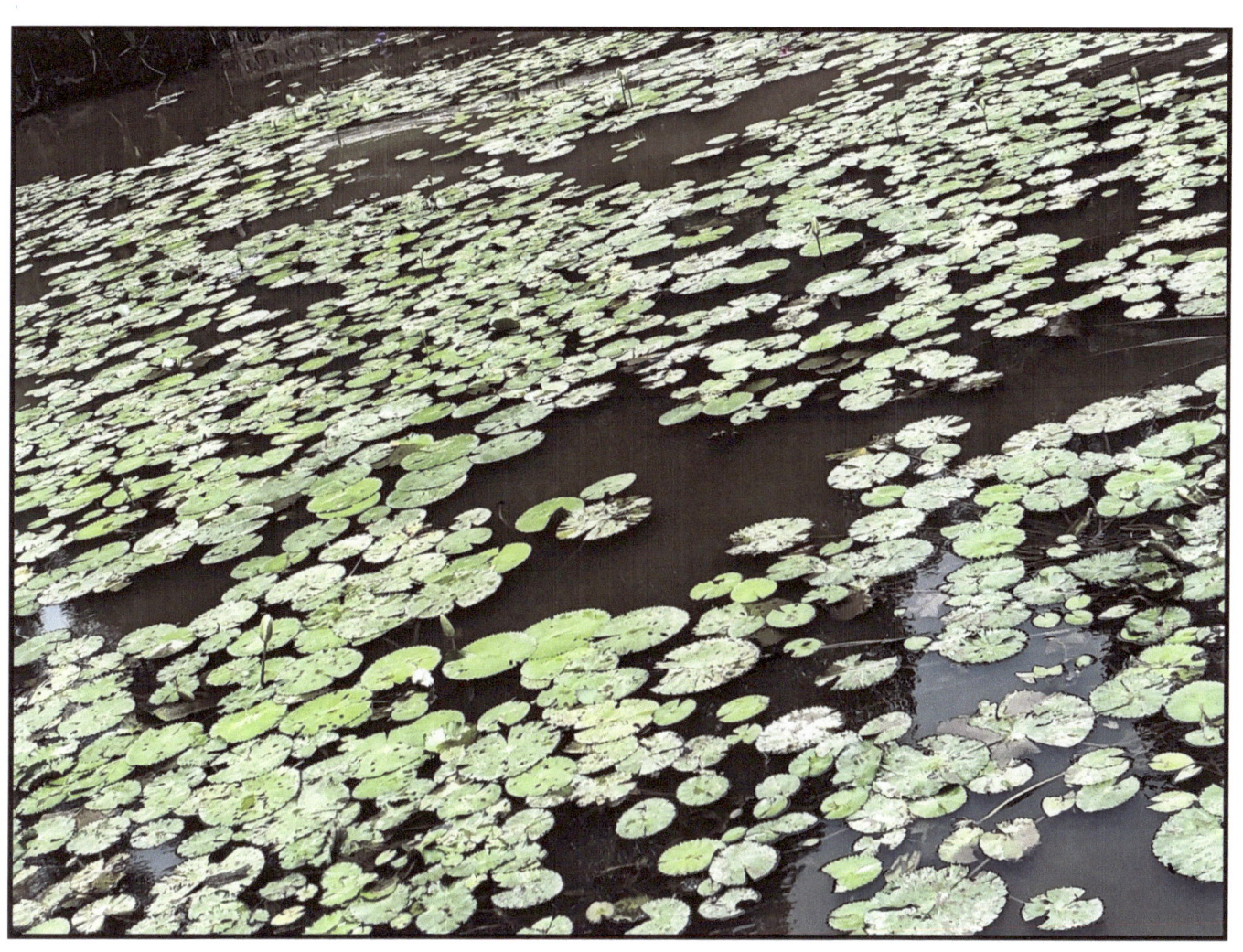

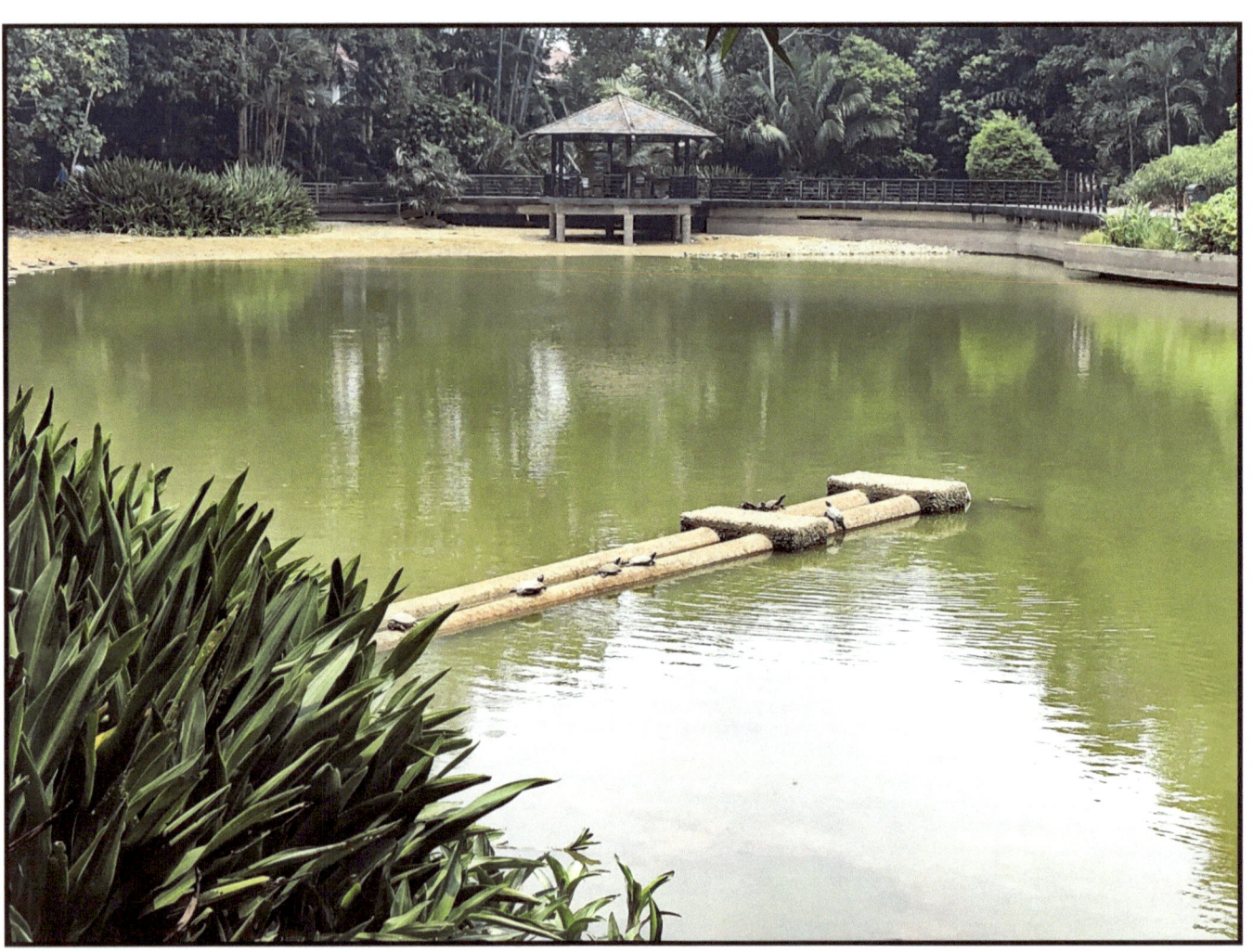

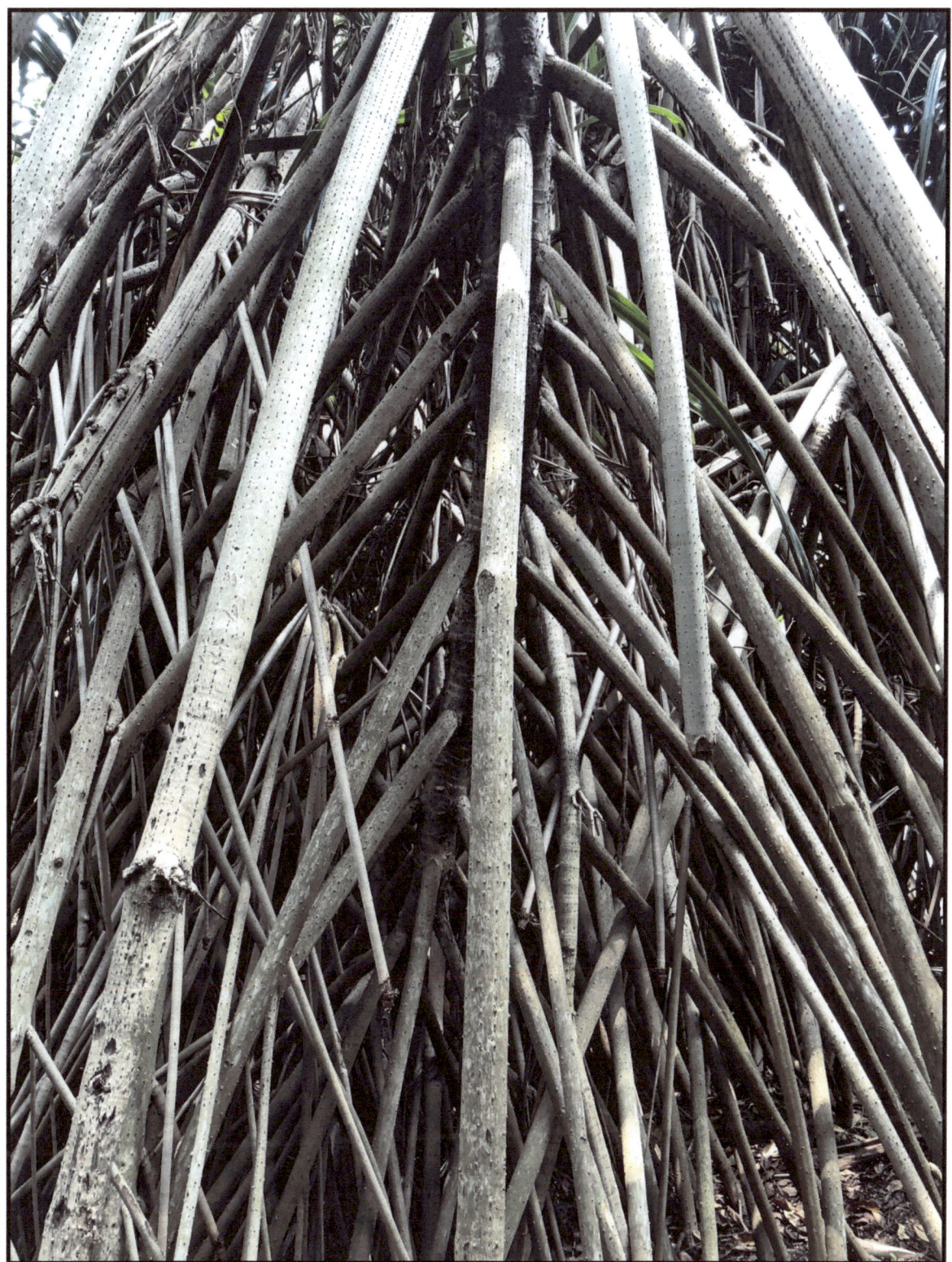

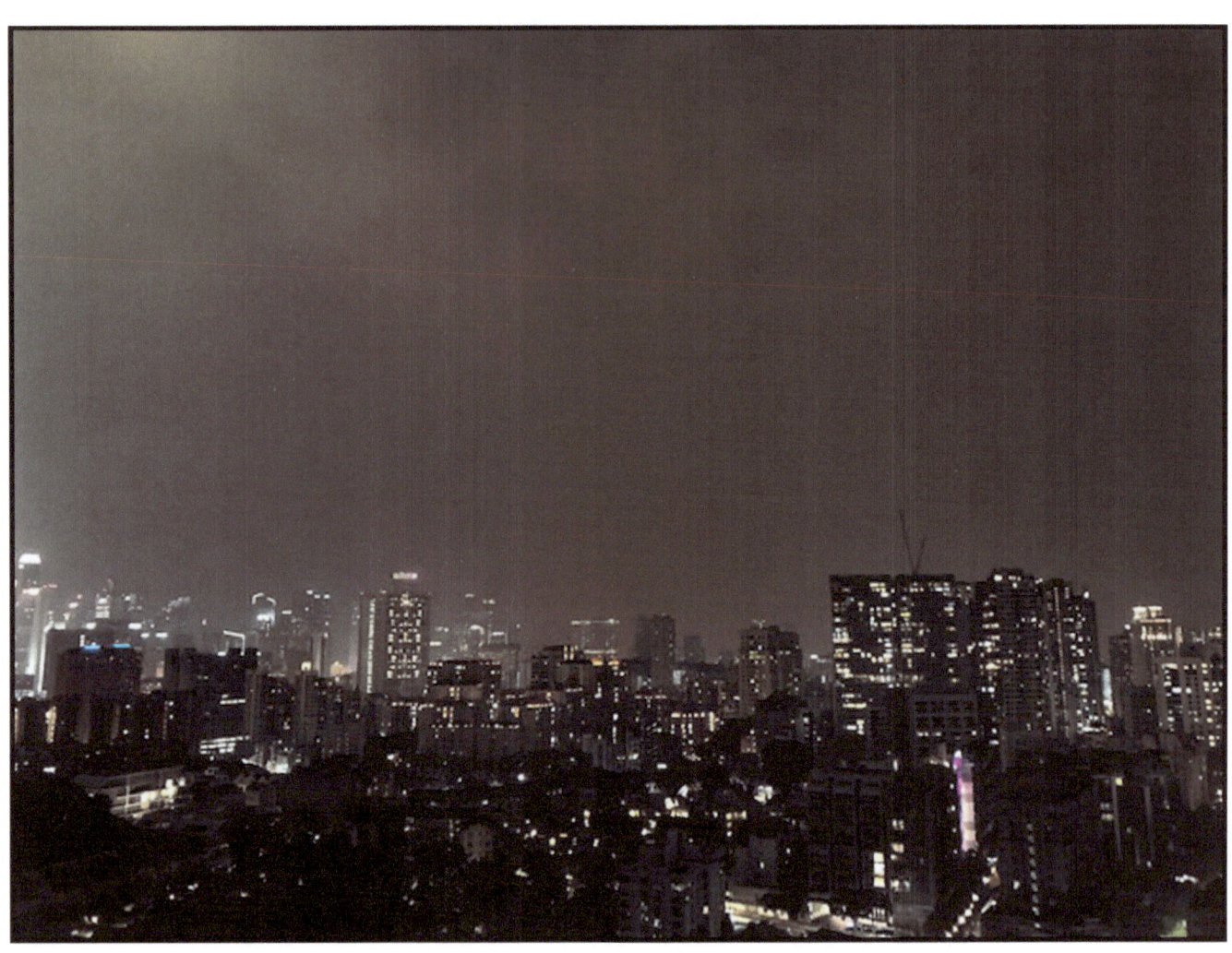

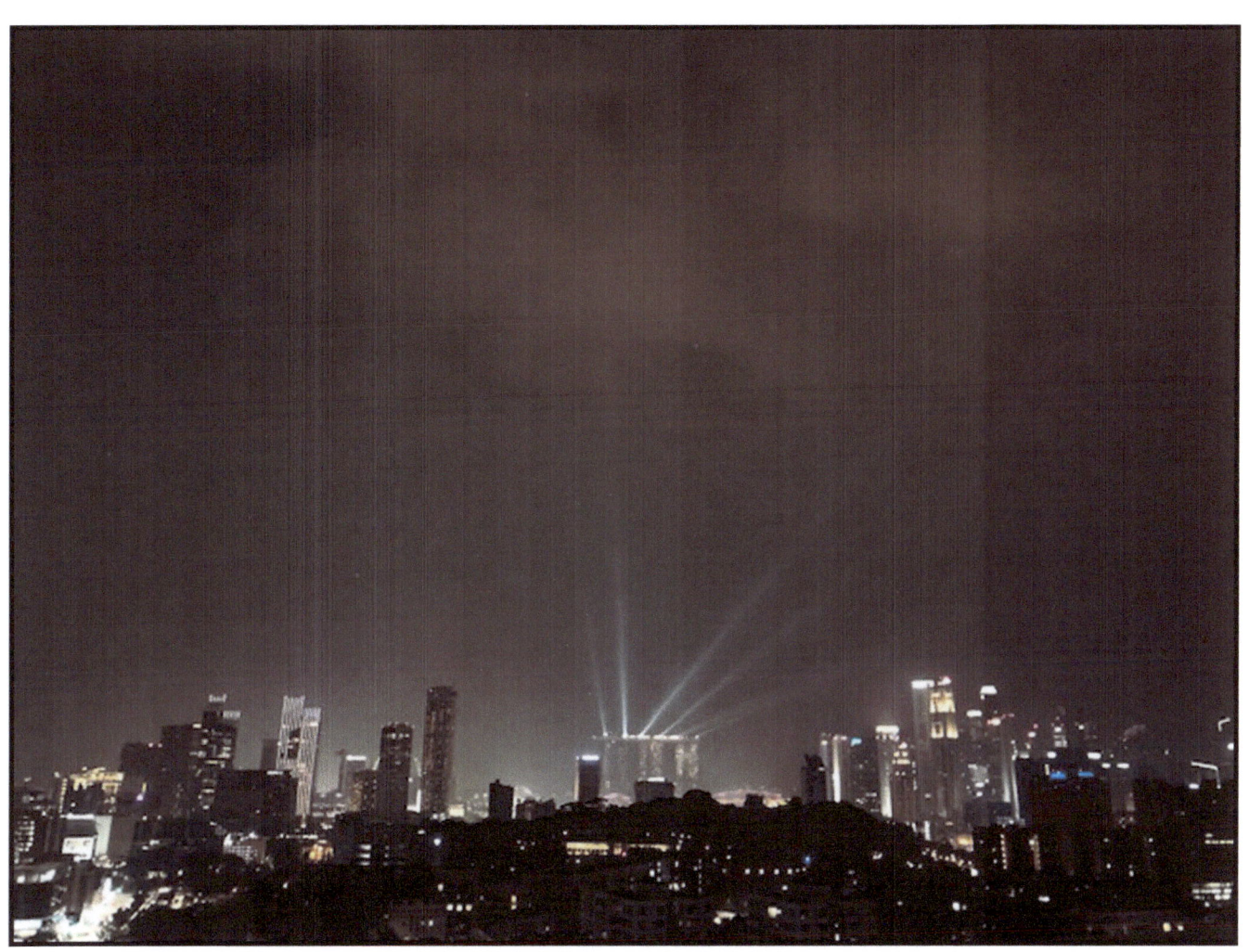

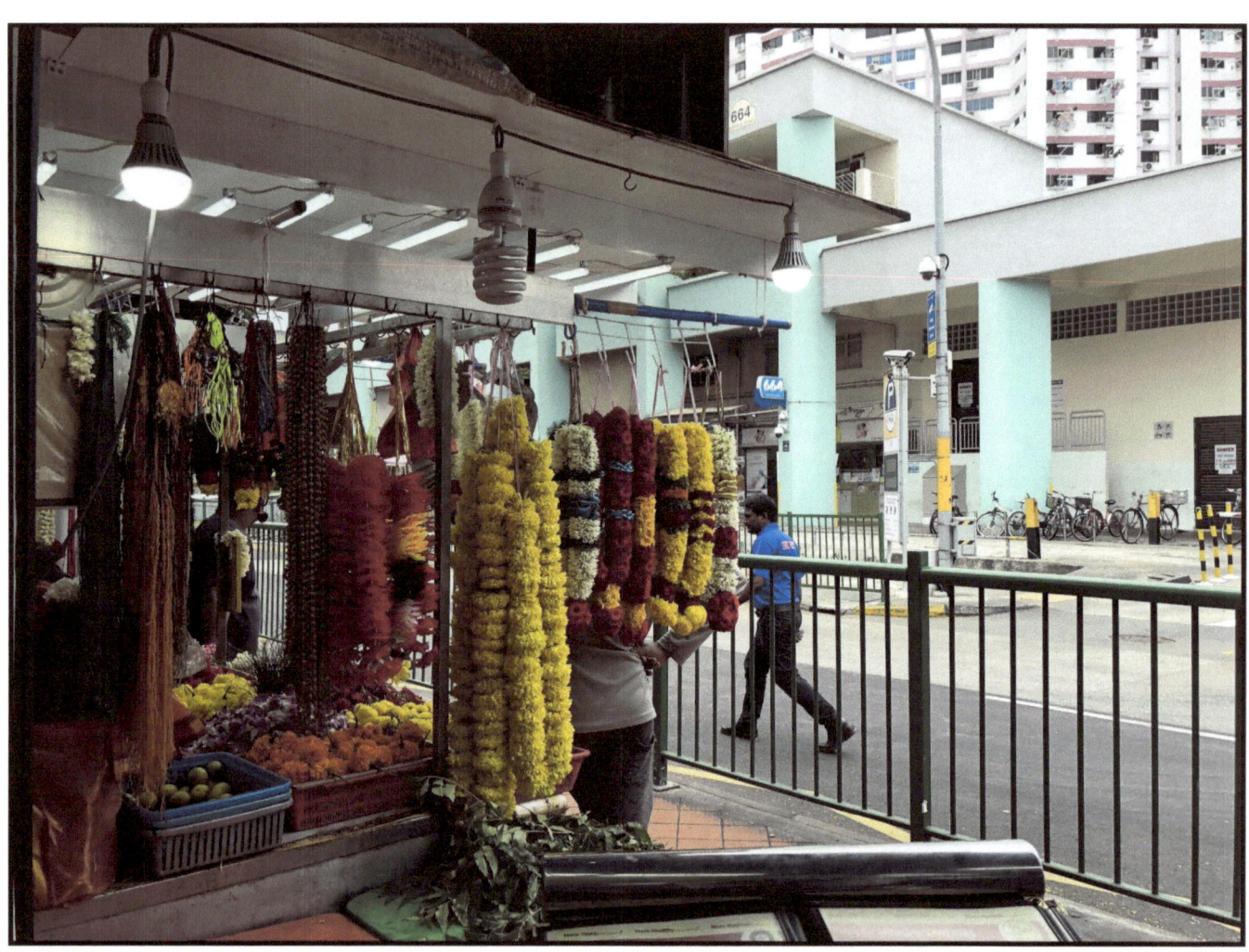

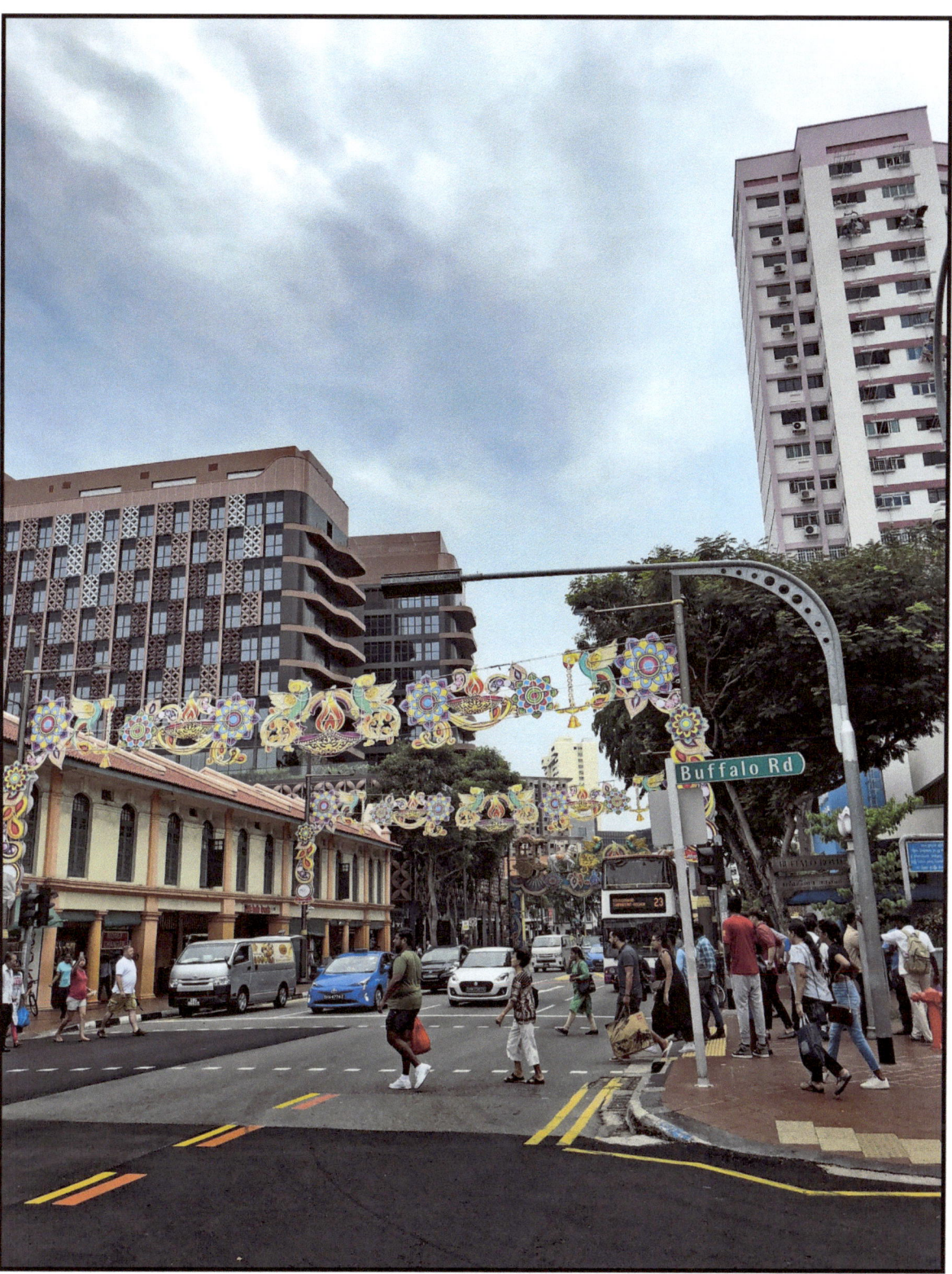

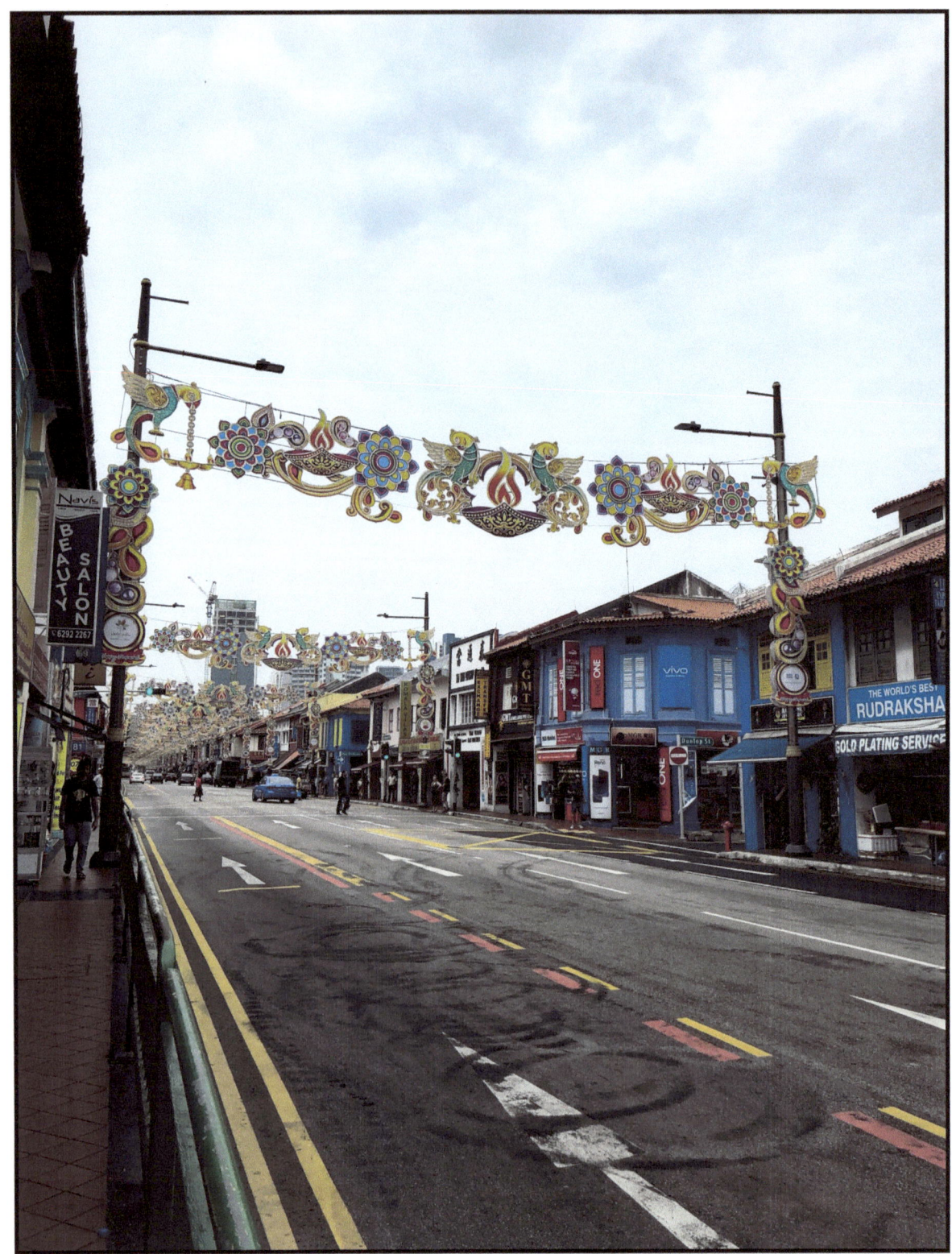

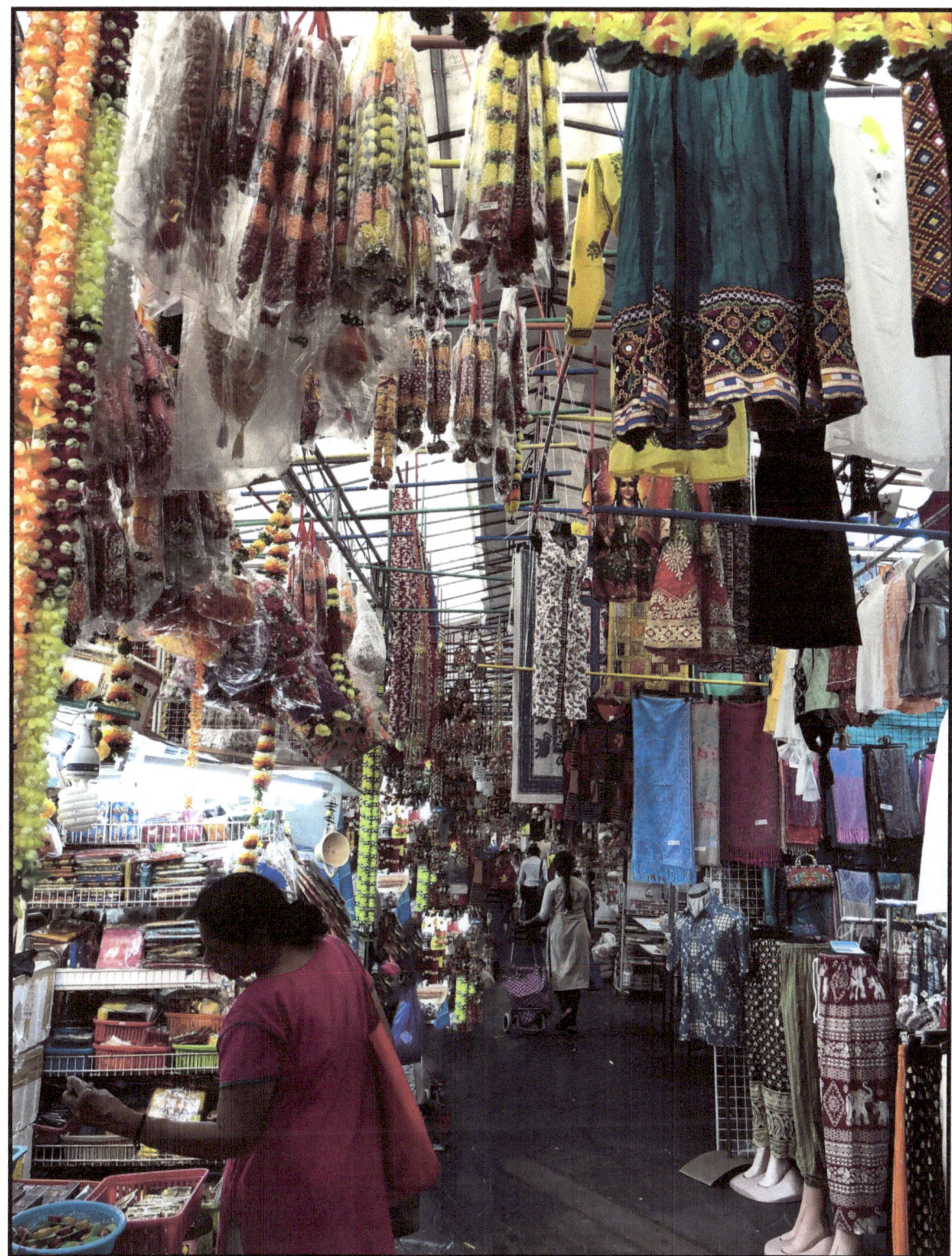

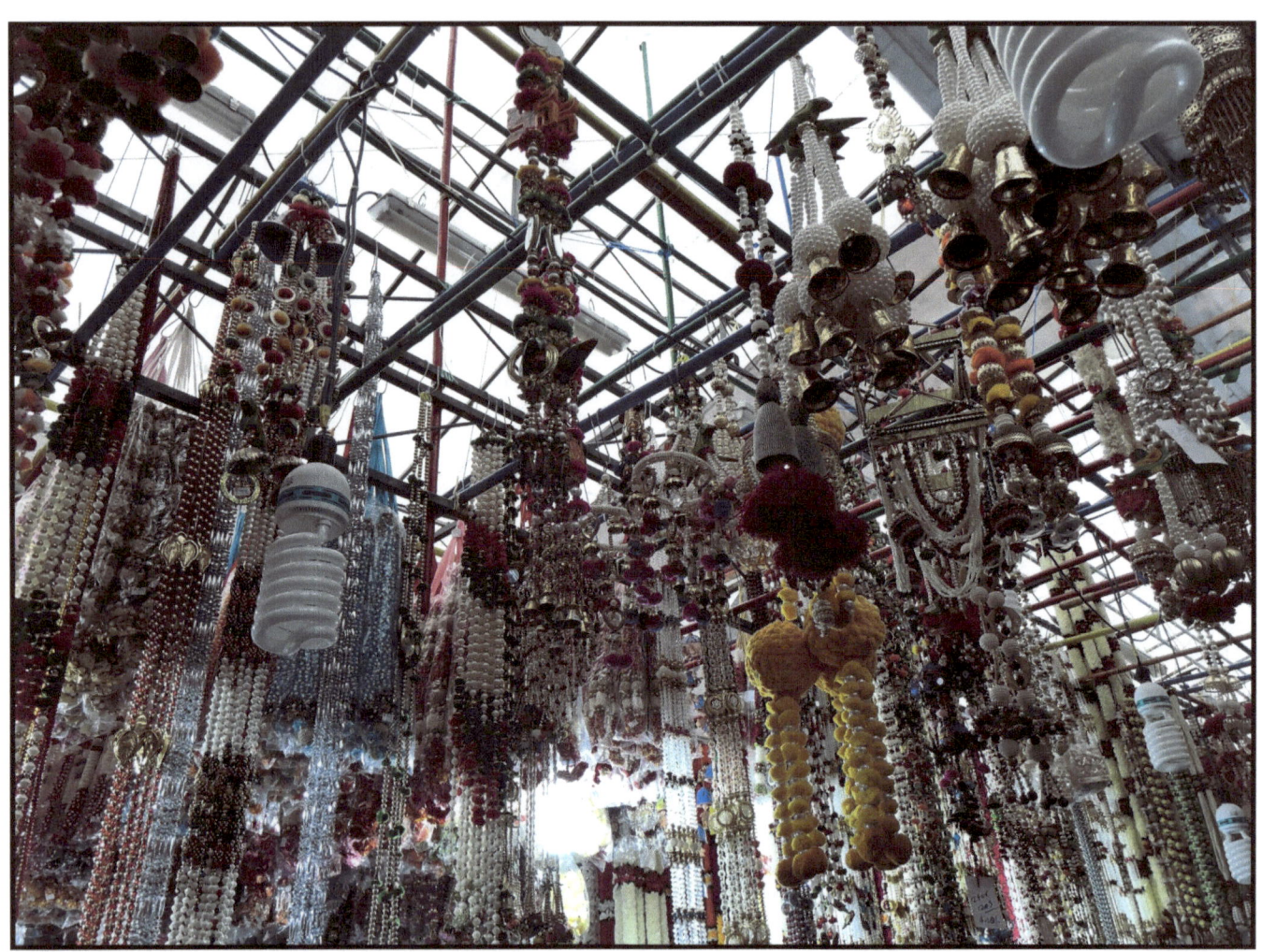

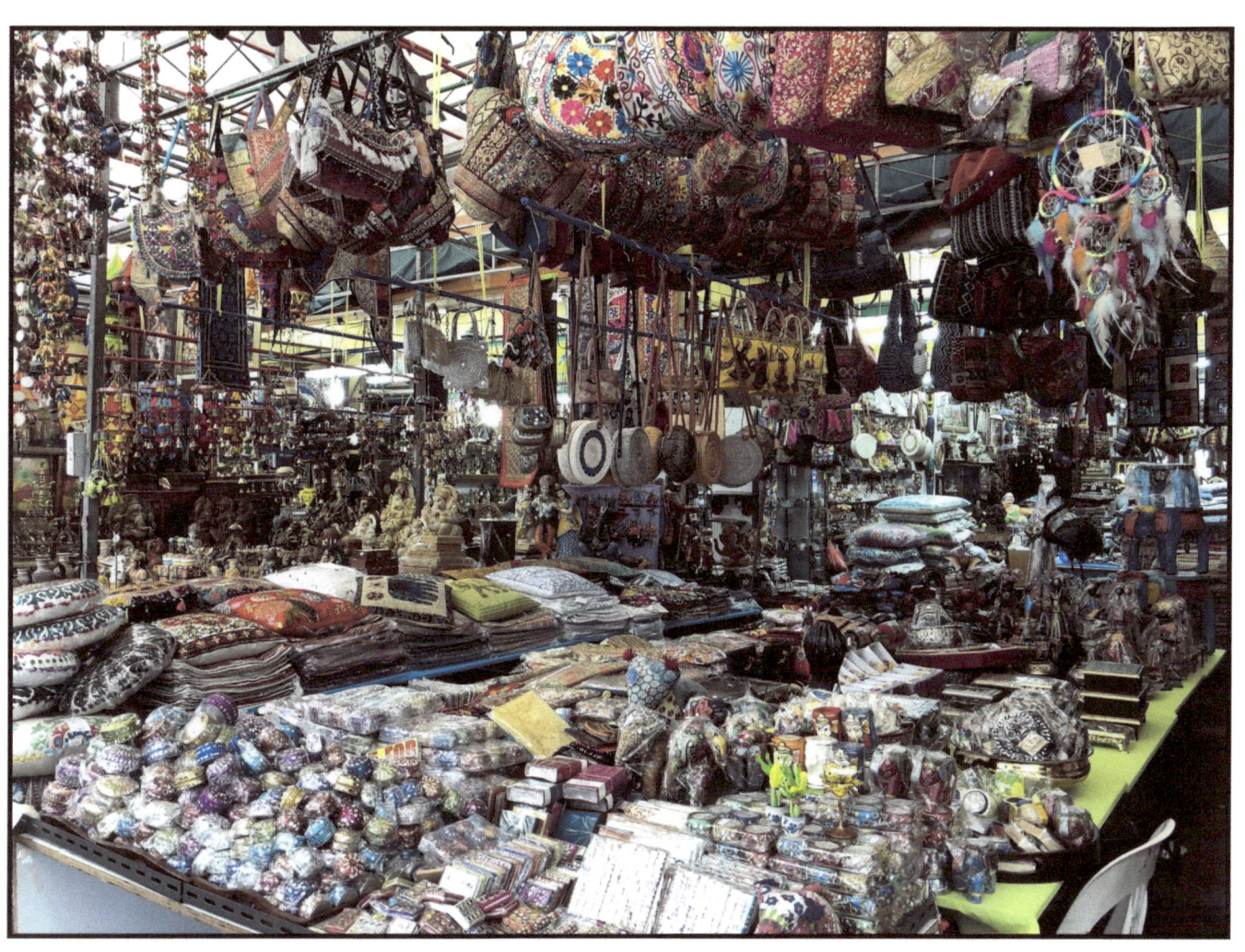

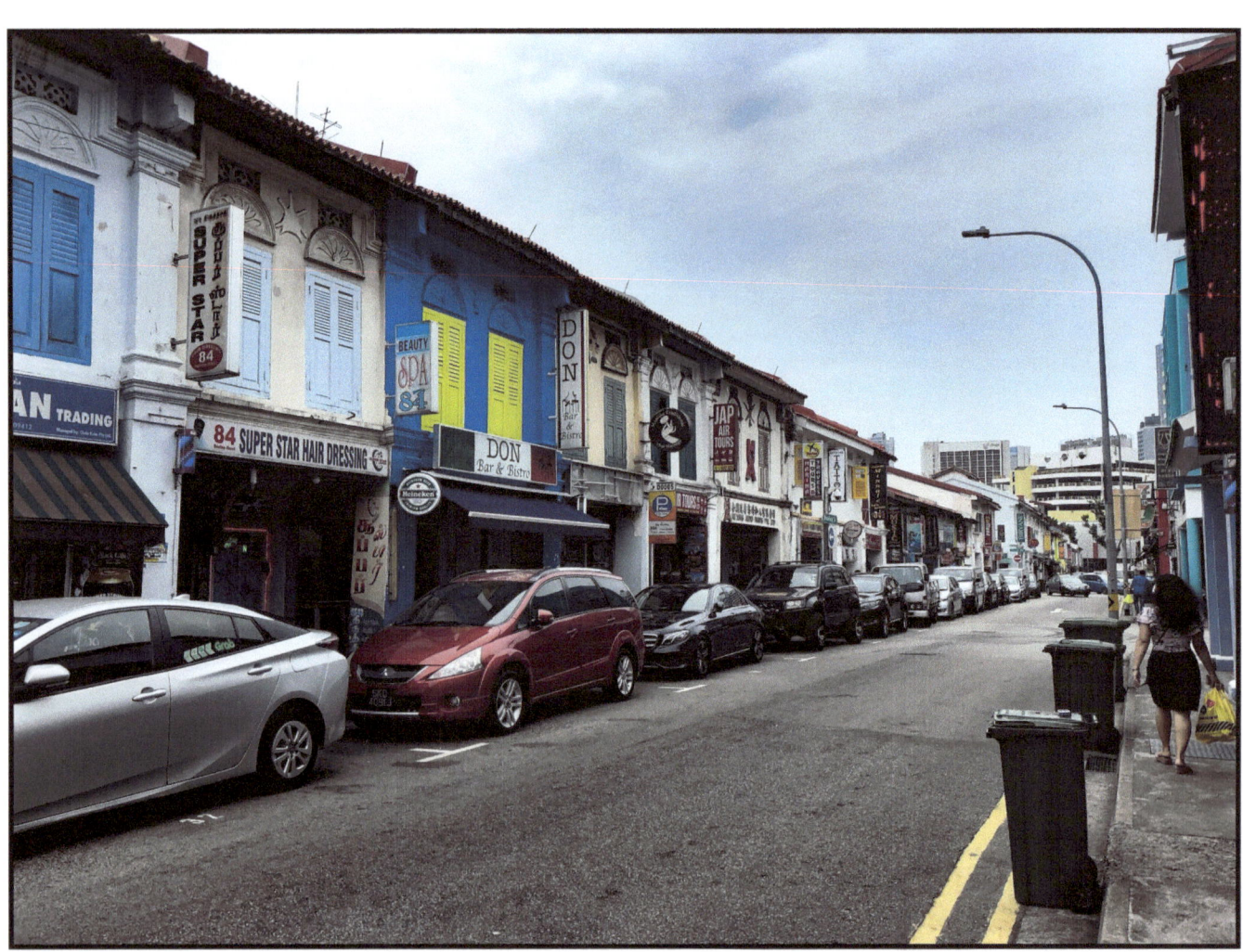

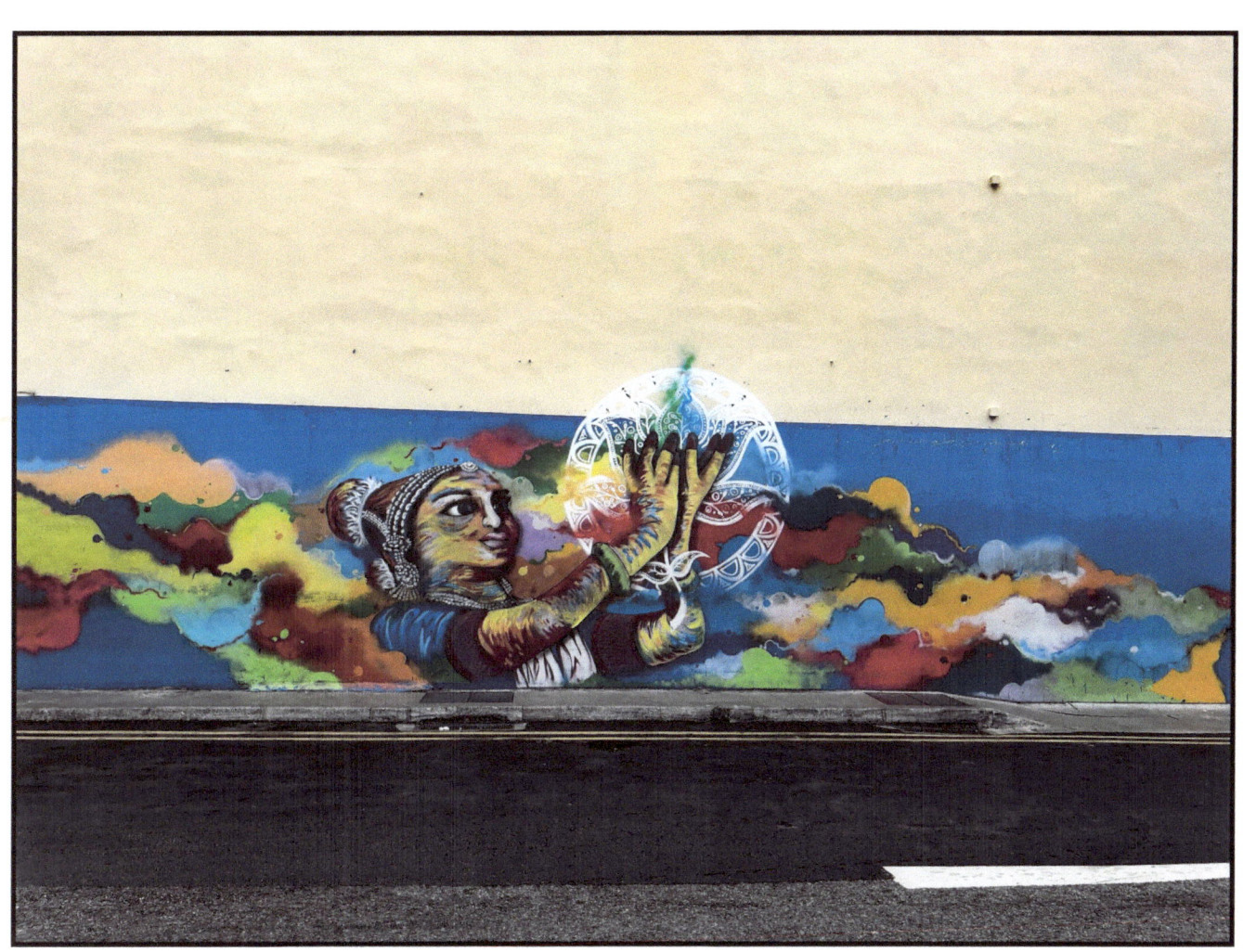

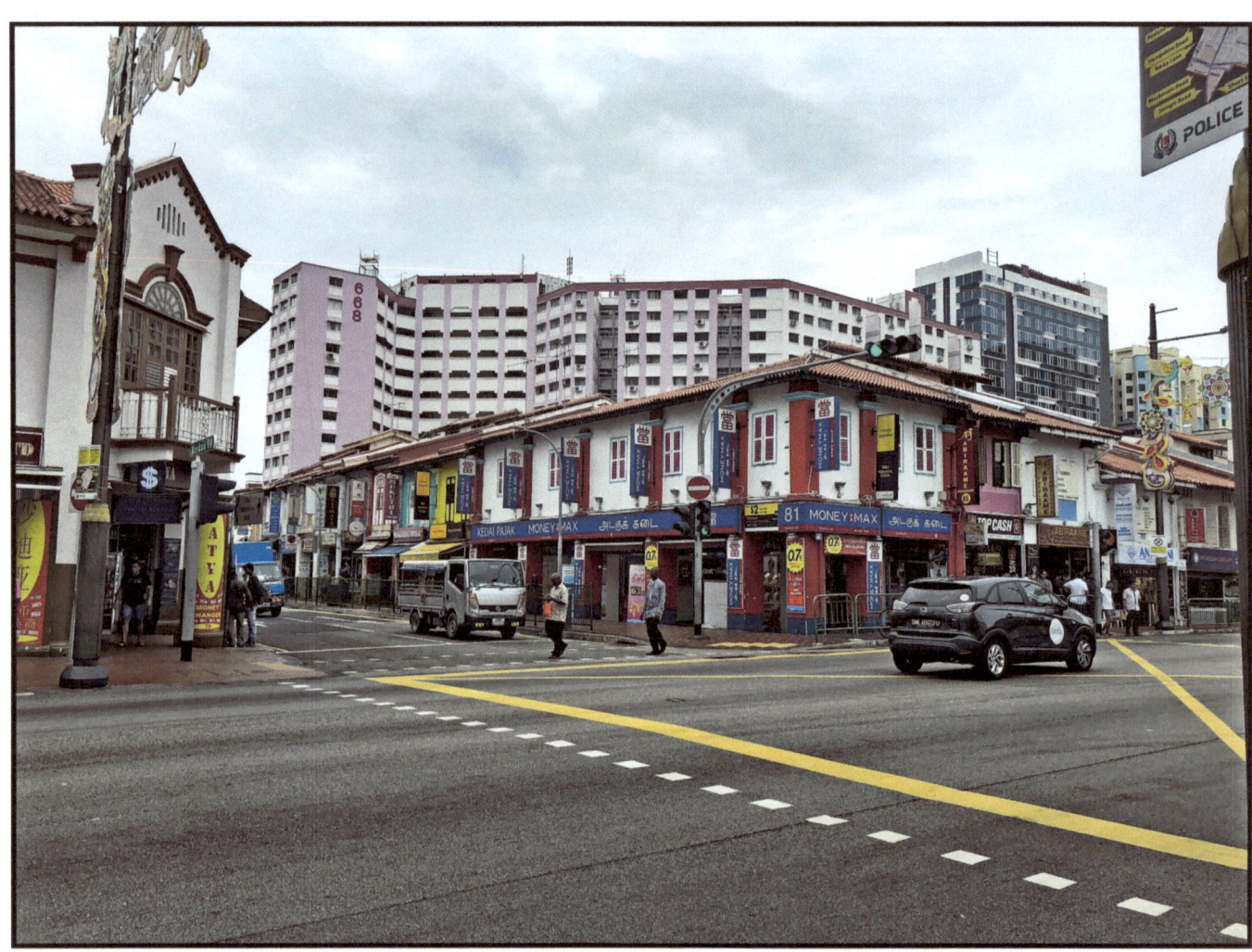

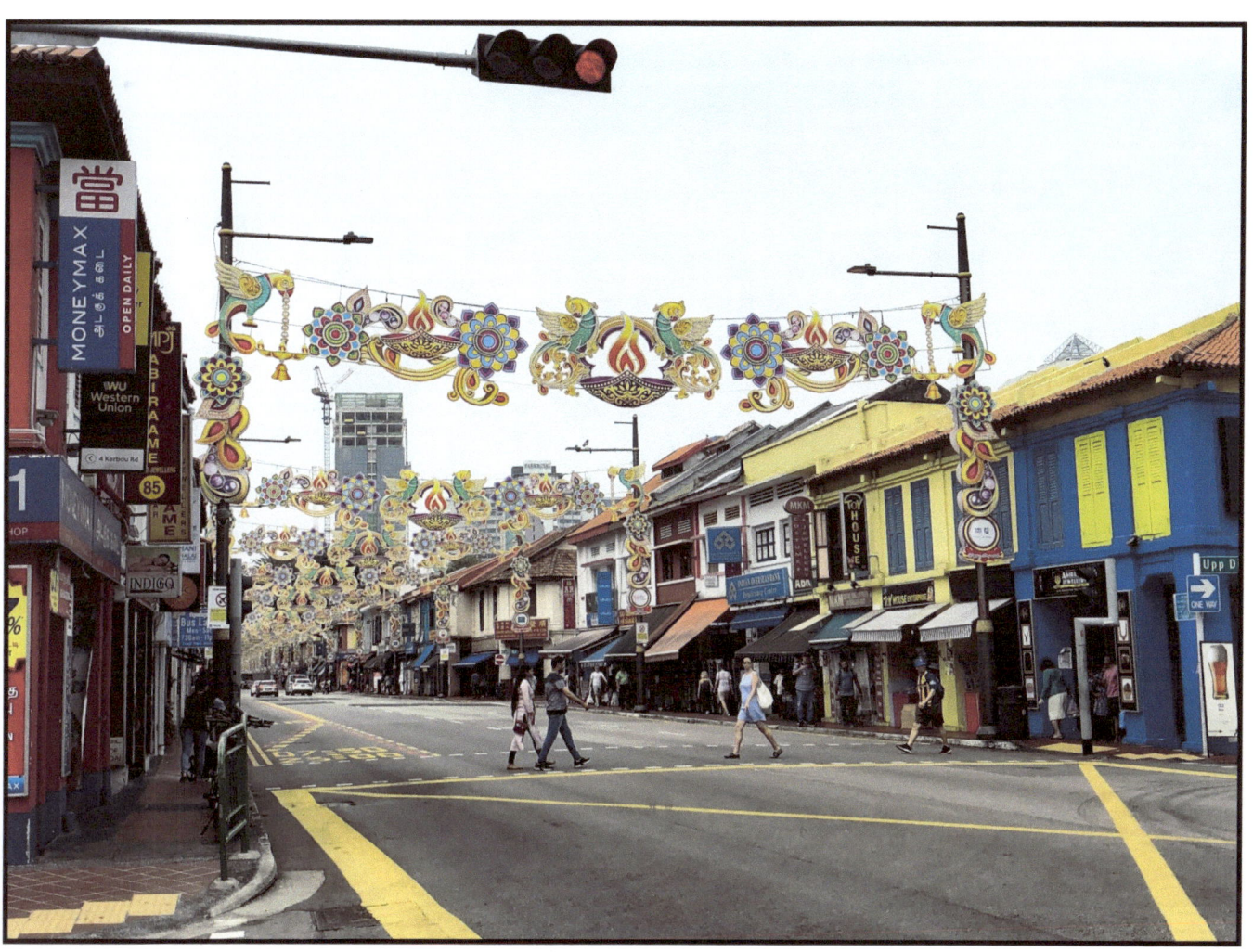

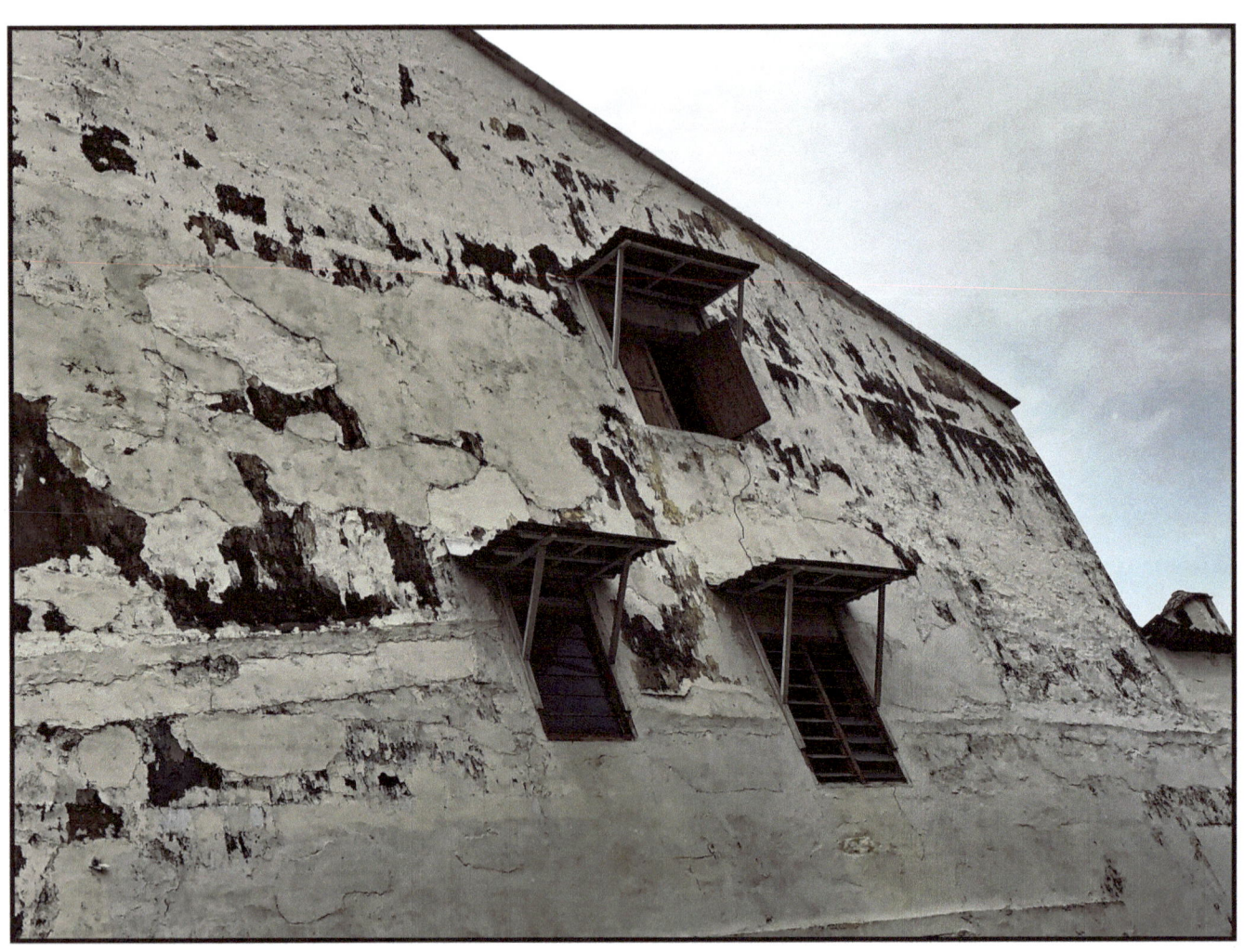

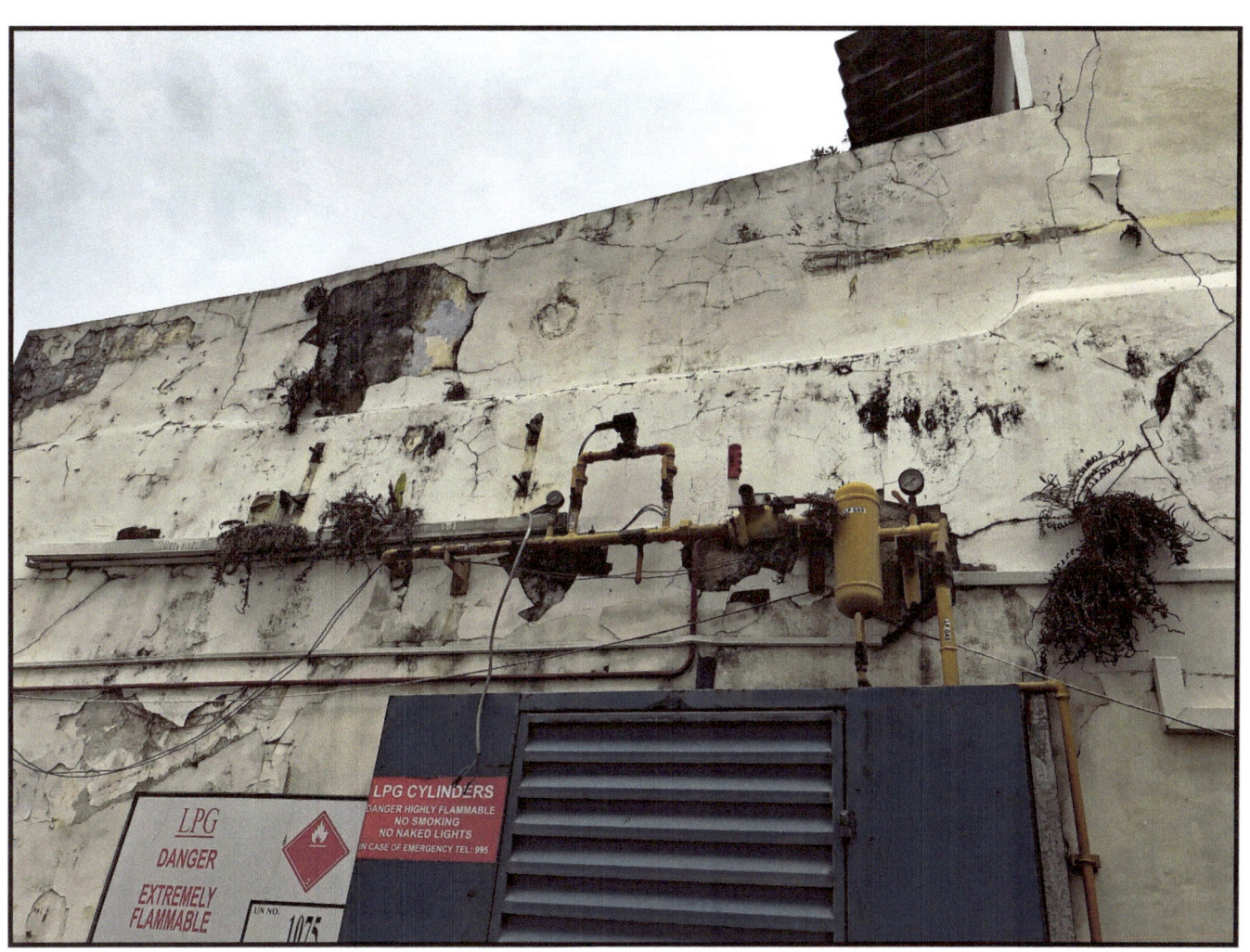

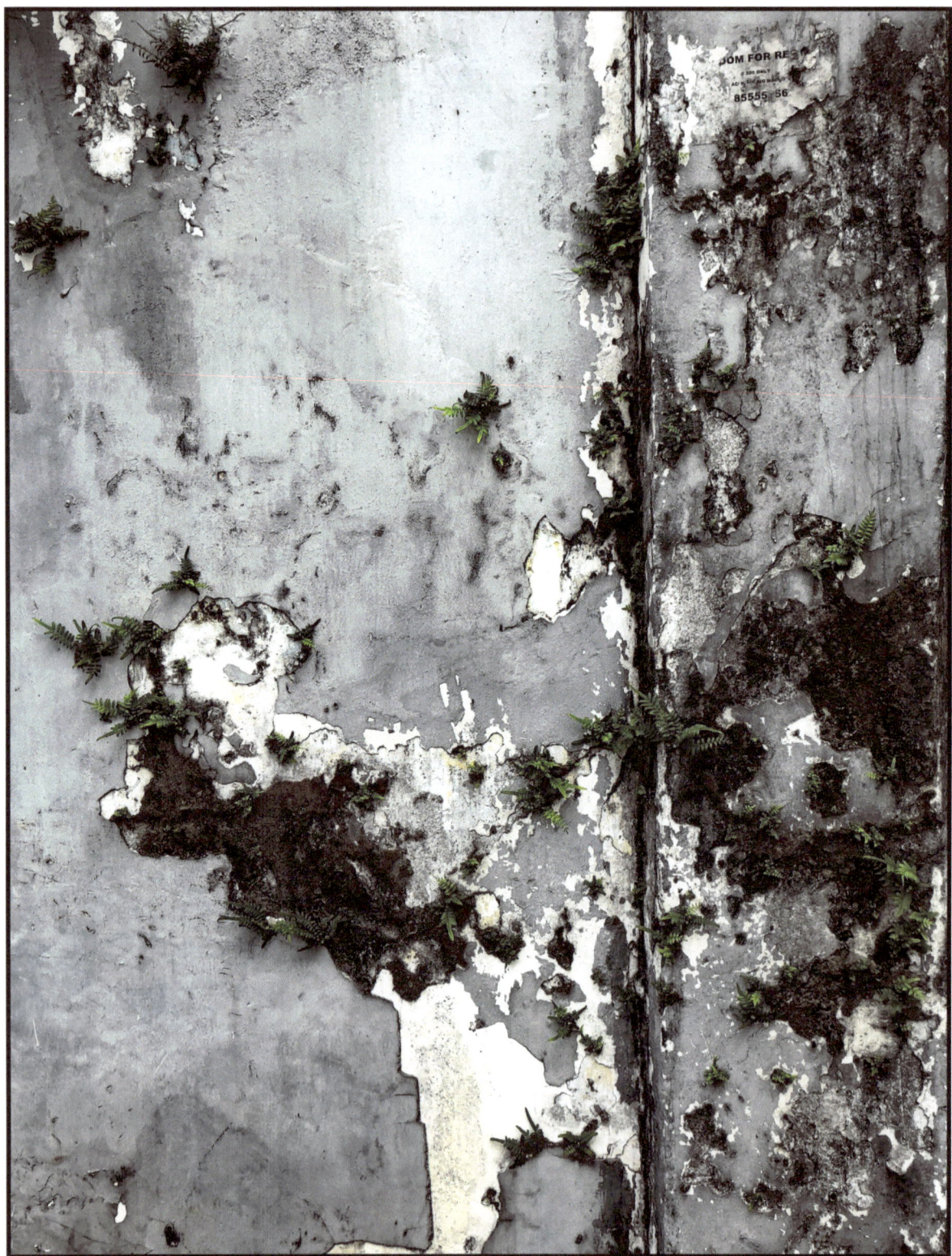

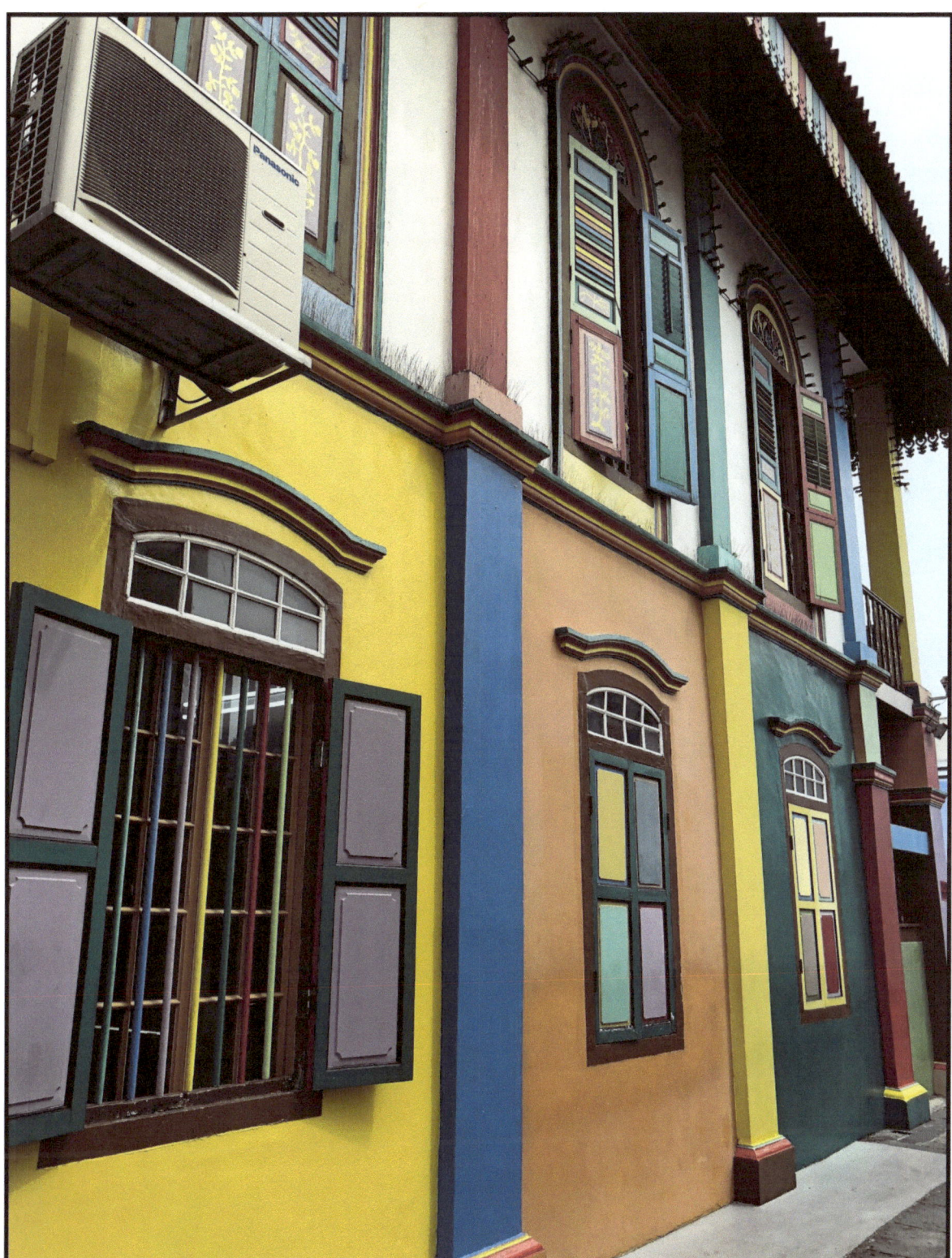

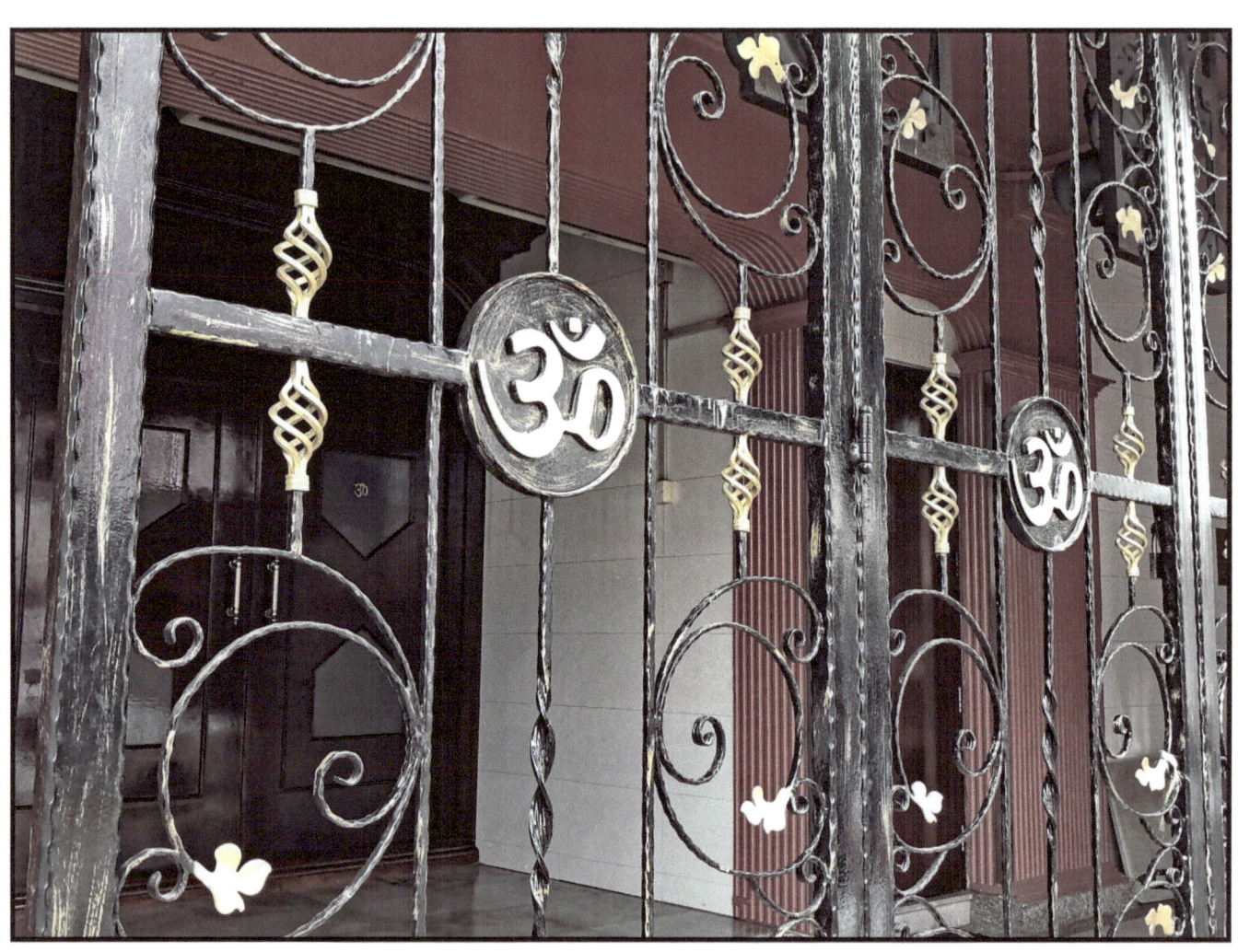

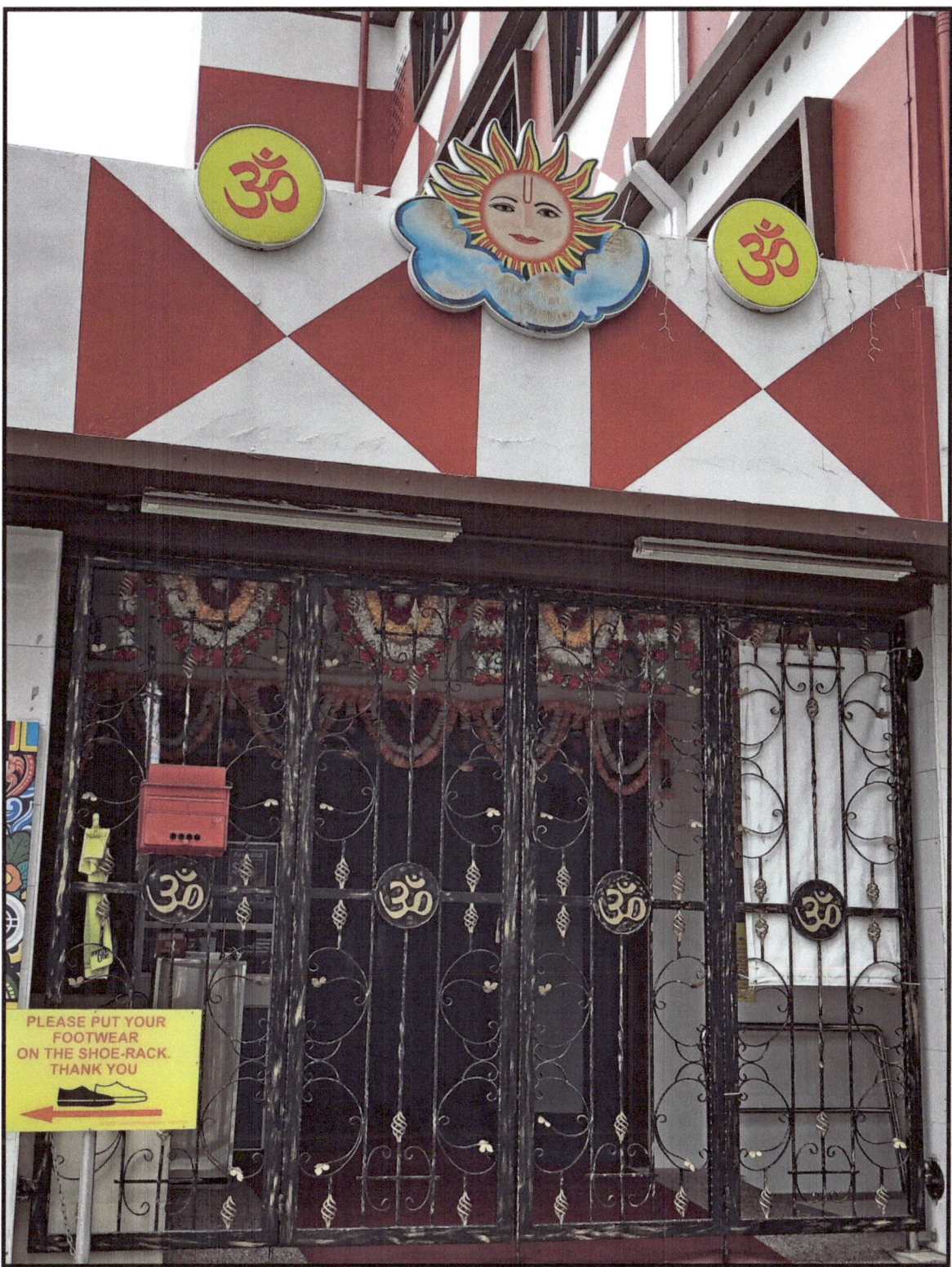

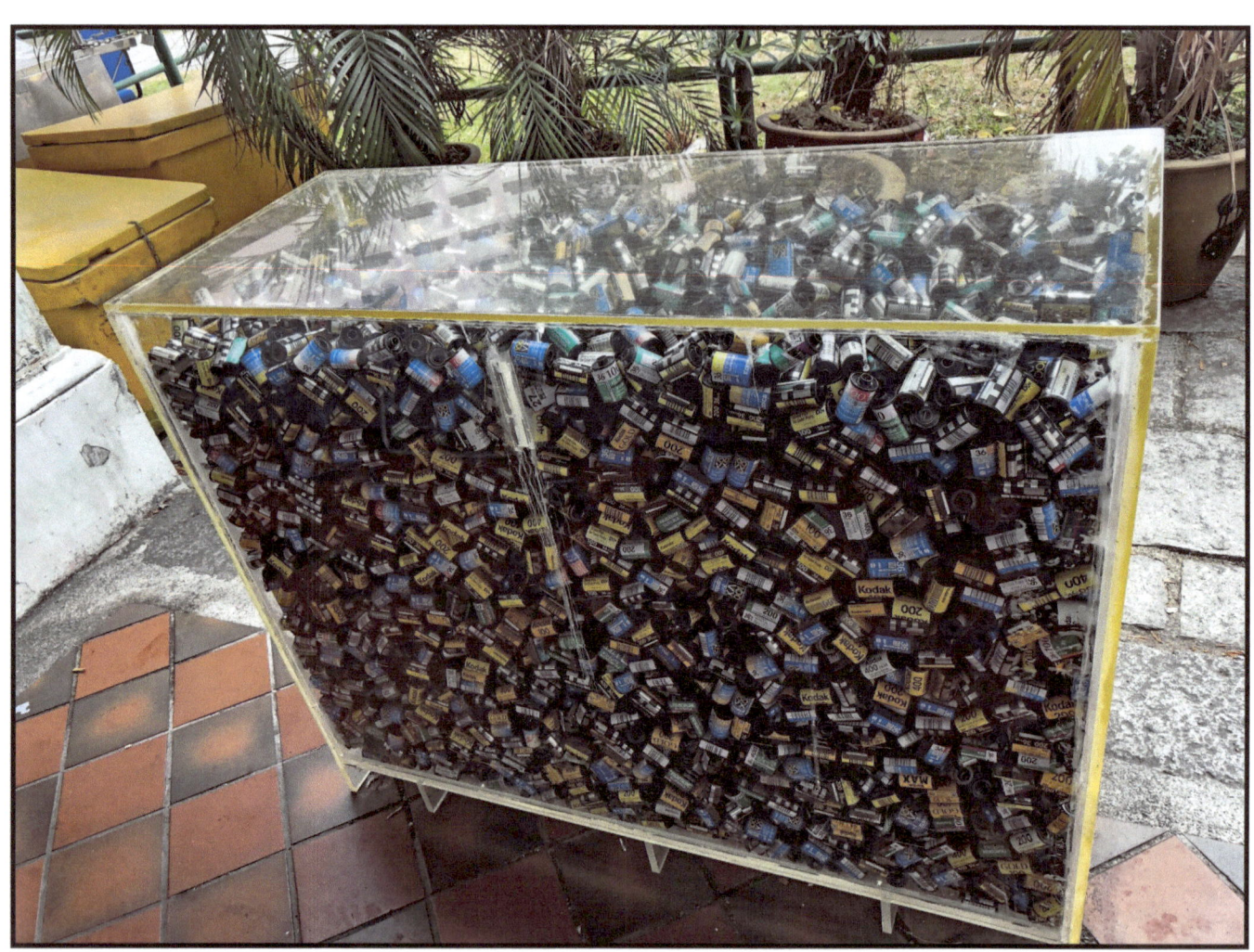

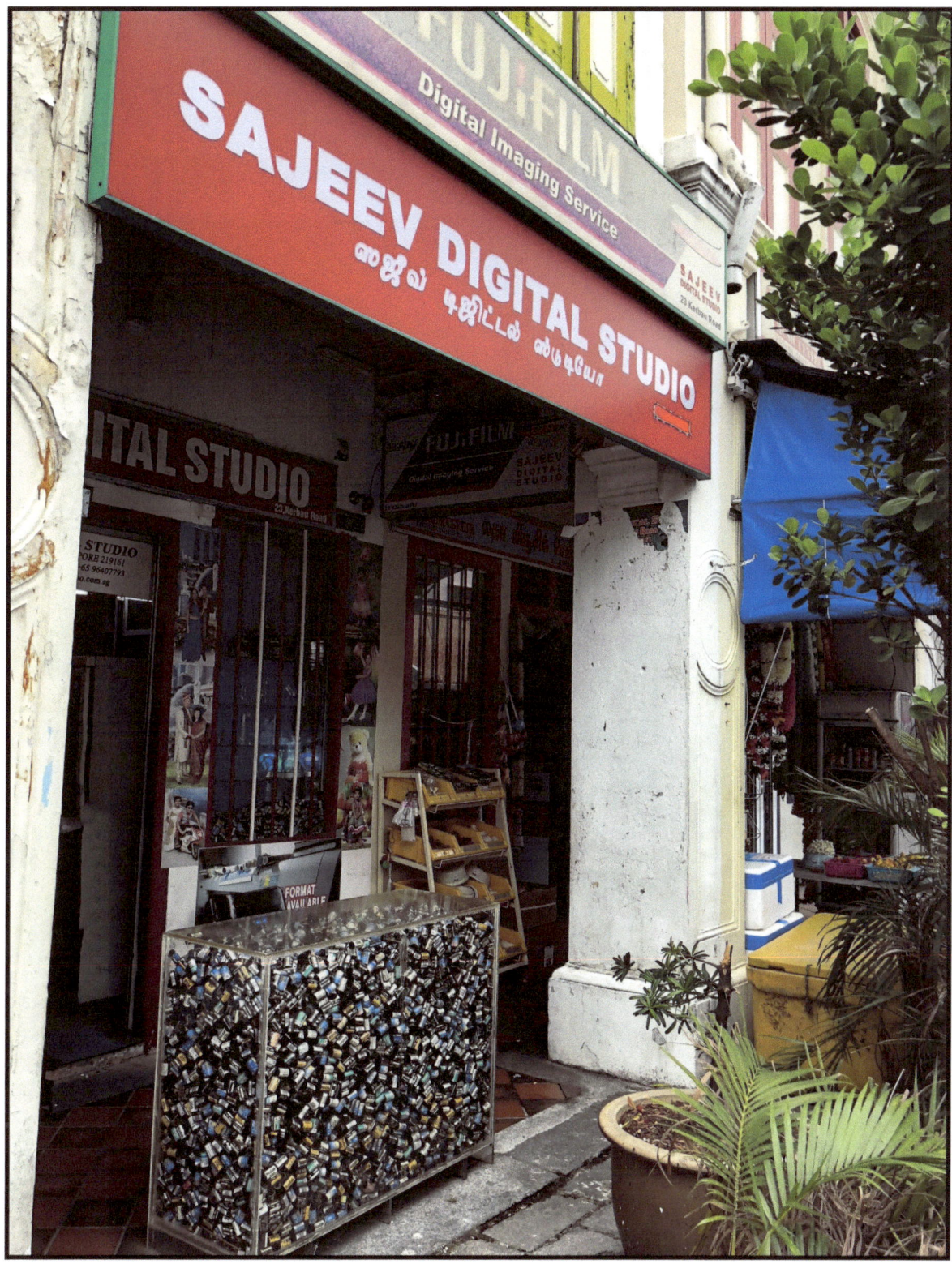

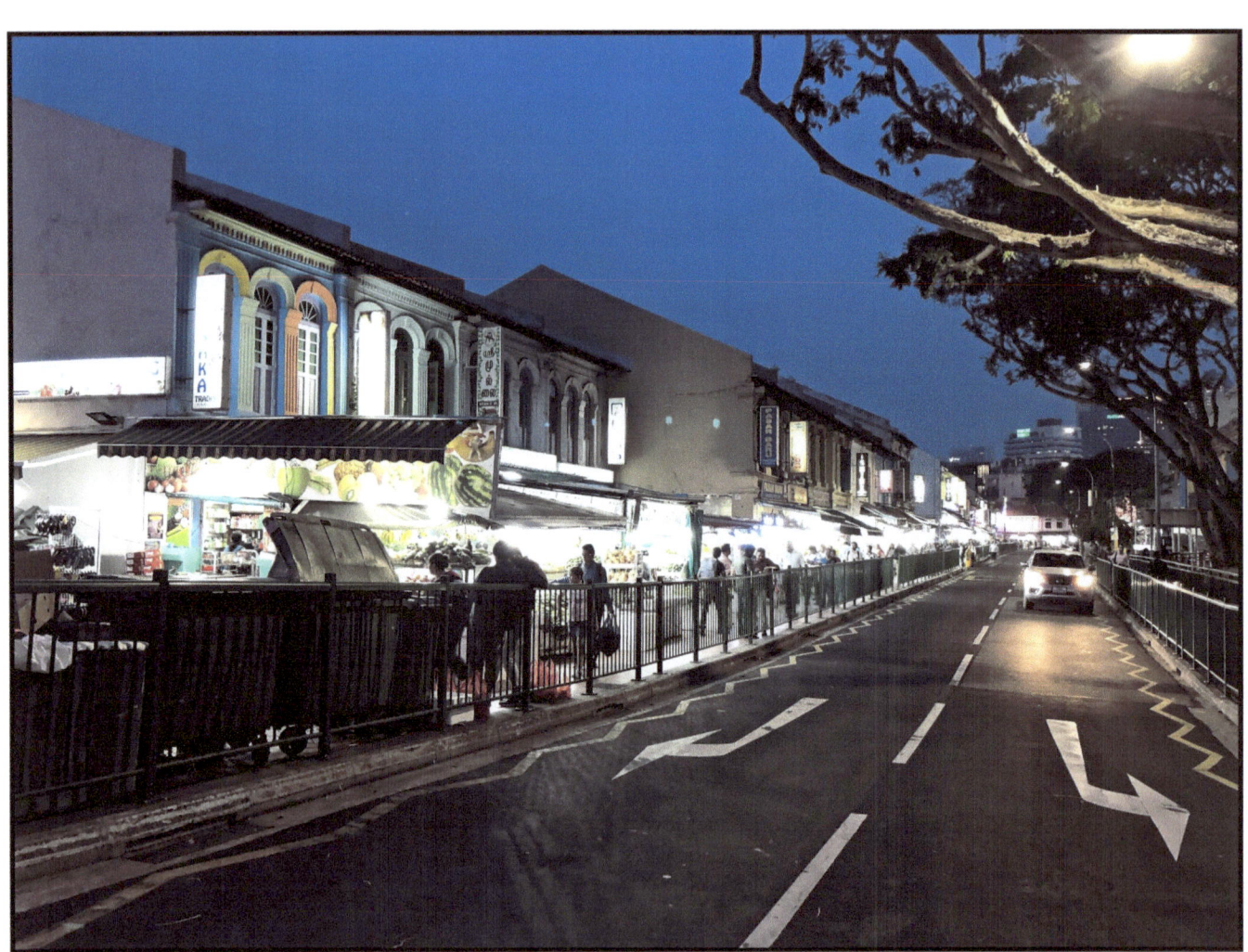

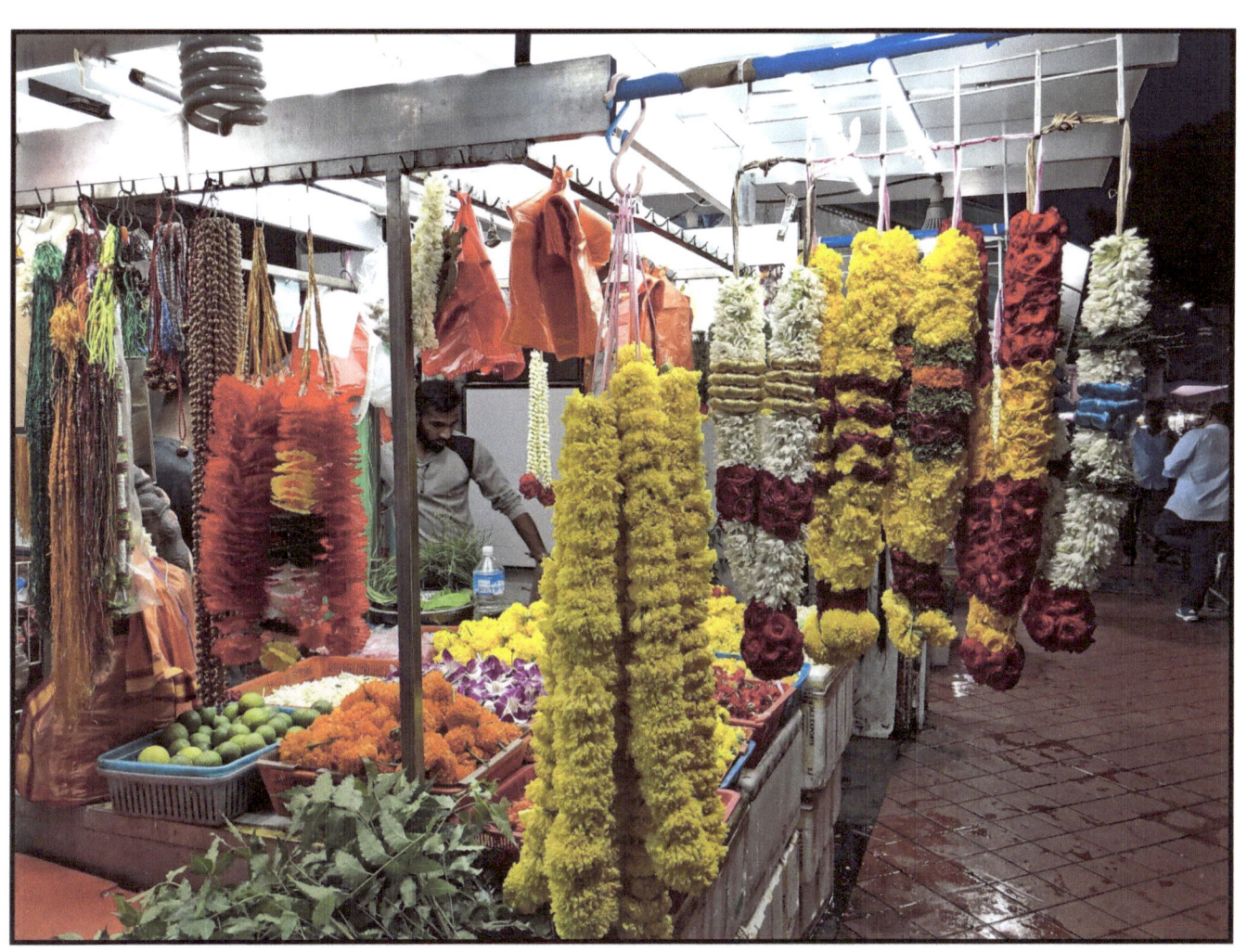

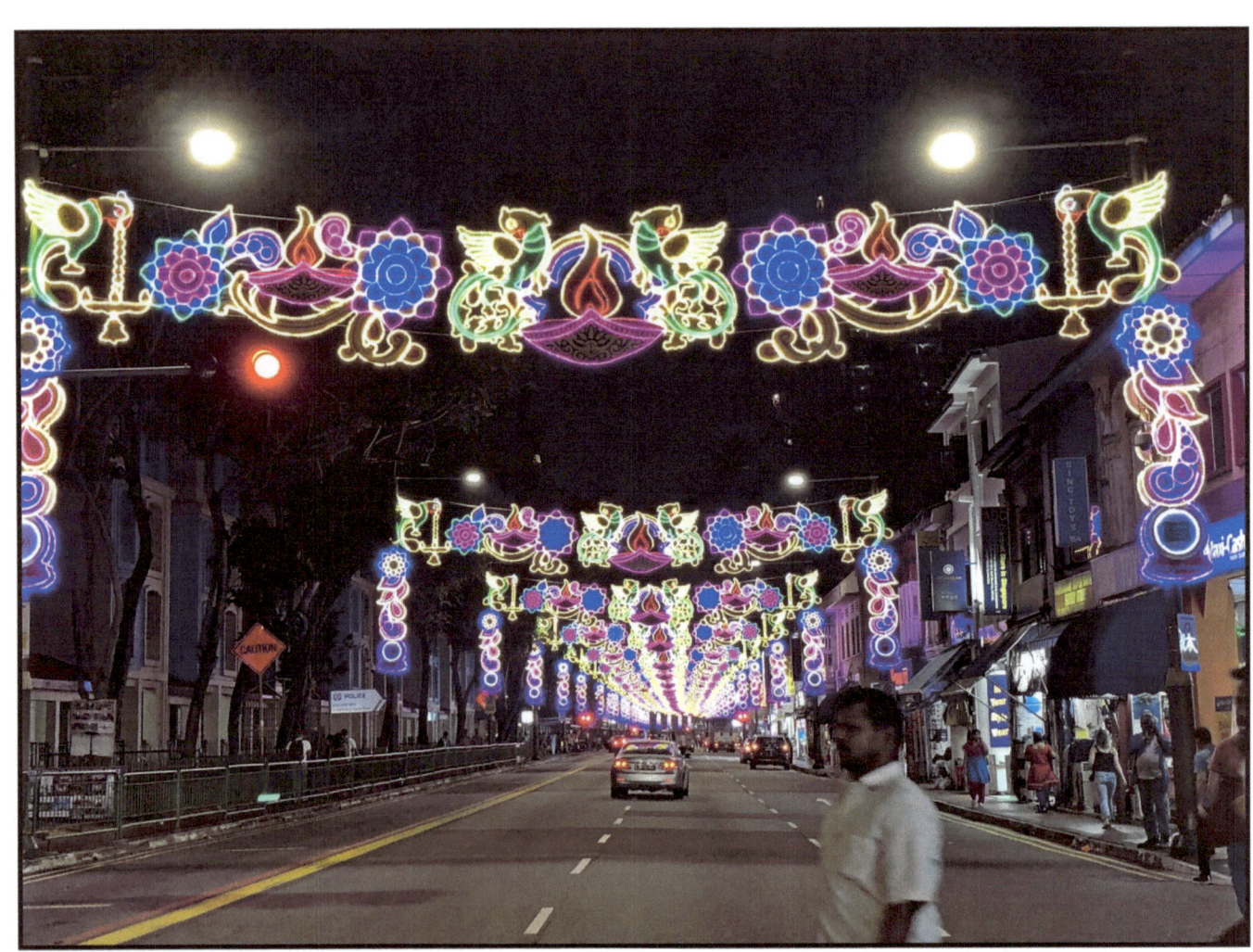

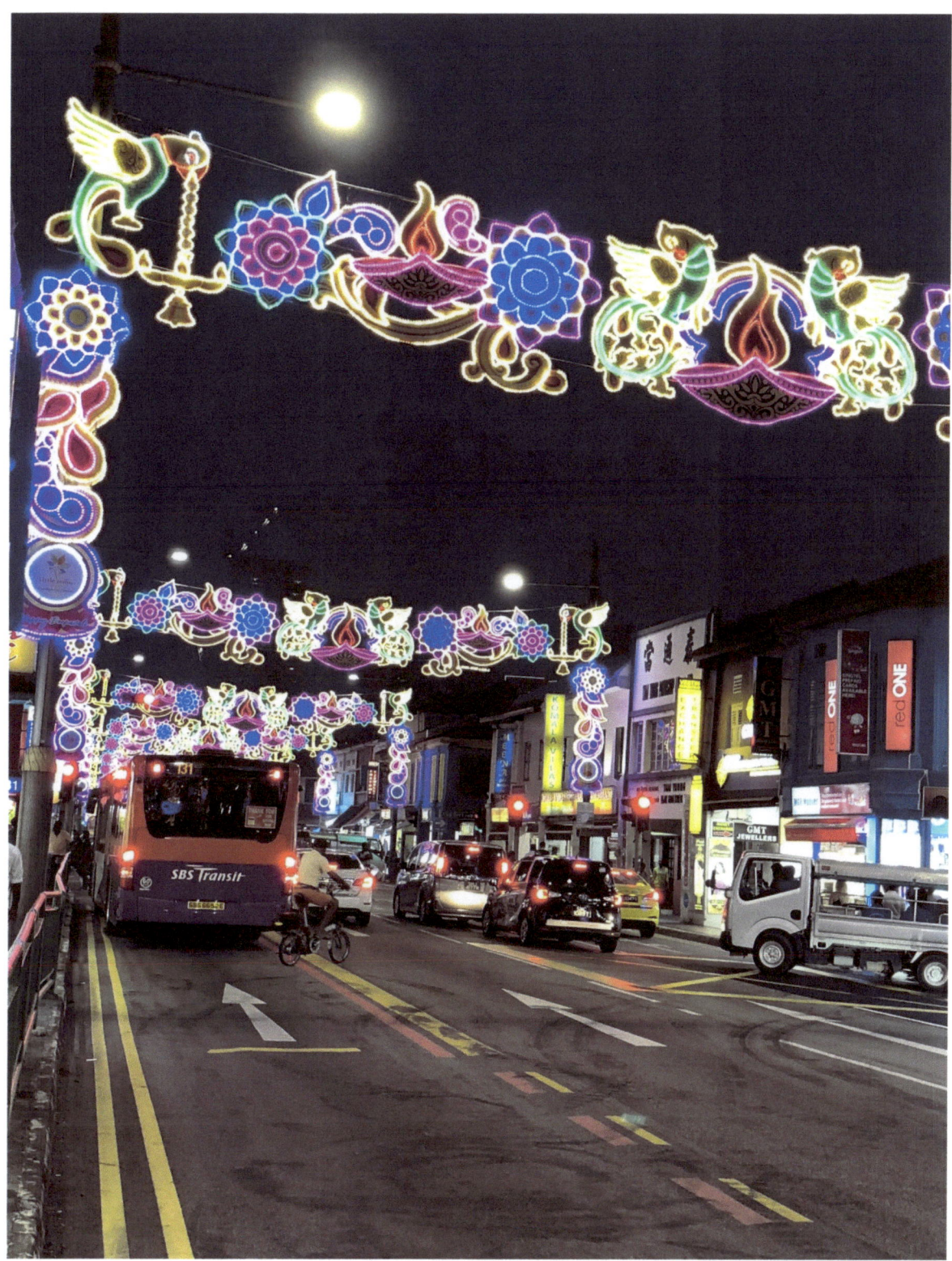

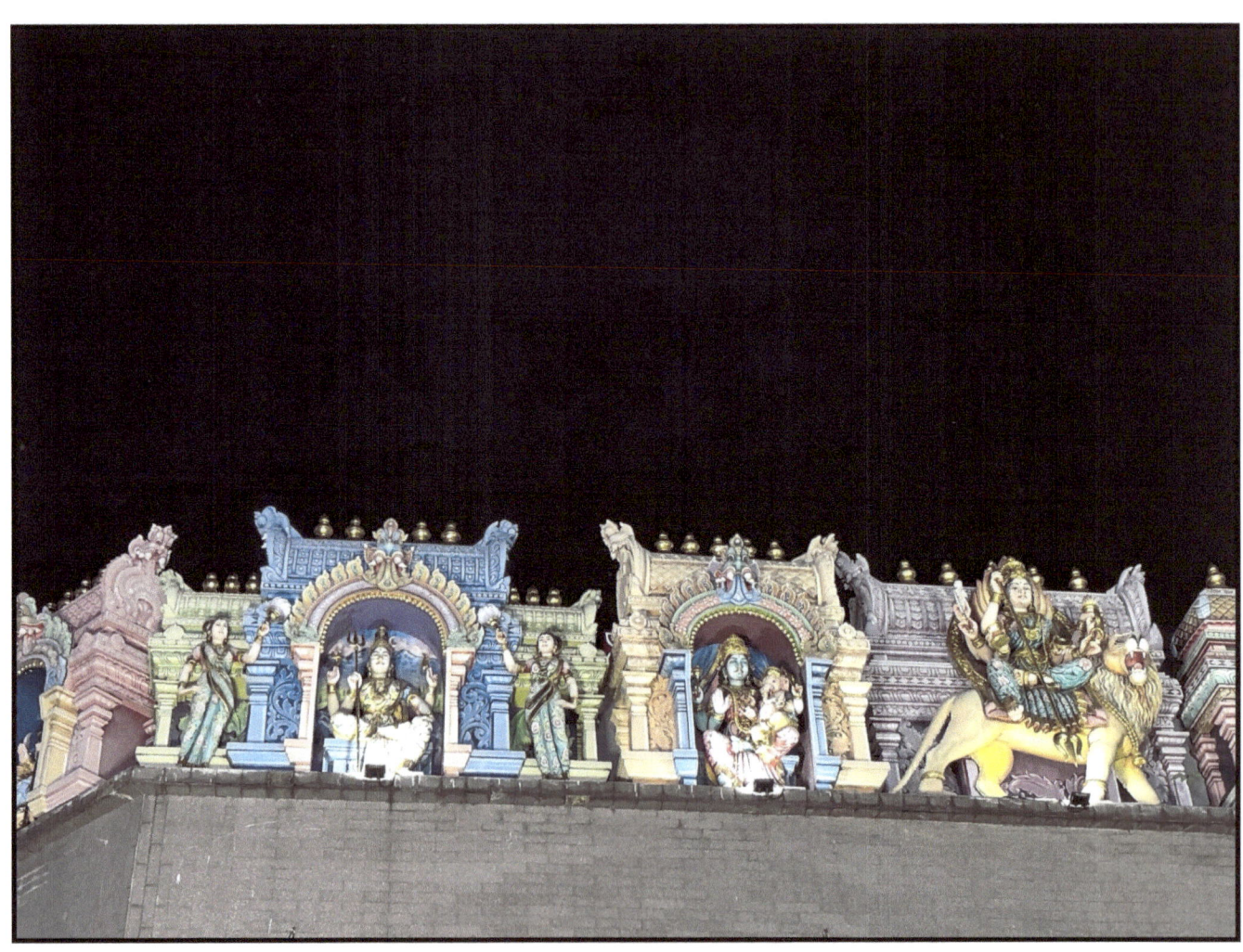

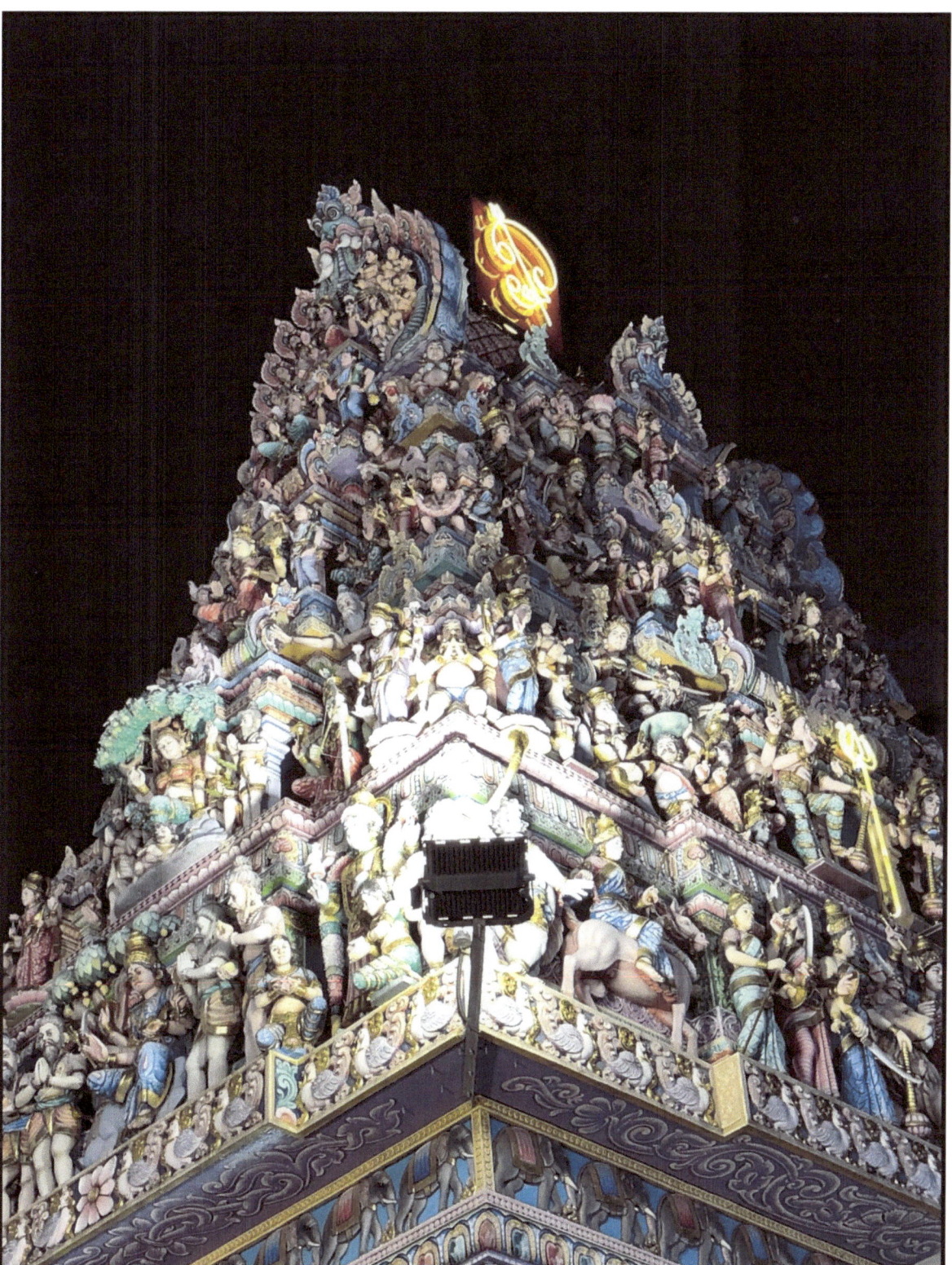

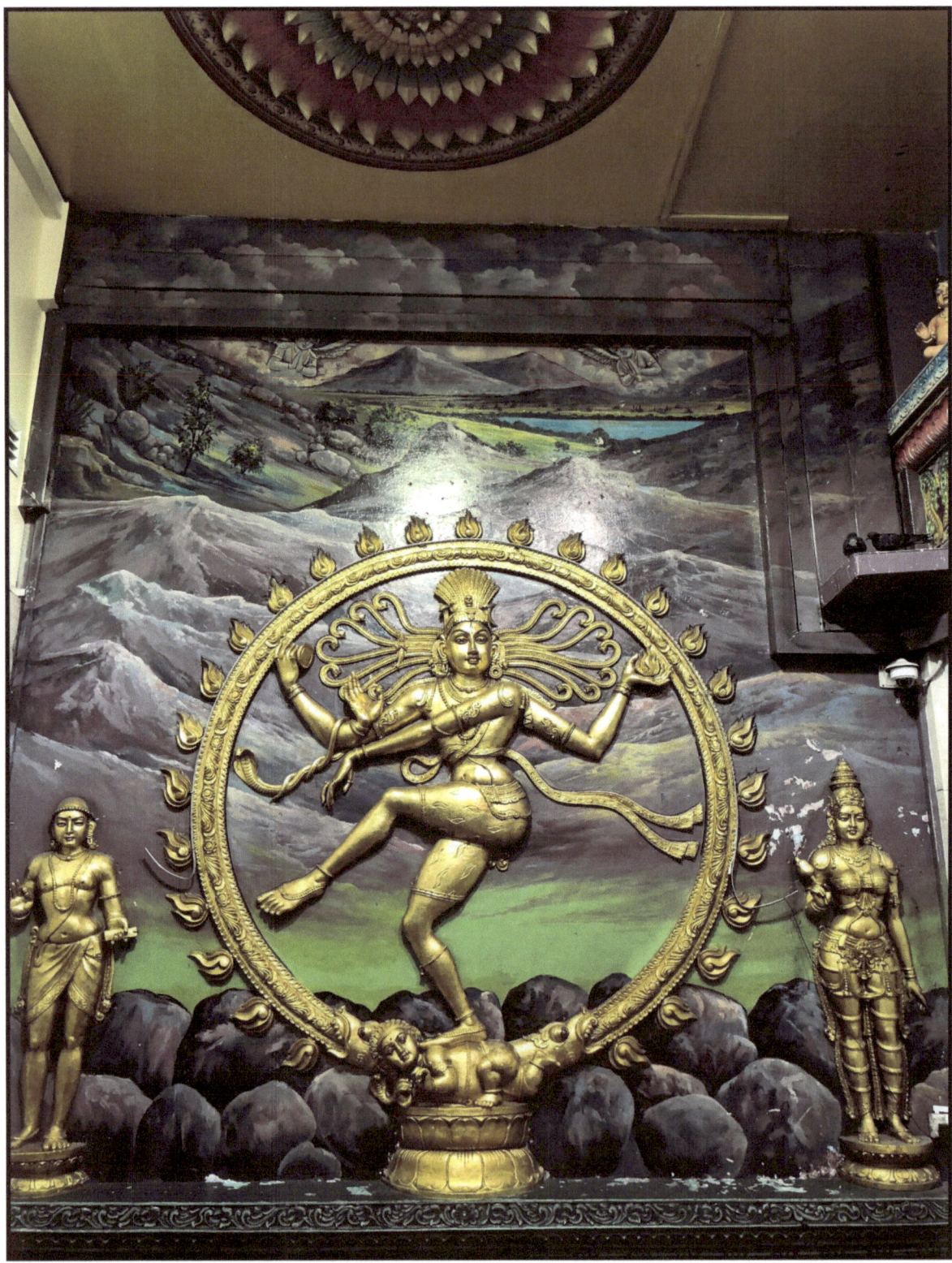

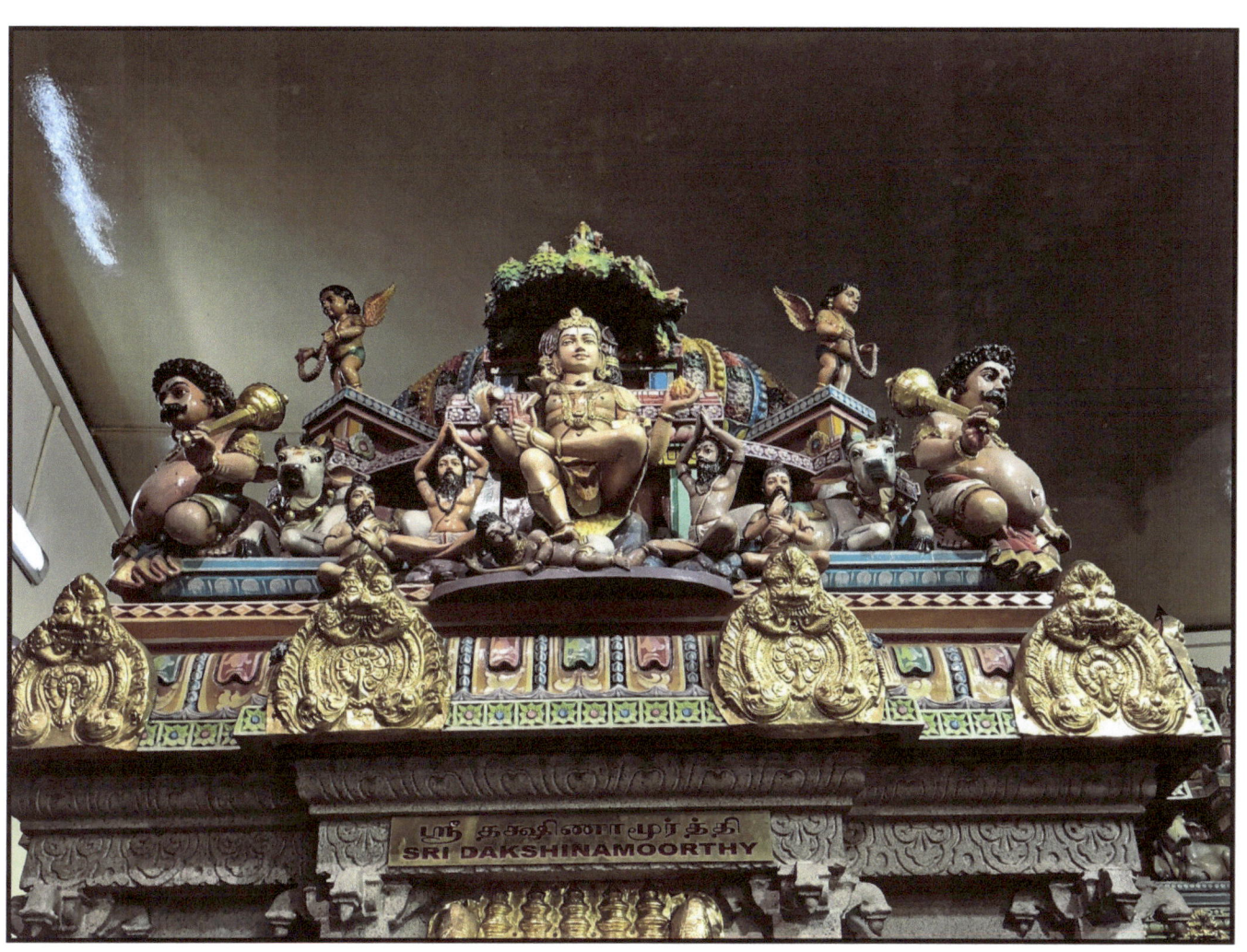

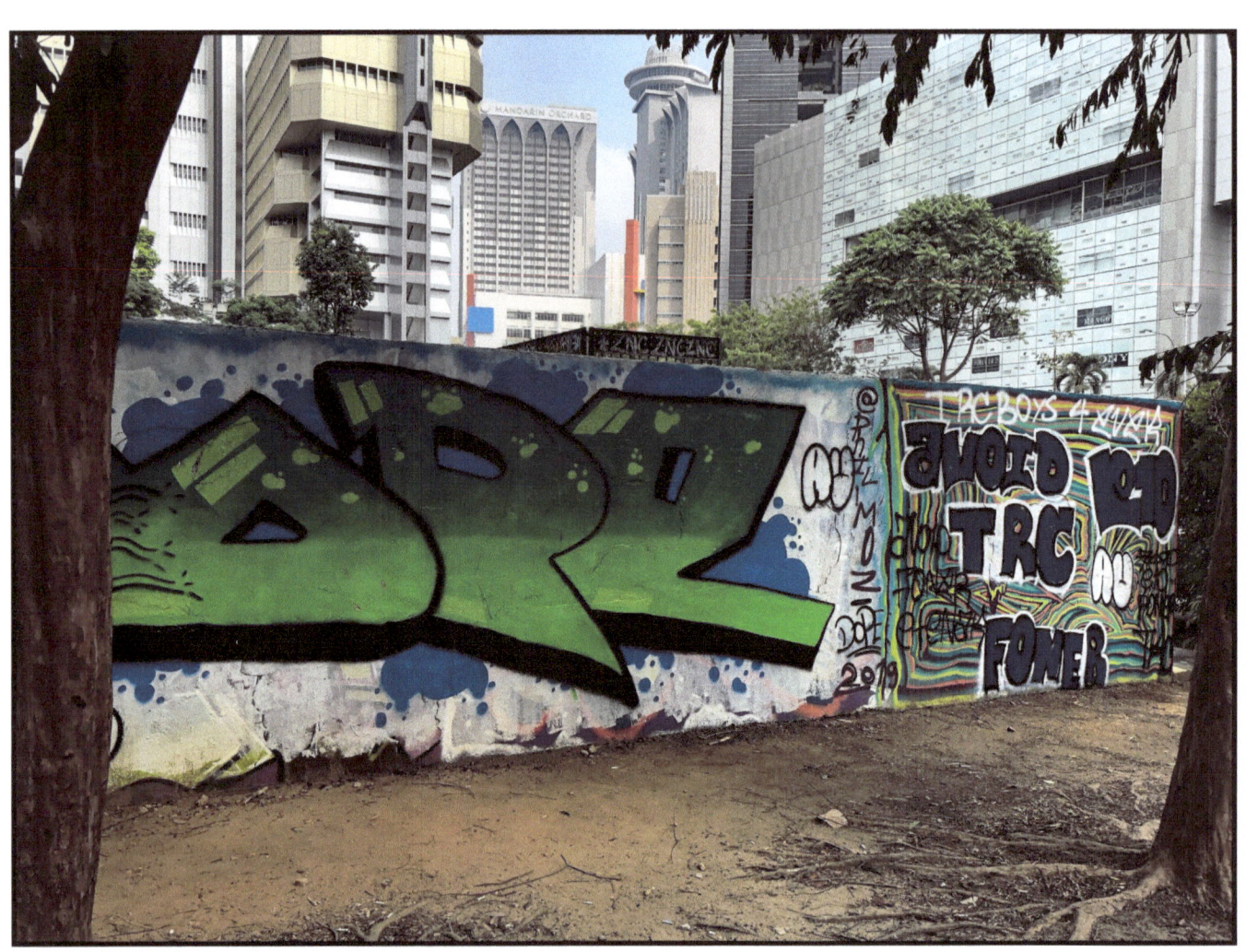

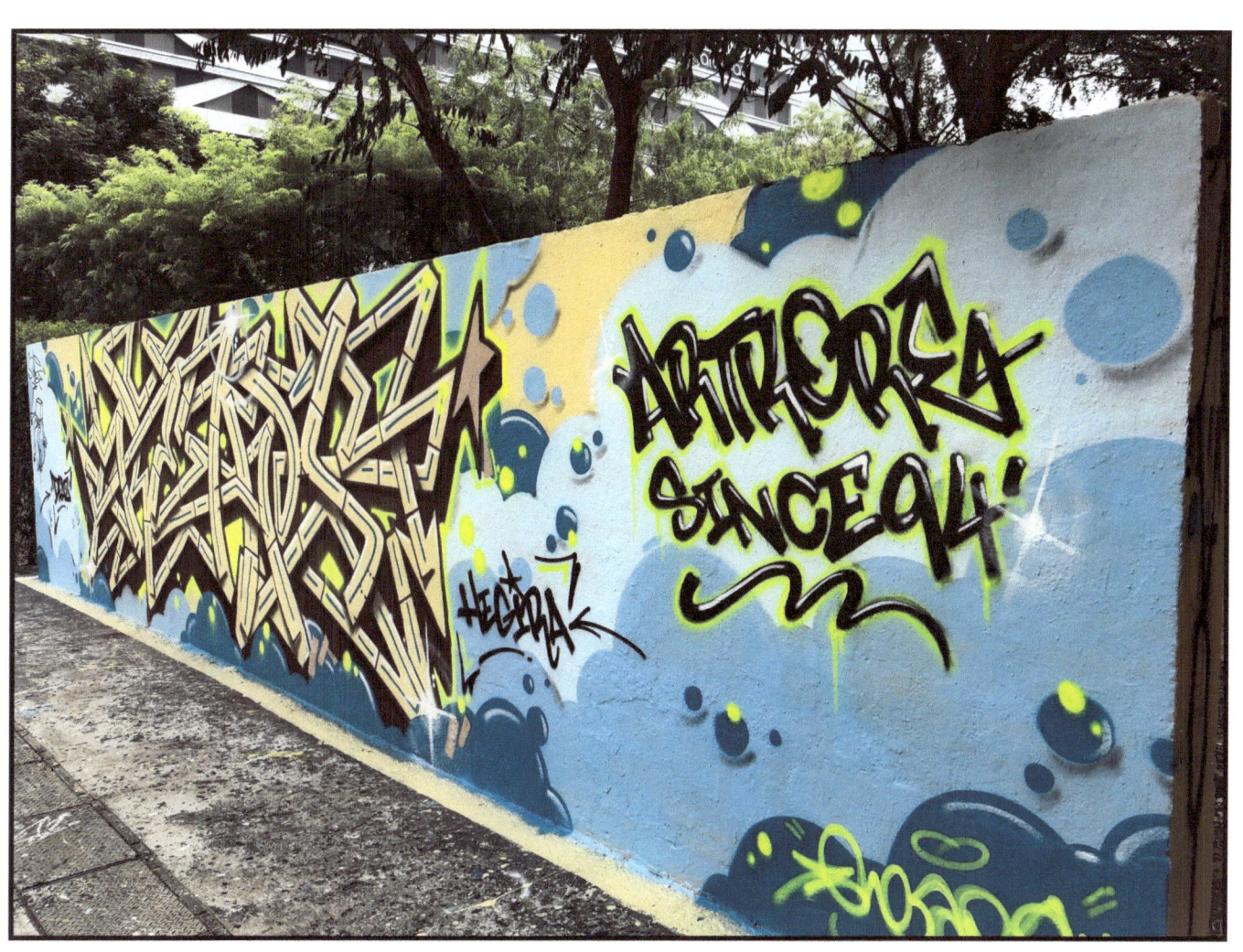

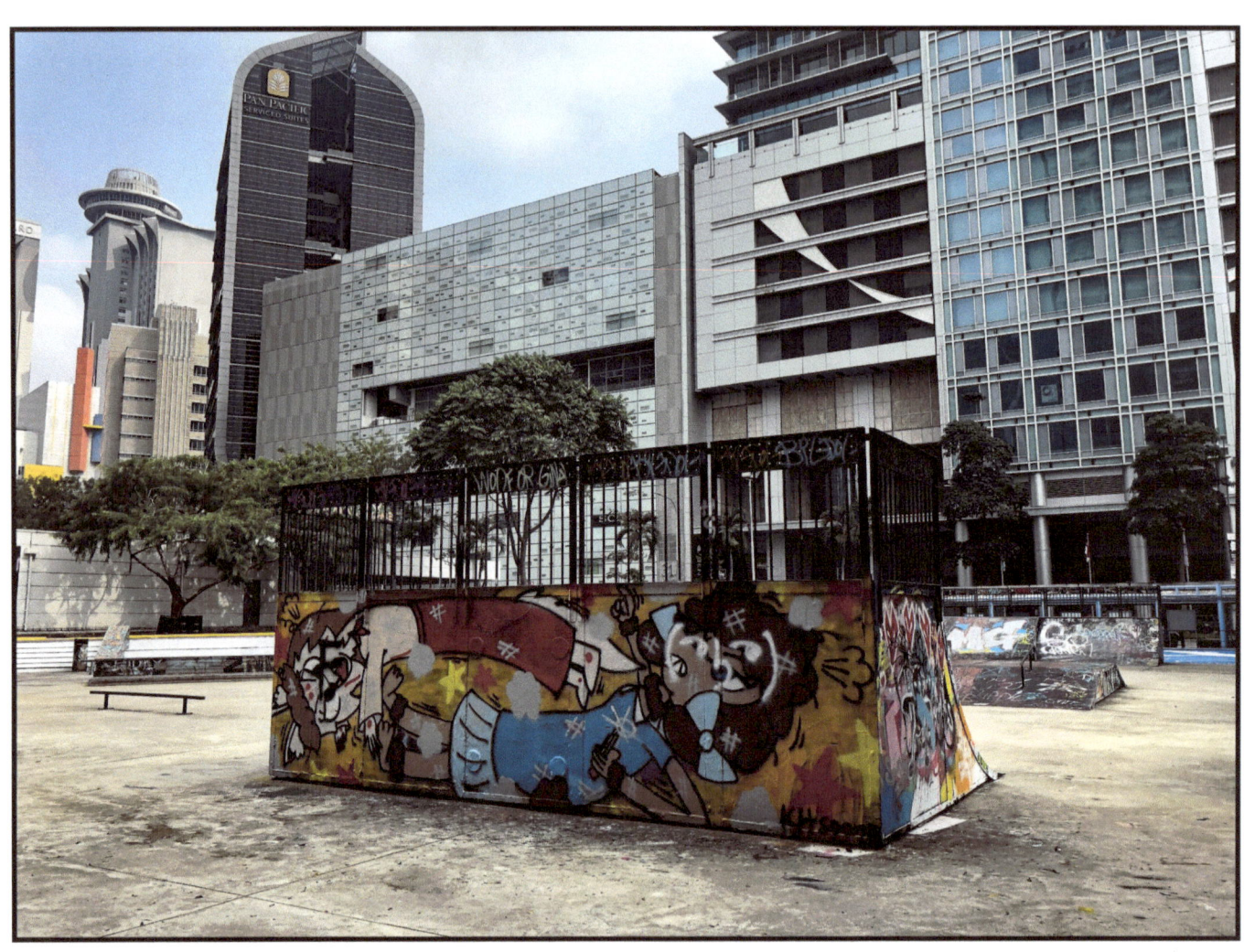

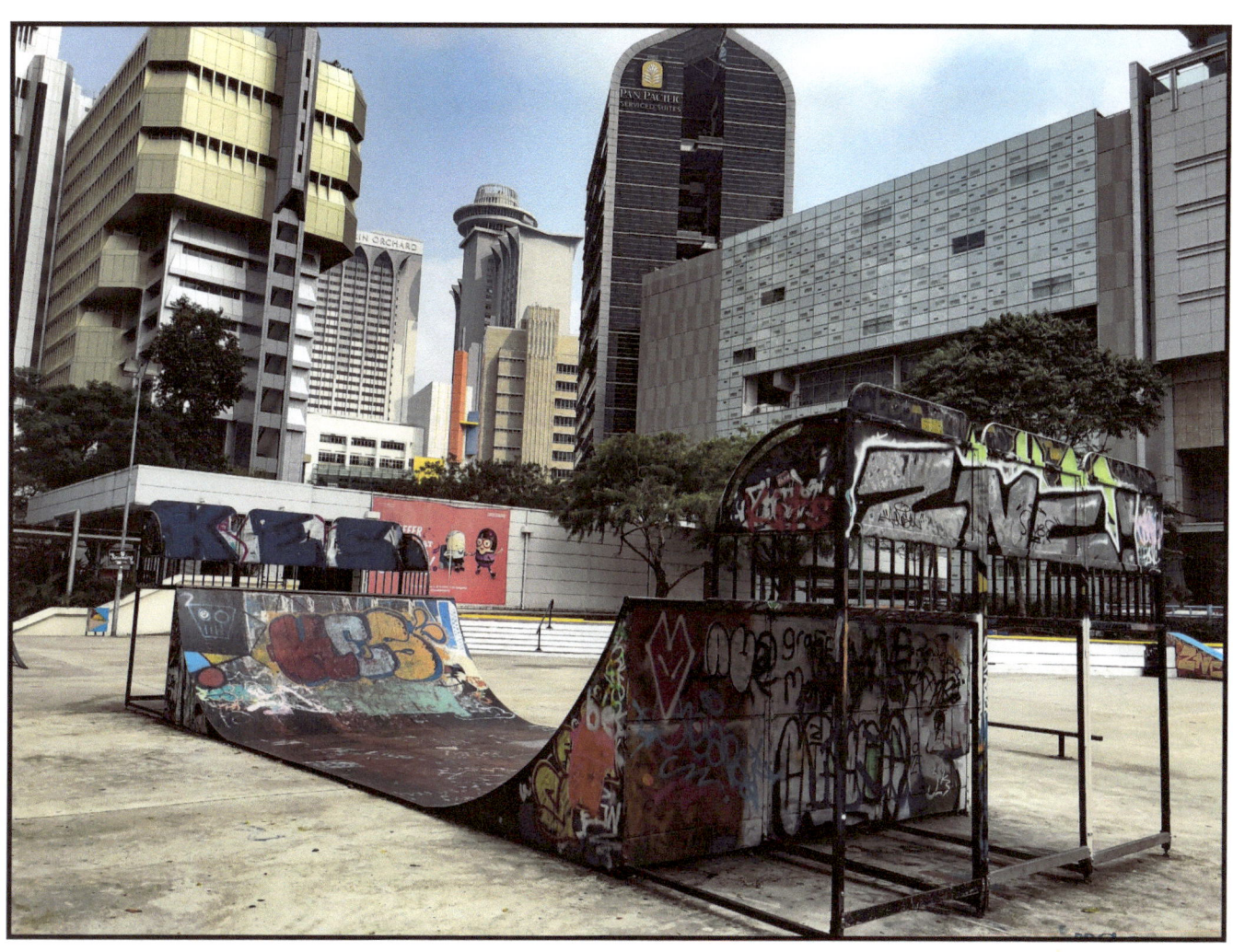

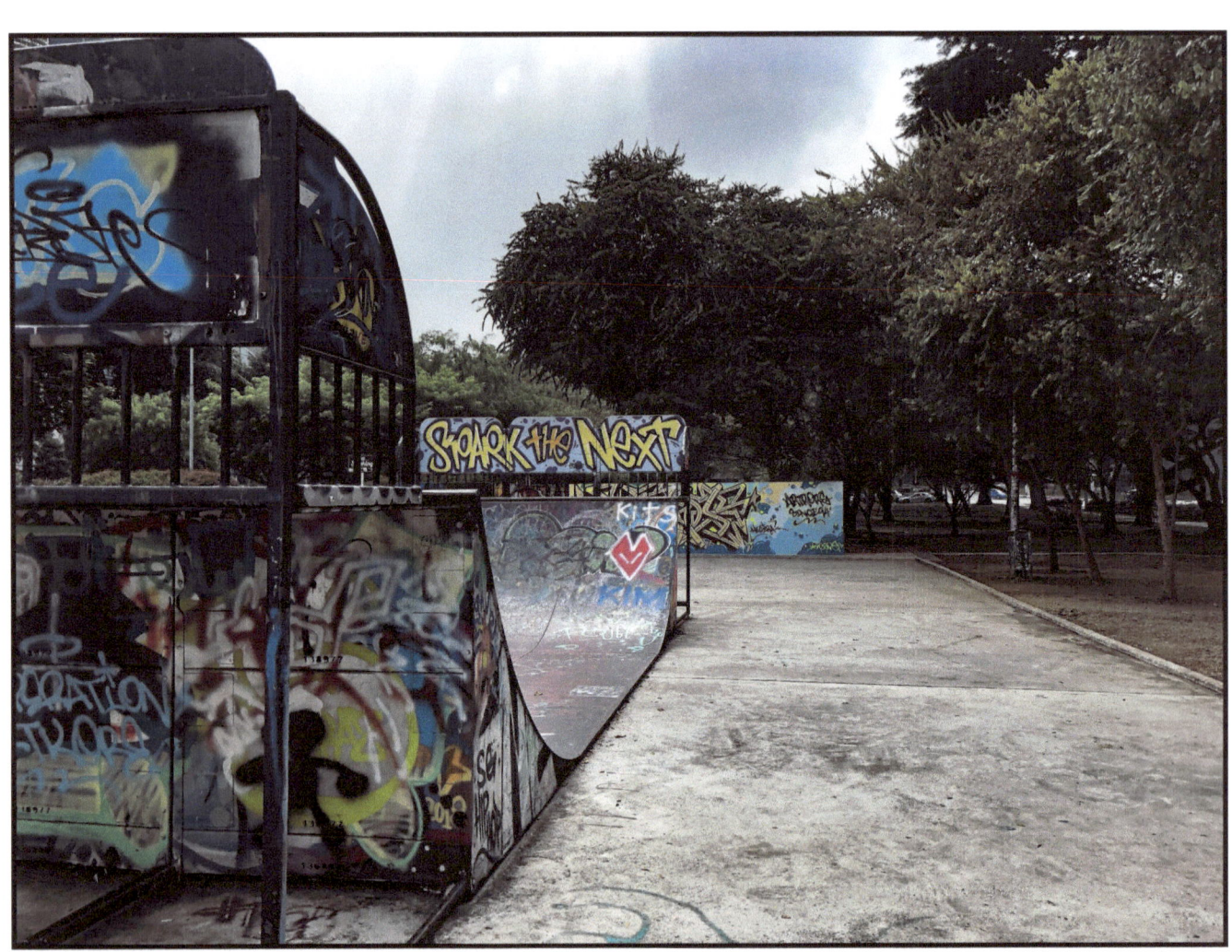

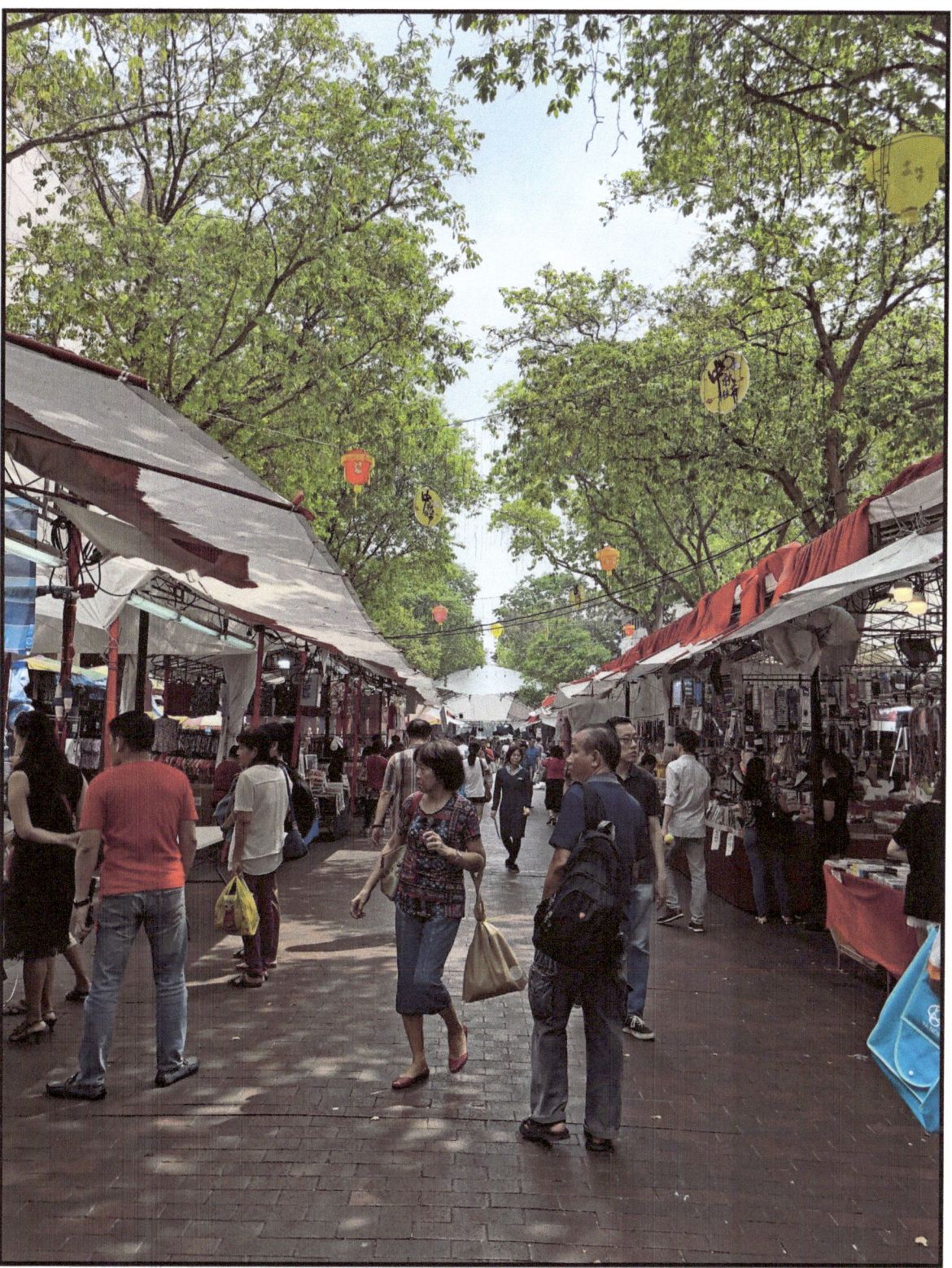

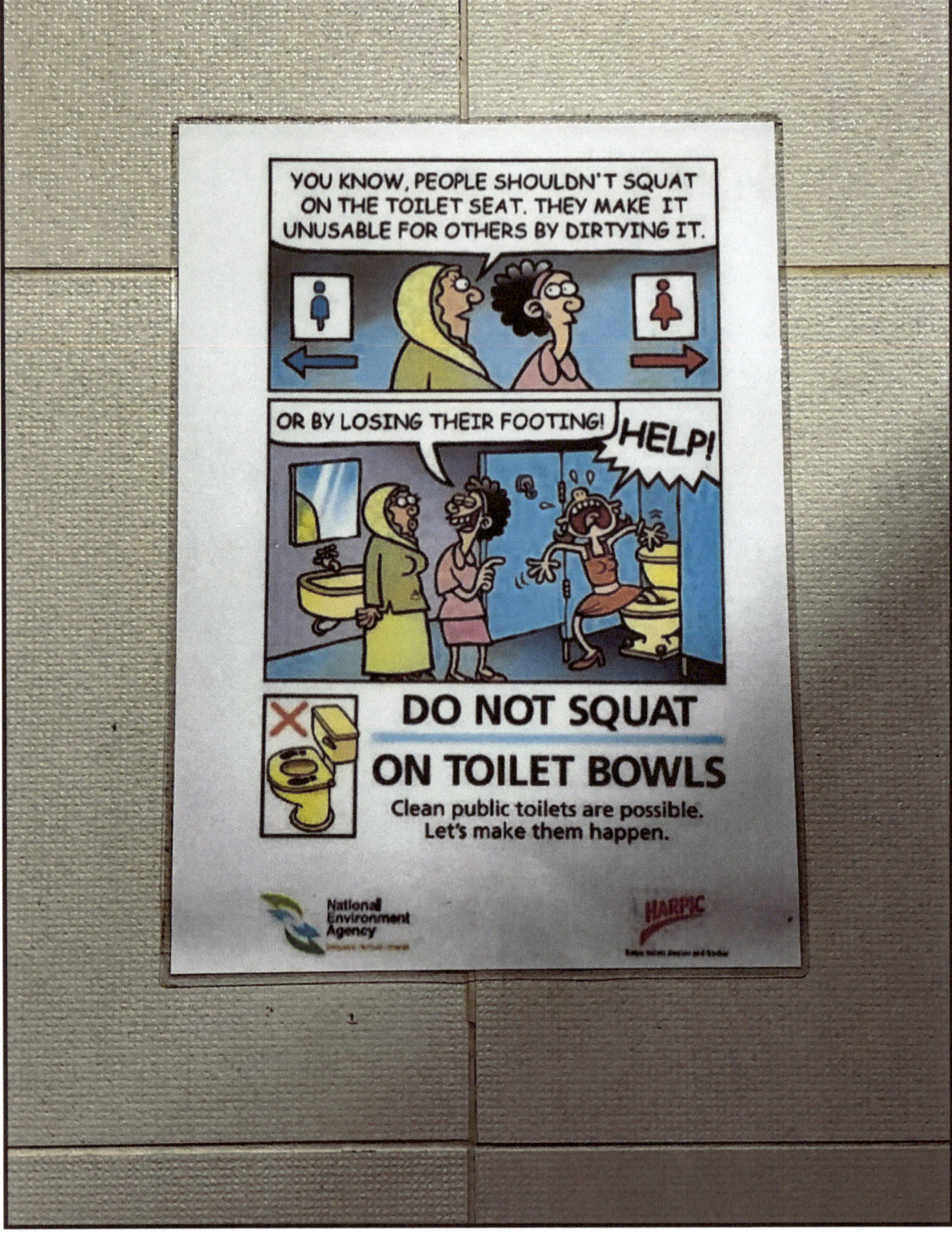

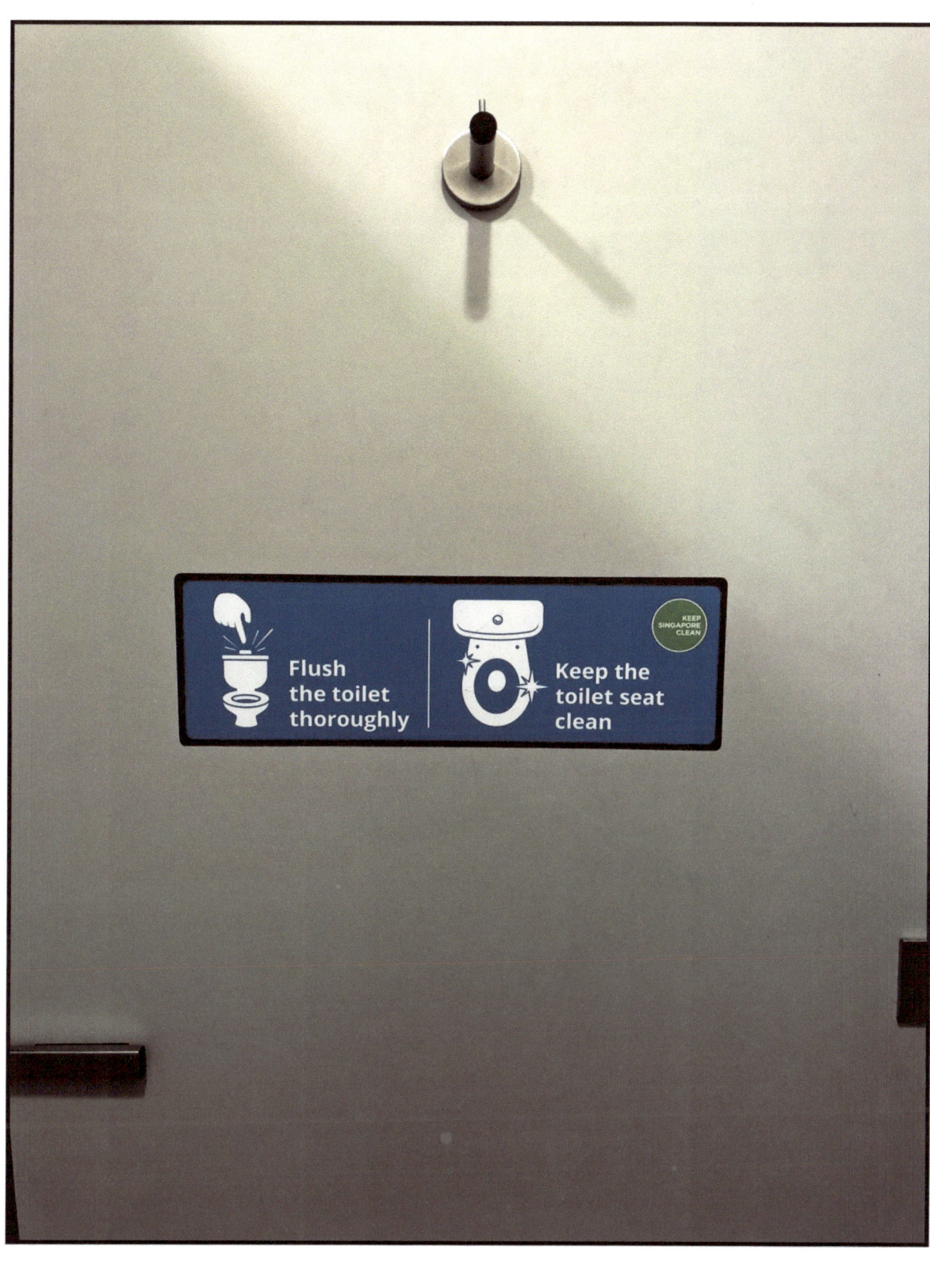

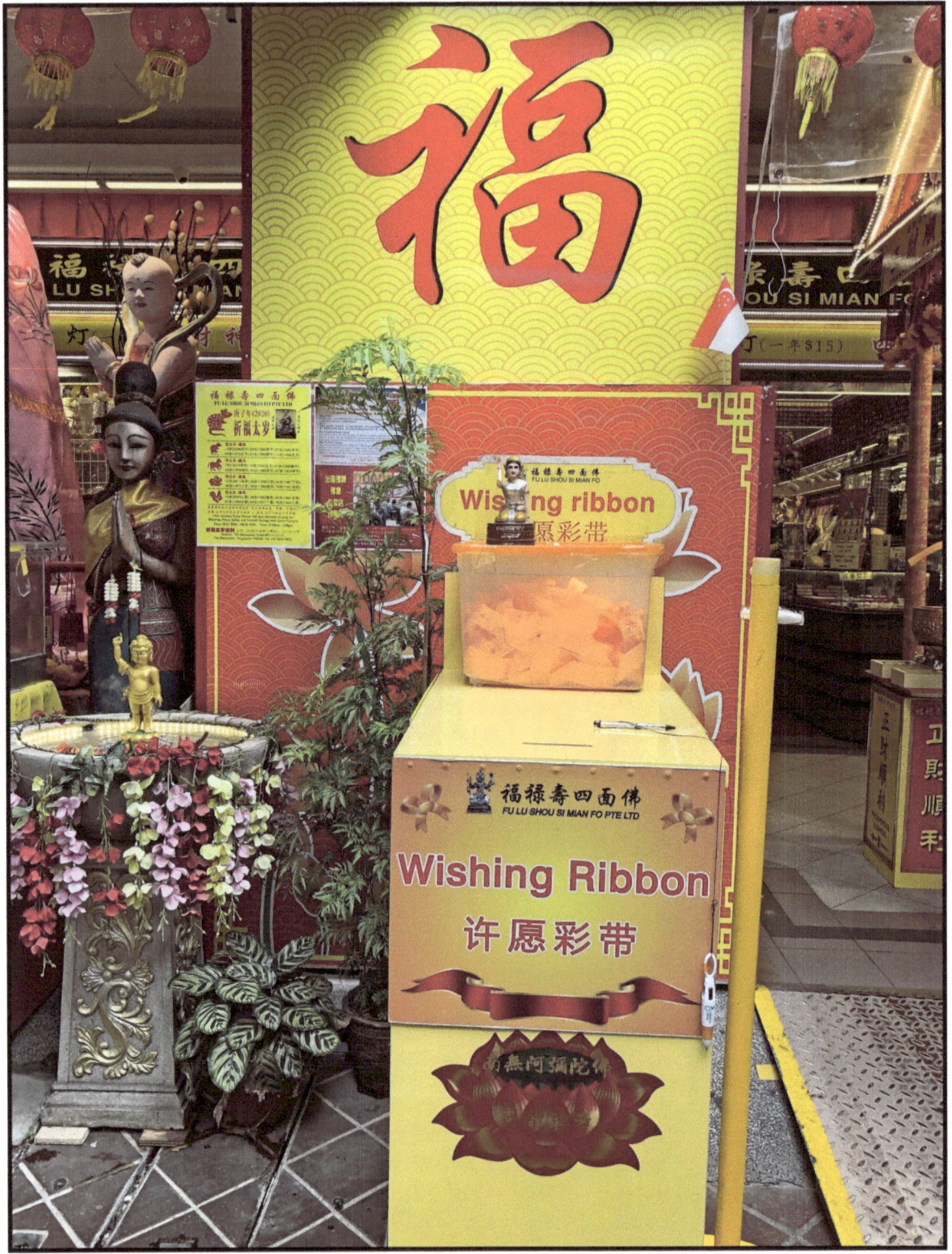

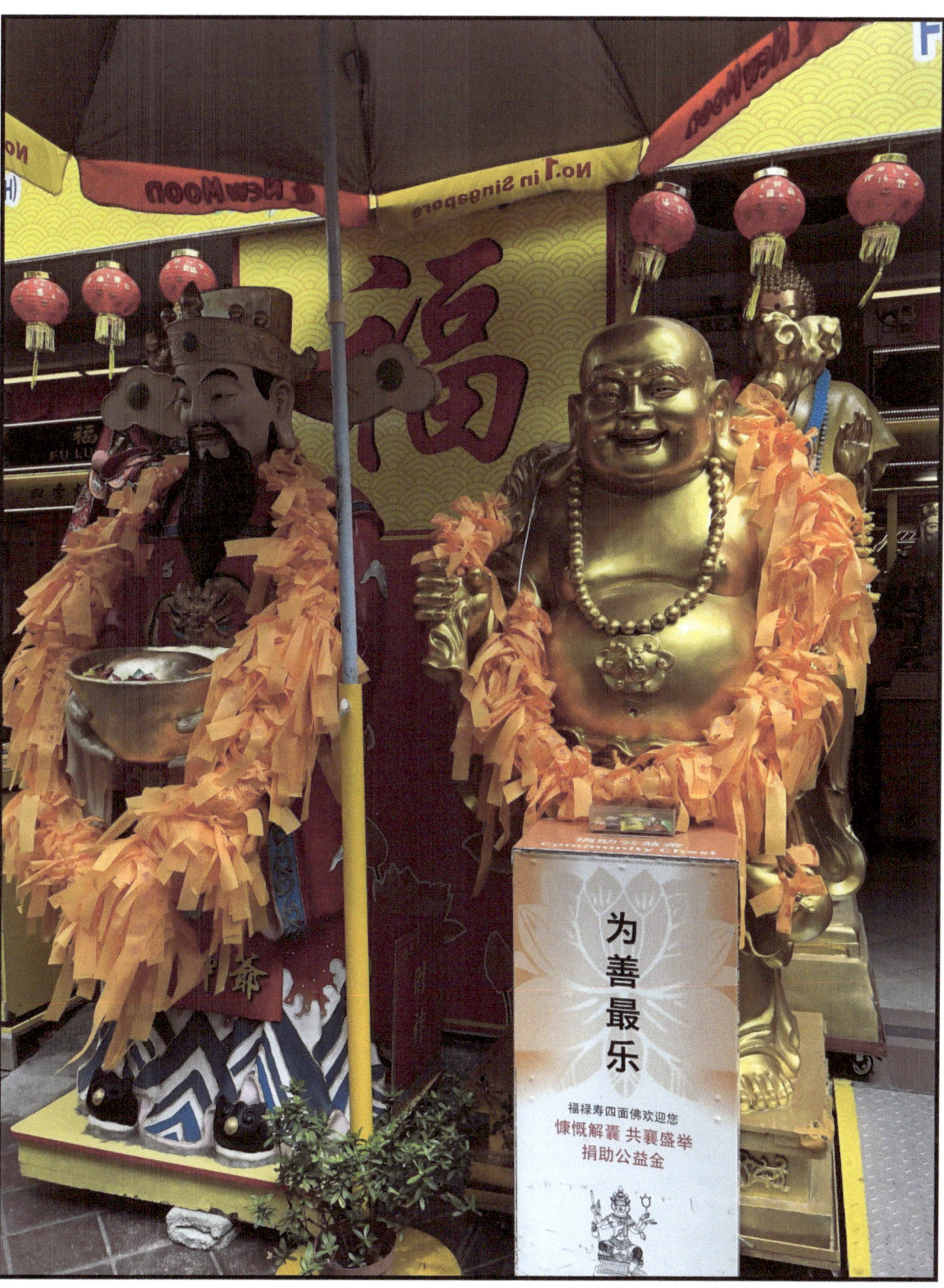

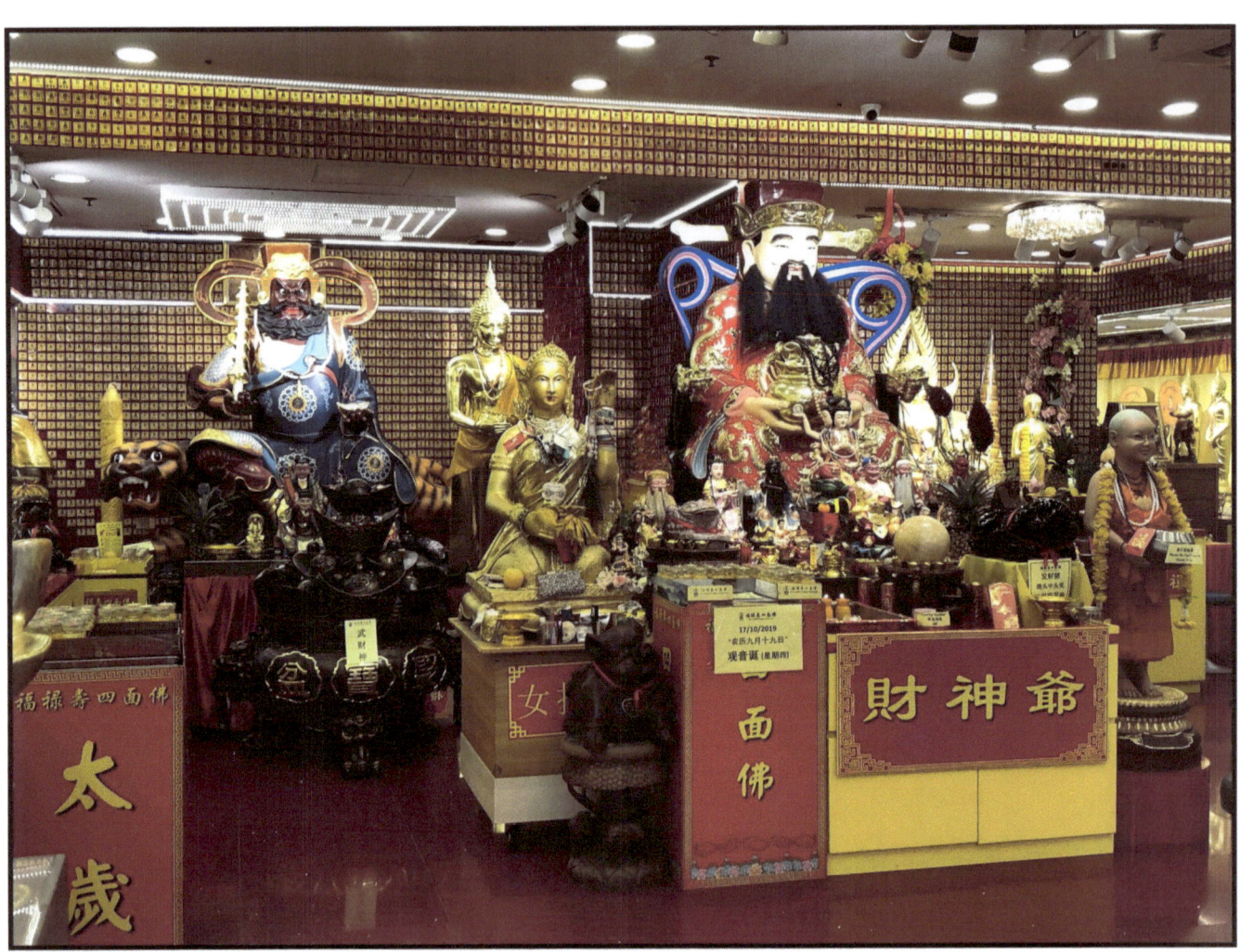

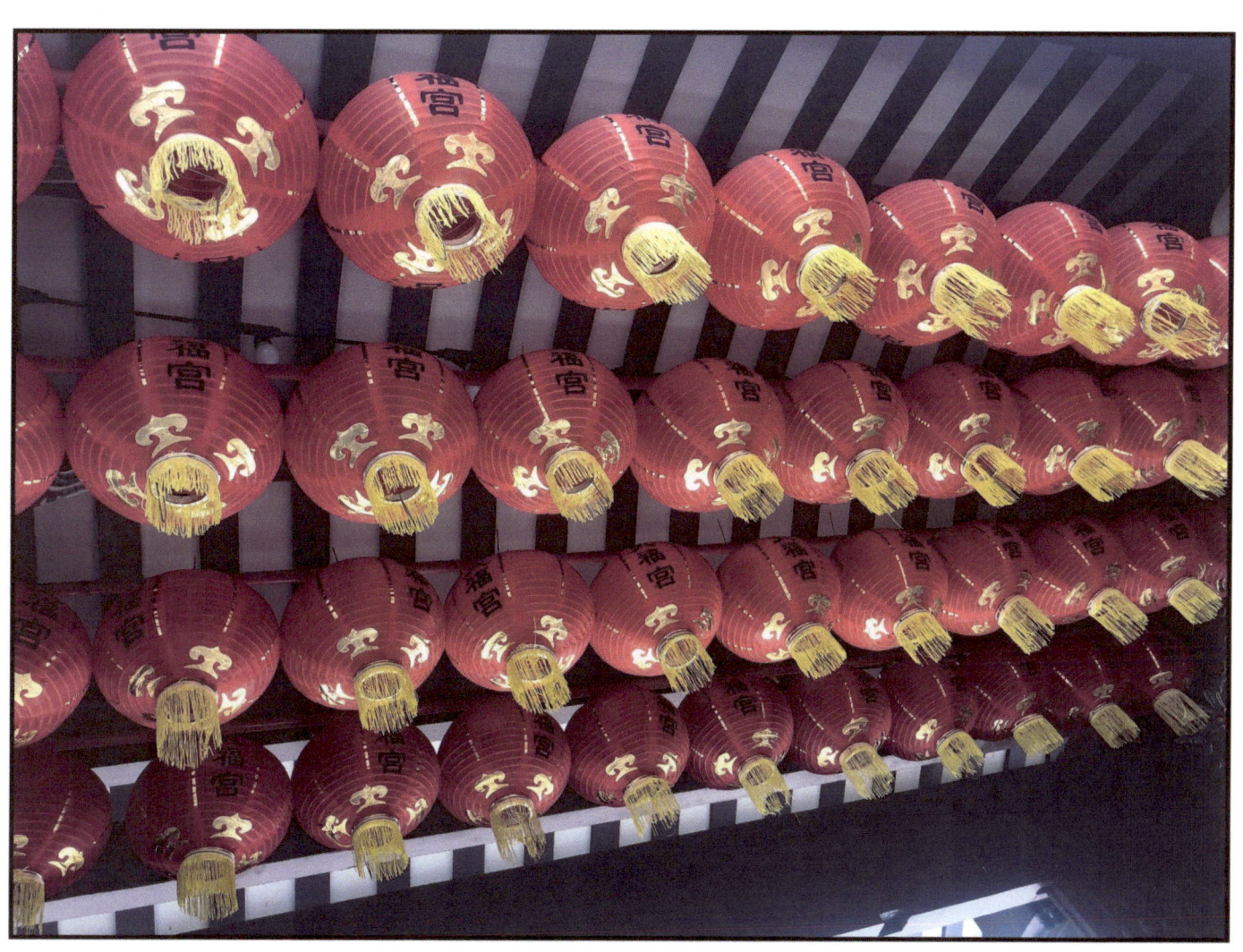

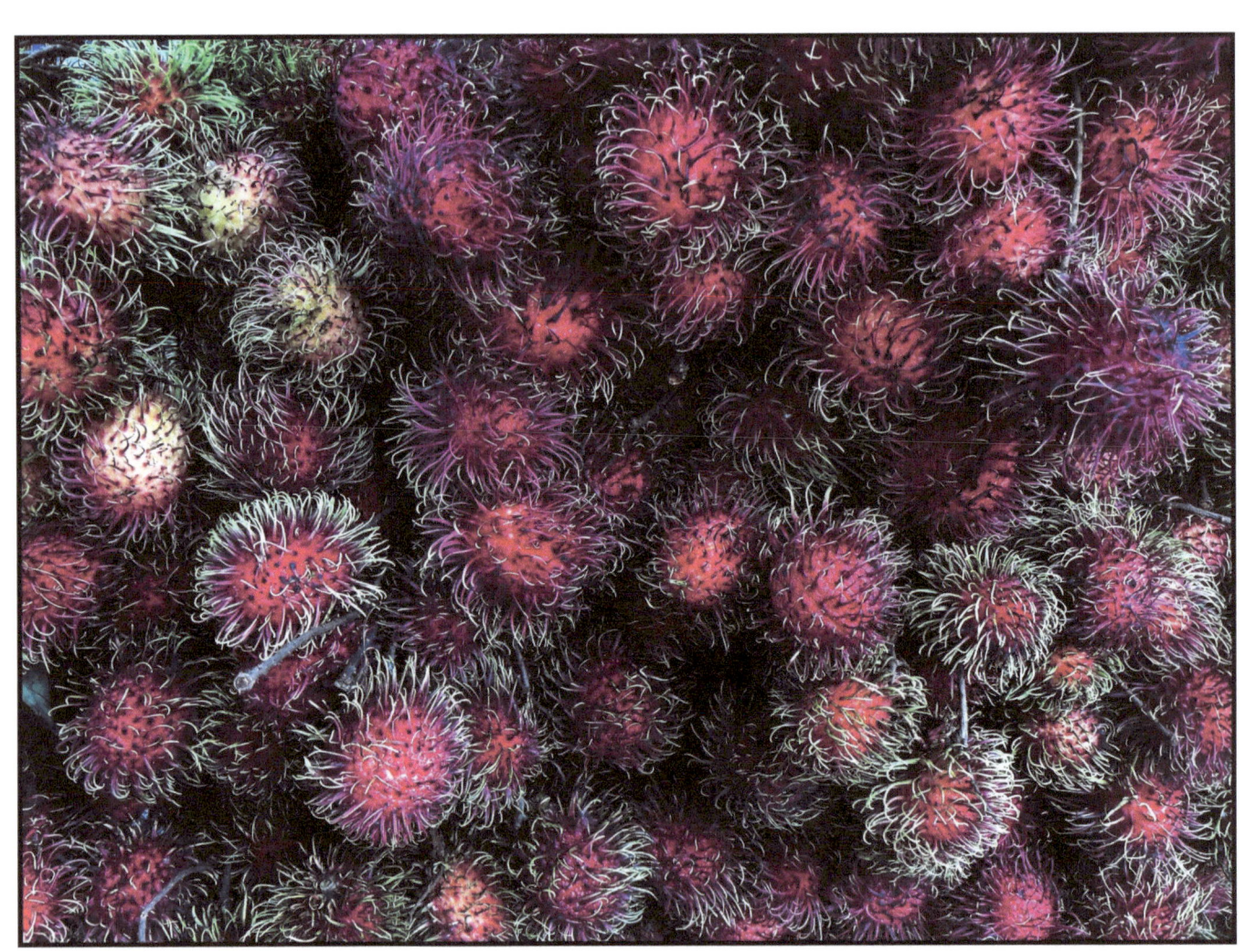

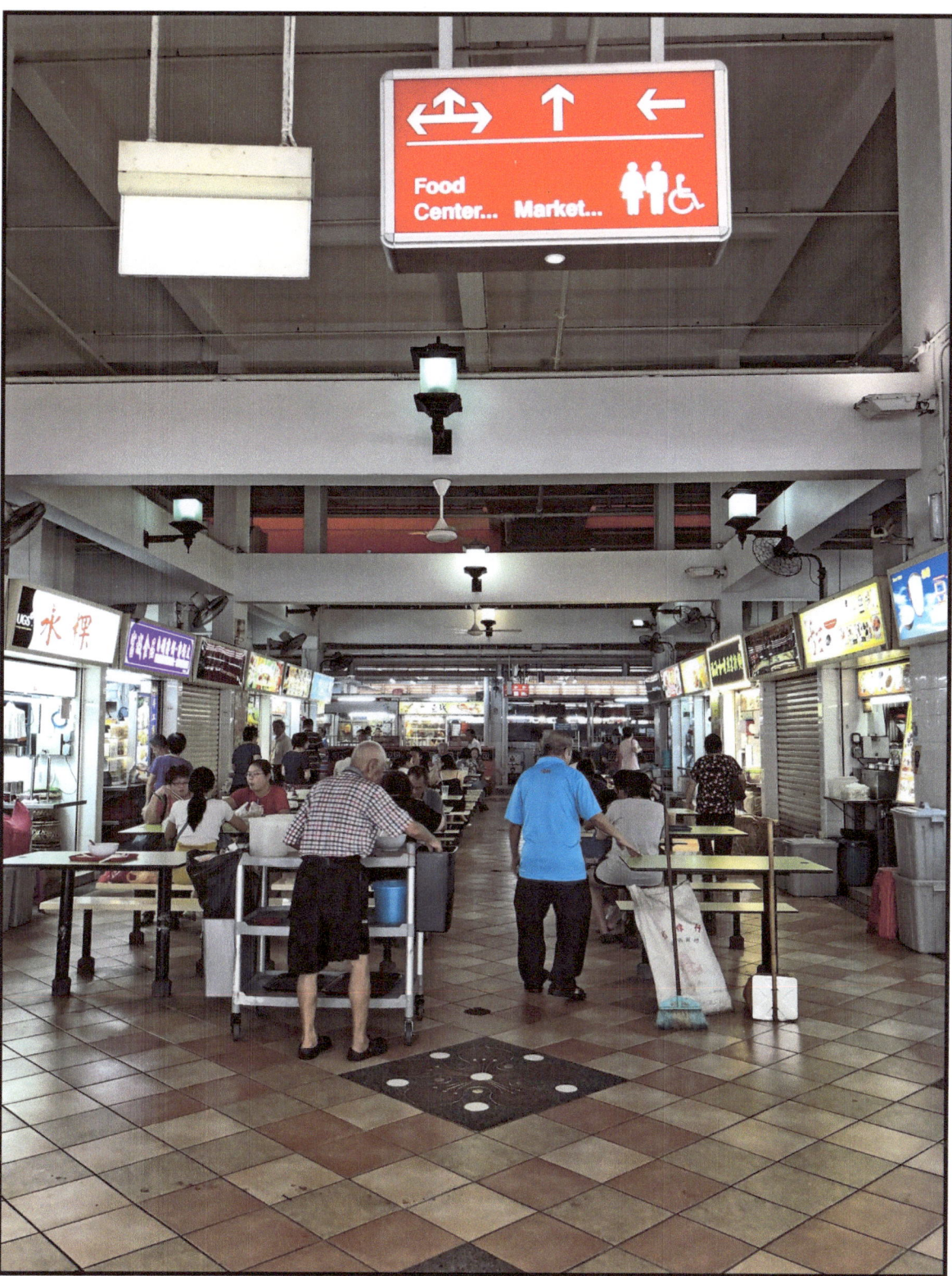

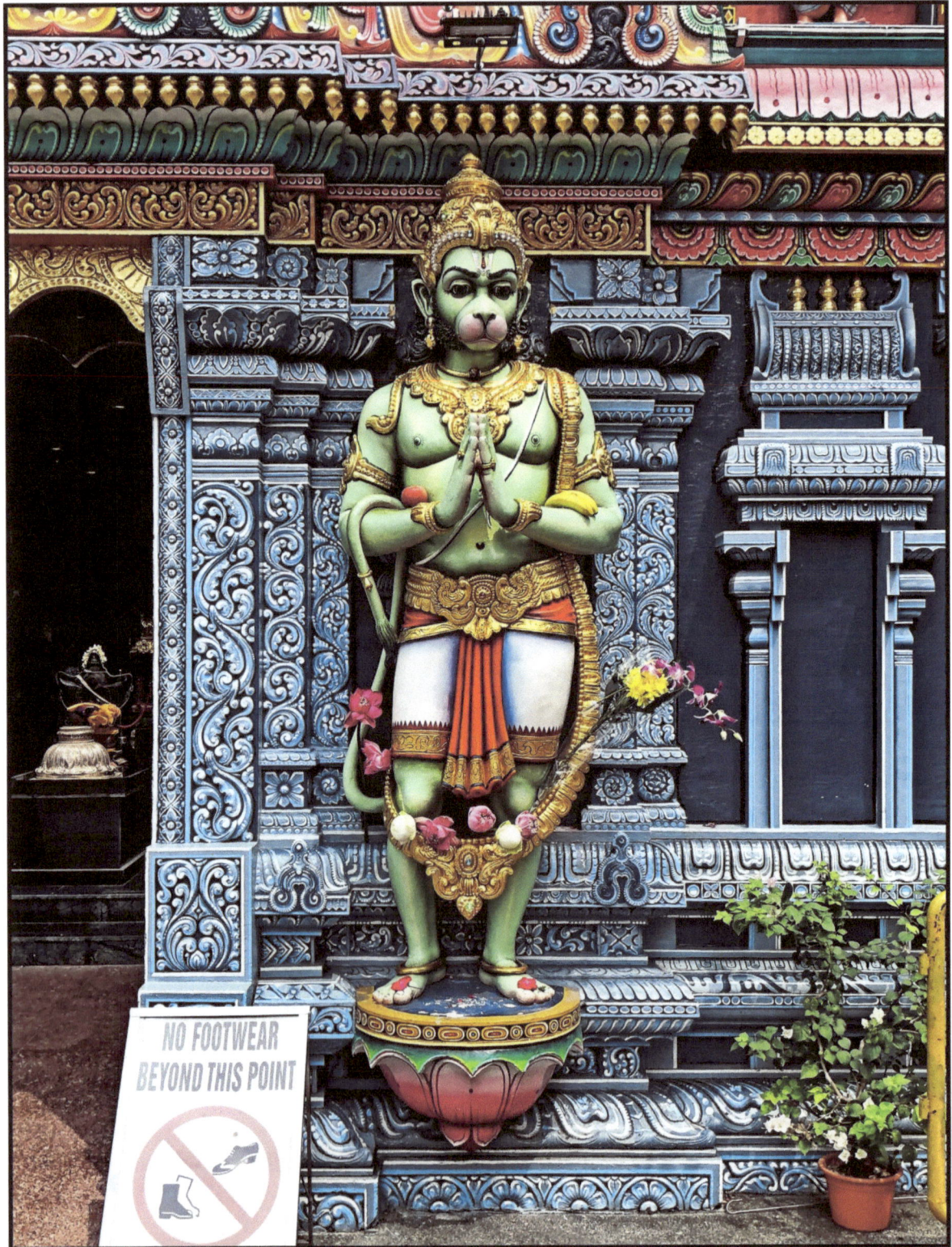

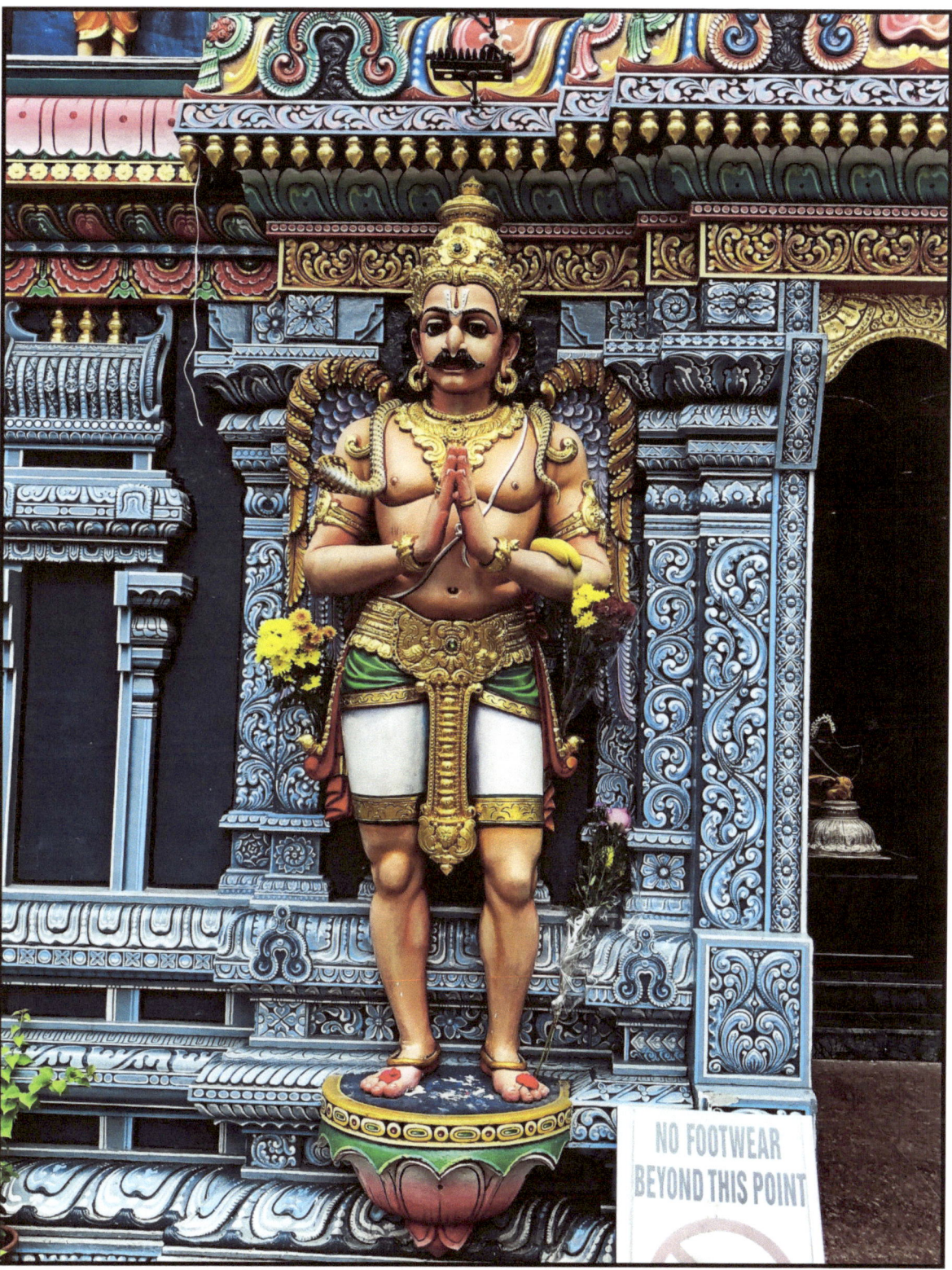

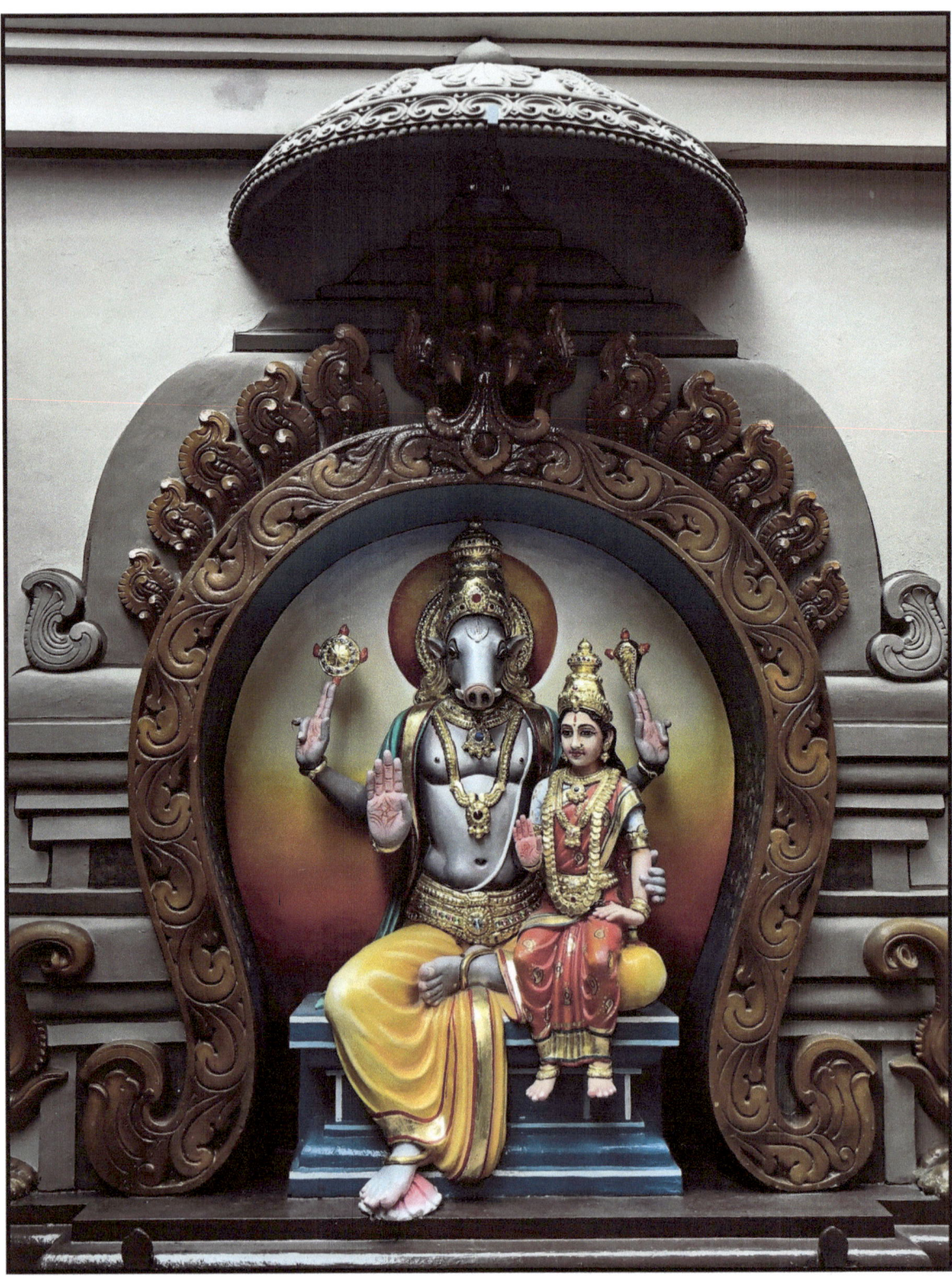

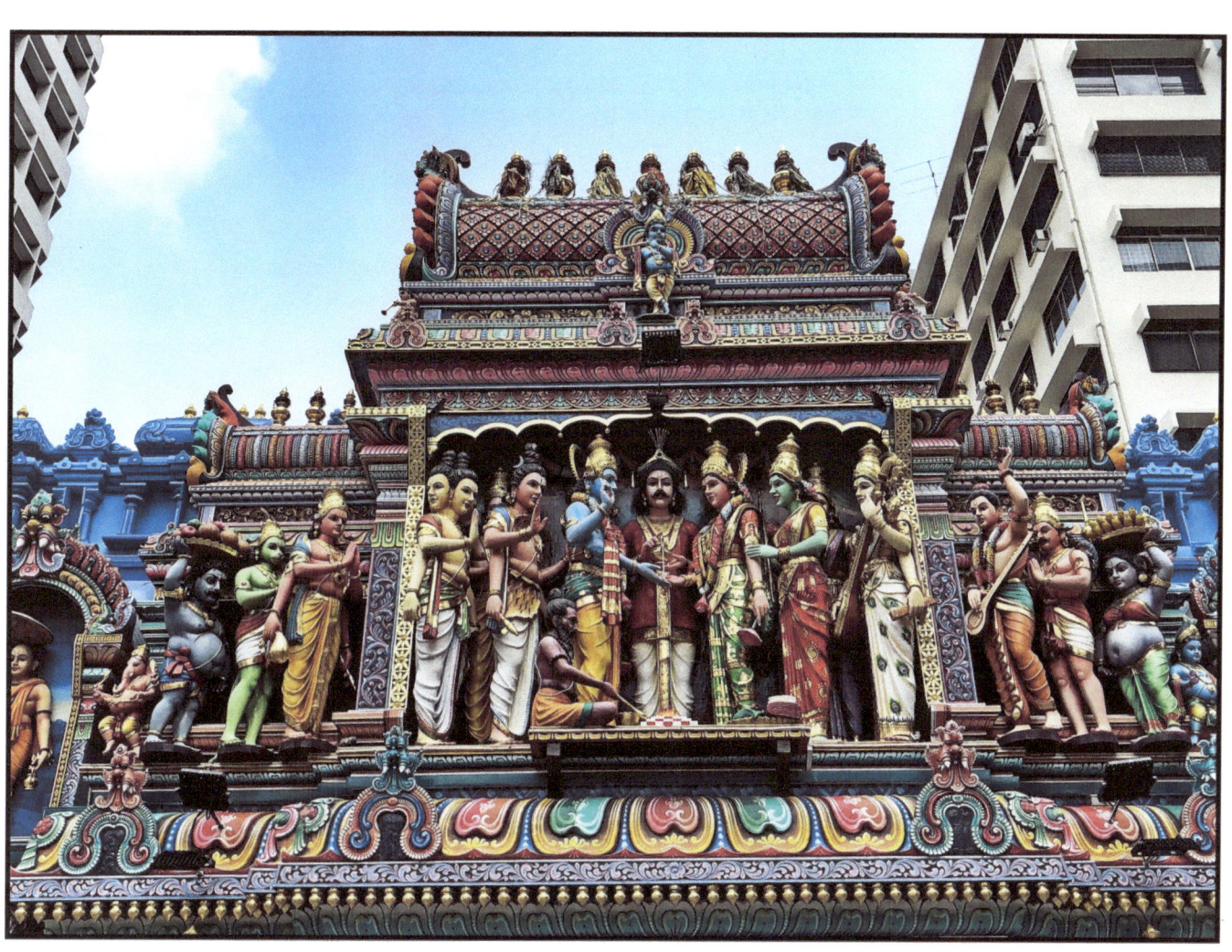

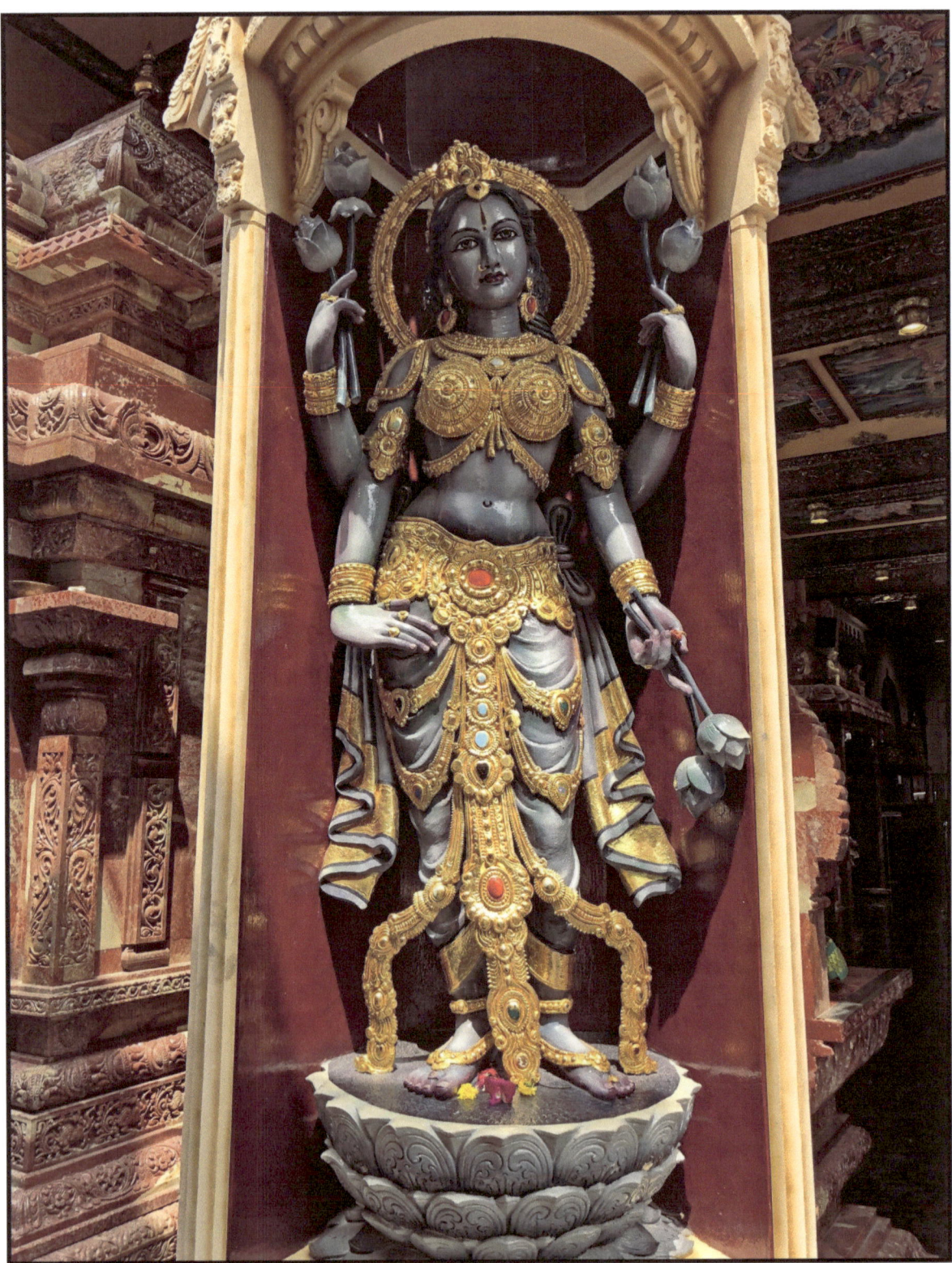

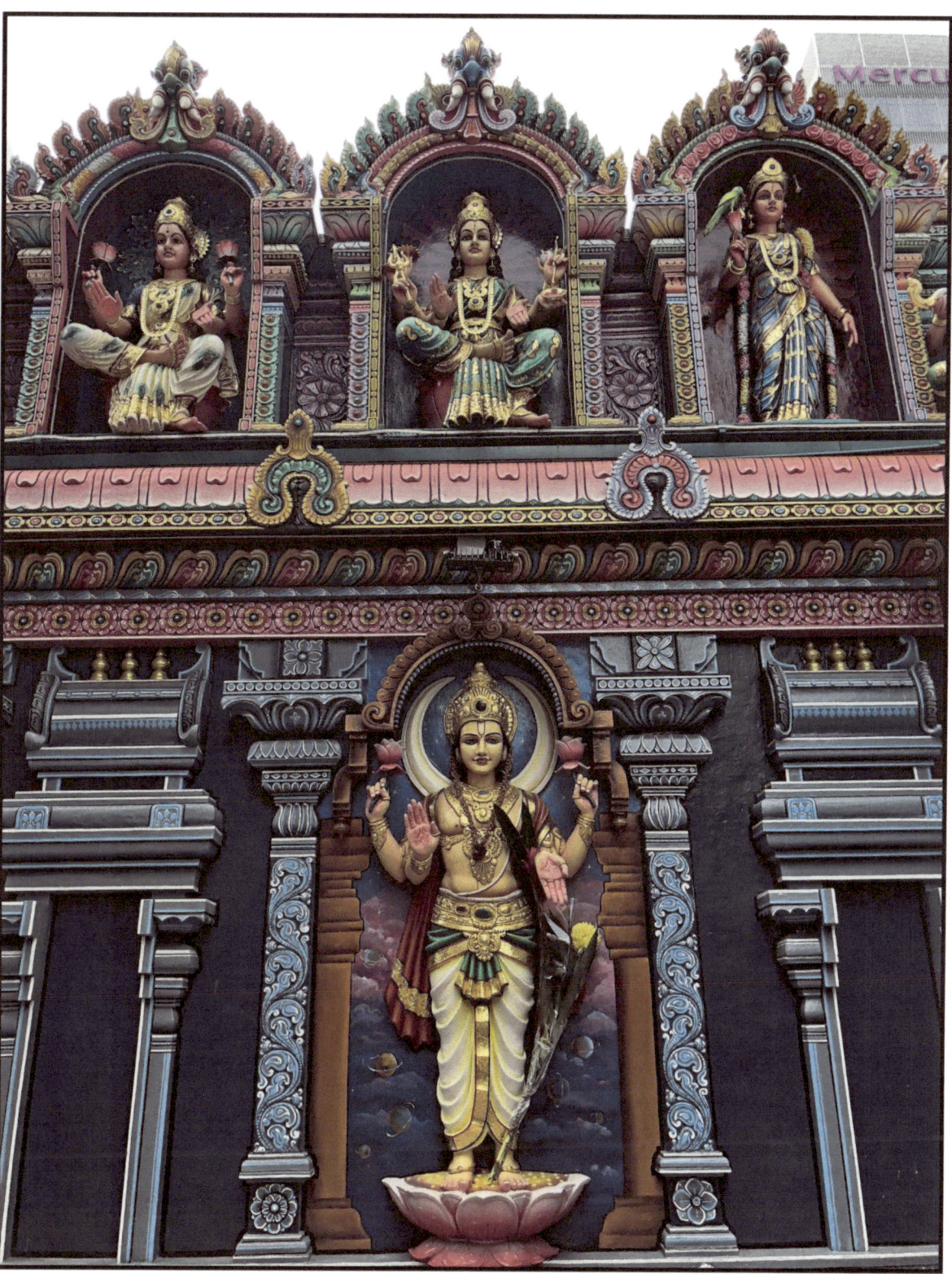

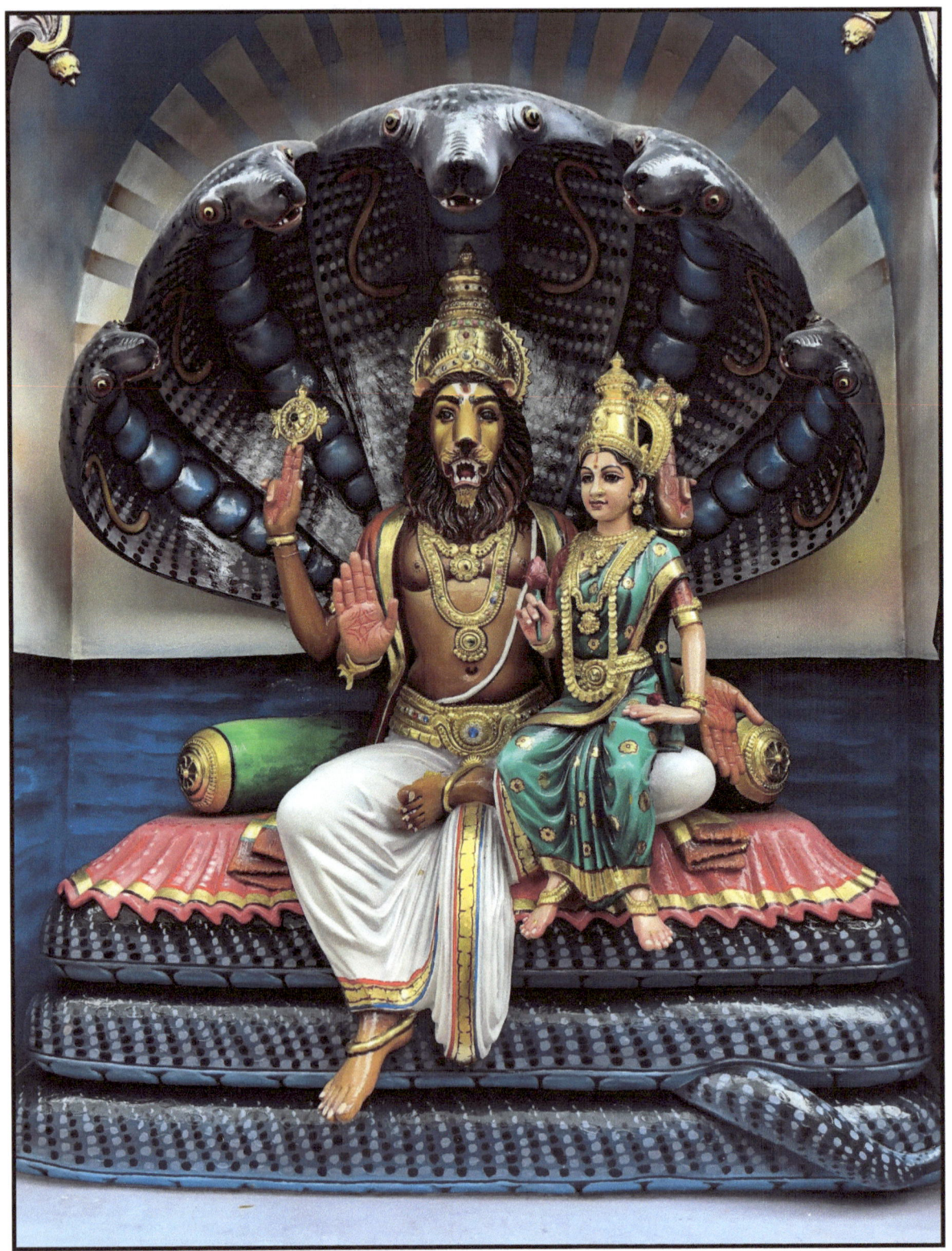

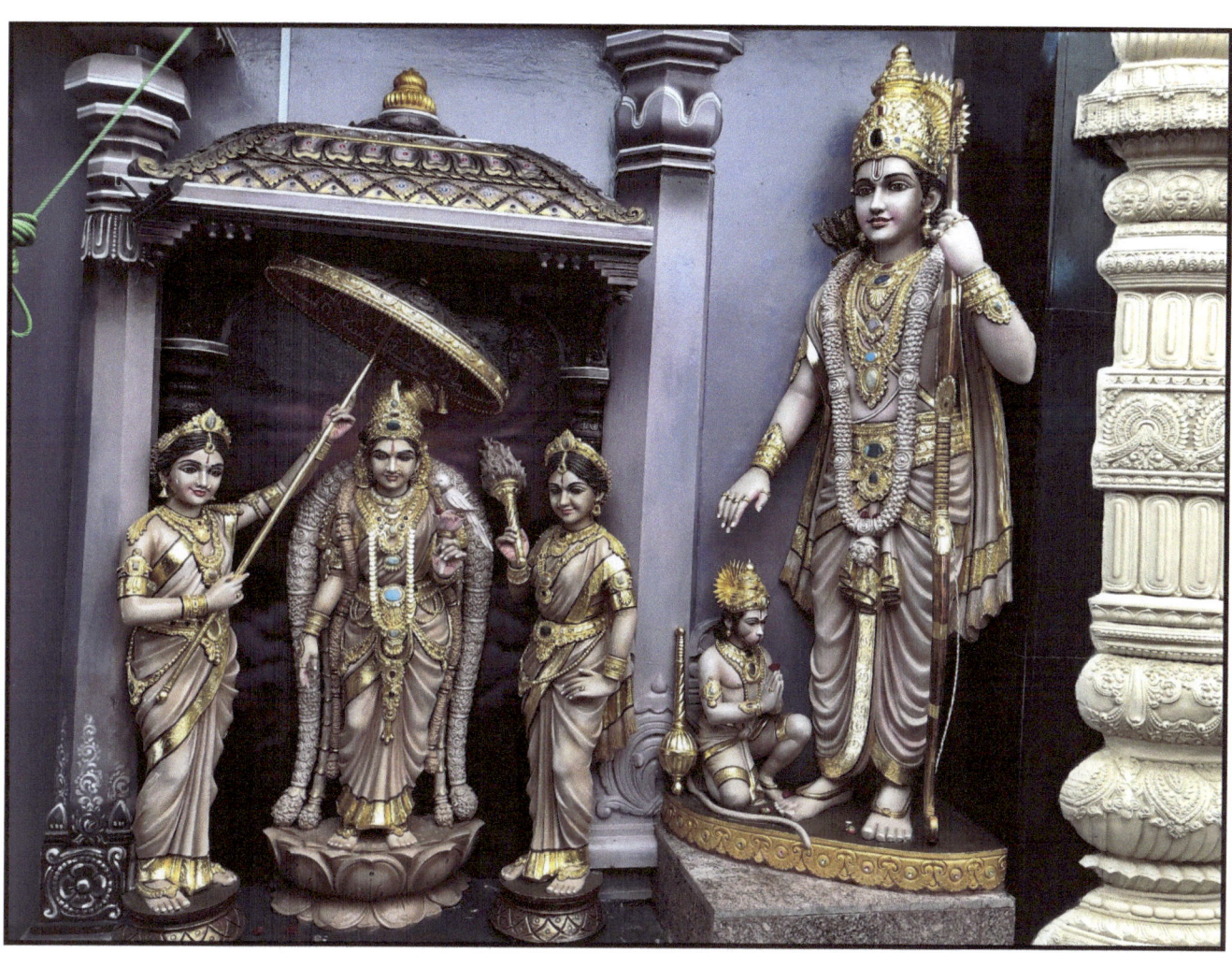

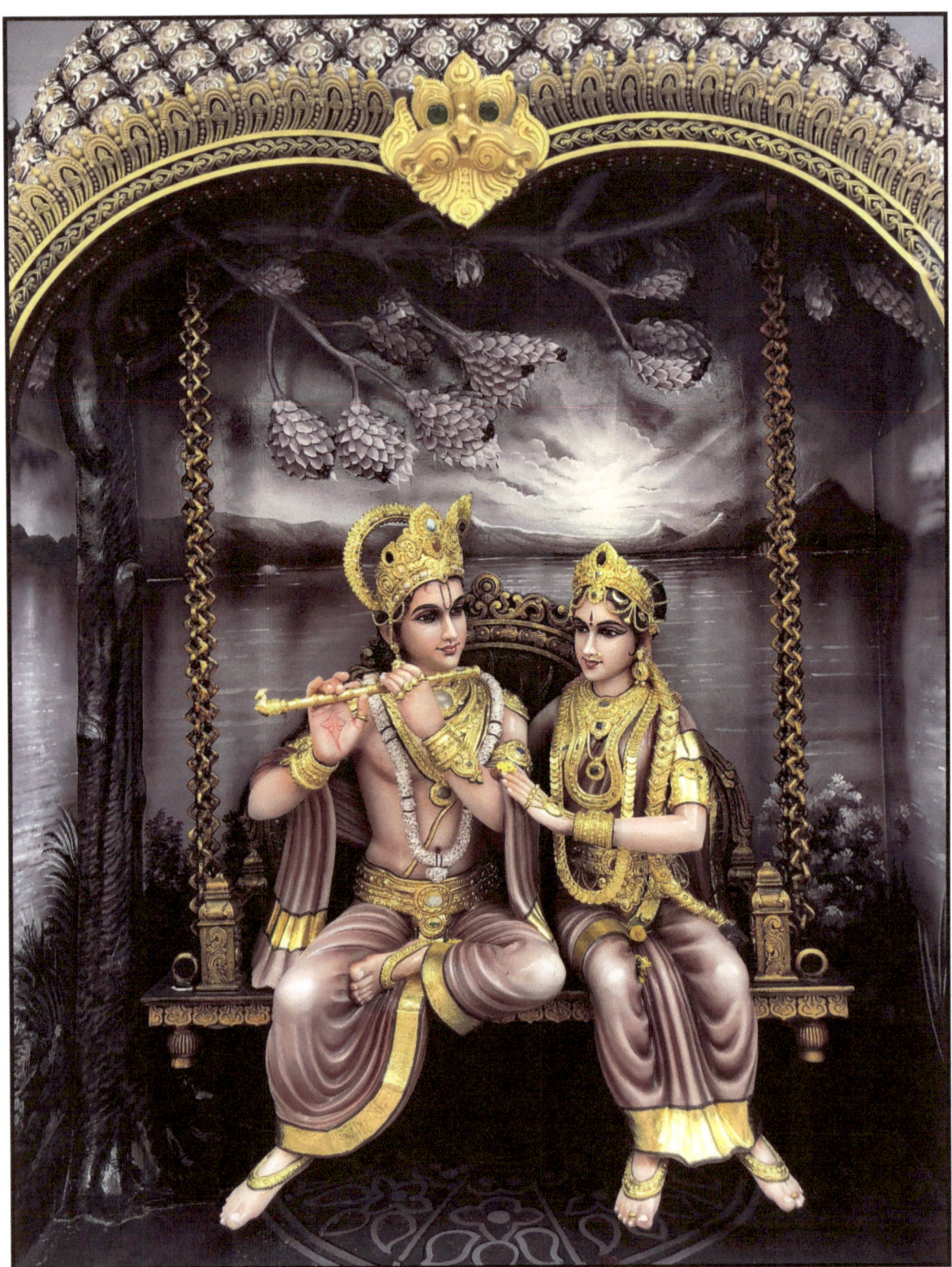

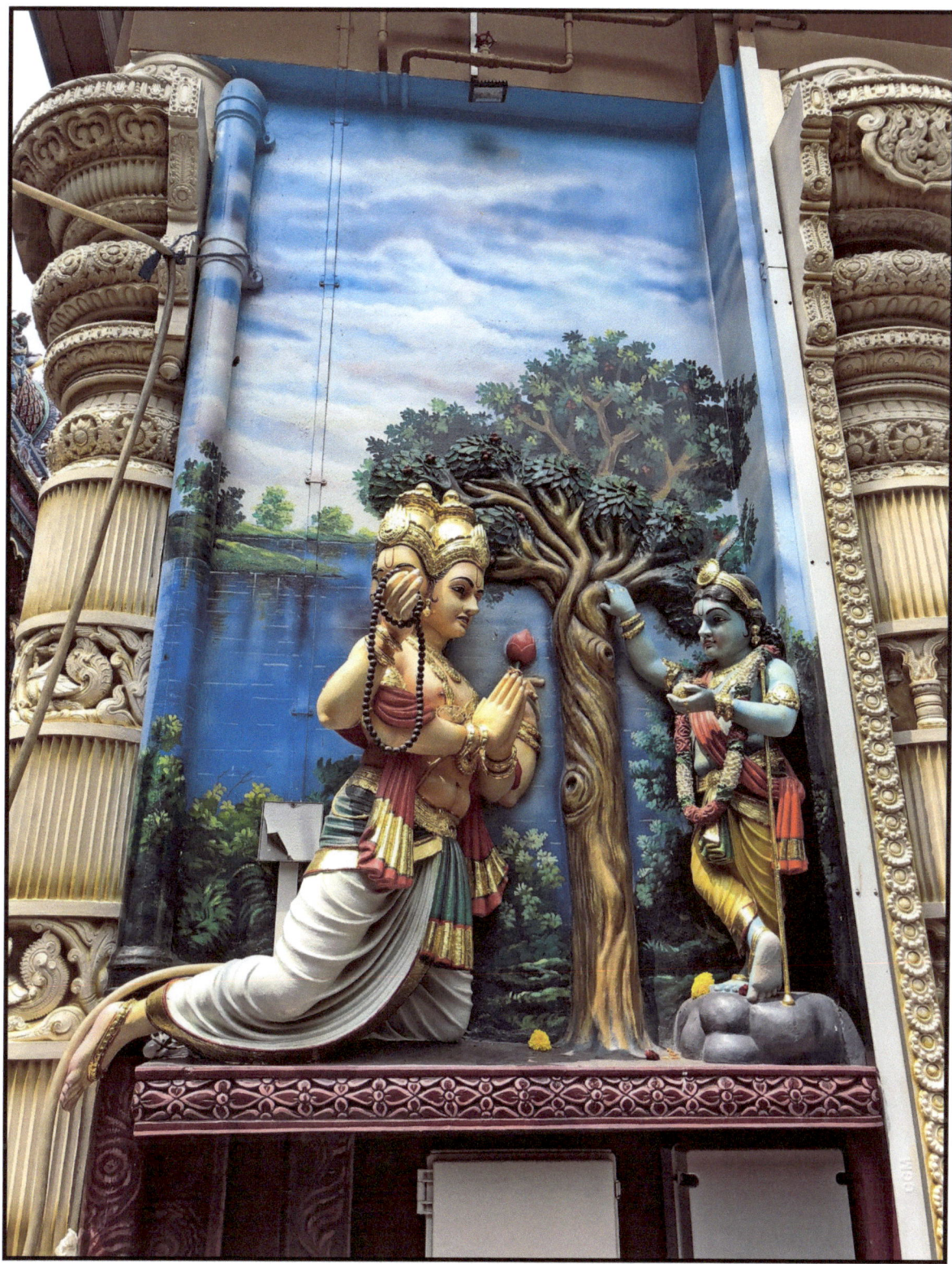

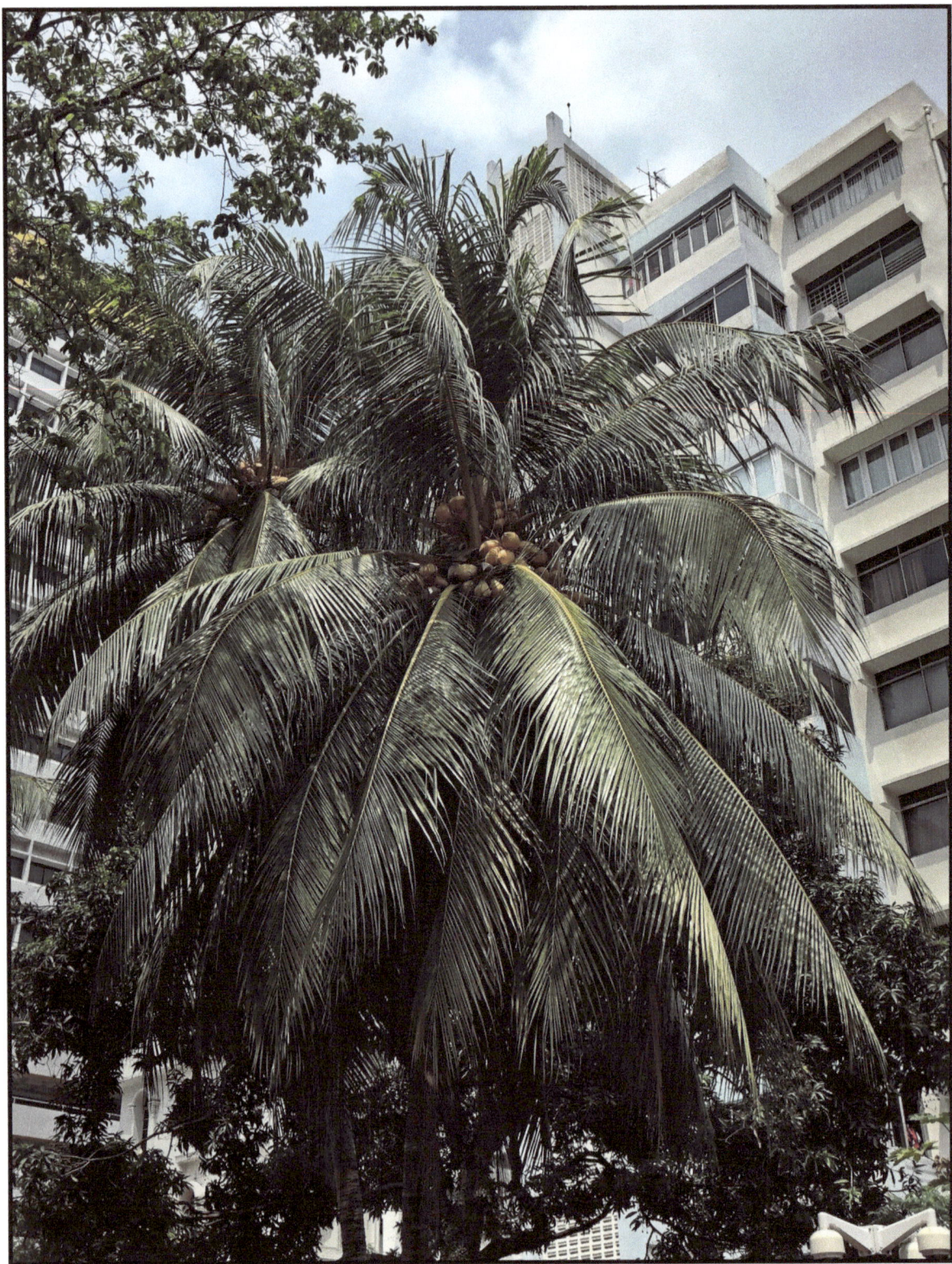

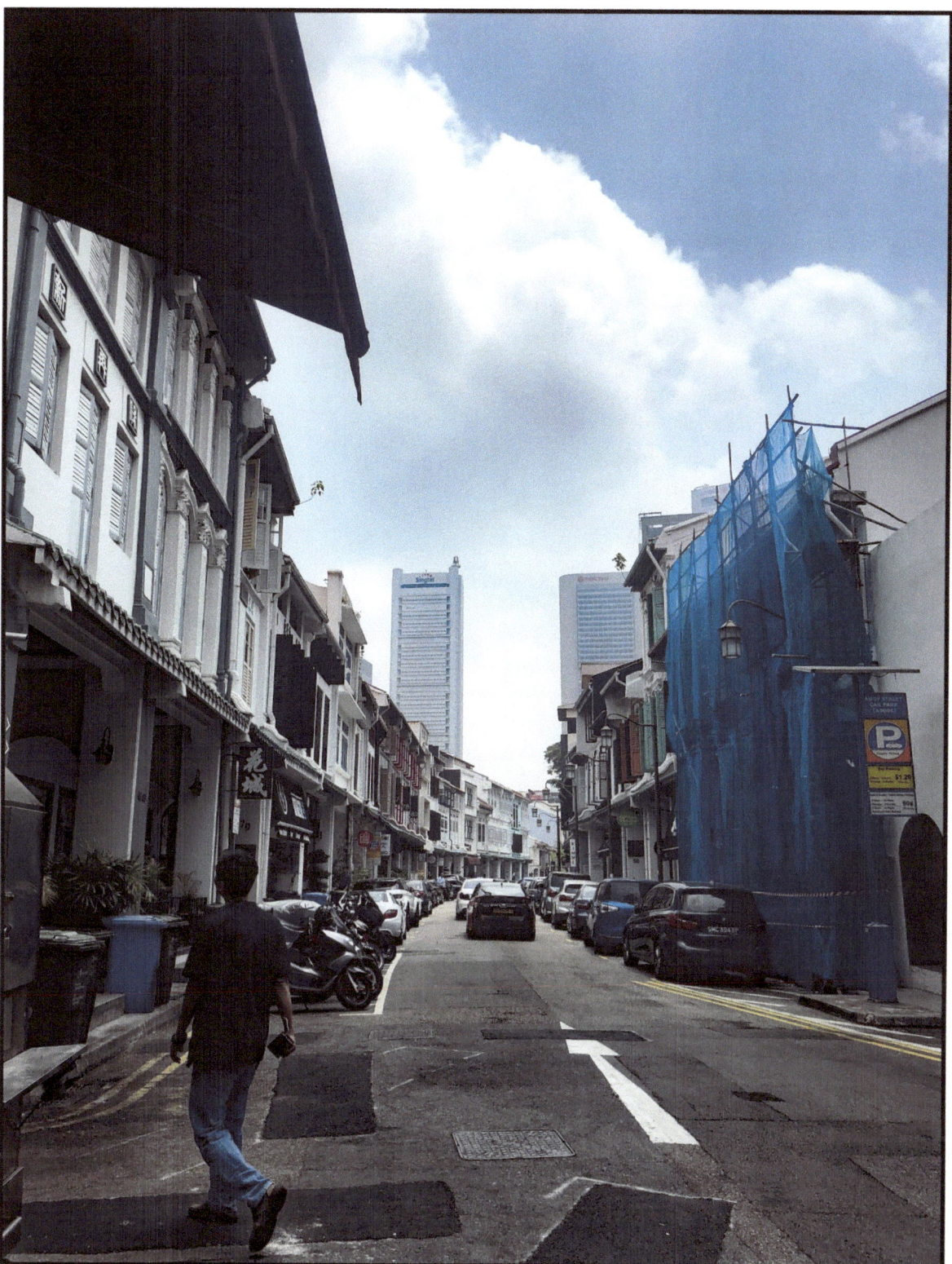

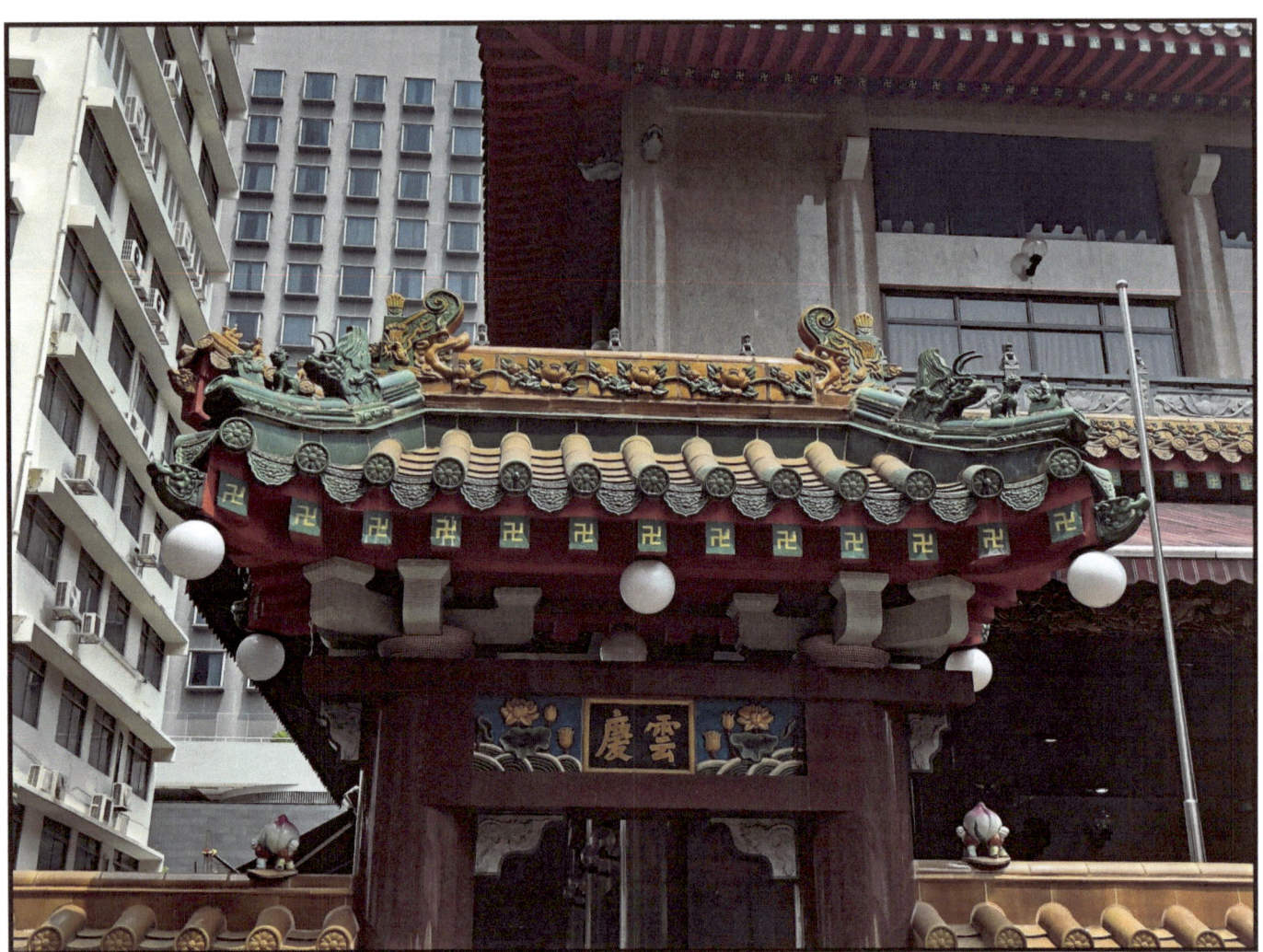

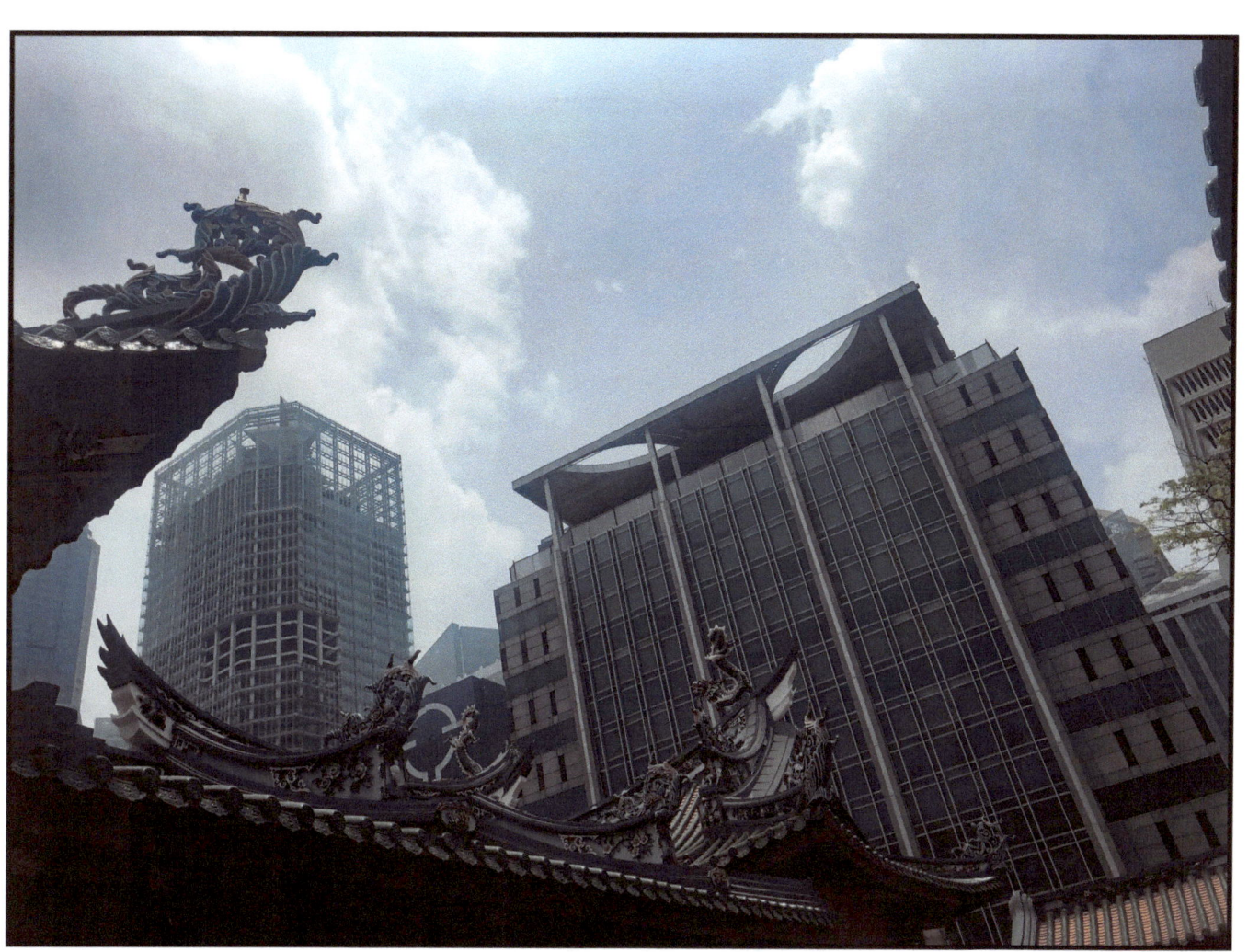

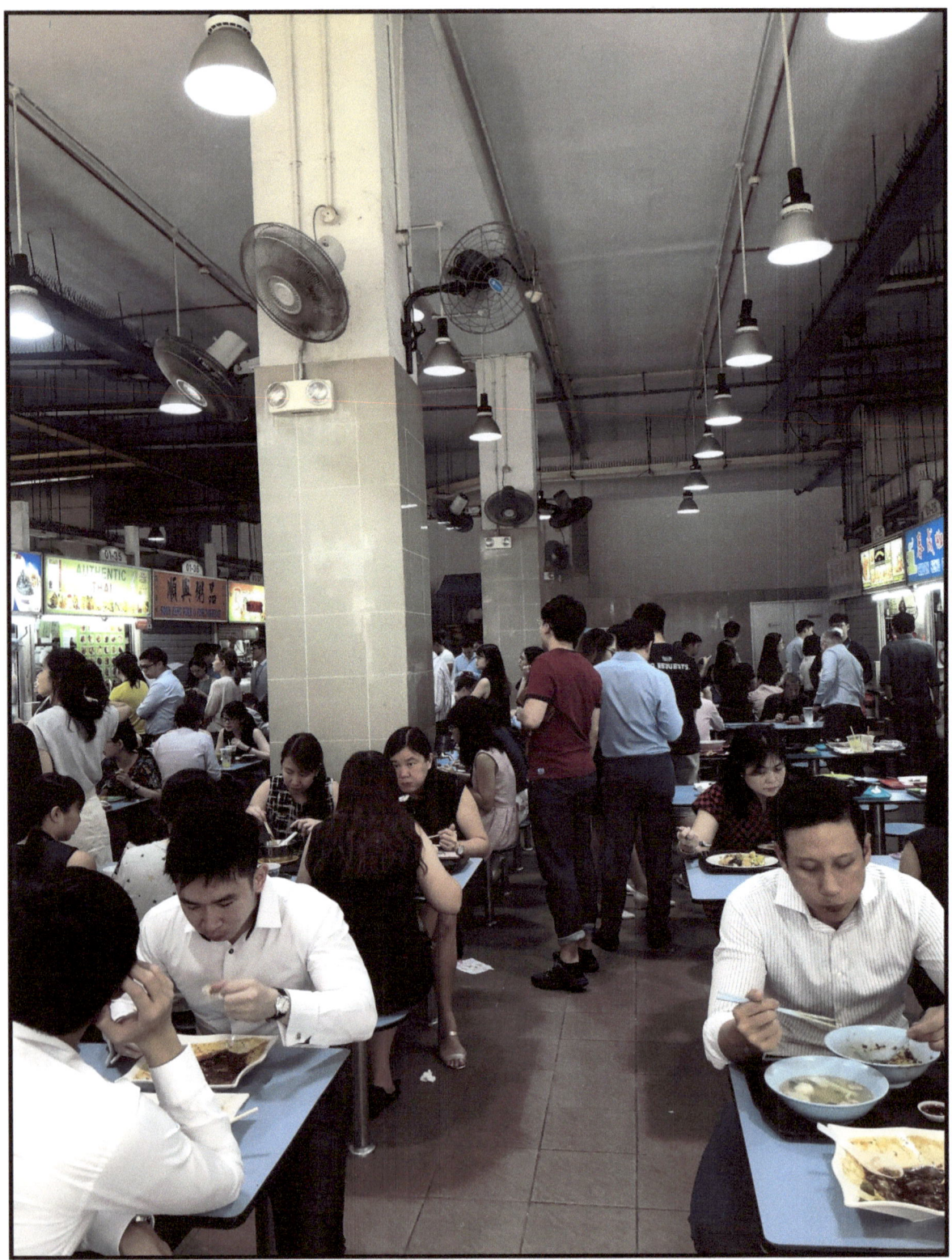

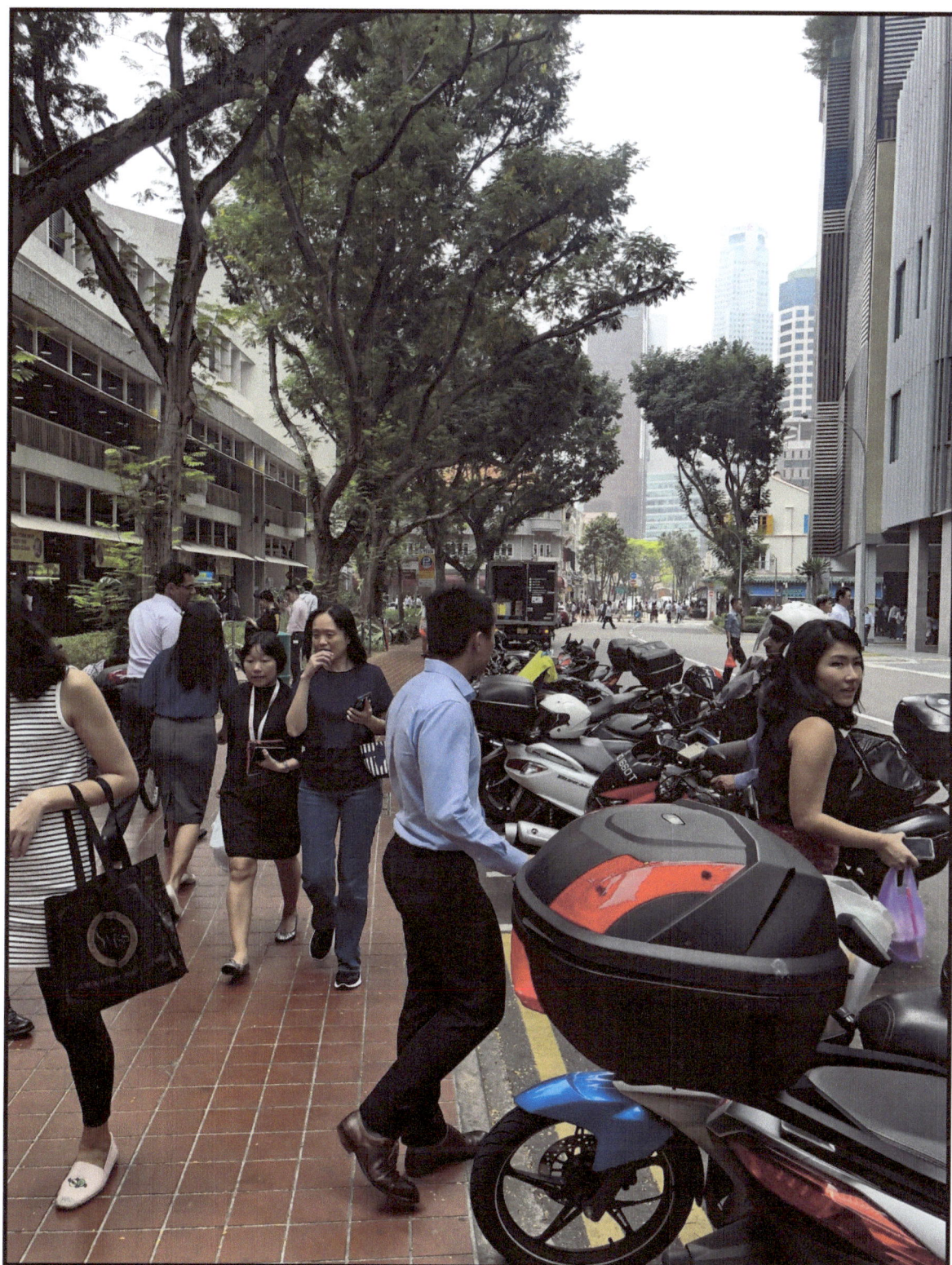

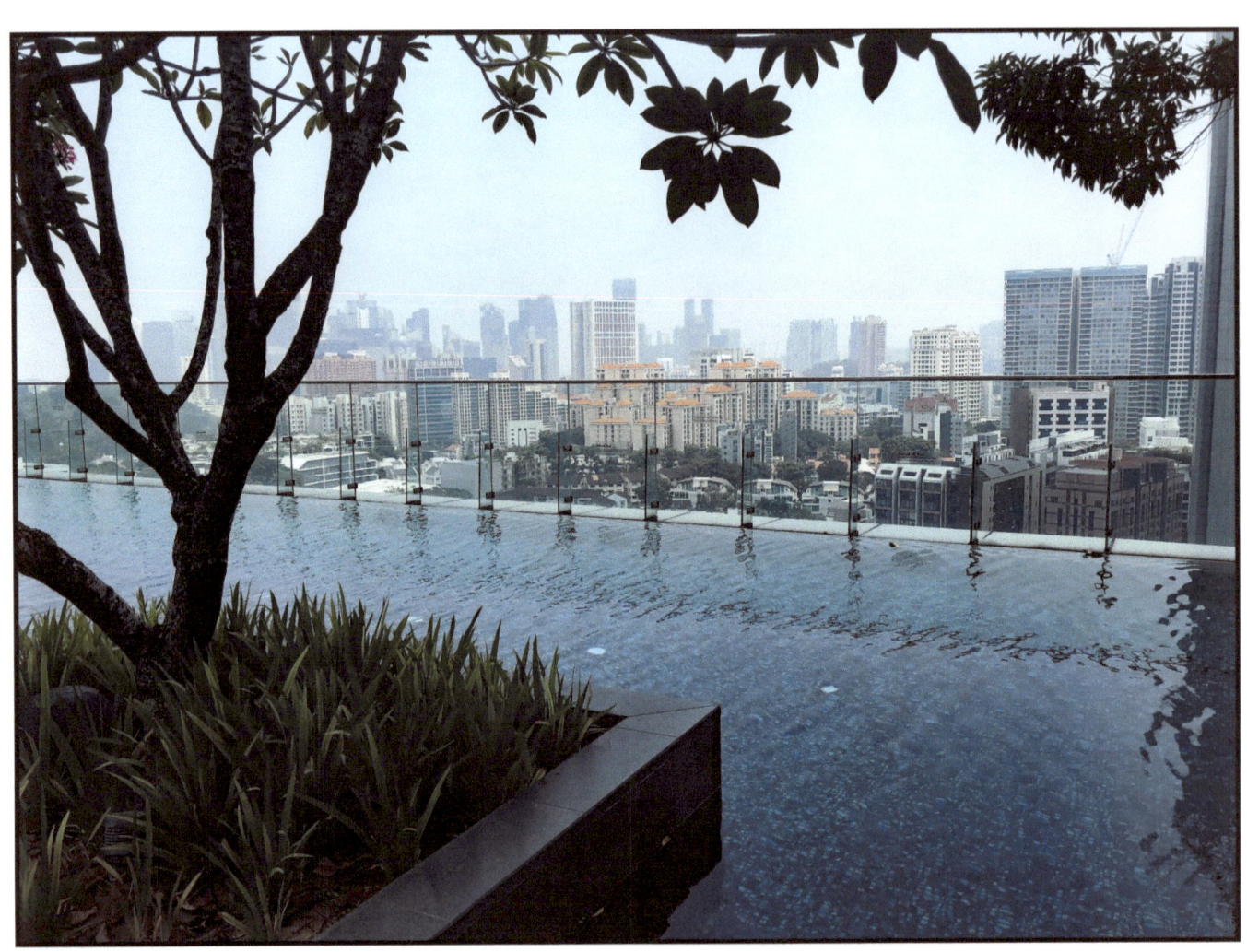

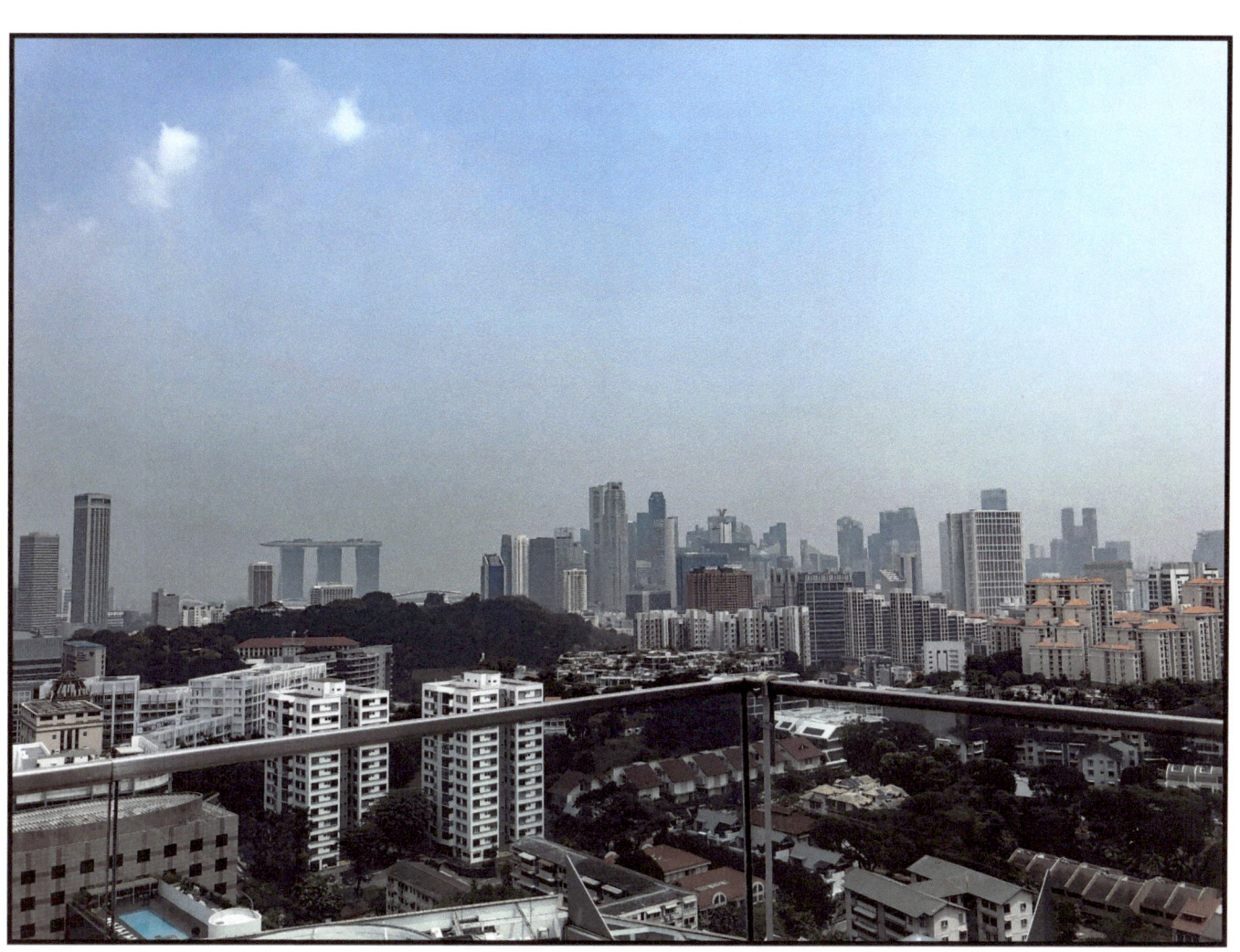

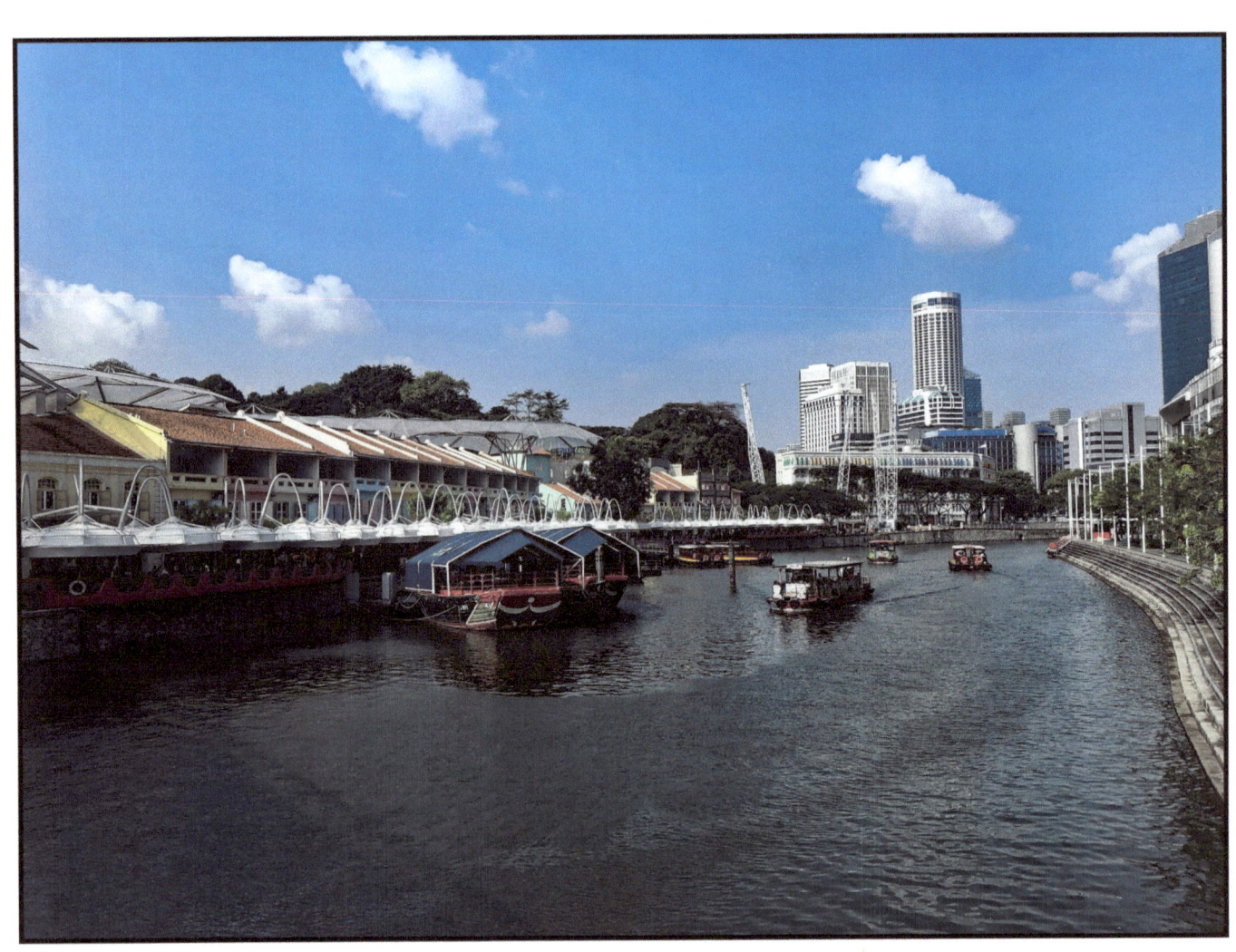

www.ingramcontent.com/pod-product-compliance
Lightning Source LLC
Chambersburg PA
CBHW051145220526
45473CB00003B/663